Principles of
Business Economics

PEARSON

Education

We work with leading authors to develop the
strongest educational materials in economics, business
and finance, bringing cutting-edge thinking and best
learning practice to a global market.

Under a range of well-known imprints, including
Financial Times Prentice Hall, we craft high quality
print and electronic publications which help readers
to understand and apply their content whether
studying or at work.

To find out more about the complete range of our
publishing, please visit us on the World Wide Web at:
www.pearsoned.co.uk

Principles of Business Economics

Joseph G. Nellis
Professor of International Management Economics
Cranfield School of Management
Cranfield University

David Parker
Professor of Business Economics and Strategy
Aston Business School
Aston University

 Prentice Hall
FINANCIAL TIMES

An imprint of **Pearson Education**
Harlow, England • London • New York • Boston • San Francisco • Toronto
Sydney • Tokyo • Singapore • Hong Kong • Seoul • Taipei • New Delhi
Cape Town • Madrid • Mexico City • Amsterdam • Munich • Paris • Milan

This book is dedicated to our families
Helen, Gareth, Daniel and Kathleen
Megan, Michael and Matthew

Pearson Education Limited
Edinburgh Gate
Harlow
Essex CM20 2JE
England
and Associated Companies throughout the world

Visit us on the World Wide Web at:
www.pearsoned.co.uk

First published in Great Britain in 2002

© Pearson Education Limited 2002

The rights of Joseph Nellis and David Parker to be identified as authors of this
Work have been asserted by them in accordance with the Copyright, Designs
and Patents Act 1988.

All rights reserved. No part of this publication may be reproduced, stored in a
retrieval system, or transmitted in any form or by any means, electronic, mechanical,
photocopying, recording or otherwise, without either the prior written permission of
the publisher or a licence permitting restricted copying in the United Kingdom issued
by the Copyright Licensing Agency Ltd, 90 Tottenham Court Road, London W1T 4LP.

ISBN 0 273 64609 5

British Library Cataloguing-in-Publication Data
A catalogue record for this book is available from the British Library

Library of Congress Cataloging-in-Publication Data
Nellis, J. G.
    Principles of business economics / Joseph G. Nellis, David Parker.
        p. cm.
    Based on the authors' The essence of business economics.
    Includes bibliographical references and index.
    ISBN 0-273-64609-5 (alk. paper)
    1. Managerial economics. I. Parker, David, 1949 Sept. 28- II. Nellis, J. G. Essence of
business economics. III. Title.

HD30.22 .N453 2002
338.5'024'658--dc21

10 9 8 7 6 5 4 3   2002024299
08 07 06 05 04 03

Typeset in 10/12¹/₂pt Sabon by 35
Printed in Malaysia

Contents

Contents

Preface

Target audience

This book is intended for students of business economics on a wide range of degree and professional programmes, at both undergraduate and postgraduate levels. It should also prove useful to managers attending continuing studies courses in which the principles of business decision-making represent an integral part. The book will be particularly attractive to those studying for a wide range of academic qualifications such as the Master of Business Administration (MBA), MSc in Management and Business Studies, Diploma in Management Studies (DMS), and BA Business Studies. In addition, the material should be relevant to those taking professional accountancy and banking examinations in which business economics is a core element.

Our aim in writing this book is to provide a text that will be accessible not only to specialist economics students and tutors but to practising and trainee managers. The rationale for the book lies in the belief that, armed with a clear understanding of the core *Principles of Business Economics*, managers are better equipped to appreciate and react appropriately to changes in the competitive environment in which their businesses operate.

Structure of the book

The book has been structured to provide a comprehensive treatment of the *Principles of Business Economics*. After an introductory chapter that provides an overview of the key terms and concepts, the text turns to the meaning of demand and the factors that make an impact upon consumer behaviour. This discussion is followed by a detailed explanation of the nature of production costs and the implications for firms' supply decisions. These two aspects of the book are then combined to look at the dynamics of price determination in the market place. Several chapters of the book are devoted to a study of different types of competitive market structures, ranging from perfectly competitive situations to situations where the market is dominated by a sole supplier. An appreciation of the fundamentals of competitive strategy then consolidates the understanding of competitive markets before a discussion of pricing strategies is presented. We also examine the markets for inputs or factors of production, namely labour, capital and natural resources including land. This is followed by an analysis of the role of government in the business environment and a concise treatment of the principles of business forecasting. The final chapter provides a checklist of the key principles explored in the book and sets out detailed lists of questions to help managers assess their understanding of the dynamics of their competitive environment and the *Principles of Business Economics*.

Key features of the book

We have endeavoured to make the book as user friendly as possible both to the student and the course tutor. To this end a number of key features have been incorporated. Each chapter contains the following sections:

- Aims and learning outcomes.
- A discussion of the core principles of the subject.
- Applications.
- Concluding remarks.
- Key learning points.
- Topics for discussion.

All of the key principles including definitions and formulae are highlighted throughout the text for easy reference and revision. This book is designed for an international readership. Consequently, throughout the text we use the $ as the normal unit of account. We have intentionally minimised the use of technical jargon and mathematical treatment throughout the book, relying instead on clear discussion augmented by graphical analyses. This supports the user-friendly approach adopted in this book. Certain concepts that may not be covered in some business economics courses, such as indifference curves and isoquants, are treated separately in appendices to the relevant chapters. The inclusion of Applications within each chapter is intended to reinforce and test the reader's understanding of key concepts. A detailed Glossary is also included at the end of the book for easy reference.

Website material

Access to supplementary material is available from the following website address:

www.booksites.net/nellisparker

This material is designed to support the work of tutors and students. The website includes the following:

- *Overhead transparency masters*
  These provide for each chapter a full set of visual aids, using PowerPoint slides, covering:
  - the structure of each chapter
  - the learning outcomes
  - highlighted text in the book including formulae and definitions
  - all tables and diagrams used in the book
  - key learning points
  - topics for discussion.
- *Guidance notes*
  These provide brief notes to tutors and students with respect to answering each of the *topics for discussion* questions that are included at the end of each chapter.

Feedback

We have endeavoured to make this book user-friendly and to serve the needs of a wide range of readers. However, we recognise that there is always room for improvement in any textbook and therefore we would appreciate feedback from readers concerning areas for further improvement and development of the text. Such feedback should be directed through the publishers via the above website address.

Acknowledgements

We are grateful to the following for permission to reproduce copyright material: HMSO for extracts from *BASF AG and Takeda Chemicals Industries Ltd: a report on the acquisition by BASF AG of certain assets of Takeda Chemical Industries Ltd*, Cm.5209, July 2001, and *New Cars: a report on the supply of new motor cars within the UK*, Cm.4600, 2000, published by the Competition Commission; and Palgrave Publishers Ltd and Perseus Publishing Group for an extract from *Can Japan Compete?* by Porter, Takenchiaad and Sakakibara, published in the UK by Macmillan Press; Simon and Schuster, Inc. for Figure 4.5 from M.E. Porter, *Competitive Advantage* (1998) and Figure 11.2 from M.E. Porter, *Competitive Strategy* (1998); Palgrave Publishers Ltd for Figure 11.8 from *The Competitive Advantage of Nations* (1990) by M.E. Porter, G. Nichols for Application 12.1 from 'How do firms "really" price their products', in *Economics Today*, Vol. 6, No. 4, Economics Today Ltd (1999); and British Bankers Association for Application 11.1 from *Annual Abstract of Banking Studies*.

Whilst every effort has been made to trace the owners of copyright material, in a few cases this has proved impossible and we take this opportunity to offer our apologies to any copyright holders whose rights we may have unwittingly infringed.

We would like to acknowledge the important contributions made to the content of this book by the current and former students whom we have taught, in various institutions around the world. Their questions, insights and experiences have helped us to shape and improve our own thinking on and understanding of the *Principles of Business Economics*. In addition, we would like to thank Chris Williams, Dawn Richardson, Rita Woods and Nicky Billington for their many hours of hard work devoted to typing and retyping drafts of the manuscript, and Catarina Figueira for assistance in the preparation of the index to the book. Any remaining errors are, of course, solely our responsibility! Finally, this book could not have been written without the support and patience of our families. We dedicate this book to them.

Joseph G. Nellis
David Parker

List of applications

List of figures and tables

List of figures

List of tables

1 Business economics: an overview

Aims and learning outcomes

Today, the economic, political, social and technological environments are changing faster than ever before. Business success depends, therefore, on managers anticipating and coping with change. To do this managers must first identify the characteristics of the environment in which they operate. That 'environment' may be examined at the following two levels:

- The microeconomic environment.
- The macroeconomic environment.

The *microeconomic environment* deals with the operation of the firm in its immediate market, involving the determination of its prices, revenues, costs, employment levels and so on. In contrast, the *macroeconomic environment* comprises the general economic conditions of the larger economy of which each firm forms a part. This larger system involves the impact of political, legal and economic decisions, both nationally and internationally. By definition, since any single firm usually represents a minute part of the larger system, it is unlikely to be able to exercise control over the macroeconomic environment in the way in which it may be able to have control over its microeconomic environment.

Analysis of the macroeconomic environment is covered in our companion volume entitled *The Principles of Macroeconomics*. In terms of Figure 1.1, this companion book deals with the impact of the wider international and domestic economies on the firm, whereas the current book is solely concerned with a study of the immediate environment of the firm, i.e. business economics.

Our aim here is to meet the needs of the manager in the daily process of decision-making. Decisions, if they are to be effective, must be soundly based on a critical awareness of the fundamental economic relationships which underlie all business operations. The manager must be able to apply this understanding and knowledge to real-world problems. An understanding of the key concepts of business economics provides a sound foundation for optimal decision-making. The subjects of marketing, strategic management, operations management, finance and so on, utilise many of the core concepts introduced here.

This overview chapter provides a foundation for understanding many of the tools, models and forms of analysis covered in the subsequent chapters. In particular, we set

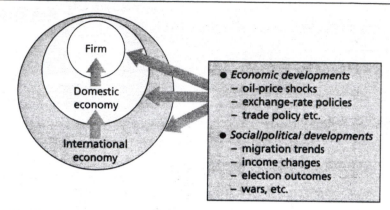

Figure 1.1 The business environment

out detailed definitions and explanations of the core concepts used in business economics as well as an overview of the nature of the competitive environment of firms. This foundation will help the reader to appreciate the significance of the strategic options facing firms in an ever-changing business environment.

Learning outcomes

This chapter will help you to:

- Understand the core *terms* and *concepts* used in business economics.

- Appreciate the nature of a firm's production decisions with respect to *what* to produce, *how* to produce and for *whom* to produce.

- Employ economic reasoning when making choices in the use of resources and to recognise the importance of *diminishing returns*.

- Comprehend the nature of *marginal analysis* in the context of business and consumer decisions.

- Recognise the different *objectives* which different firms may pursue and the consequent impact on price and output decisions.

- Distinguish between the *short run* and *long run* in business economics.

- Understand the nature of different competitive structures in market economies ranging from *perfectly competitive* to *monopoly* situations.

- Analyse the *external environment* and *internal capabilities* of a firm using core techniques in business economics and thereby understand the forces shaping the firm's competitive environment.

- Appreciate the choice of *generic strategies* facing firms in terms of *cost leadership*, *differentiation* and *focus* options.

Basic concepts in business economics

There are a number of basic concepts which lie at the heart of business economics and managerial decision-making. The most important of these are the following:

- Resource allocation.
- Opportunity cost.
- Diminishing marginal returns.
- Marginal analysis.
- Business objectives.
- Time dimension.
- Economic efficiency and equity.
- Risk and uncertainty.
- Externalities.
- Discounting.
- Property rights.

We start by briefly describing the relevance of each of these concepts to business economics.

Resource allocation

Economics is concerned with the efficient allocation of scarce resources. When purchasing raw materials, employing labour and undertaking investment decisions, the manager is involved in *resource allocation*. Decisions need to be made at three levels, namely:

- **What** goods and services to produce with the available resources,
- **How** to combine the available resources to produce different types of goods and services; and
- **For whom** the different goods and services are to be supplied.

Figure 1.2 illustrates the interrelationship between the production decision and decisions regarding these three considerations. Such decisions are sometimes described as the *allocative, productive* and *distributive* choices which exist in economies. In business economics we examine how the *price mechanism* relates to making these choices.

The price mechanism is the major determinant of the *what, how* and *for whom* decisions in market economies, though less so in the formerly centrally planned or command economies of Central and Eastern Europe and China. However, over time and in all economies firms have grown in size and importance – witness for example the resource allocation which goes on *within* companies such as IBM, Microsoft and Toyota. Resources within firms are allocated by both command and price. For example, a decision on where to locate a factory could be based upon detailed costings of alternative

3

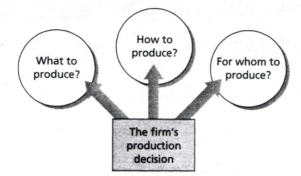

Figure 1.2 The production decision

sites (i.e. determined by price). Alternatively, the decision might be made by management on the basis of non-price factors, which may in fact be purely subjective (based, for example, on perception of the local environment).

In so far as resource allocation in firms results from command rather than price, as Professor Robertson observed, firms might be considered to be 'islands of conscious power in . . . [an] ocean of unconscious co-operation' (cited in R.H. Coase, 'The nature of the firm', *Economica*, 4 (1937), 386–405). The market represents a network of unconscious co-operation between a multitude of buyers and sellers. At the same time, the boundary between the firm and the market is constantly evolving through mergers, takeovers, divestment, management buyouts, etc. Firms are constantly reassessing their structures and strategies and attempting to answer questions such as whether or not they should undertake in-house those activities which are currently purchased in the market (e.g. by taking over a supplier), or, instead, should certain activities which are currently undertaken internally (e.g. software development in the case of a computer manufacturer) be closed down or sold off?

In other words, the degree of *vertical integration* or the so-called 'make or buy' decision needs to be constantly monitored. The American economist Oliver Williamson has referred to this as a decision about the *boundary of the firm*. Where is the boundary of the firm to be drawn? In other words, what activities should be directed by the 'conscious power' of management and what activities should be the prerogative of the 'unconscious co-operation' which is the hallmark of the market? The firm or the market is a choice between the allocation of resources in 'markets' or 'hierarchies'. Sometimes it will pay to buy in the market, while sometimes it will be more efficient to undertake an activity in-house. In economic terms, the deciding factor will be the relative costs of transacting in markets and firms (or hierarchies). These costs are referred to by economists as *transaction costs*. It is the case that sometimes it will be more economic to undertake transactions in markets and sometimes within the firm. For example, a firm may find it more cost efficient to buy components from other firms (the market place) rather than manufacture them in-house. The manager, therefore, needs to be aware of not only the current costs of producing in-house but also the costs of the alternative method of supply, i.e. outsourcing. This brings us to the economist's concept of *opportunity cost*.

Opportunity cost

Underlying business decisions is the fact that resources are scarce. This scarcity can be reflected in many ways, such as shortages of capital, physical and human resources, and time. The existence of scarcity means that whenever a decision or choice is made, a

---

Application 1.1

The dismal science?

In the nineteenth century Thomas Carlyle labelled economics 'the dismal science', thus beginning a tradition of poking fun at economists!

'If you laid all the world's economists from end to end they still wouldn't reach a conclusion.'

There's no such thing as a one-handed economist – it's always 'on the one hand this' and 'on the other hand that'!

Two economists are walking together and one spots a $10 bill in the road. 'Isn't that a $10 bill?' says one. 'No it can't be' says the other 'otherwise logically somebody would already have picked it up'.

But leaving aside the jokes – which we take on the chin! – the insights from economics are powerful. The last of these three jokes is based on the notion that people are rational and rationally somebody should already have picked up the $10 bill, if it was a real $10 bill.

Economists also use humour to make a point. The French economist Frédéric Bastiat (born 1801) teased his government regarding protection from competition. For example, he petitioned the legislature on behalf of candlemakers pointing to 'ruinous competition of a foreign rival who works under conditions so far superior to our own for production of light that he is flooding the domestic market with it at an incredibly low price'.

He had in mind the sun. The remedy he proposed was a compulsory shuttering of all windows. To protect employment in the economy he once suggested, presumably tongue in cheek, that workers should be limited to using one hand at work to slow them down and share out the available work. If that failed he advocated chopping one hand off!

Actually Bastiat was making a serious point. In protecting groups from the forces of competition and in governments intervening to provide full employment, economic welfare can be seriously damaged, albeit unintentionally. Economic activity, including economic intervention, involves an opportunity cost in terms of the use to which the state resources could alternatively have been put.

The role of economists is to point to illogical argument and to draw attention to actions that unintentionally cause serious economic loss – using or not using humour. As economists say:

'There is no such thing as a free lunch.'

Activity

Consider the importance of taking into account the opportunity cost of economic actions. Illustrate your answer with reference to state subsidies to industry.

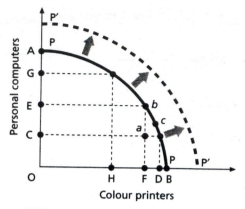

Figure 1.3 Production possibility curve

cost is incurred. Economists take a broader view of such a cost than that based purely on monetary factors as used by accountants. In economists' jargon, such costs include *opportunity costs*.

> The *opportunity cost* of any activity is what we give up when we make a choice. In other words, it is the loss of the opportunity to pursue the most attractive alternative given the same time and resources.

The concept of opportunity cost can be illustrated using a simple diagram. In Figure 1.3, the curve PP represents what is called a *production possibility curve* (sometimes known as a *production possibility frontier*).

> A *production possibility curve* shows the maximum output of two goods or services that can be produced given the current level of resources available and assuming maximum efficiency in production.

Any firm with its available *factors of production* (which may be broadly categorised as land, labour and capital) has a choice as to the products it may produce. For example, suppose as in Figure 1.3 that a company produces both personal computers and colour printers. It is able to produce OA computers or OB printers or some combination of both if it fully utilises its resources. The various alternative outputs are shown along the PP curve. Now suppose that currently the company produces OC computers and OD printers, but decides to expand its production of computers to OE. Given current resources, these extra computers can only be achieved by reducing the production of printers to OF. In other words, the opportunity cost of producing CE extra computers is DF fewer printers. Similar trade-offs between the two products are shown along the PP curve.

The shape of the production possibility curve reflects the fact that as resources are transferred from one activity to another, the resulting increase in production (in this case personal computers) is likely to be at a declining rate. This relates to the concept of *diminishing marginal returns*.

> The concept *of diminishing marginal returns* refers to the situation whereby as we apply more of one input (e.g. labour) to another input (e.g. capital or land), then after some point the resulting increase in output becomes smaller and smaller.

For example, in the case of our computer company, the transfer of equal amounts of resources from printers to the production of computers may produce an increasingly smaller addition to the output of computers if the resources transferred from the production of printers are less suitable for producing computers (for example, employees may have the wrong kind of skills). If the company continues to increase the output of computers by a given amount, it is likely to have to reduce its output of printers by a proportionately greater amount. For example, returning to Figure 1.3, an increase in the production of computers from C to E leads to a fall in the production of printers from D to F. Further increasing the output of computers from E to G (where EG = CE) leads to a fall in printer output of FH. As will be appreciated from the diagram, the reduction in printer output is now much greater – the distance FH is greater than DF.

Of course, if the company had *not* been using its resources to maximum efficiency then it could have increased the production of computers without cutting its production of printers simply by becoming more efficient (in Figure 1.3 this is shown by moving from point *a*, below the PP curve, to point *b* on the curve). Equally, it could have increased provision of *both* products by moving from point *a* to, for example, point *c*. To increase provision beyond the PP curve (as shown by P′P′) requires more resources, e.g. staff, factory space, etc. But attracting more resources to the firm means that the resources cannot be used elsewhere in the economy, *unless* there is economic growth in the economy ('a bigger economy') as a result, for example, of technological change. These sorts of choices and hence the issue of resource allocation lie at the heart of business decision-making.

Marginal analysis

The idea of opportunity cost highlights the fact that choices have to be made regarding what to produce. The concept of the *margin* reminds us that most of these choices involve relatively small (incremental) increases or decreases in production. For example, decisions have to be made regarding whether to provide an extra school classroom, an extra production shift, to generate an extra megawatt of electricity, to produce 1,000 fewer ball-bearings, to add a new product to the product range, etc. Only relatively rarely do we make decisions about all or nothing, e.g. whether to provide school education or not or whether to be a manufacturer or not! The scale of the increase or decrease in production – the extent of the 'marginal' change – will, of course, be related to the scale of the overall operation. For example, electricity generating companies are most unlikely to be concerned with decisions about whether or not to produce one more kilowatt of electricity!

The concept of the margin is central to most economic decisions and hence is referred to throughout this book, both in terms of consumer behaviour when buying products or services and the behaviour of firms when deciding whether to alter production. Consumers, through their purchasing decisions, must decide whether or not buying a particular product will add more to their well-being or *utility* than spending the same amount on some alternative. This gives rise to the notion of *marginal utility*. The satisfaction that consumers get from consuming a good or service is referred to by

Application 1.2

Economic man

Rationality and self-interest

Economists assume that consumers and producers are rational and attempt to maximise their own utility. In the case of producers this utility is reflected in business goals, e.g. profit maximisation. People are therefore viewed as driven by the pursuit of self-interest.

As we observe on a day-to-day basis, however, people appear not always to make rational choices and they sometimes act selflessly, for example when giving to charity. Also, people are not dedicated calculating machines when in the shops or workplace. Critics of economics argue, therefore, that the subject ignores the true nature of social behaviour. The result is economic predictions that are sometimes well wide of actual outcomes.

This critique is powerful but at least in part ill-judged. When economists assume rational behaviour they are not saying that people do not make mistakes. Economic decisions are often made in an environment of incomplete information about actual outcomes. What economists assume is that consumers and producers pursue their utility and make appropriate decisions, based on the information they have at the time or choose to obtain. Subsequently, mistakes may result – people may wish they had made a different choice – but all that economics assumes is that people do not *plan* to make mistakes! Equally, economists work on the reasonable premise that people learn from their mistakes and do not choose to make the same mistakes time after time. Also, when economists refer to self-interest they do not rule out the pursuit of benevolent ends, including pursuing the welfare of others. People get satisfaction (utility) from contributing to society and giving to charity. They may also recognise that their long-term utility depends upon a flourishing and stable society.

Leaving aside such arguments, if economic predictions are to be made then some assumptions about human behaviour need to be made. Human behaviour is very complicated and therefore some simplification is essential if analysis is to proceed. The pursuit of self-interest is a simplification, but it has proved superior to any alternative generalisation about human behaviour.

Activity

Consider the role and nature of economic models in terms of their predictive ability and descriptive reality. Why do economists prefer economic theories that have predictive ability even at the expense of descriptive reality? Under what circumstances might assumptions of rationality and self-interest produce incorrect predictions?

economists as the 'utility' from consumption. Similarly, at the heart of managerial decision-making is the question of whether or not the increase in output will provide enough extra revenue to compensate for the extra cost of production. The aim of the manager (i.e. the decision-maker in this case) is to find the optimal level of production. This gives rise to the concepts of *marginal product*, *marginal revenue* and *marginal cost*. More formally, these concepts are defined as follows:

- **Marginal utility** is the amount by which consumer well-being or total utility changes when the consumption of a good or service changes by one unit.
- **Marginal product** is the amount by which total product changes due to a one unit change in the amount of input used.
- **Marginal revenue** is the change in total revenue which results from increasing the quantity sold by one unit.
- **Marginal cost** is the change in total cost which results from increasing the quantity produced by one unit.

Business objectives

Traditionally, the study of managerial decision-making has focused on the single objective of *profit maximisation*. This stems from the fact that, in the past, owners of businesses were considered to be simply interested in making profit. Today, many businesses are still run with an eye to maximising profits or returns to shareholders known as 'shareholder value'. Shareholder value is increased through higher dividends on issued shares and a rise in the share price in the stock market. Both dividends and the share price are affected by the firm's profitability. However, the development of modern capitalism has led to a divorce of ownership and control in modern companies. Especially in the large companies which dominate production in advanced economies, a 'managerial class' controls the company's operations, while ownership of the company is spread amongst a multitude of shareholders. This development has led to a reassessment of the view that the pursuit of maximum profit is always the firm's primary objective, even in the longer term.

In reality, management in large companies may pursue a wide range of objectives, which may not always be wholly consistent (e.g. maximising output as against minimising environmental damage). Profit maximisation for shareholders, suitably defined, may be but one element amongst such objectives and may not be of most immediate importance in the eyes of management. Other possible objectives of managers could include the following:

- The achievement of personal goals, involving personal security and reward, status, degree of discretionary power, etc.
- Growth targets for the company in terms of scale of output, market share, geographical market, annual extension of physical capacity, size of departments or size of the labour force, etc.

- Maximisation of sales revenue.
- Pursuit of the interests of all *stakeholders* including employees, customers, suppliers, etc. as well as shareholders.

It is possible, of course, that managers at any given time may not be actively attempting to maximise any particular goal, preferring instead to achieve a *satisfactory* level of performance across a range of indicators, including the attainment of simply an adequate level of profits to satisfy shareholders' expectations and thereby retain shareholder confidence (and their own jobs!). This behaviour by management is known as 'satisficing' behaviour.

Ascertaining the objective(s) of management is, of course, important because the objective(s) pursued determines actions taken such as, for example, whether to increase or reduce output. Unless we are clear about management's objective(s) it is difficult to say anything useful about the precise decisions which should be taken. It may make sense to increase output to maximise sales revenue but to cut output to maximise profit. Therefore, to aid and simplify the analysis *we shall normally assume that managers aim to maximise profits*. We choose profit because most firms seem to strive for high profits, especially in the private sector, and because even where managers pursue other ends they are unlikely to be entirely uninterested in profitability (or at least their shareholders are unlikely to be uninterested!).

In Chapter 10 we return to the discussion of managerial objectives and observe how other objectives alter conclusions about optimal prices and outputs based on the profit-maximising assumption.

Time dimension

Managerial decisions and objectives need to be considered within a time framework – profit maximisation in the short term may not be consistent with the long-term success of the company. In certain circumstances it may even lead to the downfall of the company in the long term. For example, short-term profit maximisation might mean that workers are pushed so hard to increase production for relatively low wages that they eventually go on strike, or that goods are made which are less reliable and sold at such high prices that new competitors eventually emerge to take over the market. This suggests that profit maximisation (and other managerial objectives) can only usefully be discussed in relation to a given time dimension.

Time is a continuum, but for convenience economists normally distinguish between the following two broad time periods, which are referred to as the *short run* and the *long run*:

The *short run* represents the operating period of the business in which *at least one* factor of production is fixed in supply.

It should be noted that as the firm attempts to increase output by employing more and more of one resource or input alongside a fixed input, *diminishing marginal returns* will eventually set in. For example, employing more and more workers on an existing assembly line is likely to lead to overcrowding and a reduction in productivity, i.e. output per worker. Ultimately, there will be one level of production in the short run which is the most cost efficient and that can be attained given existing resources. This will be at some point on the firm's production possibility curve depending upon both the physical output and the input prices.

The *long run* represents the planning horizon for the business in which *all* factors of production may be varied.

During this period, more workers can be employed or made redundant, land and buildings can be acquired or sold off, and capital equipment can be bought or scrapped. In other words, the *scale* of production can be changed over the long-term planning horizon to enable the firm to arrive at its *long-run optimal level of production*, defined in terms of the least cost allocation of resources. Also, in the long run, businesses can be bought and sold, hence changing the configuration of corporations.

Economic efficiency and equity

The success or failure of firms is often directly affected by the extent to which they are managed efficiently. *Economic efficiency* is concerned with the use of scarce resources to achieve stipulated economic ends. In competitive markets, the lower the cost per unit of output, without reducing the quality of the product, the higher the economic efficiency of the firm. An alternative way of measuring efficiency is to consider the firm's *productivity*.

The productivity of the firm is the efficiency with which resources are used to produce output. One popular measure of productivity is *labour productivity*, defined as output per unit of labour employed in the production process. An alternative and more comprehensive measure takes into account all resource inputs – capital and materials as well as labour – giving rise to the term *total factor productivity*.

Sometimes profit is used as an indicator of efficiency. In competitive markets, the more efficient the firm, the more likely it is that the firm will make profits. However, in markets with little or no competition, even an inefficient firm could make profits by charging a high price to the consumer. Therefore, profit can be a misleading indicator of economic efficiency.

It is important to appreciate that economic efficiency is not necessarily equated with *equity*. Equity is concerned with the distribution of resources. Sometimes there may be a trade-off between efficiency and equity. For example, goods may be produced more cheaply by lowering wages – this raises efficiency in terms of the costs of production but such a decision may be considered to be unfair or inequitable. Another example is where incomes are equalised as a result of income tax and welfare payments – this may be considered to be equitable but there is likely to be a resultant reduction in economic efficiency as work incentives are reduced.

Risk and uncertainty

Businesses do not exist in a world of perfect information. Outcomes are usually uncertain and managerial decisions inevitably involve an element of risk. If this were not so, no company would ever fail – success would be guaranteed because managerial decisions would be based on perfect knowledge of the outcome!

Economists distinguish between *risk* and *uncertainty*. Risk occurs in economic decision-making where there is an element of chance of injury or loss. For example, there is a risk associated with fire or burglary at a business premises. Such risk affects a large number of businesses and the chance (i.e. probability) that they may affect any particular business can be calculated. As a consequence, sometimes the risk can be insured against and can therefore be converted through insurance into a known cost to the firm.

Other types of outcome, however, cannot be insured against as the chance and costs of occurrence are much more difficult (or even impossible) to estimate. These types of risk are usually labelled by economists as *uncertainty*. Examples of uncertainty in business include a loss through unforeseeable changes in the future demand for products; the effects of unforeseeable political changes, wars, natural disasters, etc. on the markets for goods and services; and the likelihood that a new business venture might succeed or fail.

In setting down the foundations of business economics, economists usually start by assuming *perfect information* and therefore the absence of risk and uncertainty. This means that cause and effect relationships can be clearly identified in order to build up, step by step, a clear understanding of the foundations of the subject, before progressing further to analysis of the complex interrelationships of the real world. This is the approach adopted in this *Principles* book.

Externalities

So far we have emphasised objectives (short-run and long-run) from the viewpoint of the firm only. Of course, it may arise that these objectives are not compatible with the interests of society in general. The annual accounts of firms may not reflect so-called *social costs* or *social benefits* (referred to by economists as *externalities*). For example, the expansion of industrial output may increase the firm's profits but damage the environment through pollution (an external social cost). Alternatively, the development of a new reservoir may enhance the quality of life for the public in general by increasing the provision of water sports (an external social benefit), while at the same time benefiting the water company.

Managers of firms operating in the private sector are likely to find it difficult to incorporate such externalities into their decision-making either because they may lose out to competitors who are less socially conscious, or because there is no direct return to the shareholders. However, it is becoming increasingly important for managers in today's society to pay greater and greater attention to these issues as public awareness of environmental issues increases – being 'green' compliant increasingly plays a part in a modern business strategy. Business decisions will then reflect both the *internal* costs and benefits of a project to the firm (the costs and benefits they directly control) and those *external* costs and benefits which also affect society.

Environmental issues are becoming of increasing concern at national and international levels. Tighter governmental regulations and initiatives such as pollution permits and taxes on waste disposal mean that firms increasingly take some external costs into consideration when making business decisions. In effect, the costs are 'internalised'; for example, a tax paid by firms on disposed waste becomes a cost of production.

Most of the discussion in this book will centre on internal costs and benefits, but this is not intended to imply that private sector managers can safely ignore externalities in the present business environment. For public sector managers concerned with pursuing social welfare, externalities should, of course, be of central concern.

Discounting

In considering the costs and benefits of an investment project it is important to appreciate that both internal and external benefits will accrue over the life of the project and should be *discounted*.

> **The concept of *discounting* is concerned with the fact that costs and benefits arising in future years are worth less to us than costs and benefits arising today.**

It is natural, for example, to have preference for money today over money tomorrow, a concept known as *time preference*. This is not simply because of uncertainty about future inflation or fears that the money may not arrive tomorrow, but rather it is the property of the passage of time. For example, a rational person faced with a choice between receiving $1,000 now or the same amount in a year's time would choose the former option. This is because the money received now could be invested and earn interest (delaying receipt has an *opportunity cost*). With an annual interest rate of 10%, the $1,000 would be worth $1,100 in a year's time. The fact that interest can be earned over time means that, even with zero inflation, all future costs and revenues must be discounted at an appropriate rate of interest (referred to as the *discount rate*) before we are able to make proper comparisons with costs and revenues expressed in nominal values.

The importance of discounting is greatest when a decision has to be made between different investment projects over different time periods, which therefore produce alternative streams of returns. The proper evaluation of these alternatives requires the use of an appropriate discount rate since an investment decision involves the commitment of resources today in order to achieve an annual stream of outputs in the future. Leaving aside the possibility of liquidating the assets, resources invested are committed for the lifetime of the project. The future values may be discounted to a *net present value (NPV)* by adapting the standard formula for compound interest. For instance, with a discount rate of 10%, a receipt of $1,100 in one year hence is equivalent to the receipt of $1,000 today. The *discounting formula* is expressed generally as:

Discounting formula

$$\text{NPV} = \sum \frac{S_t}{(1 + r)^t}$$

where NPV is the net present value of the cash flow over the life of the project, S is the future sum, r is the rate of interest or discount rate, and t the number of years elapsing before the future sum is received.

The discount rate in this formula reflects the opportunity cost of the funds invested over the life, t, of the project (note that the symbol Σ is shorthand notation for 'the sum of' such that the value of $\dfrac{S_t}{(1 + r)^t}$ for each year is summed over all years of the project's life).

A simple example should make the discounting principle clearer. Suppose a landowner expects to receive a net annual rent from his property (rent less repairs and other costs) of $5,000 each year over the life of a four-year agreement. Let us assume that the discount rate is 10%. The present value of the future stream of rental income is calculated as follows:

$$\text{NPV} = \frac{\$5,000}{(1 + 0.10)} + \frac{\$5,000}{(1 + 0.10)^2} + \frac{\$5,000}{(1 + 0.10)^3} + \frac{\$5,000}{(1 + 0.10)^4}$$

$$= \frac{\$5,000}{1.10} + \frac{\$5,000}{1.21} + \frac{\$5,000}{1.331} + \frac{\$5,000}{1.4641}$$

$$= \$4,545.45 + \$4,132.23 + \$3,756.57 + \$3,415.07$$

$$= \$15,849.32$$

The landowner should compare this net present value of $15,849.32 with alternative returns that could be earned if the property was used in other ways, with the appropriate net revenue stream similarly discounted, to check whether or not a rental income of $5,000 per year is adequate (it should be noted that there is usually no need to work through calculations such as those above using pen and paper since computer programs and discount tables are readily available and greatly simplify the computations involved).

The above is a simple example of the use of discounting in a business context. But the principles are used in more complex business investment decisions involving an initial outlay on buying an asset which will have some residual value at the end of the period analysed. In which case, the initial capital investment and *any expected future proceeds from the disposal of assets at the end of the project's life* should also be taken into consideration when deciding whether or not to invest.

Property rights

Market economies are supported by a set of institutions. These institutions have been built up over time and include the legal system with its courts of law and policing etc. that establish and maintain clear, private *property rights*.

Property rights **define the ownership of property, the uses to which property can be put, the rights of others over the property and how property can be transferred.**

The property may be tangible (e.g. land, buildings, stocks and bonds, plant and machinery) or intangible (e.g. intellectual property). Only if property rights are clearly defined and legally protected (e.g. from theft) can mutually beneficial exchange in markets flourish. Many of today's economic problems in the so called 'transition' economies (such as in Central and Eastern Europe) result from inadequate property rights.

The competitive environment

A recurring theme in this book is the question of managerial behaviour in terms of objectives and outcomes. An important factor in determining this behaviour is the nature of the competitive environment in which the firm operates. As all managers are aware, decision-making within the firm is to a large extent influenced, or at least constrained, by the fact that the firm needs to operate successfully in the market place in order to survive. Therefore, the form that the market takes influences the forms of action adopted by management and, in turn, ultimate business success or failure. In other words, the existence and the structure of the competitive environment are significant in explaining decisions taken relating to marketing, research and development, production, finance, strategic planning, distribution and so on. In this book we analyse in some detail the structure of the competitive environment, especially in Chapters 6 to 9. In essence, the competitive environment may be viewed as a spectrum of competition ranging from a perfectly competitive market structure to one which is highly monopolistic. Economists break this spectrum down into four discrete models of market structure, namely:

- Perfectly competitive markets.
- Monopolistically competitive markets.
- Oligopolistic competition.
- Monopoly.

We briefly describe the nature of each of these market structures in turn.

Perfectly competitive markets

These are markets which are made up of numerous small firms each *offering identical* or *homogeneous* products with complete freedom of entry for new firms and exit from the market. In such markets each firm has no control over the price of the product – each is a *price-taker* rather than a *price-maker* – and must accept the price determined by the interaction of the overall market supply and demand. Closest examples tend to be found in commodity markets (wheat, coffee, timber, etc.). The arrival of internet technology is leading to more competitive markets for consumer products and for firms' inputs with respect to their supply chains. It remains to be seen whether or not this technology will eventually result in more markets which are close to the perfectly competitive model.

Monopolistically competitive markets

These markets arise, as in the perfectly competitive case, where there are very many sellers but where there is also some degree of differentiation of the product or service offered by each. They may alternatively be described as *imperfectly* competitive markets. The degree of pricing discretion that each firm has is limited because the degree of product differentiation is slight and consumers can switch to alternative suppliers. Closest examples tend to be found in the retailing and services sectors, e.g. grocery sales through the use of branded products, packaging and advertising, and car repairs.

Oligopolistic competition

This form of imperfectly competitive market arises where there exists a small number of relatively large firms which are constantly wary of each other's actions and reactions regarding price and non-price competition. There is therefore a high degree of *interdependence* in oligopolistic markets between the competing firms. In principle, the products on offer may be undifferentiated, but in practice some differentiation usually exists. This type of market structure is very common in developed economies. Amongst the industries which are most obviously oligopolistic in such economies are the commercial banking sector and the brewing, motor and oil industries. For example, in UK banking the 'Big Four' banks control over 70% of personal current (cheque) accounts.

Monopoly

At the opposite end of the spectrum from the perfectly competitive market is the sole supplier or *monopolist*. At the extreme the monopolist faces no competition because there are no other producers of the same or similar products or services. For this reason, the monopolist is described as a *price-maker*, rather than a *price-taker*. In practice, it is rare to find such a 'pure' monopoly because it is usually possible to find some, albeit imperfect, substitute, e.g. gas instead of electricity for heating purposes. The definition of a monopoly, therefore, is a fairly arbitrary one and it is common, in practice, to regard a monopoly as existing where the market is dominated by one firm producing a product or service for which there are no *close* substitutes. Where substitution is highly imperfect, the firm will have wide discretion regarding either price or output.

It is important to appreciate that competition (anti-trust) law in many countries, including the European Union countries and the USA, defines monopoly more widely. The definition is based on a given market share, for example controlling more than 25% or 40% of the market. This legal definition of monopoly should not be confused with the definition used in economic theory – *a firm producing a product for which there is no close substitute*.

Pure monopoly involves *one* supplier to the market. The theory assumes that no other firms could enter the market should they wish to do so. If new firms could enter the market, and would do so if high or 'supernormal' profits could be earned, the monopolist would have to price its products *as if* the market were competitive. In other words, a monopoly strictly exists where the market is *not contestable*.

Defining the nature of the market

Sometimes it may be difficult to define precisely the form and structure of the competitive environment faced by a firm. However, there are three groups of factors which managers might consider when attempting to determine the nature of the markets in which they are currently operating or are planning to operate.

Defining the nature of the market

- The number and size distribution of the buyers and sellers in the market.
- The degree of product differentiation that exists.
- The severity of the barriers to entry and exit that face potential new entrants to the market.

Barriers to entry into a market can take many forms, including legal and natural barriers. Legal barriers give rise to a monopoly, for example, through patent rights, regulations, licensing, charters or franchises. Natural barriers may also give rise to a monopoly as a result of economies of scale in production. For example, electricity distribution is usually a *natural monopoly* because costs are minimised by having only a single electricity distribution system in each area of a country.

High capital costs associated with entering an industry may give rise to barriers to exit. This occurs where a firm wishing to leave a market is unable to recover its capital costs. A firm may wish to exit a market where it faces unexpectedly intense competition. Unrecoverable costs associated with entering a market are referred to as *sunk costs*.

The significance of these groups of factors in relation to the nature of the market structure described above is summarised in Figure 1.4 below.

Market structure

	Perfect competition	Monopolistic competition	Oligopoly	Monopoly
Number of buyers and sellers	Very high	Very many	Few suppliers	One supplier (in the extreme case of 'pure' monopoly)
Degree of product differentiation	Nil	Very low	Usually high	Very high
Market entry and exit barriers	Nil	Nil	High	Very high

Market attributes (vertical axis label)

Figure 1.4 Characteristics of markets

Porter's Five Forces Model

The above discussion of market structure can be usefully encapsulated in the *Five Forces Model* developed by Michael Porter of Harvard University, in which profitability is mainly a function of industry structure. This model describes the competitive environment and profitability as being determined by the following forces:

Porter's Five Forces Model

- **The bargaining power of buyers** – how much leverage buyers have in determining the price.
- **The bargaining power of (input) suppliers** – the competition among suppliers which determines the price of inputs to the firm.
- **The threat from potential new entrants into the market** – the degree of 'market contestability' or the extent to which firms are able to enter the market and contest for consumers.
- **The threat from substitute products or services** – e.g. mobile telephones for fixed-line services.
- **The degree of competition (rivalry) in the market.**

The interrelationship between these five forces is illustrated in Figure 1.5.

Porter argues that the interaction of these forces ultimately determines the competitive environment faced by a firm. For example, a firm which sells to consumers who have limited buying power, and operates in a market where there is little rivalry or potential rivalry, is likely to make much more profit than a firm facing the opposite circumstances. The aim of a firm's strategy must therefore be to limit the threat posed by these five forces, recognising, of course, that at various points in time some market forces will be more important than others in determining profitability.

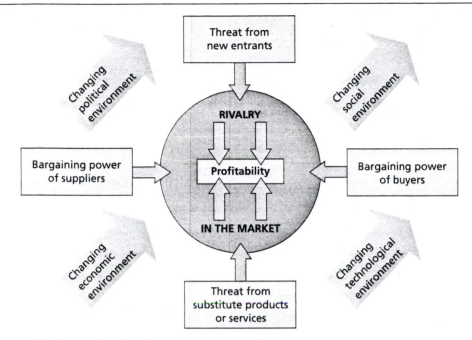

Figure 1.5 Forces shaping the competitive environment

Analysing the firm's external environment

Over time the competitive environment, as encapsulated in Porter's five forces model, will be subject to change – sometimes dramatic change. As illustrated in Figure 1.5, these changes may come in the shape of political (including legal), economic, social and technological developments which will often be difficult to predict. The challenge facing management, therefore, is a daunting one in that decisions have to be made not only to take account of the competitive dynamics of the market but also in terms of a changing and unpredictable *external environment.*

Awareness of the importance and impact of the external environment on business can be greatly enhanced through the use of PEST analysis (where PEST is shorthand for the '*Political, Economic, Social* and *Technological*' factors impacting on the business). This involves identifying the key issues and trends under these four headings that impact or are likely to impact on the markets and industries within which the firm operates. The most successful firms over time are likely to be those which best respond to changes in the external environment.

Internal analysis of the firm

A detailed PEST analysis is a stage in the strategic planning process of a firm, in that it helps management to identify emerging *opportunities* and *threats* due to developments in the external environment. Following on from this analysis, an internal assessment of the firm's *strengths* and *weaknesses* in the light of the opportunities and threats facing and likely to face the business can be conducted – giving rise to the term *SWOT analysis*.

A SWOT analysis is a combined examination of the external and internal issues and trends affecting a firm's performance. It can be applied at various levels – corporate, business unit or departmental. Whether a SWOT analysis paints a pessimistic or optimistic picture for the firm, it can be extremely useful in that:

- it helps the firm to recognise why it is doing well and where it might do well in the future;
- it helps the firm to identify where it needs to attend to problems;
- it helps to focus management's attention on important strategic issues such as resource deficiencies; and
- it can provide an opportunity to identify organisational strengths and weaknesses.

A fuller analysis of the firm will include consideration of the firm's *core competencies* and *distinctive capabilities* (see pp. 113–14).

Competitive positioning of the firm

With a clear understanding of the industry structure and its external environment, alongside a critical assessment of the firm's internal strengths and weaknesses, managers can be more confident in developing and implementing appropriate competitive positioning strategies for the different products of their business.

Michael Porter has suggested that firms can pursue three *generic strategies* to achieve competitive advantage, namely:

- Cost leadership.
- Differentiation.
- Focus.

A *cost leadership* strategy involves the firm in minimising its costs of production so as to become the lowest cost producer in the industry. By achieving lowest cost production the firm can compete successfully in the market by charging the lowest price for what otherwise is an undifferentiated product or service. Alternatively, it can charge the same price as its competitors and earn higher profits that can be ploughed back into the business to finance product and process developments to gain further competitive advantage.

Another strategy is *differentiation*. Under this strategy, through product development, branding, advertising etc., a firm can develop customer loyalty without necessarily producing at lowest cost. A differentiated product, perceived by consumers to be of better quality, can be sold at a premium price, leading to profitability, e.g. Mercedes cars.

A *focus* strategy involves the firm in using either cost leadership or differentiation in a narrow segment of the market to gain advantage over more broadly based competitors.

Porter has argued that all three of these generic strategies could be appropriate depending on the particular market conditions faced by a firm. He has stressed, however, that failure by a firm to pursue any one of these strategies consistently runs the

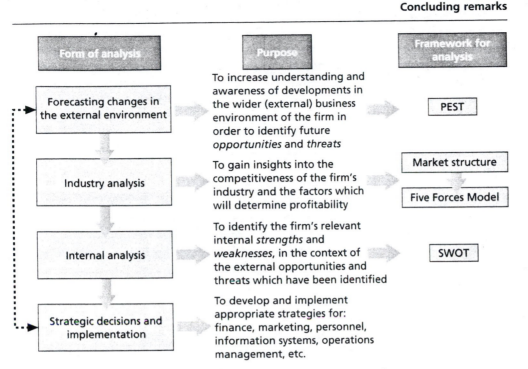

Figure 1.6 Strategy and the competitive environment – an overview

risk of becoming 'stuck in the middle'. The result could be a loss of competitiveness and lower profitability. The extent to which low cost and differentiation are alternative strategies remains, however, controversial. Some businesses, e.g. supermarkets, appear to pursue both strategies simultaneously.

Perfectly competitive markets are associated with undifferentiated products and firms are focused, therefore, on minimising production costs. A firm with costs of production higher than its rivals will quickly disappear from the market. By contrast, imperfectly competitive markets involve some degree of product differentiation. The more the focus is on product differentiation, the less competitive the market is likely to be.

Figure 1.6 provides an overview of the various forms of analysis discussed above, the purposes of each and the frameworks used. The dotted arrow on the left-hand side, linking the forms of analysis together, emphasises the need for management to monitor and adapt the firm's strategic decisions and strategy implementation in the face of an ever-changing competitive environment, at all levels.

Concluding remarks

The purpose of this chapter has been to provide an overview of the nature of the business environment and its impact on managerial decision-making. We have introduced many of the terms and concepts which form the basis of the discussions in later chapters and which lie at the heart of business economics and managerial decisions.

Managers operate in an uncertain world and their decision-making is not an exact science. It is never possible to predict the future with complete confidence. In particular, the behaviour of consumers and the actions and reactions of competitors in the market place will always be uncertain to some degree. Incomplete information dominates in the business world, but the contents of this book are based on the belief that through a systematic analysis of economic problems based on sound economic principles the manager is more likely to be able to minimise the risk of failure and maximise the market opportunities presented. Business decision-making is an art, not a science. Nevertheless, the intelligent application of the economic analysis included in this book should help the busy manager to make better choices. In this book we shall be concerned from time to time with economic models in which perfect information is assumed (even though we are all agreed that it does not exist) because by assuming that consumers and producers are perfectly informed, we can predict how purchasing and selling decisions would be made. Actual outcomes can then be compared with these predictions.

The various models developed in the book provide useful insights into the behaviour of consumers and the operation of firms in market economies. They serve as stepping stones towards a more critical awareness of the pressures and challenges facing management and allow us to explore the intricacies of business economics within a coherent framework. Once we are clear as to how perfectly informed markets work, followed by appropriate allowances for actual information shortcomings, we can better predict how *actual* markets work. In the next chapter, we begin our detailed study of the competitive environment by looking at the nature and role of consumer demand before linking this discussion to an analysis of a firm's production costs and the structure of markets, in later chapters.

Key learning points

- **Microeconomics** deals with the operation of the firm in its immediate market, involving the determination of its prices, revenues, costs and input employment levels.

- **Macroeconomics** is concerned with the interactions in the economy as a whole of which each firm forms a part.

- **Resource allocation** is concerned with decisions regarding **what, how,** and **for whom** to produce. In a market economy the **price mechanism** is the major determinant of these decisions.

- The **opportunity cost** of any activity is the loss of the opportunity to pursue the most attractive alternative given the same resources.

- A **production possibility** curve shows the maximum output that can be produced given the current level of resources available and assuming maximum efficiency in production.

- **Diminishing marginal returns** refers to the situation whereby, as we apply more of one input to a fixed amount of another input, then after some point the resulting increase in output becomes smaller and smaller.

- **Marginal analysis** reminds us that most choices involve relatively small (incremental) increases or decreases in production (or consumption).

- The **short run** represents the **operating period** of the business in which at least one factor of production is fixed in supply.

- The **long run** represents the **planning horizon** of the business in which all factors of production may be varied in order to alter the scale of production.

- **Externalities** represent wider outcomes of the market mechanism and arise when some of the benefits or costs of consuming a good or service spill over to others.

- The concept of **discounting** is concerned with the fact that costs and benefits arising in future years are worth less to us than costs and benefits arising today.

- **Property rights** are the rights to own, benefit from and transfer assets (tangible or intangible) in market economies.

- **Perfectly competitive markets** are made up of numerous small sellers each offering identical products with complete freedom of entry and exit. Each firm is a **price-taker** rather than a **price-maker**.

- In **monopolistically competitive markets** there are many sellers but there is also some degree of product differentiation. This form of market structure is also sometimes referred to as **imperfectly competitive**.

- **Oligopolistic competition** arises where there exists a small number of relatively large firms which are constantly aware of each other's actions and reactions regarding price and non-price competition.

- A **monopoly** exists where the market is supplied by one firm producing a product for which there is no close substitute. A monopolist, therefore, tends to be a **price-maker**, in that the firm is able to set a price in the face of little or no competition. In practice, the term monopoly is often applied also to markets that are *dominated* by one firm.

- **Porter's Five Forces Model** describes the competitive environment as being determined by the **power of buyers**, the **power of suppliers**, the threat from potential **new entrants**, the threat from **substitutes** and the degree of **rivalry** in the market.

- The **external environment** of business is determined by changes in **political, economic, social** and **technological** factors, i.e. **PEST** influences.

- A **SWOT analysis** involves consideration of a firm's internal strengths and weaknesses in the context of the opportunities and threats which it faces.

- **Generic strategies** refer to the choice between pursuing a market strategy based on cost leadership, differentiation or focus.

Topics for discussion

1 What do you understand by the 'microeconomic environment' and 'macroeconomic environment' of the firm? List some of the key issues which management should be aware of under both of these headings.

2 Consider the main issues that management might take into consideration when deciding how to allocate the firm's resources.

3 What do you understand by the term 'opportunity cost'? Give examples from the decision-making of (a) a government policy-maker, (b) a private-sector manager, and (c) a public-sector manager.

4 From your own experience, give examples of diminishing marginal returns from economic activity.

5 What do you understand by the term 'externalities'? When are they likely to be important?

6 Compare and contrast the different forms of competition found in market economies. What are the possible implications for government economic policy?

7 What methods might be used to assess a firm's competitive environment?

8 How might a firm decide on the appropriate strategies to adopt in order to achieve and maintain a competitive advantage?

9 Select a company with which you are familiar. Conduct a detailed assessment of its competitive environment in terms of:

(a) A PEST analysis.
(b) Porter's Five Forces Model.

In the context of this assessment, conduct a SWOT analysis of the company.

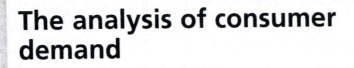

The analysis of consumer demand

Aims and learning outcomes

It should not be surprising to discover that successful firms expend considerable time and effort analysing the demand for their products. A firm is unlikely to make adequate profits, and hence remain in business for very long, unless it has a good knowledge of the demand conditions facing it in the market place. Complete ignorance of these conditions means that it will have no clear basis – other than guesswork – for deciding how much to produce, what quantity it can expect to sell, and at what price. By contrast, the successful firm plans effectively how to allocate its resources so that it can respond positively to any changes in the demand for its products. For example, it will hold sufficient finished stocks (inventories) and maintain an adequate stream of work in progress to meet expected surges in demand.

In this chapter we develop a number of economic concepts which are useful to an understanding of consumer behaviour. The key aim is to identify the factors that determine the demand for a firm's product and to show how management can proceed to measure the magnitude and impact of these factors. Therefore, much of what is presented in this chapter provides a foundation for various aspects of business management. For example, if management can estimate the importance of factors such as price, advertising or the rate of interest in determining the quantity demanded, then this will help in planning a useful marketing strategy. At the same time, if it is possible to predict (albeit with some margin of error) the volume of sales that can be expected when one or more of these factors is altered, this will have important implications for the firm's overall financial and business strategies.

Some of the factors affecting the demand for a firm's product are under the direct control of management (such as the advertising spend) while other factors that influence demand are external to the business. External factors include consumers' incomes, the prices charged by competitors, demographic trends and changes in the weather. As they lie outside the firm they may be described as 'uncontrollable' conditions of demand. Business planning should nevertheless incorporate some estimate of how these forces might change in the future and what the ultimate impact of possible changes will be on sales. This leads us into the area of *forecasting* and forecasting methods which we shall return to later in Chapter 17. For the moment, however, we shall focus on the measurement and determination of demand, linking the concepts introduced in this chapter to the determination of revenues received from sales and to the overall structure of the industry in question. This provides a useful introduction to the more detailed analysis of market structure and the nature of competition provided in Chapters 6 to 9.

In this chapter the following central concepts are discussed:

- The market demand curve.
- Utility and the demand curve.
- Consumer surplus.
- The determinants of demand.
- The classification of goods.
- Concepts of elasticity.
- The relationship between price elasticity and sales revenue.

Much of what is presented in this chapter represents a simple and practical approach to understanding demand, based on a theoretical foundation developed by economists over many years. Various models of consumer behaviour have been put forward by economists to provide insights into the decision-making process of consumers. However, they all draw on the (common-sense) observation that consumers, when spending their hard-earned money, attempt to maximise their *utility* (i.e. overall satisfaction from their limited budgets). In other words, it is assumed that all consumers are *rational* in that they desire to maximise their own well-being. The assumption of rationality is not uncontroversial. Sometimes consumers may appear to act irrationally. However, as a broad assumption, it seems more sensible to assume that consumers are rational, rather than irrational, in spending their incomes. Where consumers act rationally, given imperfect information, this is referred to as *bounded rationality*. For example, a consumer may buy a car and later regret the decision because the vehicle proves unreliable. This does not mean that the consumer acted irrationally when purchasing the car in the first place because the consumer was unaware at the time of purchase that the car would prove to be unreliable.

Learning outcomes

This chapter will help you to:

- Understand why changes in price affect consumer demand and, in particular, why demand curves are normally downward sloping, i.e. the *law of demand*.
- Understand why demand curves may shift in response to changes in various factors, other than price, which impact upon demand (known as *the conditions of demand*).
- Analyse the nature of the relationship between *marginal utility* and the demand curve for any product or service.
- Appreciate the meaning and importance of *consumer surplus* in the context of pricing strategies.
- Interpret the relative importance of *income* and *substitution effects* on demand when the price of a good or service changes.

- Classify goods and services according to how demand responds to changes in price and income, giving rise to the terms *normal, inferior, Giffen* and *Veblen* goods or services.
- Calculate *price, cross-price* and *income* elasticities of demand and interpret the significance of the results.
- Appreciate the relationship between *price elasticity, marginal revenue* and *total revenue* arising from the sale of goods or services.

The market demand curve

When economists discuss the 'demand' for a product, they mean the *effective demand*, that is, the amount consumers are willing to buy at a given price and over a given period of time. Demand, in the economists' sense, does not mean the wants, desires or needs of people since these may not be backed up by the ability to pay (you may *want* a Jaguar sports car but, unless you actually go out and buy one your desire will have no bearing on the demand for Jaguar cars!). Managers refer to demand in the same way, hence readers should have no difficulty with this treatment.

At any given time and for any good or service it is possible to perceive of a consumer's demand curve.

A *consumer's demand curve* relates the amount the consumer is willing to buy to each conceivable price for the product.

Clearly, we would normally expect the consumer to be willing to buy more of something the lower its price. From the notion of a relationship between an individual consumer's demand for a product and its price we can derive the total demand of all consumers in the market – the latter in turn gives rise to the notion of an *aggregate* or *market demand curve* for a good or service.

The *market demand curve* for a good or service is derived by summing the individual demand curves of consumers horizontally for any given price.

A market demand curve is shown in Figure 2.1. Suppose that there are only two potential buyers, Adam and Eve. $D_A D_A$ represents the demand for the product by Adam at various price levels, while $D_E D_E$ represents the corresponding demand by Eve. Summing horizontally, it will be seen that, for example, at a particular price P_1, a total quantity of $Q_{(A+E)}$ is demanded, which is equal to the sum of the individual quantities demanded, Q_A and Q_E, at that price. It follows, therefore, that $D_{(A+E)}$ is the market demand curve.

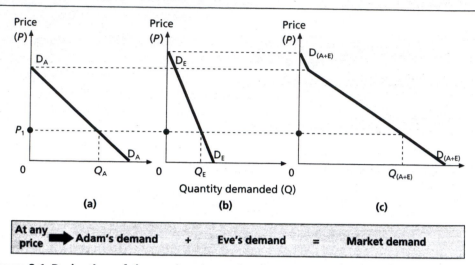

Quantity demanded (Q)

Figure 2.1 Derivation of the market demand curve

The law of demand

A demand curve, relating to either an individual or the market, shows the relationship between different possible prices of the good in question and the quantity of the good which the firm can expect to sell.

> **In general there is a central *law of demand*, which states that there is an inverse relationship between the price of a good and the quantity demanded *assuming all other factors that might influence demand are held constant*.**

Thus, if price increases (decreases), it is normally the case that less (more) will be bought. In other words, a *rational* consumer prefers to pay less rather than more for something.

It is important to be aware of the significance of the expression 'assuming all other factors that might influence demand are held constant'. Economic activity is complex and usually more than one thing is changing at any given time. For example, at the time a firm is changing the price of a product household incomes may also be increasing, advertising expenditure may be rising, consumers may be revising their attitude to the product, and so forth. In order to study the relationship that exists between price and demand, it is necessary to 'freeze' the picture. We can then later study how behaviour changes as we introduce other factors which might impact on demand, step by step. The assumption of 'all other factors held constant' is, therefore, merely a convenient framework to begin the study of what is a much more complex demand relationship in practice. The assumption is often abbreviated and stated in its Latin form as *ceteris paribus* (or simply, *cet. par.*). Also, by initially examining how demand changes only in relation to changes in price we are able to illustrate the demand relationship in a simple, two-dimensional, diagram – as in Figure 2.1 above.

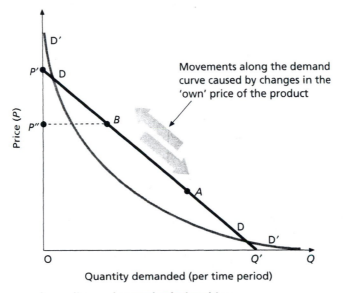

Figure 2.2 Linear and non-linear demand relationships

We stated above that if price increases (decreases), demand *normally* falls (rises). The word 'normally' is very important and later we shall examine cases where the law of demand may not apply. For the moment, however, we shall assume that the demand curve is downward sloping from left to right, with price measured on the vertical axis and quantity demanded on the horizontal axis, as shown by the line DD in Figure 2.2. Note that if price is continuously increased, a point must eventually be reached where nothing will be demanded, point *P′* in Figure 2.2. Likewise, if supply is continuously increased management will eventually discover that the only way it can sell more is to give the good away! (i.e. charge a zero price – point *Q′* in the figure). The line DD in Figure 2.2 is referred to, generally, as a demand 'curve' – despite the fact that in this diagram it is shown as a straight line. Economists frequently use linear demand relationships as approximations for true relationships between price and demand which may in fact be non-linear (such as D′D′ in Figure 2.2). This is purely for convenience and illustration in textbooks, though over small sections of the curve a linear representation will often provide a close enough approximation to predict actual changes in demand.

Utility and the demand curve

Why do consumers buy more of something the lower its price? One explanation put forward by economists relates to the concept of *utility*. A good or service has utility if consumers want it, in other words if it satisfies a want or a need.

The term *utility* describes the pleasure, satisfaction or benefit derived by a person from the consumption of goods or services.

When people consume more of something in a given time period the *total utility* from their entire consumption usually rises but the *marginal utility* will tend to fall.

Marginal utility is the addition to total utility as a consumer purchases each extra unit of a good or service.

The decline in marginal utility with increasing consumption is associated with the *law of diminishing marginal utility*. Like other 'laws' in economics, it is not incontrovertible but identifies a tendency. The idea that we obtain less additional utility from extra units of a good consumed will not necessarily be true, especially where tastes change or incomes alter, but it will *tend* to be true.

If the additional utility obtained by a consumer from each extra unit purchased is falling then it follows that the consumer will only be willing to buy extra units at progressively lower prices. The price paid by the consumer for a particular good or service represents purchasing power that could have been spent on other goods or services. The consumer will therefore distribute expenditure between goods and services so that the total utility obtained from a given income is maximised. This will occur where the consumer can no longer continue to redistribute expenditure to obtain a higher total utility. This is a situation known as *consumer equilibrium*, which can be expressed in notation form as follows:

Consumer equilibrium

$$\frac{MU_a}{P_a} = \frac{MU_b}{P_b} \ldots = \frac{MU_z}{P_z}$$

where

MU	= marginal utility
P	= price
$a, b, \ldots, z$	= various goods and services consumed

This equilibrium condition means that when the consumer considers whether to buy a particular unit of a product, he or she is deciding whether the marginal utility derived exceeds the marginal utility that would be obtained from buying an alternative good with the same money. In other words, in order to maximise their total utility, consumers distribute their expenditure so that the ratio of marginal utilities for all the goods and services they consume at any given time is equal to their relative prices.

Assume two goods only, a and b and initially $MU_a/P_a = MU_b/P_b$. If the price of, say, good a rises, the ratio MU_a/P_a falls. Now $MU_a/P_a < MU_b/P_b$. This means that the price rise has disturbed the consumer equilibrium. To restore the equilibrium, the consumer will buy less of good a and buy more of good b (assuming that the consumer always spends all of his or her income). As this happens, the marginal utility from good a will rise and that from good b will fall (the law of diminishing marginal utility operates), until once again $MU_a/P_a = MU_b/P_b$. At this point there is no incentive for the consumer further to redistribute spending between goods a and b.

The concept of marginal utility helps us to understand why some goods which are necessary for life (e.g. water) cost less in the market than other products which are considered to be luxuries (e.g. diamonds). The marginal utility of the first unit of water consumed will be very high but we consume lots of water. Hence, the utility from the *last* unit of water consumed is relatively low. By contrast, diamonds are scarce and the marginal utility from 'consumption' tends to be very high. The outcome is that water is sold at a much lower price than diamonds. Although water is a necessity and diamonds are a luxury, utility theory explains the apparent paradox that some necessities are priced lower than luxuries. This example is often referred to as the *paradox of value*.

The purpose of utility theory is simply to help us understand why consumers tend to buy more of something (or less of something) when its price falls (rises). But, of course, consumers are not computers and economists do not believe that consumers consciously calculate marginal utility-to-price ratios as they do their shopping! All that is implied in utility theory, and the concept of the consumer equilibrium, is that consumers when spending act *as if* they are balancing the utility they obtain from additional purchases of goods and services against the price they have to pay for them. Therefore, when spending, consumers are taking into account the alternatives that they could buy with their money and the satisfaction (utility) that such purchases would provide.

An alternative approach to the analysis of consumer demand, *indifference curve theory*, is set out in Appendix 2.1 to this chapter. It should be noted that not all business economics courses deal with consumer demand using the theory of indifference curves – hence the reason for placing the discussion in an appendix.

Consumer surplus

The negative slope of the demand curve, illustrated earlier in Figure 2.2, gives rise to a concept that is influential in guiding economic policy on competition, known as *consumer surplus*. The concept of utility forms the basis for an understanding of this concept.

> *Consumer surplus* is the excess of the price which a person would be willing to pay rather than go without the good, over that which he or she actually does pay.

This is also sometimes referred to as *consumer's rent*. The magnitude of consumer surplus can be approximated by the area under the demand curve, which represents the additional aggregate payment consumers would pay in excess of the amounts actually paid for a good at the going price. For example, in Figure 2.2 consumer surplus is the triangular area $P'P''B$ if the product was sold at price P''.

One way of appreciating the meaning of this concept is to imagine that goods are sold on an open auction basis so that each potential consumer is able to bid the price that he or she is willing to pay for each unit – each bid will thus reflect the marginal valuation placed on that good by each individual and (presumably), therefore, the marginal utility which he or she expects to derive from the good. If the good is being sold to each consumer on the basis of the highest price each is willing to pay, this would ensure that no consumer surplus remains. This type of behaviour on the part of the seller (i.e., the auctioneer in this case) gives rise to the notion of a *discriminating monopolist* (see the analysis of price discrimination set out in Chapter 12). In other words, everyone will have paid a price that just equals the valuation they have each placed on each unit of the good consumed. This is equivalent in Figure 2.2 to every individual unit demanded being sold at the price shown for that unit by the demand curve. For example, every unit between B and P' in Figure 2.2 would be sold at a progressively higher price along the demand curve thereby eliminating the consumer surplus. By way of an example, suppose a petrol retailer is free to charge customers different prices on the basis of their willingness to pay. To maximise profits, the retailer would charge each customer the highest possible price. So, for example, someone who has to use a car to get to work would be charged more for each litre of petrol than someone whose car use was more optional.

Application 2.1

Marginal utility and water shortages

Demand and supply in disequilibrium

Water shortages have been a common feature in many areas of the UK in recent years as demand has outstripped supply. This has led to frequent bans on the use of hosepipes and appeals to the public to reduce consumption.

Rising living standards (and, to a lesser extent, a rising population) have been responsible for the rising level of demand for water by households. As real incomes have grown so more households have cars to wash, gardens to water, and appliances that use large quantities of water (e.g. dishwashers). Most houses do not have water meters. Instead, water bills commonly vary according to the size of the property and are unrelated to the actual amount of water used. Water to industry (and to some households) is metered – and hence there is a real price for each unit of this water consumed.

On the supply side, periods of drought coupled with widespread leakages from old pipes have led to water shortages in some parts of the country. There is, as yet, no national water grid to move large volumes of water from one area to another.

The industry faces the task in future years of bringing the market for water into genuine market equilibrium – instead of relying on emergency rationing measures and appeals to the public for voluntary restraint to reduce demand during times of inadequate supply.

The marginal utility of water

The present fixed charge system for water supply to most households means that these consumers treat water as a free good, not an economic good. Given that these households pay the same in water charges per year regardless of actual consumption, they have an incentive to consume water up to the point where the marginal utility equals zero. In this way, they maximise *consumer surplus*.

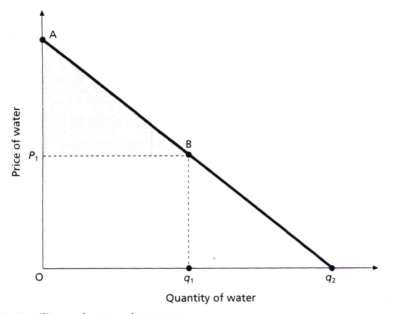

Marginal utility and water shortages

The figure illustrates this point. Under the present system, consumption will be q_2 for the household using unmetered water. For the consumer the price is effectively zero and the consumer surplus is the whole area under the demand curve (area AOq_2).

However, if water were priced by a meter at P_1 per unit then the demand for water could be expected to fall to q_1. Consumer surplus would be reduced to the shaded area AP_1B.

Water metering is clearly an attractive option, based on economic grounds. Critics argue however, that there may be adverse affects for poorer families and public health issues if incentives are put in place to use less water.

Activity

How would you solve the 'water' problem? Justify your views.

The determinants of demand

As we have stated above, the study of consumer behaviour generally shows that as the price of a good falls, consumers will choose to buy more of it, *ceteris paribus*. However, a change in the price of the good itself is only one determinant of the total quantity of the good demanded. For example, we would expect the demand for butter to be affected by the price of margarine (a *substitute good*) and the price of bread (a *complementary good*).

A listing of the most important factors which determine demand might include the following:

Determinants of demand

- The 'own price' of the good itself (P_o).
- The price of substitute goods (P_s).
- The price of complementary goods (P_c).
- The level of advertising expenditure on the product in question, a, as well as on complementary and substitute products, $b, \ldots, z$ (denoted $A_{a,b,\ldots z}$).
- The level and distribution of consumers' *disposable* incomes (Y_d), i.e. income after state direct taxes and benefits.
- Wealth effects (W) caused by, for example, stock market booms, rising house prices, windfall gains, etc.
- Changes in consumers' tastes and preferences (T).
- The cost and availability of credit (C).
- Consumers' expectations concerning future price rises and availability of the product (E).
- Changes in population (POP), if we are examining the total market demand.

In relation to particular products some of these factors may be more important as determinants of demand than others. The factors other than 'own price' which affect demand may generally be described as representing the *conditions of demand* (i.e. the 'environment' within which consumers decide how much to purchase at any given price). We can summarise these conditions in a *demand function*, which in shorthand notation expresses the quantity demanded of a product (Q_d) over a given time period.

Demand function

$$Q_d = f(P_o, P_s, P_c, A_{a,b,\ldots z}, Y_d, W, T, C, E, POP)$$

Thus, the demand curve (either DD or D′D′) in Figure 2.2 above shows the quantities of the good in question that will be bought (Q_d) at different prices (P_o) *with all the other factors in the demand function held constant*. Clearly, as P_o changes, there will be a *movement along* the demand curve, say from A to B (in the case of a price rise) or B to A (in the case of a price fall). However, if any of the other factors in the demand function should change, then there will be a *shift* in the demand curve, as illustrated in Figure 2.3. This highlights the fact that, as the conditions of demand change (except for P_o, the 'own price'), there will be a new price–quantity relationship established. For example, a stock market boom is likely to mean that at any given price, P_o, more will be demanded arising from a wealth effect, shown by the increase from Q_0 to Q_1 in Figure 2.3. Likewise, stock market and property crashes (as in Japan in the 1990s) will tend to lead to a leftward shift in demand curves.

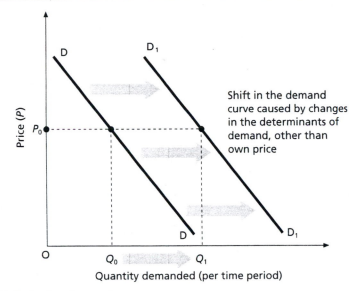

Figure 2.3 Shift in the demand curve

The distinction between a *movement along* a product's demand curve and a *shift* in the curve is useful because it helps to identify the causes and nature of changes in demand.

When the own price of a product changes, the outcome is a *movement along the demand curve* and when any other determinants of demand change, there will be a *shift of the demand curve* (either to the left, showing a fall in the quantity demanded, or to the right, showing a rise) depending on the nature of the change.

Some examples of shifts in demand curves are presented in Figure 2.4.

The classification of products

There are two distinct reasons why more (less) of a good is usually demanded as its price falls (rises). These are referred to as the 'income effect' and the 'substitution effect':

- **The income effect.** As its own price falls, consumers are in effect better off and hence able to buy more of the good. The fall in price has raised their effective purchasing power, while the opposite applies in the case of a price rise. The change in price is equivalent, in effect, to a change in income (though *actual* income is unchanged).

- **The substitution effect.** As the price of a product falls, it becomes relatively cheaper than alternatives. Hence, there is a tendency for consumers to switch towards the product in question, substituting more of it for other goods. The opposite outcome occurs, of course, where there is a rise in the price of the product.

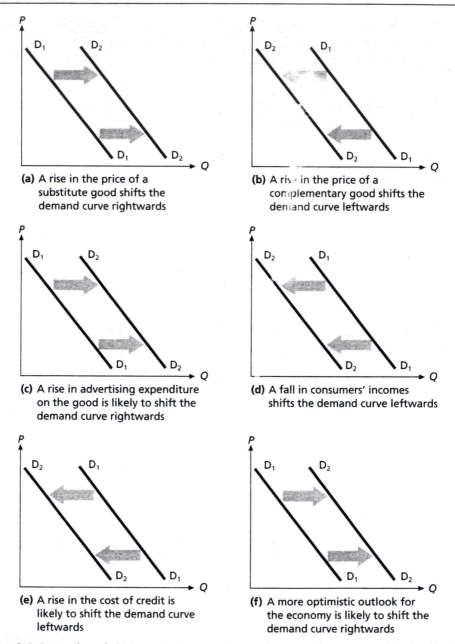

(a) A rise in the price of a substitute good shifts the demand curve rightwards

(b) A rise in the price of a complementary good shifts the demand curve leftwards

(c) A rise in advertising expenditure on the good is likely to shift the demand curve rightwards

(d) A fall in consumers' incomes shifts the demand curve leftwards

(e) A rise in the cost of credit is likely to shift the demand curve leftwards

(f) A more optimistic outlook for the economy is likely to shift the demand curve rightwards

Figure 2.4 Examples of changes in the conditions of demand (demand curves DD refer to the good in question)

The substitution effect on demand of a price change will always be opposite in direction to the price change (assuming rational behaviour on the part of the consumers) or zero if no substitutes exist at all (this is unlikely). The income effect, however, can either increase or reduce demand depending not only on the direction of the income change but also on the nature of the good or service. The direction of the income effect allows us to classify the nature of products under the following particular headings:

- Normal products.
- Inferior products.
- Giffen products.
- Veblen products.

We explain the meaning and significance of each of these in turn.

Normal products

Goods and services may be classified as 'normal products' if the quantity demanded rises as incomes rise and falls as incomes fall. (Here, as throughout the rest of the chapter, income refers to a change in *real purchasing power* rather than simply a nominal change which may be neutralised by a proportionate price change.) For example, family cars would be classified as 'normal' since as household incomes rise, the demand for such cars also generally rises. Note that the key factor is the link between quantity demand and *income* – we would still expect an inverse relationship between *price* and quantity demanded.

Inferior products

Certain products are classified as 'inferior' because the demand for them *falls* as incomes *rise* (and vice versa). For example, as household incomes rise, there may be a tendency to switch from buying cheaper, lower-quality 'junk' food to higher-quality foods. The switch from inferior to superior products is common as real incomes rise over time. For most inferior goods, however, there is still likely to be an overall increase in demand as their price falls. This is because the *positive substitution effect* (i.e. a switch towards the relatively inexpensive product) more than offsets the *negative income effect* on demand.

Giffen products

A special case of the inferior product arises when, as price *rises*, more of the good in question is bought – resulting seemingly in an *upward* sloping demand curve, contrary to the normal law of demand. Such products are classified as Giffen products, named after a nineteenth-century English economist who studied the response to changes in the price of potatoes in Ireland. Giffen found that as the price of potatoes rose, the Irish at that time bought more since they could not now afford to buy as much of the more expensive foodstuffs such as meat. This response to a price change is still found today in developing countries – for example, as the price of rice rises, people may be forced to buy less meat and fish in order to be able to continue buying sufficient quantities of rice to stay alive – hence the vicious circle of famine and malnutrition so common in many parts of Africa and other developing regions. In the case of Giffen products, the income effect of a price change is so large that it swamps the substitution effect, leading to an overall rise (fall) in demand for the product as its price rises (declines).

Veblen products

It has been suggested that 'luxury type' products also display perverse price–demand relationships, though for different reasons to that of the Giffen products case. These are sometimes referred to as Veblen products, after the American economist, Thorstein Veblen, who explored the phenomenon. For example, as the price of a piece of jewellery rises, the demand for it may also rise because consumers attach a higher 'snob' value to owning and displaying the item. Equally, as the price falls there is the possibility that the product could lose its up-market image – 'everyone can afford it, so why bother to buy it'! This situation reflects a change in tastes, determined by the perception of the product in relation to its price. The existence of a positive Veblen effect is, of course, very advantageous to some producers of luxury goods since it enables them to charge premium prices for their products.

Concepts of elasticity

The discussion so far has been concerned with the broad direction of relationships between price changes, changes in other possible determinants of demand and the quantity demanded. However, in addition to understanding the *nature* of demand, it would of course be very useful if management were able to estimate the *extent* to which demand is likely to respond to a price change. Gauging this responsiveness is referred to by economists as *the measurement of price elasticity*. In addition, because, as we have seen, demand is affected by many factors, we can calculate elasticity (i.e. responsiveness of quantity demanded) with respect to a wide range of variables other than price, notably the price of other goods and income. Thus we can define the following three key concepts:

- *Price elasticity of demand.* This measures the responsiveness of quantity demanded of a product to changes in its 'own price'. For example, if the price of alcohol increases, what happens to the quantity of alcohol demanded?
- *Cross-price elasticity of demand.* This measures the responsiveness of quantity demanded to changes in the prices of other goods (both complements and substitutes). For example, if the price of one brand of coffee rises, what happens to the demand for another coffee brand? Or, if the price of petrol falls, what happens to the demand for cars?
- *Income elasticity of demand.* This measures the responsiveness of demand to a change in the income of consumers. For example, if incomes are rising, on average, by $50 per month, what will happen to the demand for housing?

In general terms, a *coefficient of elasticity* can be calculated for each of the above categories using the following general formula:

$$Coefficient\ of\ elasticity = \frac{\text{Percentage change in quantity demanded}}{\text{Percentage change in the relevant variable}}$$

We will now examine each of these three elasticity concepts in more detail.

Price elasticity of demand

Based on the general formula, the (own) price elasticity of demand for a product, denoted E_d, may be measured as:

Price elasticity of demand

$$E_d = \frac{\text{Percentage change in quantity demanded}}{\text{Percentage change in the price of the product}}$$

Where a product has a downward sloping demand curve (the usual case), the value of the price elasticity of demand will always be negative – because when price rises demand falls and when price falls demand rises. Conventionally, however, the negative sign is omitted when the value of elasticity is stated. We follow this convention in the following discussion.

Two different types of price elasticity (E_d) can be calculated, as follows:

- **Arc** elasticity of demand.
- **Point** elasticity of demand.

Arc elasticity of demand

With reference to Figure 2.5, *arc elasticity* measures the responsiveness of demand between two points on the demand curve such as X and Y, whereas, as the name suggests, *point elasticity* is concerned with the elasticity at only one given point of the curve. Since managers are usually concerned with estimating the effect on demand of, say, a 5% rise in price, the price change causes a movement along a section of the demand curve and hence the arc elasticity formula is the relevant one.

Using the notation shown in Figure 2.5, we can calculate arc elasticity as:

Arc elasticity of demand

$$Arc\ E_d = \frac{(Q_2 - Q_1)/\frac{1}{2}(Q_2 + Q_1)}{(P_2 - P_1)/\frac{1}{2}(P_2 + P_1)}$$

$$= \frac{(Q_2 - Q_1)}{(P_2 - P_1)} \times \frac{(P_2 + P_1)}{(Q_2 + Q_1)}$$

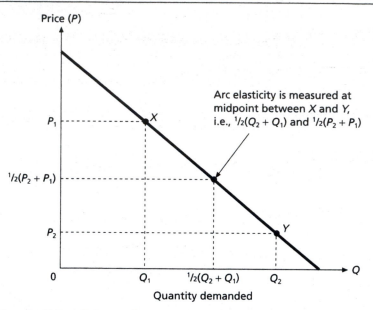

Figure 2.5 Arc elasticity of demand

It is important to appreciate the reason why arc elasticity is expressed on the basis of the average quantity, $\frac{1}{2}(Q_2 + Q_1)$, and average price, $\frac{1}{2}(P_2 + P_1)$. When there is an appreciable price change, the value of elasticity calculated on the basis of X as the starting point will differ from that calculated on the basis of Y as the starting point (as in Figure 2.5) – we end up with two different values for the sensitivity of demand to price changes, which may not be very useful in business decisions. Using the midpoint, however, ensures that price elasticity is the same regardless of the direction of movement on the demand curve and, because it is based on the average price and average quantity, it will be closer to the true estimate of elasticity over the price range than that based on either of the two extreme points, X and Y.

Point elasticity of demand

It should be intuitively clear from Figure 2.5 that as X and Y come closer together, the arc shrinks in size and the two values for elasticities calculated at X and Y separately get closer to each other. If the distance is negligible, the arc will end up as a single point and therefore on the right-hand side of the arc elasticity equation $(P_2 + P_1)/(Q_2 + Q_1)$ collapses to P/Q at point X.

The *point elasticity* formula, therefore, is:

Point elasticity of demand

$$\text{Point } E_d = \frac{(Q_2 - Q_1)/Q_1}{(P_2 - P_1)/P_1} = \frac{(Q_2 - Q_1)}{(P_2 - P_1)} \times \frac{P_1}{Q_1}$$

While point elasticity is expressed here in relation to Q_1 and P_1 it will be appreciated that since the difference between Q_1 and Q_2 and P_1 and P_2 will be infinitesimally small, it no longer matters whether we use the initial or final price and quantity values. In business, of course, management is unlikely to be interested in 'infinitesimally' small changes in price since it is impractical to introduce, say, a 0.0001% change in the retail price of most products! However, while arc elasticity seems to be the more useful estimator for managers wrestling with the likely effects on the demand for their product of a price change, point elasticity has a role in demand forecasting based on the mathematical techniques introduced later in Chapter 17.

The terms 'elastic' and 'inelastic' are often used to describe different degrees of elasticity. In general (and ignoring the negative sign):

- Products with a price elasticity of demand of less than 1 are said to have a relatively inelastic demand with respect to price – they are said to be **price inelastic.**
- Products with a price elasticity of demand greater than 1 are said to have a relatively elastic demand – they are said to be **price elastic.**
- Products with a price elasticity of demand exactly equal to 1 are said to have a **unit (or unitary) elasticity** of demand.

Irrespective of the precise method of calculation, the value of the resulting price elasticity of demand will vary depending upon the nature of the demand for the good or service in question. In Figure 2.6 three extreme price elasticities are illustrated (a, b and c) together with a representation (d) of the range of elasticity values along a downward sloping demand line:

- *Perfectly inelastic demand.* When the demand for a product is entirely unresponsive to any change in price, the demand curve will be a vertical line as shown in Figure 2.6(a) with E_d equal to zero at every point. This is referred to as a *perfectly inelastic demand.*
- *Perfectly elastic demand.* Where the demand curve is horizontal, any quantity of the product can be sold at a certain price, P_1, in Figure 2.6(b). Demand is said to be *perfectly elastic* with a value of infinity at this price. Any increase in the price, no matter how small, will result in none of the product being sold. If the price is reduced, even marginally, demand (theoretically) becomes infinite.
- *Unit or unitary elasticity of demand.* A further special case arises when the shape of the demand curve is a rectangular hyperbola, as in Figure 2.6(c). At any point on it the value of elasticity is equal to *unity* (the area under the curve remains constant as price changes).

The three cases above are, in practice, unlikely to be found and should be treated as theoretical benchmarks for an analysis of actual price elasticities. Small stretches of a demand curve though may closely equate to one or other of these extremes. Figure 2.6(d) shows a situation where the value of elasticity varies between zero and infinity

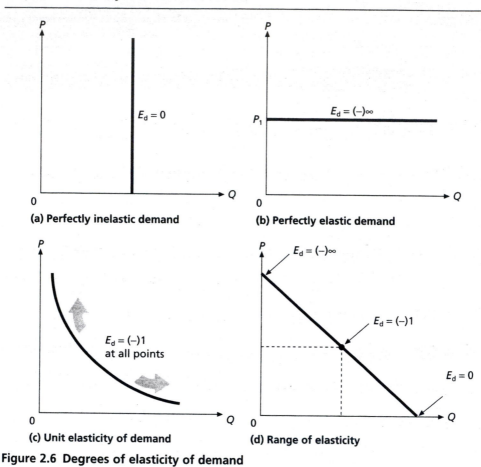

Figure 2.6 Degrees of elasticity of demand

along its length and with a straight-line demand curve the value of 1 is at the midpoint. It is important to appreciate that (excluding the cases of vertical and horizontal demand curves) even where a product has a linear demand curve, its elasticity changes as price is altered. This follows because the original price and quantity figures, which enter into the elasticity calculation (see above), change. This means that price elasticity *must* be recalculated for every price change. If the price elasticity was, say, 0.6 when the price was last increased by 5%, a linear demand curve exists and in the meantime none of the conditions of demand have altered, i.e. the demand curve has not shifted (which in itself is most unlikely), a further 5% increase in price will be associated with a price elasticity above 0.6.

Given that the price elasticity of demand is a numerical measure of the responsiveness of quantity demanded to changes in price, there is a relationship between the value of the elasticity and the total sales revenue received by the firm. This has important implications for pricing strategy and we shall return to it later in this chapter. Before that, however, we discuss the other elasticity of demand measures noted earlier, namely, *cross-price* and *income elasticity*.

Cross-price elasticity of demand

Cross-price elasticity of demand (sometimes simply referred to as 'cross-elasticity') indicates the responsiveness of the demand for one product to changes in the prices of other goods or services. The concept has most relevance where there are obvious substitute or complementary commodities and it is, therefore, of key importance to businesses which face major competition or whose sales vary directly with the sales of other goods, e.g. mortgages and mortgage protection insurance.

If A is the good or service we are interested in and B is the other product whose price is altering, we can calculate the value of the cross-price elasticity of demand for A with respect to B as:

Cross-price elasticity of demand

$$\text{Cross-price } E_d = \frac{\text{Percentage change in the demand for A}}{\text{Percentage change in the price of B}}$$

In the case of substitutes, the resulting figure will be *positive* since a rise in the price of a substitute will lead to fewer sales of the substitute and hence a rise in the demand for the other product being considered. In the case of complementary products, the resultant value will be *negative*. If the demands for the two goods are unrelated then, of course, the cross-price elasticities between them can be expected to be negligible or zero.

The terminology regarding the degree of cross-price elasticity (ignoring the sign) is the same as for price elasticity, namely:

- 1 = unit cross-price elasticity.
- Less than 1 = inelastic cross-price elasticity.
- Greater than 1 = elastic cross-price elasticity.

Income elasticity of demand

As noted earlier, demand is also likely to be responsive to factors other than 'own price' and the price of complements and substitutes. One important factor is real income (i.e. nominal income adjusted for inflation). Income elasticity of demand is defined as:

Income elasticity of demand

$$\text{Income } E_d = \frac{\text{Percentage change in demand}}{\text{Percentage change in real income}}$$

The value of the income elasticity will usually be positive, suggesting that more is bought as real income rises, though for certain products it may be negative as we saw earlier. The actual values of income elasticities can be used to classify products into the following two broad categories:

43

Inferior goods

These are goods of which consumers buy less when real incomes rise. The value of income elasticity is, therefore, negative. Examples might be potatoes, unbranded clothing, cheap package holidays, etc.

Normal goods

These are the most common goods with demand generally rising as real income rises. They can themselves be further subdivided into two categories:

- *Necessities*. These are goods and services which exhibit a positive income elasticity of demand, though the value will tend to be less than 1. Articles such as basic foodstuffs and ordinary day-to-day clothing fall into this category. Consumers will purchase a certain amount of these goods at very low levels of income, but they will tend for any given percentage increase in real income to increase their spending on the goods by a smaller proportion.

- *Luxuries*. At very low income levels, nothing will be spent on these but, once a certain threshold income level is reached, the proportionate rise in demand for luxury goods is greater than the proportionate rise in real income, e.g. foreign holidays, dining out and DVD players.

From the above classification it is obvious that it will pay firms which want to expand output very quickly to concentrate on selling products with high income elasticities when living standards are rising. With greater purchasing power, people will tend to buy disproportionately more of luxury-type goods. On the other hand, firms producing goods with low income elasticities will tend to face a more stable market for their products and will be less affected in times of economic downturn. The food retailing industry is usually an example of this.

Application 2.2

Demand and price elasticity

Public good versus pay-per-view TV

Public (or social) goods are paid for out of general taxation and not by individual consumers buying in the market place. Traditionally, television viewing has been regarded as a public good with viewers paying a fixed licence fee, regardless of the length of viewing time. The emergence of signal scramblers, cable, satellite and digital broadcasting has significantly reduced the public good characteristics of television in the UK.

The new technologies now mean that households can be excluded from watching a broadcast. The consequence is that charging viewers directly for watching a specific channel or event is increasingly common.

The first pay-per-view TV event in the UK took place in 1996, when satellite operator BSkyB broadcast a heavyweight boxing match between Frank Bruno and Mike Tyson. Over 600,000 BSkyB subscribers watched the fight, representing about 15% of all BSkyB subscribers at that time. The fight was also broadcast to more than 2,000 pubs and clubs throughout Britain. The success of this experiment, which made a small profit, was ascribed to the relatively low price of £9.99 for basic household access. At this time, in the USA, pay-per-view boxing of a similar quality, was priced at just over the dollar equivalent of £25.

In June 2000 the cable company, NTL, paid £328 million to win the rights for three years to broadcast 40 English Premier League football matches per season on a pay-per-view basis. Charges have been set at around £5 per game.

Activity

What factors are likely to influence the overall market for pay-per-view sport in television in the years ahead? What factors will affect the price elasticity of a pay-per-view event?

The relationship between price elasticity and sales revenue

In addition to income elasticity, a firm's fortunes are affected by price elasticity because demand, and hence the firm's revenue, changes as a result of price changes. The total receipts or *total revenue* (TR) earned by a business from sales is calculated by multiplying the total output sold (Q) by the average unit price (P), i.e. $TR = P \times Q$.

$$\text{Total revenue} = \text{price} \times \text{quantity sold}$$

$$TR = P \times Q$$

The resulting value of total revenue is illustrated by the shaded area in Figure 2.7 with price at P_1 and quantity demanded equal to Q_1. Where there is unit elasticity of

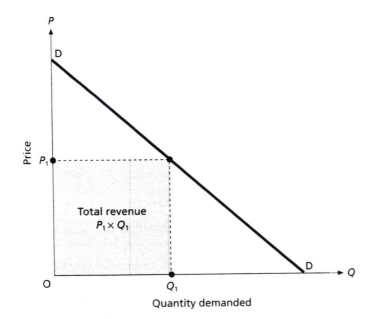

Figure 2.7 Demand and total revenue

45

demand, as the price is varied the total revenue earned from sales remains unchanged. For example, a 1% fall in price will bring about a 1% rise in sales, leaving total revenue (the area under the demand curve) unaltered. However, as we indicated earlier, unit elasticity is an extreme case and unlikely to be found over more than modest stretches of a demand curve. It will usually be the case that the value of elasticity will vary along the demand curve, as shown earlier in Figure 2.6(d). As price changes by a certain proportion, the quantity demanded usually changes by a greater or lesser proportion.

In general, we can derive the following rules concerning price elasticity and total revenue:

Price elasticity and total revenue

- **With a price inelastic demand:**
  (a) an increase in price causes a reduction in quantity demanded, but total revenue increases;
  (b) a fall in price causes an increase in quantity demanded, but total revenue earned declines.
- **With a price elastic demand:**
  (a) an increase in price causes such a large fall in quantity demanded that total revenue falls;
  (b) a reduction in price causes such a large increase in the quantity demanded that the total revenue rises.

Hence, it is clear that estimates of price elasticity are vital to business decision-making. Putting this another way, complete ignorance of the market response to price changes is likely to be a recipe for disaster!

The link between total revenue and price elasticity results from the fact that, faced with a downward sloping demand curve for a product, management must lower price if they want to sell more (other factors held constant). But if extra sales compensate for the lower unit price, then total revenue will not decline. Similarly, management might raise the price of a product to raise revenues, but the resulting collapse of demand may actually cause total revenue to contract. In other words, the precise *responsiveness* of demand to a price change determines the effect of a price change on revenue received. This introduces another important concept, which will be used throughout much of the remainder of this book, namely, *marginal revenue*.

Marginal revenue

Marginal revenue (MR) is defined as the change in (Δ) total revenue (TR) as a firm sells one more or one less unit of its output (Q).

$$MR = \frac{\Delta TR}{\Delta Q}$$

The size of a 'unit' will vary from firm to firm – for example, the smallest unit of water which is charged to domestic users is likely to be much more than a single litre, while the car dealer may be concerned with the sale of a single car. To be mathematically correct, marginal revenue is the change in total revenue resulting from an infinitesimally small change in quantity sold. But it can be approximated by looking at the change in total revenue resulting from a small, quantifiable, change in output.

Figure 2.8 shows the relationship between elasticity, total revenue, marginal revenue (MR) and the demand curve (DD). The demand curve is also the average revenue (AR) curve because it shows the price at which each unit is sold.

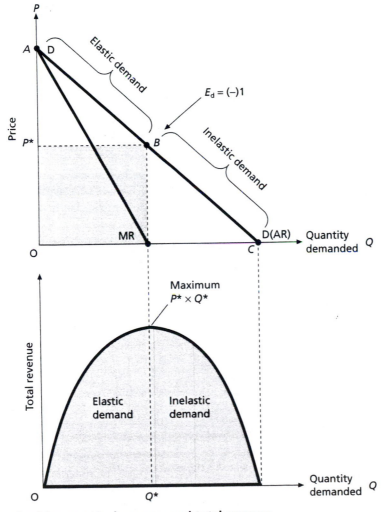

Figure 2.8 Elasticity, marginal revenue and total revenue

Average revenue (AR) is the total revenue (TR) divided by output (Q) or the revenue earned on average for each unit sold.

$$AR = \frac{TR}{Q}$$

Provided that when units are sold they are all sold at the same price, price and average revenue must be identical – and hence the demand curve is also the average revenue curve.

Based on Figure 2.8, the key relationships to note are as follows:

- **Marginal revenue falls as output rises.** Since the demand curve slopes downwards, the addition to total revenue from producing and selling extra units declines.

- **Average revenue exceeds marginal revenue.** When the demand curve is downward sloping, the marginal revenue from selling one more unit falls faster than the average revenue from selling the total output.

- **The marginal revenue curve declines at twice the rate of the demand (average revenue) curve.** Hence, the marginal revenue curve cuts the horizontal axis at a point midway between the origin and point C in Figure 2.8. A proof of this mathematical relationship is given in Appendix 2.2 at the end of the chapter.

- **When total revenue is increasing, marginal revenue is positive.** This results from the fact that demand is elastic between points A and B on the demand curve DD in Figure 2.8.

- **When total revenue is falling, marginal revenue is negative.** A negative marginal revenue results from demand being inelastic between points B and C in Figure 2.8.

- **Total revenue is maximised when marginal revenue is zero which occurs when the price elasticity is unitary.** Therefore, further attempts to increase total revenue by lowering price below P* will fail because the sales volume will not increase sufficiently to compensate for the price fall.

Marginal revenue is concerned with changes in total revenue resulting from small changes in sales. Since many business decisions hang on whether to increase or reduce sales, the concept of marginal revenue is central to much of the discussion relating to business decision-making in subsequent chapters. It is important, therefore, that the reader should not proceed further until the concept and its relationship to total revenue and average revenue are fully understood.

Concluding remarks

This chapter has been concerned with consumer demand and, specifically, with shedding light on the relationship between utility, the price of a product, the quantity demanded and firms' revenues. As we have seen, normally when the price of a product is reduced the quantity demanded by consumers rises. The precise relationship between demand and price depends upon the shape of the product's demand curve and can be measured using the concept of *price elasticity*. But for some goods and services demand may be as much, or more, affected by changes in the *conditions of demand*, notably the price of substitutes or complementary products and changes in consumers' incomes. This chapter has also, therefore, been concerned with exploring the relationship between demand and certain non-price factors. The relationship between price and revenue and the importance of non-price factors in the *marketing mix* (the mix of factors taken into account by managers when deciding their marketing strategies) is probed further in Chapter 12.

Of course, the practising manager might object that he or she has insufficient information to construct relevant demand curves. Often the manager may possess, at best, only an intuitive feel for the effect of a price increase or reduction. The demand relationship is also likely to be clouded by uncertainty as to how rival producers might react to a price change – an issue pursued at length in Chapter 9. Economists recognise that normally business decisions have to be made in the face of incomplete, and often very fragmentary, information. The analysis in this chapter has been designed simply to provide a framework for decision-making. It is not intended to imply that economists believe that managers can (or should) estimate their full demand curves. But it is important that managers appreciate that their products *do* have demand curves, even if they find it difficult or impossible to construct them accurately. When the price of a firm's product changes or there are changes in other factors, such as consumers' incomes, demand is very likely to be affected. An ability to separate out the different influences on the demand for a product and an awareness of the likely elasticities are important assets for any manager planning a business strategy. Also important is a knowledge of the nature of the relevant costs of production, the subject to which we turn in the next chapter.

Key learning points

- A **demand curve** relates the amount that consumers are willing to buy to each conceivable price for the product.
- In general, the **law of demand** states that there is an inverse relationship between the price of a good and the quantity demanded, assuming all other factors that might influence demand are held constant (i.e. *ceteris paribus*).
- **Utility theory** helps explain why consumers buy more of something the lower its price.

- **Marginal utility** is the addition to total utility as a consumer purchases each extra unit of a good or service.

- **The law of diminishing marginal utility** is concerned with the tendency for marginal utility to fall as more units of a good or service are consumed at any given time.

- **Consumer equilibrium** describes how consumers maximise their total utility by distributing expenditure so that the ratio of marginal utilities for all the goods and services they consume, at any given time, is equal to their relative prices.

- **Consumer surplus** is reflected by the excess of the price which a person would be willing to pay rather than go without the good, over that which he or she actually does pay.

- When the own price of a good changes, the outcome is a **movement along the demand curve** and when any other determinant or condition of demand changes, there will be a **shift of the demand curve**.

- The impact of a change in price on quantity demanded is made up of two distinct effects: an **income effect** and a **substitution effect**. The income effect arises from the fact that as the own price of a good falls, consumers are in effect better off and hence able to buy more of the good. The substitution effect reflects the fact that as the price falls, the product becomes relatively cheaper than alternatives and hence there will be a tendency for consumers to substitute more of it for other goods.

- Goods and services are classified as **normal products** if the quantity demanded rises as (real) incomes rise and falls as incomes fall.

- In contrast, goods and services are classified as **inferior products** if the quantity demanded falls (rises) as incomes rise (fall).

- A **Giffen product** is a special case of an inferior product and has what appears to be an upward sloping demand curve, contrary to the normal law of demand, because the income effect outweighs the substitution effect.

- A **Veblen product** also has seemingly an upward sloping demand curve because of 'snob' effects, i.e. it is demanded because it is expensive and therefore exclusive. Many luxury products fit into this category.

- The (own) **price elasticity of demand** for a product may be defined in general terms as:

$$E_d = \frac{\text{Percentage change in quantity demanded}}{\text{Percentage change in the price of the product}}$$

- The value of E_d may be calculated on the basis of a movement along a section of the demand curve, giving rise to a value of the **arc elasticity**. This is expressed on the basis of the average quantity and average price, as follows:

$$\text{Arc } E_d = \frac{(Q_2 - Q_1)}{(P_2 - P_1)} \times \frac{(P_2 + P_1)}{(Q_2 + Q_1)}$$

- For very small price changes, elasticity may be calculated with reference to a single point on the demand curve, giving rise to a value of the **point elasticity**, as follows:

$$\text{Point } E_d = \frac{(Q_2 - Q_1)}{(P_2 - P_1)} \times \frac{P_1}{Q_1}$$

- Products with a price elasticity of demand of less than 1 (in absolute terms) are said to have a relatively inelastic demand with respect to price – they are said to be **price inelastic**. In this case, total sales revenue will tend to rise (fall) as price rises (falls).

- Products with a price elasticity of demand greater than 1 (in absolute terms) are said to have a relatively elastic demand – they are said to be **price elastic**. In this case, total sales revenue will tend to fall (rise) as price rises (falls).

- Products with a price elasticity of demand equal to 1 (in absolute terms) are said to have a **unit or unitary elasticity** of demand. In this case, total sales revenue will remain unchanged as price rises or falls.

- The value of price elasticity of demand can range from infinity (in absolute terms) to 0. A product with a **perfectly inelastic demand** will have a value of E_d equal to 0 at every price, while a product with a **perfectly elastic demand** will have a value of E_d equal to infinity at a particular price.

- **Cross-price elasticity of demand** indicates the responsiveness of the demand for one product to changes in the prices of other goods and services and may be calculated as:

$$\text{Cross-price } E_d = \frac{\text{Percentage change in the demand for A}}{\text{Percentage change in the price of B}}$$

- **Substitutes** will tend to have a positive value for cross-price E_d, while **complements** will tend to have a **negative** value.

- **Income elasticity of demand** measures the responsiveness of quantity demanded with respect to (real) income variations as follows:

$$\text{Income } E_d = \frac{\text{Percentage change in quantity demanded}}{\text{Percentage change in real income}}$$

- **Necessities** exhibit a positive income elasticity of demand though the value will tend to be less than 1. In contrast, **luxuries** will tend to have an income elasticity of demand greater than 1.

- **Marginal revenue** is defined as the incremental change in total revenue and is usually measured as a firm sells one more or one less unit of its output.

- The **marginal revenue curve** declines at twice the rate of the demand (average revenue) curve.

- When total revenue is increasing (decreasing), marginal revenue is positive (negative) such that **total revenue is maximised when marginal revenue is zero**. This occurs when the price elasticity of demand is equal to 1.

Appendix 2.1 (see page 53)

- An **indifference curve** shows all combinations of two goods or services that yield the same level of utility or satisfaction so that the consumer is indifferent between each combination.

- The slope of the **budget line** is determined by the relative prices of the two goods or services and the position of the line by the consumer's income.

- Together, the **indifference curve mapping** and the budget line determine the combination of the goods or services that the consumer will choose to buy.

- Indifference curve analysis can be used to show the **income** and **substitution** effects of a price change.

Topics for discussion

1 A marketing manager at the Ford Motor Company in Belgium is preparing a briefing on consumer demand for a new model to be sold mainly in other parts of Europe. Consider the issues that this briefing should contain.

2 Draw what you consider may be the demand curve for this new Ford model in, say, the United Kingdom. Illustrate the effect of:

   (a) a fall in the sterling–euro exchange rate,
   (b) a recession in the United Kingdom, and
   (c) an increase in the price of Peugeot cars made in the UK.

3 Using the concept of consumer surplus, explain why a supplier might wish to charge more to one group of consumers than another.

4 Contrast the likely marketing strategies of:

   (a) a food retailer selling via the internet and
   (b) a fine wines retailer.

   Explain the reasons for the differences based on the classification of goods outlined in this chapter.

5 A bus company operates two routes. On route 1, research suggests that the price elasticity is (–)0.8 and on the other route (–)1.3. The company has decided to revise fares upwards on both routes by 10% this year. Comment on the decision. What alternative pricing strategy would you suggest?

6 An international hotel chain calculates that this year demand for its accommodation in Kuala Lumpur will rise by 15%. The incomes of customers are estimated by the hotel management to be rising by around 10%.

   (a) Assuming all other conditions of demand are unchanged, what do these figures suggest about the income elasticity of demand for the hotel accommodation?
   (b) In practice, what other factors would need to be taken into consideration before accepting this income elasticity figure as the sole basis for estimating the hotel's future demand?

Appendix 2.1 Indifference curve analysis

The meaning of indifference curves

In this chapter we have approached consumer demand using utility theory. Utility is the satisfaction someone obtains from the consumption of goods or services in a given time period. In economic theory there are various approaches to analysing demand, the most commonly found being utility theory, as discussed in the chapter. But another popular approach involves *indifference curve theory*. Not all courses on Business Economics include indifference curve analysis, hence the decision to place this discussion in an appendix. By so doing, the discussion can be skipped by those studying courses which exclude indifference curve theory.

An *indifference curve* details all combinations of two goods or services that yield the *same* level of utility or satisfaction.

Given that the consumer obtains the same utility from all combinations of goods and services along the curve, the consumer will be indifferent between them. This is the basis of the indifference curve approach to consumer demand.

A typical indifference curve I is shown in Figure A2.1 with combinations of goods X and Y to which the consumer is indifferent. The curve shows that the consumer can obtain the same utility if a quantity of one good is given up to consume more of the other good. For example, a movement from *A* to *B* on the curve involves consuming less of Y and more of X, yet the consumer's satisfaction stays the same. The indifference curve is non-linear (not a straight line) because consumers will be willing to give up increasingly smaller amounts of one good, say Y, to obtain additional units of the

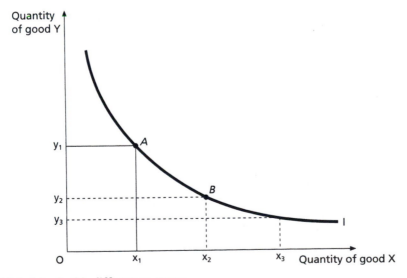

Figure A2.1 A typical indifference curve

other good, X. This follows from the same logic as *the law of diminishing marginal utility*, discussed earlier in the chapter. For utility to remain the same, it must be the case that consumers will require increasingly large amounts of the good they are acquiring to offset the utility lost from the good they are increasingly giving up. In Figure A2.1, the movement from A to B means trading off y_1 to y_2 of good Y to obtain x_1 to x_2 of good X. The same increase in the consumption of good X, from x_2 to x_3, requires a smaller sacrifice of good Y, from y_2 to y_3. This result is consistent with the law of diminishing marginal utility. The consumer is obtaining more and more of good X from which an increasingly smaller addition to total utility is obtained (declining marginal utility). By contrast, each extra unit of good Y given up involves an increasingly larger loss of marginal utility.

The above analysis can be extended to include an *indifference curve mapping* showing a consumer's different utility levels reflected in different indifference curves. The further out the indifference curve lies from the origin, the more goods and services the consumer receives. Assuming that these are goods that individuals wish to consume more of, the rational consumer will wish to be on the highest indifference curve possible. For example, indifference curve I_3 will be preferred to indifference curves I_2 or I_1, in Figure A2.2. This is the case because the individual can then consume more of one good without forgoing some of the other good or can consume more of both goods. For example, in Figure A2.2, by moving from indifference curve I_2 to I_3 the individual can consume x_1 to x_2 more of good X, without giving up any consumption of good Y, *or* y_1 to y_2 of good Y, without forgoing any of good X. Equally, the consumer might choose, say, combination x_3, y_3 and therefore consume more of both goods.

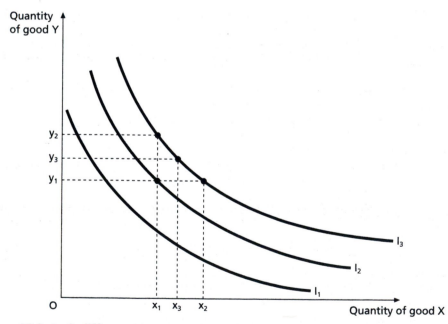

Figure A2.2 An indifference curve map

The rational consumer will always attempt to move to the highest possible indifference curve above the origin. The actual curve to which the consumer moves will be restricted by income because it can be safely assumed that in a market economy the goods and services will have to be purchased! This introduces the notion of a *budget constraint* or *budget line*.

The budget constraint

Assuming that consumers cannot borrow to purchase, the budget constraint is determined by the consumer's income. If the prices of goods X and Y are P_x and P_y respectively and the consumer's income is m, the budget constraint can be written as:

Budget constraint

$$P_xQ_x + P_yQ_y \leq m$$

This notation simply states that the total outlay on goods X and Y (their prices, P_X and P_y, multiplied by the number of units bought, Q_x and Q_y respectively) cannot exceed the consumer's income, m.

In Figure A2.3, the budget constraint is shown as a budget line. The line is determined by the prices of goods X and Y and the income, m. For example, if all of the income m were spent on good X then the consumer could buy the number of units of

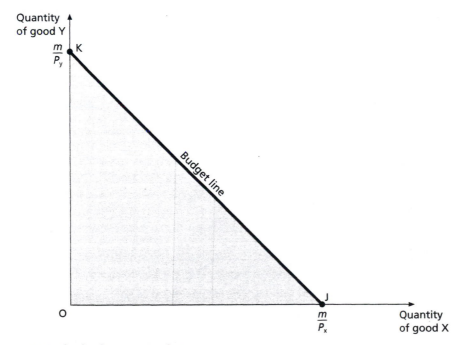

Figure A2.3 The budget constraint

X shown by the point where the budget line meets the Q_x axis, i.e. point J (given by m/P_x). If all of the income was spent on good Y then the maximum consumption of Y is given by point K, where the budget line meets the Q_y axis (given by m/P_y). It follows, therefore, that a consumer with income m could choose either to buy quantity J of X or quantity K of Y or any combination of X and Y as shown along the budget line, KJ. A consumer could also buy any combination of the goods within the triangle formed by the budget line and the axes and shaded in Figure A2.3. But buying a combination of goods *within* the budget line would imply that not all of the consumer's income was spent.

The *slope* of the budget line is determined by the relative prices of the two goods and the *position* of the line by the consumer's income.

The budget line will change, therefore, whenever there is a change in the prices of goods X or Y or a change in the individual's income. For example in Figure A2.4 an increase in income is shown by an outward movement of the budget line from M_1 to M_2 revealing that more of both goods can now be bought. A reduction in the price of good X from P_{x1} to P_{x2}, which allows more of good X to be bought with the same income, is shown by a movement from point A to point B on the X axis. Note that there is no change in the point at which the budget line meets the Y axis because the price of good Y remains unchanged.

The budget line is a constraint on consumption determined by income and the prices of goods. Given that consumers wish to maximise utility from any given income, the consumer will wish to operate on the highest indifference curve from the origin. By

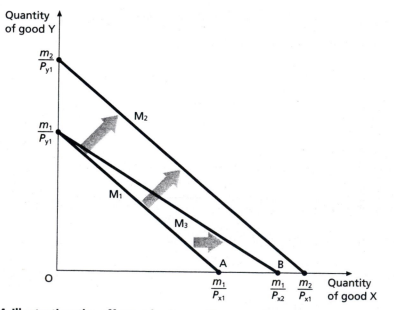

Figure A2.4 Illustrating the effects of price and income changes

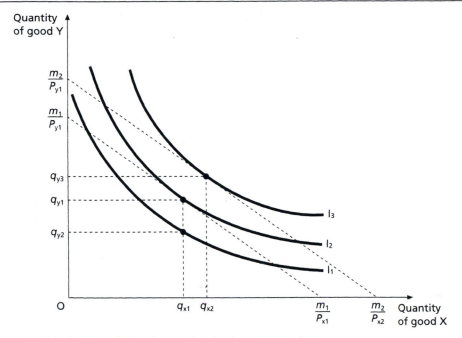

Figure A2.5 Utility maximisation with a budget constraint

putting the indifference curve mapping and the budget line on the same diagram, it is possible to discover the combinations of goods X and Y that the consumer will actually choose. In Figure A2.5 with income m_1 this combination is q_{x1}, q_{y1}. The consumer could purchase q_{x1} and q_{y2}, for example, but this would not be a rational choice because the utility obtained from the given income would not be maximised. The same X but less Y would be consumed. The consumer would be on an indifference curve nearer to the origin. By contrast, the consumer would prefer to consume the combination q_{x2}, q_{y3}, as this is on a higher indifference curve (meaning higher utility) but is unable to do so because of the limited income. This consumption pattern or other combinations of X and Y as shown along I_3 become possible only if the prices of the goods or the consumer's income changes. For instance, if income rose from m_1 to m_2 in Figure A2.5 then this combination could be chosen.

Income and substitution effects

By adopting indifference curve analysis it is possible to identify clearly the *income and substitution effects* of a price change. As discussed in the main body of the chapter, substitution effects occur because of changes in relative prices as the price of one of the goods changes. The consumer can be expected to switch to the good that is now relatively cheaper. Income effects occur because, following a reduction in the price of a good, consumers effectively have more income left over to spend on both that good and on other goods. The opposite income effect would occur if the price of a good increased.

57

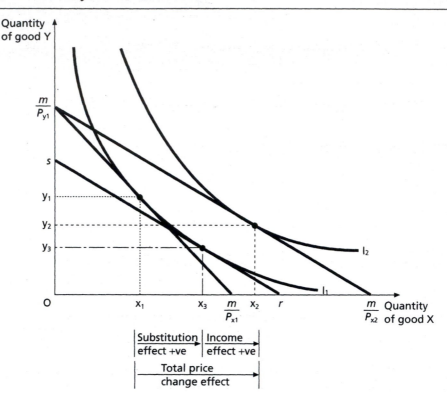

Figure A2.6 Substitution and income effects of a price change for a normal good

The result might be a rise (fall) in demand for that good and for other goods because the consumer suffers a positive (negative) income effect.

The income and substitution effects of price changes can be easily identified using indifference curve analysis – this is one of the important benefits of this approach to analysing consumer demand. Suppose that the price of good X fell from P_{x1} to P_{x2} while the consumer's money income remains the same. This would imply that the budget line changes. In Figure A2.6 the original budget line is shown by line m/P_{x1}, m/P_{y1} and the consumer buys x_1 of good X and y_1 of good Y, as determined by the budget line and the indifference curve I_1. With the reduction in the price of good X the budget line becomes m/P_{x2}, m/P_{y1}. The result is that the consumer can purchase a larger combination of goods because X is cheaper. In other words, the consumer can operate on the indifference curve labelled I_2. The individual now consumes x_2 of good X and y_2 of good Y. The increased consumption of good X, shown by the distance x_1 to x_2, is the *total effect* of the price change.

To identify the separate income and substitution effects within this total price change effect, suppose that the consumer loses the maximum amount of income compatible with him or her being able to obtain the *original* level of utility given the new price level. This is shown by drawing a new budget line, *sr*, tangential to the original indifference curve, I_1. The consumer is constrained to operate on the original indifference curve and therefore obtains the same level of utility as before. The consumer would now choose to purchase x_3 of good X and y_3 of good Y. As the income effect of the change in price of good X has been removed by moving the consumer back to the original indifference curve and therefore utility level, any change in the demand for good X must now be the result of a *substitution effect*. In Figure A2.6 the additional amount of good X purchased, as shown by the movement from x_1 to x_3 can now be attributed to the *substitution effect*. It follows, therefore, that the additional consumption shown by the extra consumption x_3 to x_2 resulting from the price change is the consequence of the *income effect*.

In summary, the total price effect, x_1x_2, is composed of a substitution effect, x_1x_3 and an income effect, x_3x_2. Income and substitution effects will be found for all goods and services when there is a price change. In this example, good X is a normal good – more of it is bought as its price falls. However, some goods may be *inferior goods*, where the income effect *reduces* the total price change effect by offsetting some of the substitution effect. This is shown in Figure A2.7. The approach to identifying the income and substitution effects is identical to that used when discussing Figure A2.6, but in this case the total price effect is x_1x_2, the substitution effect x_1x_3 and the income effect *reduces* the increased consumption of good X. The income effect is x_3x_2. If the income effect were sufficient to lead to an overall fall in the demand for good X when the price of the good was reduced (i.e. if $x_3x_2 > x_1x_3$), the result is a *Giffen good*. You might like to try

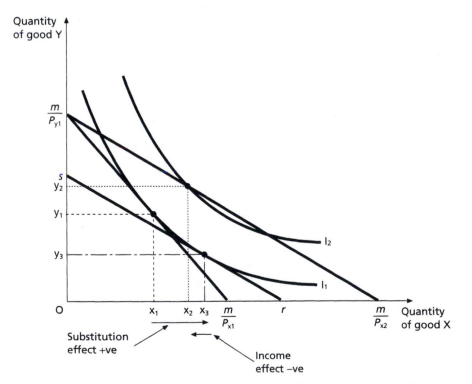

Figure A2.7 Income and substitution effects for an inferior good

to draw a diagram similar to Figure A2.7 but showing the Giffen effect. The income effect will be negative and larger than the positive substitution effect. In consequence, the demand for good X *falls* as the price of good X is *reduced*. It should be obvious from the above that while the substitution effect of a price change is always positive, the income effect can be positive or negative, depending on the nature of the good. Normal goods always have a positive income effect, whereas inferior goods and especially Giffen goods have a negative income effect.

The above discussion of indifference curves has dealt with the indifference curves of an individual. Through a fuller understanding of income and substitution effects provided by indifference curve analysis, the reason why total consumer spending changes with price changes can be better understood. Indifference curve analysis confirms that an individual's demand curves normally slope downwards. Market demand curves also slope downwards because they result from combining the spending patterns of all individuals in the market.

Appendix 2.2 Marginal revenue and the demand curve

Proof that the marginal revenue curve declines at twice the rate of the demand curve

The equation of a linear demand relationship is:

$$P = a - bQ \qquad (2.1)$$

Total revenue (TR) $= P \times Q$

Total revenue (TR) $= (a - bQ) \times Q$ (substituting for $P = a - bQ$)

Total revenue (TR) $= aQ - bQ^2$

Marginal revenue (MR) is defined as the change in total revenue with respect to a unit change in sales. In terms of differential calculus:

$$MR = \frac{\Delta TR}{\Delta Q} = \frac{\delta TR}{\delta Q}$$

$$= \frac{\delta(aQ - bQ^2)}{\delta Q} \qquad \text{(substituting for TR} = aQ - bQ^2)$$

$$= a - 2bQ \qquad (2.2)$$

Thus, comparing the equation for marginal revenue (eqn 2.2) with that for the demand curve (eqn 2.1) we see that both have the same intercept on the vertical axis (equal to a) but that the marginal revenue curve has a slope that (in absolute terms) is twice that of the demand curve (i.e. $2b$ compared with b).

This simple relationship between the demand (i.e. average revenue) and marginal revenue curves will, of course, not apply where the demand curve is non-linear. In such cases the relationship between the two curves is mathematically more complex.

The analysis of production costs

Aims and learning outcomes

In the previous chapter we discussed the behaviour of consumers and how they react to changes in prices and other variables determining the demand for goods and services. In this chapter we examine the internal operations of business by analysing the nature of costs of production and the impact costs have on business decision-making. Some of the questions which managers face are as follows:

- Whether to increase or reduce production at the margin?
- Whether to increase production using more labour?
- Whether or not to increase the overall scale of production by expanding to a new plant size?

Just as consumers, given limited incomes, make decisions about what goods to buy and in what quantity, so managers must make decisions about *how much* to produce (the size of output) and *how* to produce, in terms of the combination of inputs used (i.e. labour, raw materials, capital equipment and so on), again with limited resources. These decisions will depend heavily on the relevant costs of production.

In this chapter, the following concepts are covered:

- The production function.
- Variable costs versus fixed costs.
- Production decisions in the short run and long run.
- Diminishing returns in production.
- The relationship between production and costs.
- Maximising profit and the production decision.
- Economies and diseconomies of scale.
- Economies of scope.
- Organising production.
- The experience curve.
- Product and process innovation.
- The relationship between short-run and long-run costs.
- Optimal scale and X-inefficiency.
- The importance of information and knowledge.

In managerial decision-making, an understanding of the firm's costs of production and how they change as output is increased or reduced is essential. Of course, behind increases and reductions in costs of production lie considerable changes in the internal workings of the firm. Hence the good manager constantly keeps in mind the impact of output decisions on the so-called stakeholders in the firm: employees, shareholders, suppliers, customers, etc. Other management subjects such as organisational behaviour deal more specifically with the internal decision-making process within firms and the effect this has on outcomes. In contrast, economists are more concerned with the nature of the relationship between the firm and its market – the *competitive environment* – and more specifically the relationship between output, price and costs of production, which in turn affects the employment of factors of production. We therefore start this chapter by considering the relationship between inputs and outputs as described by the *production function*.

Learning outcomes

This chapter will help you to:

- Understand the relationship between the firm's factor inputs, its outputs and its costs of production in the short-run and long-run.

- Differentiate between *total*, *average* and *marginal* costs of production and how these costs affect output decisions and profitability.

- Determine the level of output which maximises profit for any given cost structure and demand conditions.

- Distinguish between *variable* and *fixed* costs of production and their role in determining when a firm should shut down production.

- Appreciate the meaning of *diminishing returns* in the context of short-run production decisions.

- Understand the nature of *external* and *internal* economies of scale as the size of a business alters.

- Appreciate the significance of *innovation* in sustaining a firm's competitive advantage over the long run.

- Distinguish between scale inefficiencies in production and inefficiencies that result from the poor management of resources (i.e. *X-inefficiency*).

- Realise the growing importance of information and knowledge in business decision-making as factors of production in their own right.

The production function

Firms are essentially involved in adding value by converting inputs into outputs. Firms employ labour, purchase materials and components, and invest in land, buildings, plant and equipment with a view to maximising the amount of output that can be derived from these inputs. These inputs can be combined in different ways (e.g. labour-intensive versus capital-intensive production) and we might expect the decision as to the precise combination used to be directly related to the costs of different forms of production to produce a given output. This decision depends on two particular issues, namely the *technical efficiency* of the factors of production (inputs) which is related to engineering considerations, labour skills, etc. and the relative *prices* of the factor inputs. (A more detailed analysis of this decision-making process, using *isoquant curves* and *isocost lines* is set out in an appendix to this chapter.)

In the following discussion of production we adopt the position that managers are interested in minimising the cost of producing any given output, though we acknowledge that in practice there may be constraints (e.g. union agreements on the size of the workforce) which prevent the kind of smooth adjustment process as set out below. Throughout most of the analysis in this chapter it is assumed that the firm is not wasting resources – that is to say, it is assumed that it is minimising its costs of production at any given output. We directly address the issue of this kind of 'inefficiency' towards the end of the chapter.

Production function

The production function is a mathematical expression which relates the quantity of all inputs to the quantity of outputs, assuming that managers employ all inputs efficiently. In general terms the production function for any firm may be expressed as follows:

$$Q = F(I_1, I_2, I_3, \ldots, I_n)$$

This expression is a shorthand notation to show that the quantity (Q) of output produced is determined by (or is a function (F) of) a range of inputs (I_1 to I_n). The inputs or factors of production I_1 to I_n are usually classified by economists under the general headings of *labour*, *land* and *capital*, though the production function can equally relate output to different *types* of labour, capital, etc.

From the production function, a corresponding *cost function* can be derived. Whether it is economic to produce depends on the costs of producing the output and not simply the physical input–output relationship depicted by the production function. Profit-maximising businesses are concerned to produce output while minimising cost. The cost function shows the relationship between the cost of the output and the cost of inputs used. This means that the manager needs to know the price of each input as well as the quantity of each input required in the production process. By taking into account the input prices, the cost function can be derived from the production function. There are various forms of cost functions, as there are of production functions, but they may be expressed in a general form as:

Cost function

$$C = F(Q, p_1, p_2, p_3, \ldots, p_n)$$

where the cost, C, is expressed as a function of the quantity of output, Q, and the prices $p_1, p_2, p_3, \ldots, p_n$ of the corresponding inputs $I_1, I_2, I_3, \ldots, I_n$.

It may not always be obvious to managers what the precise economic relationship is between their firms' inputs, outputs and costs. However, it must be the case that there is a relationship and economists have derived a number of general mathematical forms to describe typical relationships. A discussion of these mathematical relationships is, however, beyond the scope of this *Principles* book.

Variable costs versus fixed costs

In the production process some costs are *fixed costs* in the sense that they *do not* vary as output changes. For example, the lease rent on an office and the capital cost of a computer (including interest charges) are examples of costs which once incurred usually remain the same as output rises – these are known as *fixed factors of production*. In contrast, those costs which *do* change with output are known as *variable costs*. If more goods or services are produced, more inputs are employed and variable costs increase. The kind of inputs involved are raw materials, components, energy, telephone usage and, often, staffing levels – these are referred to as the *variable factors of production*.

It is useful to analyse the way in which fixed costs and variable costs behave as the level of production changes. Such analysis allows us to identify whether or not resources are being used most efficiently. The *total costs of production* (TC) are made up of *total fixed costs* (TFC) and *total variable costs* (TVC). Figure 3.1(a) shows the typical shape of these various cost curves. If total fixed costs and total variable costs are averaged over the different levels of output, we can derive values for *average fixed costs* (AFC) and *average variable costs* (AVC). Combining the AFC and the AVC gives *average total costs* (ATC). These costs are illustrated in Figure 3.1(b).

The key points to note about the nature of these costs are the following:

- **Total fixed costs (TFC)** are fixed at all levels of output.
- **Total variable costs (TVC)** and, therefore, **total costs (TC)** rise as output increases.
- **Average fixed costs (AFC)** decline continuously as the fixed costs are distributed across more and more output, until at very large output levels they may be negligible. The AFC curve is a rectangular hyperbola, i.e. the area under the curve remains constant as output changes.
- **Average variable costs (AVC)** may fall initially but after a certain level of output they begin to rise. This occurs because of what economists term the *law of diminishing returns*, mentioned in Chapter 1 and discussed more fully below. It is, of course, possible for average variable costs to rise continuously as output expands, while in some businesses there may be a large output range over which they are constant.
- **Average total costs (ATC)**, being the combination of AFC and AVC, tend to decline initially and then rise after a certain level of output (Q) is reached. Average

total cost is often referred to by accountants as the *unit cost*. It is also often simply referred to as the *average cost*.

- **Summary**

$$TC = TFC + TVC$$

$$AVC = TVC/Q$$

$$AFC = TFC/Q$$

$$ATC = AFC + AVC = TC/Q$$

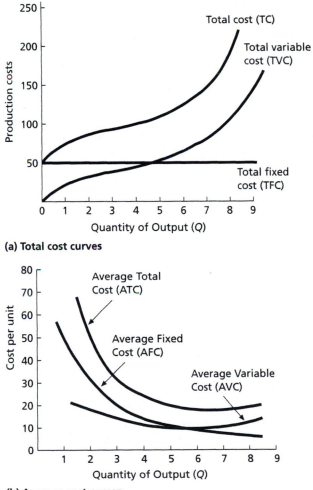

(a) Total cost curves

(b) Average cost curves

Figure 3.1 Total and average costs of production

The extent to which a firm can alter its factors of production is dependent upon the time period concerned. In general, the longer the time period the more scope a firm has to vary its inputs. The importance of the *time dimension* in production decisions gives rise to the concepts of the *short run* and *long run*, which we introduced earlier (Chapter 1, pp. 10–11).

Production decisions in the short run and long run

Economists single out two general time periods: the short run and the long run. These are defined as follows:

The *short run* is the time period during which the amount of at least one input is fixed in supply (e.g. the amount of capital equipment installed or in some organisations the number of personnel employed) but the other inputs can be altered.

In essence, the short run is the *operating period* of the firm, where the management has already made a technical decision about the production process: for example, in a bank so many cashiers are employed based on a given branch network. To expand the volume (output) of service it may be possible to employ more staff relatively quickly, but to expand the number of the branches and to incorporate more capital equipment will usually take much more time and planning.

The *long run* represents a sufficient length of time for management to be able to vary *all* inputs into the production process.

The long run is also known as the *planning horizon* of the firm in contrast to the current operating period. For example, in order to meet a growing demand from customers the bank's management may decide over the next five years to open more bank branches and employ a much larger number of staff. The bank will, therefore, over this period have moved from one *scale* of operation to another, which in turn will give rise to a different set of cost relationships. Alternatively, the bank may decide to pursue a totally different strategy by introducing an internet-based banking service. This will also give rise to a new set of cost relationships.

It is important to appreciate that the terms *short run* and *long run* should not be interpreted too rigidly. They are defined according to the extent to which the firm is able to alter its inputs and this will vary from business to business and circumstance to circumstance. For example, in large-scale manufacturing plants with high set-up costs, it is obviously difficult to expand production quickly beyond the capacity of the plant, though it may be possible to achieve this over a longer time period through more investment. The length of time to expand output significantly in the case of nuclear power generation may be many years, while, by contrast, in service-orientated businesses (such as retail banking) the planning period may be relatively short. In parts of the service sector a shortage of skilled labour may be the major constraint on the expansion of output in the short run. It may be quicker to buy and install a new microcomputer than to recruit and train new staff.

Diminishing returns in production

Assuming that the firm is using its existing resources efficiently, the extent to which output can be increased is dependent upon the extent to which inputs can be varied. This introduces the concept of *diminishing (marginal) returns*.

The law of diminishing (marginal) returns

In the short run, when one or more factors of production are held fixed, there will come a point beyond which the additional output from using extra units of the variable input(s) will diminish.

The law of diminishing returns suggests that there will be an output beyond which the employment of more variable factors of production, e.g. labour, in combination with a given fixed factor of production, e.g. capital, will lead to a decline in output per employee (known as the *average physical product of labour*). The increment in total output which arises from employing each extra unit of the variable factor of production is known as the *marginal physical product* (physical because it is measured in terms of the number of units produced). The law of diminishing returns states that beyond some output level (which will vary from case to case) the marginal product of the variable factor will decline and the rate of increase of the average product will therefore slow down.

Although labour is usually the variable factor because the number of hours worked, if not the number of employees, can be altered quickly, this need not always be the case. Where labour is highly specialised and in short supply it might be quicker and simpler to alter the amount of capital equipment to boost output.

Table 3.1 provides an example of the law of diminishing returns. In this table total physical product (TPP), average physical product (APP) and marginal physical product (MPP) are defined as follows:

- *TPP* is the total output when labour is applied to capital.
- *APP* is the total output or physical product divided by the number of units of labour employed.
- *MPP* is the addition to total physical product as each extra unit of labour is employed.

As more labour is employed total output continues to rise, albeit at a decreasing rate after the third person. The fall in the marginal product causes the rise in the total and average products to slow down, and once the marginal physical product is below the average physical product, the average physical product declines. The total physical

Table 3.1 Example of the law of diminishing returns

(1) Units of capital input	(2) Units of labour input (*n*)	(3) Total physical product (TPP)	(4) Average physical product of labour (APP) = (3) ÷ (2)	(5) Marginal physical product of labour (MPP)
10	1	8	8	8 (8 – 0)
10	2	20	10	12 (20 – 8)
10	3	35	11.7	15 (35 – 20)
10	4	40	10	5 (40 – 35)
10	5	42	8.4	2 (42 – 40)
10	6	43	7.2	1 (43 – 42)

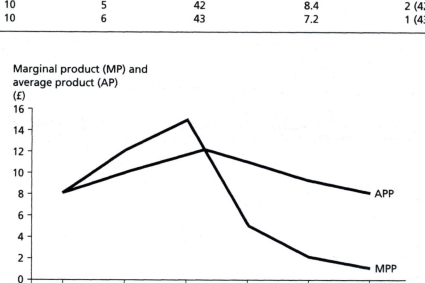

Figure 3.2 Diminishing returns

product would fall if the marginal product became negative. Presumably no sensible firm would allow this to happen. Figure 3.2 is based on the data in Table 3.1. Note that the marginal physical product curve intersects the average physical product curve when that curve is at its maximum. This must always be so – if the marginal physical product of an extra person employed is greater than the average physical product, then the average must increase. Similarly, if the marginal physical product is less than the average physical product then the average physical product must fall. Only when the marginal physical product is the same as the average physical product will the average product neither rise nor fall. If you have difficulty understanding this relationship, think about the effect on the average score of a sports team when the last or marginal player scores more or less than the average scored by the previous players.

It is easy to think of cases where diminishing returns will occur in manufacturing. For example, if the Ford Motor Company faces a sudden surge in demand for its range of cars and attempts to meet this extra demand by simply employing more workers on a given assembly line, a point will be reached when manning exceeds the optimal level given the scale of plant and unit costs rise. Therefore, if the company believes that the increase in demand is permanent, it would be better to begin planning an increase in overall capacity. Diminishing returns also apply in the service sector. For instance, imagine a retail store attempting to serve more and more customers by simply employing additional sales assistants but without extra cash registers – in this case, long customer queues at tills would be a reflection of diminishing returns.

The relationship between production and costs

The data in Table 3.1 can easily be converted into cost data. Suppose, for example, that each unit of labour cost $10 and there are capital costs of $100. We can then derive a table, Table 3.2, from the data in Table 3.1 showing costs of production. The law of diminishing returns causes costs per unit to rise eventually. This has considerable implications for the behaviour of firms as we shall see later. (Note that the law of diminishing returns could operate from the first unit of output produced, in which case costs per unit rise from the outset.)

Another name for TPP is output. The output at which average costs are at their lowest is known as the *technically optimum output*. This optimum is represented by output 40 in Table 3.2. At this point the factors of production are being combined so as to minimise average costs, at $3.5 per unit. To pursue the discussion of costs further, we now return to the concept of the *margin*.

Marginal cost

The change in total costs of production as output is changed incrementally is referred to as the *marginal cost*. Given a total cost function, it is technically the 'first derivative', that is, the slope of the total cost curve at each level of output ($\Delta C/\Delta Q = \delta C/\delta Q$). Where the total cost curve is linear, the marginal cost is a constant, and it is easier to refer to *the* marginal cost of output.

Table 3.2 Deriving cost data from product data

(1) Cost of capital employed $	(2) Cost of labour employed $	(3) Total cost = (1) + (2) $	(4) Total output	(5) Average cost per unit = (3) ÷ (4) $
100	10	110	8	13.7
100	20	120	20	6.0
100	30	130	35	3.7
100	40	140	40	3.5
100	50	150	42	3.6
100	60	160	43	3.7

Marginal cost is the additional cost incurred of producing a very small increment in output, normally *one more unit of output*, though in practice it is often applied in general terms to any appropriate increment in production, e.g. the addition to total electricity generating costs of bringing into service the marginal generating set. In such cases, however, it is more correct to describe the change in cost as the *incremental cost* rather than marginal cost, incremental cost being the change in total costs associated with a specified change in output which is not necessarily a single unit. By so doing, we are able to distinguish the incremental cost from the marginal cost.

Incremental cost

The *incremental cost per unit* is the total change in costs caused by the output increment (this is equal to the sum of the marginal costs over the increment in output), divided by the change in output. In other words, incremental cost equals the 'average' marginal cost over the range of outputs.

Marginal costs in the short run will depend only on changes in variable costs because fixed costs are unaltered. In the long run, marginal costs reflect changes in the total costs of production because all inputs are variable. Hence, when discussing changes in output we need to distinguish the impact on marginal costs in the short run and long run. Figure 3.3 illustrates a typical relationship between short-run marginal cost and output (the nature of the long-run marginal cost is addressed later in this chapter involving a discussion of *economies* and *diseconomies of scale*).

At the margin, as output is increased the additional costs of production will tend to fall at first but rise as diminishing returns set in, as illustrated in Figure 3.3. There is an important relationship between marginal and average total costs as shown in this figure. As long as the marginal cost (MC) is less than the average total cost (ATC) of

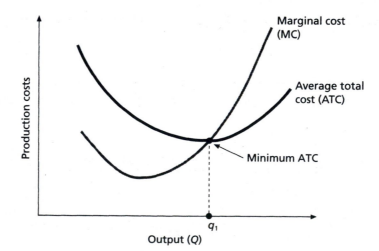

Figure 3.3 Marginal cost and output

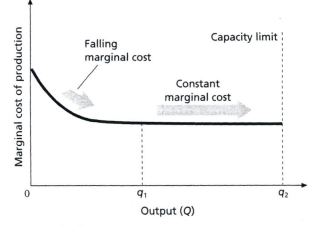

Figure 3.4 Constant marginal costs

production, then the latter must be falling. Once marginal cost exceeds average total cost the latter will be rising. The relationship is similar to that for average and marginal products discussed earlier.

In Figure 3.3, the marginal cost curve fell and then rose. However, empirical studies of firms suggest that sometimes marginal costs do not vary greatly with the level of output but instead are broadly flat over a certain range of output, resulting in *constant marginal costs* as shown in Figure 3.4.

The flatness of the marginal cost curve between outputs of q_1 and q_2 in Figure 3.4 means that average variable costs between these two outputs remain constant until around capacity output is reached; once capacity output is reached the marginal cost curve can be expected to be vertical because no more output is possible. Only variable costs have a bearing on short-run marginal costs because fixed costs are fixed. Often, of course, marginal costs will start to rise before absolute full capacity working is reached as management tries to squeeze further output from the plant under conditions of diminishing returns.

We can now put together our discussion of production and costs by reviewing the relationship between each of the costs and output. Table 3.3 relates to a cost schedule of a firm. Note that you can also tell that it is concerned with the short-run period since there are fixed costs. Remember that the long run is defined as a period where there are no fixed factors of production and hence no fixed costs. The data produce the (short-run) MC, AVC and ATC curves shown in Figure 3.5.

Maximising profit and the production decision

The general rule regarding whether or not a firm should expand production relates marginal costs to sales revenue. Where a firm is attempting to maximise its profits, as long as the marginal cost of producing one more unit of output is less than the addition to revenue resulting from producing and selling that unit, then it will pay the firm

Table 3.3 Cost of production: a worked example

Quantity of output (units)	Variable cost ($)	Fixed cost ($)	Total cost ($)	Marginal cost ($)	Average variable cost ($)	Average fixed cost ($)	Average total cost ($)
Q	VC	FC	TC	MC	AVC	AVC	ATC (8) = (4)/(1)
(1)	(2)	(3)	(4) = (2) + (3)	(5)	(6) = (2)/(3)	(7) = (3)/(1)	= (6) + (7)
0	0	48	48		–	–	–
1	20	48	68	20	20	48	68
2	30	48	78	10	15	24	39
3	36	48	84	6	12	16	28
4	40	48	88	4	10	12	22
5	48	48	96	8	9.6	9.6	19.2
6	60	48	108	12	10	8	18
7	80	48	128	20	11.4	6.9	18.3
8	112	48	160	32	14	6	20
9	156	48	204	44	17.3	5.3	22.6

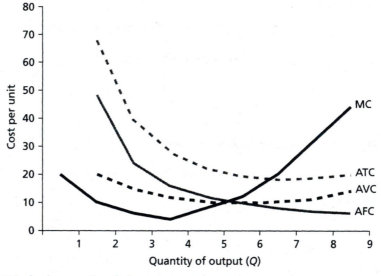

Figure 3.5 Worked example of short-run cost curves

to continue expanding production (marginal revenue exceeds marginal cost). This is illustrated in Figure 3.6 where MR is the marginal revenue or the addition to total revenue from selling and producing one more unit. From the discussion in Chapter 2, most firms face a downward sloping demand curve for their product, hence increasing sales is associated (*ceteris paribus*) with a lower price. It follows, therefore, as we saw in that chapter, that the marginal revenue curve will also be downward sloping. To the right of output q^* marginal cost exceeds marginal revenue, and thus the marginal output beyond q^* costs more to produce than the extra revenue generated. By contrast, units

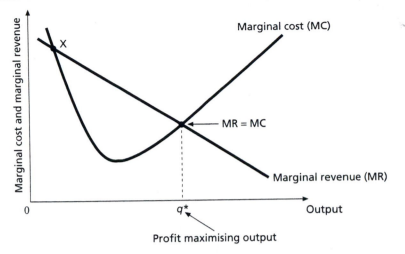

Figure 3.6 Profit-maximising output

of output before q^* raise more revenue than they add to costs. It follows, therefore, that profits are maximised at output q^*, where marginal cost equals marginal revenue.

The profit maximisation rule

Profits are maximised where marginal cost (MC) equals marginal revenue (MR). It is possible that over the firm's full potential range of outputs there are two points where MC = MR (in Figure 3.6 the two points are shown at X and at output q^*). Producing at point X would not profit maximise because outputs up to X are produced where MC > MR. Technically, profits are maximised where MC = MR *and the MC curve is rising* (not falling), as at q^* output in Figure 3.6.

Comparing marginal cost and marginal revenue is vital in deciding whether it pays to *increase* or *reduce* current output. It does not on its own, however, clarify whether the *total* production is profitable. To know this we need to calculate profit over the entire, not just the marginal, output range. One way of doing this is to compare total revenue with total cost. Another way, used here, is to compare price (average revenue) with average total cost. Multiplying the difference by the total output allows us, of course, to calculate the total profit or loss.

In Figure 3.7 it will be seen that provided the price per unit is above P_1, price exceeds the average total cost (ATC) of production and hence profits are made. These profits are described as *supernormal* (or *pure*) profits as opposed to *normal* profits. This follows from the need for ATC to include the opportunity cost of the capital invested (i.e. the best return that could be earned on the capital if it were invested elsewhere) because unless the firm covers this cost it would pay to shut down production in the long run (i.e. not reinvest in the firm) and put the capital to other use. Profit which *just* covers this opportunity cost is called a *normal profit*.

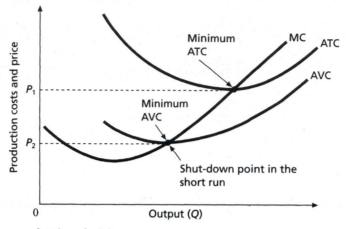

Figure 3.7 The production decision

- *Normal profit* is the minimum profit which must be earned to ensure that a firm will continue to supply the existing good or service. In incorporated firms it is equivalent to the 'cost of capital', namely the interest charges on loan capital plus the return to equity investors that must be paid if creditors and investors are to put their capital into the firm. In non-corporate enterprises (sole traders and partnerships) this is the profit that ensures that a sufficient number of people are prepared to invest, organise production and undertake risks in an industry (including the return to risky 'entrepreneurship'). The normal profit will differ from industry to industry, according to the degree of risk involved. Costs of production, in an economic as opposed to an accounting sense, include an allowance for normal profit.
- *Supernormal profit* is any profit earned above normal profit and is a form of *economic rent* (see pp. 143 and 308).

For incorporated enterprises that borrow and raise equity funds through the capital market, the normal profit equates to the cost of raising this capital. In such cases, the total cost of capital is a weighted sum of the costs of raising the loan and equity funds. A popular method of calculating this total cost is the so-called *Capital Asset Pricing Model* (a topic dealt with on specialist finance courses).

In Figure 3.7, if the price is between P_1 and P_2, although profits are not made, the price exceeds the average variable costs and hence a 'contribution' is made towards the fixed costs (AFC). As the fixed costs have to be met whether production occurs or not, they are not relevant to the decision as to whether to produce or not in the short run. Should the price be below P_2, then the firm is not even covering its variable costs (AVC) and, if this is likely to be more than a very temporary situation, the firm would be well advised to shut down. Continuing in production, given that the variable costs are not being met, must mean a higher loss than if no production occurred at all.

Assuming the firm is in business to make profits, in the long run when all factors of production are variable in supply, whether the firm continues producing depends on whether it makes profits or not. In other words, the revenue earned must cover *all* costs (remember: including a normal profit). Hence price must at least equal average total cost, i.e. price must be at or above P_1 in Figure 3.7.

In the long run the concept of diminishing returns is not relevant since it relates to a situation in which at least one factor of production is in fixed supply. With all factors of production variable the firm can change its *scale* of production. This could involve shutting down one plant (with a certain cost structure and associated marginal and average cost curves) and opening up another plant (with its own set of short-run cost relationships). In other words, there is a particular cost structure for production in the short term (the operating period) for each scale of output. A discussion of the nature of production costs in the long run requires an appreciation of *economies* and *diseconomies of scale*.

Economies and diseconomies of scale

In the long run, management decisions will be concerned with how production costs change as the size of the business alters. Opening up new factories, offices and shops is associated with a change in the scale of output. There are broadly three possibilities, as follows, which may arise:

- **Constant returns to scale.** This arises when the volume of output *increases in the same proportion* to the volume of inputs.
- **Increasing returns to scale.** This arises where the volume of output *rises more quickly* than the volume of inputs.
- **Decreasing returns to scale.** This arises where the volume of output *rises less quickly* than the volume of inputs.

These three possibilities are associated with *constant cost, decreasing cost* and *increasing cost* production in the long run, respectively. For example, increasing returns to scale should result in decreasing average or unit costs (this is usually the case, but whether or not average costs do in fact fall also depends on what is happening to input prices as output changes).

The existence of increasing and decreasing returns to scale is explained by the presence of both *internal* and *external economies* and *diseconomies of scale* in production. These are described below.

Internal economies of scale

Internal economies of scale arise in industries such as chemicals, oil extraction, retail banking, etc., where there must be a large output of goods or services to minimise long-run average costs. Economies stem from the more effective use of available resources resulting in higher productivity and lower costs. A number of internal economies of scale can be readily identified in relation to the following factors:

- Labour.
- Investment.
- Procurement.
- Research and development.
- Capital.
- Diversification.
- Product promotion.
- Transport and distribution.
- By-products.

The importance of each of these factors is discussed briefly here.

Labour

Better use may be made of specialised labour and managerial skills in large firms and there may be economies in training costs. Also, by offering better career prospects, large firms can often attract and retain better quality staff. In addition, a superior division of labour may be achievable, which is likely to lead to the development of expertise on the part of staff and a consequent growth in overall productivity.

Investment

There is likely to be a minimum level of investment which is viable in many businesses – a bank cannot buy half of a computerised money transfer system even though it may only require that much capacity! Investment economies of scale are likely to be more evident in large-scale rather than small-scale enterprises.

Procurement

Large firms usually have considerable bargaining power and are more likely to be able to gain cost savings through bulk purchasing from suppliers. This is particularly evident in grocery retailing, for example in the United Kingdom where the market is dominated by a small number of supermarket chains, namely, Tesco, Sainsbury, Safeway, ASDA-Walmart and Somerfield, which are able to exercise considerable bargaining power over food producers and distributors. A firm which purchases all or most of a supplier's output will be able to exert considerable *monopsony* (i.e. single or dominant buyer) power and drive down prices.

Research and development

In industries such as aerospace and pharmaceuticals the pursuit of competitive advantage requires heavy investment in R&D. To be viable, the cost must be spread over the very large output which only large-scale enterprises can hope to achieve.

Capital

Large firms can often raise loan finance more easily and cheaply than smaller businesses since they usually offer greater security to lenders. Also, many larger firms are publicly quoted and hence have access to the equity markets, both domestic and overseas.

Diversification

Many large firms spread risk by operating in a number of different markets. For example, the well known business grouping, Virgin, operates in many separate sectors, such as airline services, soft drinks, train companies and finance. A collapse of one market should not, therefore, jeopardise the whole company.

Product promotion

Large firms are likely to be able to make more effective use of advertising, specialist sales forces and distribution channels.

Transport and distribution

Only firms producing a large output are likely to be able to employ economically their own transport fleet or be able to negotiate preferential rates with haulage companies (monopsony power again).

By-products

In large enterprises such as oil companies, the opportunity exists to produce a wide range of by-products in quantities which are commercially exploitable.

External economies of scale

Internal economies of scale relate to the operations and decisions made by the individual firm. They are therefore directly under the control of *the firm*'s management. In contrast, *external economies* arise at the industry level and are generally associated with growth in output over time in *the industry*. Three main types of external economies may arise relating to:

- Labour force.
- Suppliers.
- Social infrastructure.

The significance of these with respect to external economies of scale may be summarised as follows.

Labour force

Where firms in an industry group together there is often a large and skilled labour force in the locality which all firms can utilise.

Suppliers

As an industry grows, it is often the case that specialised ancillary firms become concentrated in the locality, supplying components, transport, consultancy services, etc. For example, with the development of the financial services industry in London, New York and Tokyo, it is not surprising that there is also a concentration of accountancy and legal advisory services to be found in these cities (as well as many wine and coffee bars!).

Social infrastructure

A concentration of industry in a particular area will also lead to the development of educational and training facilities, roads, airports, rail networks and a greater availability of housing for workers, all of which may help to reduce the overall costs to local industry. Indeed industry and government often co-operate to ensure that these facilities are developed in areas of business expansion, e.g. through new town developments and regional expansion schemes.

It should be noted that external economies are important in the creation and maintenance of *industrial clusters*. Good examples of firm clustering include Silicon Valley in California and the small hi-tech firms which have increased in number in science parks adjacent to many universities around the world, such as around Cambridge University in the UK.

Internal diseconomies of scale

A growing firm is likely to benefit from economies of scale which are internal to its operations. However, as growth continues a point may be reached where certain internal *diseconomies* of scale arise. These result in rising long-run average costs. Once this occurs the firm needs to consider whether or not further expansion is desirable (this will depend on what is happening to revenues as well as costs). Such diseconomies may relate to the following topics.

Management

The larger a firm's operations become, the more complex the managerial structure often needs to be. There is a danger that management will become bureaucratic and unresponsive. This leads to 'organisational slack' and the internal decision-making process slows down and staff become alienated, leading in turn to industrial relations problems. The firm may also become less responsive to changes in the external market place. How often do we hear the criticism that a firm has 'too many layers of management' resulting from inadequately managed growth?

Labour

It is a well-known fact that industrial disputes are more likely to occur in large rather than small companies. This arises because, as the labour force increases, the gap between 'management' and 'the workers' grows and consequently loyalty to the firm falls. At the same time unionisation increases and this can bring with it more rigid wage-bargaining processes leading to friction between management and the workforce. Costs may rise because of lowered productivity and the need for greater managerial supervision of the labour force. Absenteeism and slacking in work also tend to be more prevalent in large firms.

Other inputs

As the firm grows its demand for inputs increases. If the supply of these inputs is limited, then their unit cost will rise as the firm's output expands. This applies not only to materials and components but to certain skilled labour requirements.

External diseconomies of scale

Sometimes costs rise as the whole industry expands in a particular area. For example, growth in the number of local companies and in business generally can put pressure on the price of housing and transport and this may ultimately feed through to higher wage demands and increased distribution costs. There may be additional costs associated with road congestion and other environmental hazards.

Long-run average costs

As firms expand production over the long run and move to different scales of operation, if internal and external economies of scale exist unit costs will fall as the volume of output increases. This represents *increasing returns to scale* or *decreasing cost production* as defined above. Presumably, however, unit costs will not always decline (otherwise they would approach zero) and hence we would expect them eventually to level out. The firm is then said to operate under *constant cost production*. It is conceivable that at some very large level of output internal and external diseconomies of scale cause unit costs to rise, leading to *increasing cost production*. These three possibilities – increasing, constant and decreasing returns to scale – are illustrated in Figure 3.8. Also shown

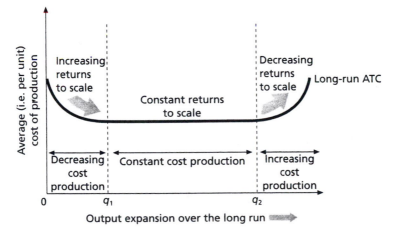

Figure 3.8 The long-run average cost curve

Application 3.1

E-commerce and costs of production

Recent years have seen an explosion in the number of 'business to business' (B2B) internet exchanges. These are sites designed to bring firms in contact with other firms. They enable firms to buy in from suppliers more cheaply. By providing market information, the internet makes it easier to find the best deal and to process transactions with lower transaction (e.g. administration) costs. British Telecom, for example, has estimated that online buying may reduce its cost of processing transactions by up to 90% and reduce the direct costs of the goods and services it buys by an average of 11%. Also, B2B e-commerce should enable businesses to reduce and in some cases even eliminate their stocks of raw materials, components and finished products.

What does this all mean for the structure of markets? Competition is restricted when dominant firms use their size to protect their position. Being big and gaining *economies of scale* enables firms to prevent the emergence of competitors in an industry. But since the internet helps *all* businesses to reduce costs, it should reduce the minimum efficient scale (MES) or optimal size of firms (see Figure below). The implication is that the cost barriers to the entry of firms into markets will be reduced. The impact of the 'new' economy could make 'old' economy markets more open to the forces of competition.

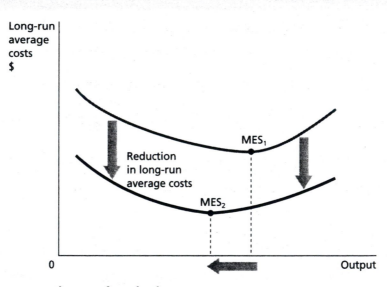

E-commerce and costs of production

Activity

Consider how firms might respond to reduce the threat from the internet to their competitive position.

are decreasing, constant and increasing cost production (ignoring the complication of input prices – see p. 75 above).

The art of good management is to capture the benefits of internal and external economies and, of course, to avoid the onset of internal and external diseconomies. Ideally, firms will want to operate at the level of output which corresponds to minimum unit costs over the long run or what is sometimes termed the *minimum efficient scale* (MES). This represents the technical long-run optimum scale of production for the firm. In Figure 3.8, an output of at least q_1 must be achieved to minimise long-run average costs and hence this is the MES. As there is constant cost production between outputs q_1 and q_2 there is no *single* optimum scale – instead, any of the outputs in this range represents a technical optimum. However, if the long-run average cost curve were U-shaped there would be *one* scale of output, at the bottom of the U, which represents the technical optimum. Achieving MES gives a firm a strong competitive advantage in the market place over higher-cost producers.

Economies of scope

In addition to economies of scale firms may benefit from *economies of scope*. Economies of scope arise when the costs of producing two or more different outputs by one firm are lower than would be the case if each output was produced in separate firms.

A firm can achieve economies of scope by:

- Sharing common inputs over a range of its activities.
- Jointly promoting its range of products and services; or
- Jointly distributing its range of products and services.

A good example of economies of scope is found in banking where existing staff, branches, IT systems, etc. are used not only to provide current (cheque) accounts but to offer customers a wide range of other financial services such as mortgages, savings accounts, insurance and foreign currency transactions. Each of these services could be supplied by a separate, dedicated financial institution but economies of scope are reaped by sharing inputs, promotion and distribution channels.

Organising production

Management must strive to avoid long-run average costs rising. As one of the major diseconomies of large-scale production is managerial breakdown, firms have tended to establish sub-units, separate operating companies and so on to avoid this. This gives rise to what is often called an 'M-form' (multi-form) structure in which parts of the company operate with considerable managerial independence, especially in terms of day-to-day decision-making. This reduces bureaucracy and speeds up decisions. The most extreme example of this is where a *holding company* is set up (e.g. The News

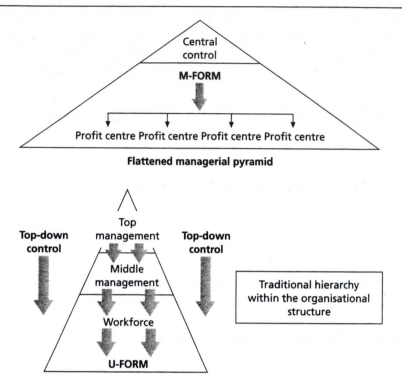

Figure 3.9 Organisational structures

Corporation). In this case a small number of senior managers and support staff seek to co-ordinate and oversee the activities of the much larger subsidiary companies spread around the world. (The News Corporation has activities worldwide in publishing such as *The Times* and *Sun* newspapers, and other media such as BSkyB satellite broadcasting, organised into separately managed subsidiary businesses reporting their financial performance to the parent company.) In contrast, smaller firms tend to be managed more from the centre through a clear managerial hierarchy and with little decentralised decision-making. This structure is often referred to as a 'U- form' (unitary form) structure and makes sense where tight control must be imposed from the centre on day-to-day operations. Figure 3.9 highlights the key features of the M-form and U-form organisational structures.

Other ways in which firms attempt to avoid the onset of diseconomies of scale may involve one or more of the following decisions:

● **Relocation of operations** which may be at the lower end of the added-value scale, e.g. Japanese electronics and car companies moving assembly operations out of Japan and into other parts of South East Asia to avoid costs associated with congestion and labour shortages in Japan; American companies moving production from the higher-cost north-east of the United States to the lower-cost southern states.

New technological breakthrough can be incorporated at this level of production

luction

Loesberg, M.D.

52-53

List of Errors
✓ 52-53
62-64
Intro tech
Pg 69

Chpt 6 - 9

Chp 12

Figur ...osts

- (...*tment* (selling-
  ...h management
  ...by management

- ...the managerial
  ...d, more recently,

...vity in production
...10 this leads to a
...n volume of output

...ductions. Static cost
...h improving *existing*
...from efficiency gains
...ducts and production
...ong run and result both
...arising from *experience*

curve (or *learning* c...

The experience curve

Economies and diseconomies of scale relate to the behaviour of long-run production costs as the *scale* of output changes. It is also likely that unit costs will fall over time as experience of producing and selling a good or service increases. In other words, costs of production decline as the *cumulative volume* of output rises.

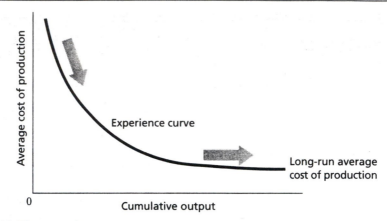

Figure 3.11 The experience curve

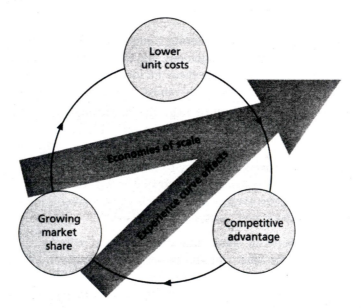

Figure 3.12 The 'virtuous circle'

Figure 3.11 provides an example of a typical *experience curve*. This is also sometimes referred to as a *learning curve*. By combining the notion of costs related to scale and experience, we can conclude that the achievement of competitive advantage through lower costs than competitors lies in growth of production, which in turn implies (at least in a relatively static market) capturing a larger market share. Indeed, we can see how a 'virtuous circle' could build up in which lower unit costs enhance competitiveness, drive up market share and permit a further cost-reducing expansion in output due to economies of scale and experience curve effects, as illustrated in Figure 3.12.

Equally, a loss of competitive advantage leading to a fall in market share can reduce output and force up unit costs leading to a 'vicious circle' of competitive decline.

Product and process innovation

The global markets of today are highly dynamic and *innovation* is a critical factor in sustaining competitive advantage over competing producers and therefore survival in the long run. By developing R&D skills or an R&D *core competence* (see Chapter 4, p. 113) the firm can maintain a constant stream of new products and services to stay ahead in the market. For example, Sony has maintained a lead in the consumer electronics market through innovative products such as the Walkman cassette player and high definition televisions. Such companies are described as being leaders in *product innovation.*

By contrast, some companies pay more attention to *process innovation.* This involves re-engineering the business supply chain or particular stages of the production process so as either to reduce the cost of supply or increase the quality and reliability of supply of goods and services provided to the market place. In the UK Tesco has been at the forefront of grocery supply-chain management and *logistics.*

This discussion of innovation links to the subject of *generic strategies* mentioned in Chapter 1, p. 20. Product innovation permits firms to differentiate themselves in the market place in terms of supplying superior outputs (a *differentiation strategy*). This permits the goods and services to be offered at premium prices. Process innovation can support product differentiation by enabling firms to supply higher-quality output and goods and services that are more responsive to changing consumer demands. But process innovation can also support a *cost leadership strategy* by reducing the cost of production.

The relationship between short-run and long-run costs

Each scale of production can be represented by a set of short-run cost curves. In Figure 3.13 a firm is producing on a small scale and at high unit cost as represented by $SRAC_1$ (short-run average cost).

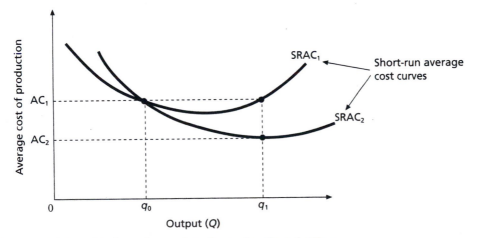

Figure 3.13 Benefits from increasing the scale of production

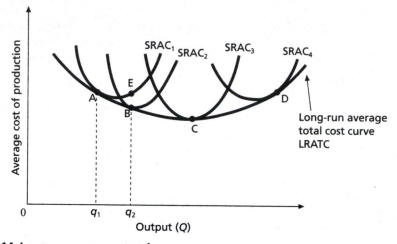

Figure 3.14 Long-run average total cost curve

If this firm were to invest in new plant and machinery or extend its premises or in some other way increase its capacity, then its new short-run cost curve would be $SRAC_2$. This new cost curve is below $SRAC_1$ beyond output q_0, representing a higher output at a lower unit cost provided output is above q_0. For instance, the output q_1 is now being produced at a unit cost of AC_2 but would have been produced at a unit cost of AC_1 if the fixed factors of production (i.e. the scale of production) had not been altered. With increasing output (presumably reflecting increasing sales) provided the firm benefits from economies of scale (decreasing cost production) each change in the scale of production will lead to lower costs.

In Figure 3.14 a number of possible short-run average cost curves have been drawn representing progressive scales of production for a firm. Tangential to these short-run curves, a long-run average cost curve has been introduced. This is commonly referred to as the *envelope curve*. This helps us to see how the average costs of production change as output is expanded over the long run. For example, if the firm were to expand output to q_2 using the same scale of production (based on the short-run average cost curve, $SRAC_1$) unit costs would rise to the level indicated at point E. By increasing the scale of production unit costs can be reduced to the level indicated by point B. So the envelope curve is mapped out along points ABCD etc. In Figure 3.14, beyond scale C average costs rise.

This is a simplified diagram showing only four possible scales of production. In reality we would expect to find a very large number of different scales of production. Technically, the envelope curve is the product of a large number of possible scales of production (short-run average cost curves). Where a large number of small changes in scale can be made the result is a smooth LRATC curve as shown in Figure 3.14. Where small changes in scale are not possible (e.g. in nuclear electricity generation or steel production) then the 'lumpiness' of investment will lead to a LRATC curve which is

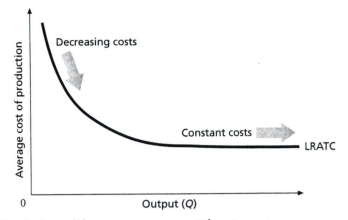

Figure 3.15 The 'L-shaped' long-run average total cost curve

not smooth. Lumpiness or 'indivisibilities' in the capital stock lead to periods of under-utilisation and over-utilisation of capacity until the new investment comes on stream.

The long-run average cost curve has been drawn to show the long-run average costs of production falling initially as output and the scale of production rise, i.e. decreasing costs (increasing returns to scale) are experienced. Later, however, increasing average costs (decreasing returns to scale) are experienced. Hence, the result is a 'U-shaped' long-run average cost curve, as shown in Figure 3.14.

In so far as diseconomies of scale can be avoided, a firm's long-run average cost curve may not be 'U-shaped'. However, as we noted earlier, long-run average costs cannot, presumably, decline for ever, otherwise eventually the cost of producing goods and services would be negligible.

Empirical research suggests that in a number of industries average costs fall at first but eventually level out, producing an 'L-shaped' long-run average cost curve over a wide range of outputs – see Figure 3.15.

Optimal scale and X-inefficiency

Companies may not always be able to identify exactly their short-run or long-run technical optimum, as this requires considerable knowledge of the nature of production costs as output rises. Even in the presence of complete information there may not always, of course, be sufficient demand for the firm's product to justify increasing output to reach the optimal long-run scale of production.

Companies' unit costs may be higher than is technically feasible – a 'production-cost' gap may arise – for the following two broad reasons:

- The firm is not producing at its *optimal scale of production*.
- The firm wastes resources and its costs are higher than necessary at its *existing* scale of production. This type of inefficiency is often referred to as X-*inefficiency* because

Application 3.2

Large goods vehicles: an example of economies of scale

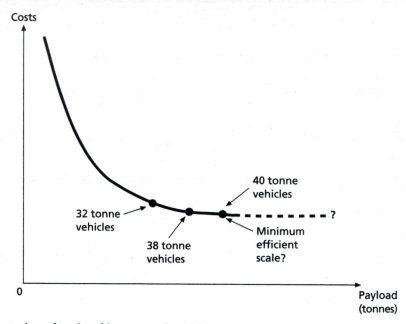

Economies of scale of large goods vehicles

The above figure summarises what happens to costs as the size of commercial vehicles rises. Larger trucks are able to carry bigger loads but still need only one driver. Also, if the choice is between two smaller truck loads or one large truck load, there can be economies of scale in terms of the cost of one truck – a large truck may cost less to buy or hire than two smaller trucks; there may also be savings in licensing costs, road tolls paid and fuel use.

The figure refers to the maximum weight of goods that can be carried on each vehicle. Switching from 32 tonne to 38 tonne vehicles, for example, lowers unit costs. The European Union (EU) recommendation of a maximum of 40 tonne lorries on EU roads lowers average costs further, albeit only slightly. However, given current vehicle technology it appears that the industry may now be at its minimum efficient scale. If this is so, introducing even larger vehicles, such as 44 tonne trucks, may not lead to cost savings.

Activity

Explain the meaning of minimum efficient scale in the above example. The figure shows the average costs to the road haulage firms of operating larger vehicles. Why should wider (external) costs be taken into account, such as the effects on road maintenance and environmental pollution, when governments take a decision on the maximum weight of vehicle to permit on the roads?

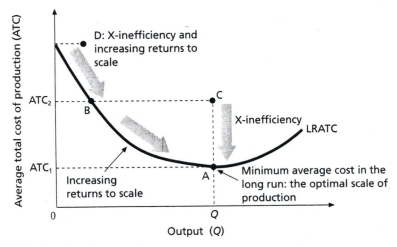

Figure 3.16 The 'production cost' gap

it can exist to any degree. Remember that so far we have been assuming that the firm uses its resources efficiently – there is no waste or slack in the business. In other words, we have assumed in the above analysis of production costs that X-inefficiency does not exist; this is probably unrealistic – otherwise why employ management consultants to improve the organisation of production!

Four possible situations are illustrated in Figure 3.16. These show the following:

- A firm at point A on the long-run average cost curve is operating at the optimal scale of output where unit costs are minimised (at ATC_1). In addition, it is operating at maximum efficiency in terms of avoiding waste of resources – i.e. it is on the long-run average cost curve which represents the minimum cost of producing at any output (there is no X-inefficiency present).

- A firm at point B could reduce its unit costs (ATC_2) by increasing its scale of output. Once again, however, as the firm is operating on the achievable long-run average cost curve there is no X-inefficiency. In other words, while firm B is not operating at its most efficient scale of production, it is nevertheless minimising its costs given its existing capacity.

- A firm at point C is operating at its optimal scale of production but its unit costs are higher than could be achieved if efficiency was maximised. Costs could be lowered to point A by reducing waste or organisational slack. The difference between C and A is the X-inefficiency gap for this firm.

- Management of a firm at a point such as D has the greatest challenge of all – and the firm is at the greatest risk of failure! It is not cost efficient in terms of using the available resources (it is not operating on its long-run average cost curve). Also, it is failing to take full advantage of economies of scale (it is producing below optimal scale). Not to mince words, the firm has the potential to reduce its production costs significantly, and if this potential is not recognised by the current management, then perhaps the solution is for the firm to be taken over by new management!

Since X-inefficiency represents a waste of resources, a function of management is to minimise it. Some economists argue that X-inefficiency is a very common phenomenon, especially in state-owned companies where the profit motive does not exist and hence the drive for efficiency may be reduced. In terms of private sector joint-stock companies, the shareholders (the owners or 'principals' of the firm) appoint directors as their 'agents' to manage the firm efficiently – a *principal–agent relationship* exists. This raises the whole question of the objectives of firms and management and the subject of *corporate governance*, which we address at length in Chapter 10. Profit maximisation and hence the drive for a more efficient use of resources, though presumably desired by shareholders, may not always be the primary goal of managers – some managers may seek glory in being in charge of a worldwide company, with the authority to hire and fire and with responsibility for large sums of discretionary expenditure. The pursuit of goals may therefore lead to inefficiency even in private sector firms. It is suggested, however, that the threat of takeover by new management, alongside the need to sell products in competitive markets, should limit X-inefficiency in the private sector. If management do not endeavour to maximise profits the shareholders may well sell their shares in the capital market, leading to a lower market valuation of the company and great vulnerability to a hostile takeover bid, and banks etc. may be less willing to advance loans. Loan creditors may perceive a greater risk that the firm will fail to repay its debts. At the same time, however, the extent to which the private 'capital market' (shareholders and loan creditors) does effectively constrain non-profit behaviour by management is the subject of on-going debate. For example, evidence suggests that profitability may be a poor predictor of a firm's vulnerability to a hostile bid. The relationship between shareholders and directors (top management) of companies is a highly topical issue today and is at the heart of the debate about corporate governance in modern economies.

The importance of information and knowledge

To draw our discussion of production costs to a close, we turn briefly to the consideration of an important emerging issue in business economics – the so-called *information revolution*.

In dealing with the analysis of production costs for this chapter, there is an implicit assumption that managers have full or complete knowledge of the nature of the firm's production function, resulting in a full understanding of the relationship between factor inputs and the firm's output. In the real world, decisions are made in an environment of *imperfect information*. This can result in decisions concerning production that seem to be correct or optimal, given the information available, but would be deemed to be sub-optimal if managers were perfectly informed.

The importance of information and knowledge has come to the fore in the study of economics in recent years. This has largely been due to a growing recognition of the significance of information and knowledge in business decision-making in modern economies. This significance is based on information and knowledge as vital inputs into decision-making on both the demand and supply side of markets. In particular, global economic forces (e.g. the globalisation of markets and companies as well as the rapid growth of internet technology) are leading to a radical rethink about the role of information and knowledge in increasing competitive pressures and the power of consumers. For this reason, information and knowledge can be viewed increasingly as factors of production in their own right.

New industries are forming (e.g. e-commerce businesses) and old ones are being restructured (e.g. traditional banking and retailing) based on the new technologies that rely on the importance of information and knowledge. Whereas the industrial revolution created economies reliant on the production of tangible or 'weighty' products (such as iron and steel, machine tools, etc.), the current 'information revolution' is leading to the growth of economies increasingly based on less tangible or 'weightless' inputs and outputs. The outcome is the so-called *weightless economy*, where information and knowledge, although embodied in capital and labour (e.g. a highly educated workforce) need to be recognised as critical inputs to the economy. For example, in so far as internet technology increases information and knowledge for customers and producers, we should expect competition to intensify.

Concluding remarks

On first reading, much of what has been included in this chapter may appear as fairly esoteric and removed from the real world of business decision-making. But nothing could be further from the truth. The cost concepts introduced are fundamental to any analysis of actual business operations, for the extent to which costs change as output varies has obvious implications for pricing and competitiveness. A successful competitive strategy cannot be developed in isolation from a full appreciation of the firm's cost structure. Moreover, the nature of the firm's costs will have an important bearing on decisions regarding whether to consolidate, expand capacity, cut back production, and ultimately whether to shut down. Operational and planning decisions can only be based on a clear picture of the changing nature of the cost structure facing the firm.

In the following chapters we build on the foundations established in this chapter and the previous chapter on consumer demand. In Chapter 4, we derive and explain the firm's supply curve in a perfectly competitive market and the degree to which supply responds to price changes. This chapter also looks at the firm's supply chain, while Chapter 5 brings together demand and supply in the determination of prices. Chapters 6 to 9 deal with the different types of competitive environment that firms may face and the strategies they might adopt. Chapter 10 builds on these chapters and analyses the implications of different managerial objectives for production decisions and pricing outcomes.

Key learning points

- The **production function** is a mathematical expression which relates the quantity of all inputs to the quantity of outputs.

- **Total physical product** (TPP) is the total output from the factors of production employed.

- **Average physical product** (APP) is the TPP divided by the number of units of the variable factor of production employed.

- **Marginal physical product** (MPP) is the change in TPP when an additional unit of the variable factor of production is employed.

- **Fixed costs** are costs of production which *do not vary* as output changes.

- **Variable costs** are costs of production which *do vary* with output.

- **Average total cost** (ATC) is total cost divided by output (TC/Q) and is made up of average fixed cost (AFC) plus average variable cost (AVC), where AFC = TFC/Q and AVC = TVC/Q. TFC is total fixed cost; TVC is total variable cost; and Q is output.

- The **law of diminishing (marginal) returns** states that, in the short run, when one or more factors of production are held fixed, there will come a point beyond which the additional output from using extra units of the variable input(s) will diminish.

- The output at which average costs are at their lowest is known as the **technically optimum output.**

- **Marginal costs** (MC), defined as the additional costs incurred when producing a very small increment or one more unit of output, will only depend on changes in variable costs in the short run because fixed costs are unaltered as output changes. In the long run, however, marginal costs reflect changes in the total costs of production since all inputs are variable.

- The **marginal cost curve** will always be below (above) the average cost curve when average costs are falling (rising).

- **Profits** are maximised at the level of output where marginal cost equals marginal revenue and when marginal costs are rising.

- Economists include a **normal profit** in costs.

- **Normal profit** is defined as the minimum profit which must be earned in order to ensure that a firm will continue to supply the existing good or service.

- **Normal profit** is earned when price is set equal to average total cost.

- **Supernormal profit** is earned when price is set above average total cost.

- The **shut-down point** in the short-run exists when price has fallen below average variable costs. In the long run a profit-maximising firm must cover its average total costs if it is to remain in business.

- **Constant returns to scale** arise when the volume of output increases in the same proportion to the volume of inputs.

- **Increasing** and **decreasing returns to scale** arise when the volume of output rises more quickly or less quickly, respectively, than the volume of inputs.

- The existence of increasing and decreasing returns to scale is explained by the presence of both **internal** and **external economies** and **diseconomies of scale**, which relate to the behaviour of long-run production as the scale of output changes.

- **Decreasing, constant** and **increasing cost production** relate to what happens to the costs of production as the scale of production is changed.

- The **minimum efficient scale (MES)** represents the technical optimum scale of production for the firm, corresponding to minimum unit costs over the long run.

- **Economies of scope** exist where a range of goods use joint inputs, promotion or distribution resulting in a reduction in the long-run average costs of production.

- **Static cost reductions** tend to occur in the short run and are associated with improving *existing* production methods.

- **Dynamic efficiency gains** are more clearly associated with new developments in product and production processes over time.

- The **experience (learning) curve** relates to declining unit costs of production over time as the *cumulative volume* of output rises.

- **Innovation** occurs within firms in the form of both products and processes. *Product* innovation involves the introduction of new goods and services; while *process* innovation is concerned with improving the existing methods by which outputs are produced so as to lower the costs of production.

- **X-inefficiency** indicates the extent to which the costs of production are above the minimum average cost due to waste and organisational slack given the existing scale of production.

- The **envelope curve** shows how total costs of production change as output continues to rise over the long run. This represents the *envelope* of all possible short-run average total cost curves relating to different scales of production and is appropriate where there are no significant 'indivisibilities' in the capital stock.

- **Information and knowledge** are of growing importance as factors of production in their own right in the new information-led or 'weightless economy'.

Appendix 3.1 (see p. 95)

- An **isoquant curve** shows in graphical form different combinations of factor inputs that can be used to produce a given quantity of a product.

- An **isoquant map** is a collection of ranked isoquant curves that shows in graphical form a firm's increasing output when moving outward from the origin using larger quantities of factor inputs.

- The **marginal rate of technical substitution (MRTS)** is the ratio of the marginal physical product of two inputs in the production process; i.e. the amount by which it is possible to reduce one factor input and maintain a given level of output by substituting one extra unit of the other factor input. In notation form:

$$MRTS_{KforL} = (-)\frac{MP_L}{MP_K}$$

- An **isocost line** shows the combination of two inputs which can be purchased for the same total money outlay.
- An optimal combination of inputs in the production process takes place when the ratio of the marginal products of the factor inputs is equal to the ratio of the input prices; i.e.

$$(-)\frac{MP_L}{MP_K} = (-)\frac{P_L}{P_K}$$

or, alternatively

$$\frac{MP_L}{P_L} = \frac{MP_K}{P_K}$$

Topics for discussion

1 Explain the distinction between *variable* and *fixed* costs of production.

2 Using an appropriate diagram, discuss the relationship between marginal cost, average fixed cost, average variable cost and average total cost.

3 Using the discussion of costs included in this chapter and the discussion of demand in Chapter 2, explain the success of a large international motor car manufacturer such as Toyota.

4 The Meetoo Company produces shirts at a factory in Singapore. The shirts currently sell from the factory at $15 each but cost $18 each to produce (AFC = $4, AVC = $14). Mike Smart, chief accountant, has advised the board in New York to shut the Singapore factory. What is your view? What other information might you need before reaching a decision?

5 Offscale, an office equipment supplier, has expanded its operations dramatically over the last ten years. As sales rose, at first unit costs fell and then levelled out. Now there are signs of rising costs. Investigation suggests that diseconomies of scale have set in. Offscale is still run by its founding director and two sons. Explain, using an appropriate diagram, what has been happening to costs over the last decade. Make suggestions as to what actions might be taken to prevent diseconomies of scale.

6 Choose a firm in a sector with which you are familiar and consider the role of innovation within the firm in sustaining its competitive advantage.

7 Assess the significance of new information-based technology for the future of the retail banking industry. Illustrate your answer using appropriate cost diagrams.

8 Using isoquant and isocost analysis (see Appendix 3.1) discuss how the optimal combination of factor inputs employed by a firm should be decided.

Appendix 3.1 Isoquants, isocosts and the optimal combination of inputs

To decide on the optimal combination of factor inputs to employ in the production decision, both the technical efficiency of the inputs and the relative input prices must be taken into consideration. In the case of only two inputs, capital and labour, any desired level of output can normally be produced by a number of different combinations of these inputs. The key task facing the firm is to determine the *specific* combination of capital and labour which should be selected in order:

- *either* to maximise output for a given production cost;
- *or* to minimise production cost subject to a given output.

The task of determining the optimal combination of inputs introduces a number of important concepts including:

- Isoquant curves and isoquant maps.
- The marginal rate of technical substitution.
- Isocost lines.

This discussion has been included in an Appendix to the chapter analysing production costs because not all Business Economics courses cover isoquant–isocost analysis.

Isoquant curves and isoquant maps

An *isoquant curve* shows in graphical form the different combinations of factor inputs (such as capital and labour) that can be used to produce a given quantity of a product per time period with a given state of technology.

Figure A3.1 illustrates one isoquant curve relating to a particular level of production (say, 100 units per time period).

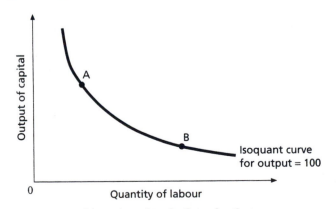

Figure A3.1 Isoquant curve for a given level of production

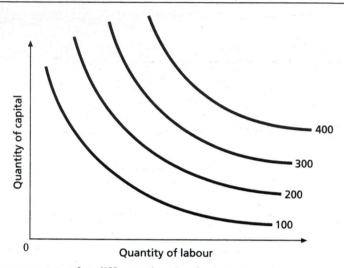

Figure A3.2 Isoquant map for different levels of production

It is important to remember that for any movements *along* a particular isoquant curve, for example from A to B in Figure A3.1, the level of output produced remains *constant* while the input ratio (of capital to labour) changes continuously.

A different isoquant curve will exist, therefore, for every possible level of production, giving rise to an *isoquant map*.

> An *isoquant map* is a collection of ranked isoquant curves that shows in graphical form a firm's increasing output per time period when moving outward from the origin using larger quantities of two factor inputs (such as capital and labour).

Figure A3.2 shows an isoquant map with the higher quantity of output per time period represented by the distance of each isoquant from the origin.

There are several important properties of isoquant curves which should be noted:

- Isoquants slope downwards from the left to the right because the two inputs can be substituted for one another in the production process.
- Isoquants are convex to the origin because the inputs, while substitutable for one another, are *not perfect* substitutes.
- Isoquant curves never cross one another because two crossing curves would lead to inconsistent or irrational choices by the firm between the two factor inputs.

The marginal rate of technical substitution

The slope of an isoquant curve and its convexity to the origin reflects the substitut-ability of one factor (say capital) for the other factor (say labour) in the production process. This introduces the notion of the marginal rate of technical substitution (MRTS), defined as follows:

The *marginal rate of technical substitution* (MRTS) is the ratio of the marginal physical products (MP) of two inputs in the production process; i.e. the amount by which it is possible to reduce one factor input (e.g. capital) and maintain a given level of output by substituting an extra unit of the other factor input (e.g. labour).

In notation form, we can define the marginal rate of technical substitution between capital and labour as:

$$MRTS_{\text{Capital for Labour}} = (-)\frac{MP_{\text{Labour}}}{MP_{\text{Capital}}}$$

From Figures A3.1 and A3.2 it should be appreciated that the MRTS of capital for labour diminishes as more and more labour is substituted for capital. It should not be difficult to understand this property of isoquants and factor substitutability. For example, consider what would happen to the marginal productivity of labour on a particular car assembly line as more and more workers are added to the line – beyond a certain level of manpower, the extra output arising from the use of more workers employed with a fixed amount of capital would fall. The same situation would apply if we added more and more capital to a fixed quantity of labour, ensuring the principle of a diminishing marginal rate of technical substitution between capital and labour.

Isocost lines

So far, we have shown that any desired level of output can normally be produced by a number of different combinations of inputs. We now must determine the *optimal* way in which these inputs should be combined. This involves the producer paying attention to relative input prices in order *either* to minimise the cost of producing a given output *or* to maximise output for a given level of cost. The incorporation of relative input prices into the production decision introduces the concept of the *isocost line*.

The *isocost line* shows the combination of the two inputs (capital and labour) which can be purchased for the same total money outlay.

In notation form, if K and L denote the quantity of capital and labour employed respectively, and P_K and P_L their respective unit prices, then the total cost, C, of using any volume of K and L is given by the equation of the isocost line as:

$$C = P_K K + P_L L$$

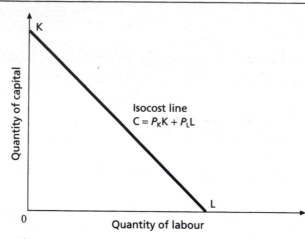

Figure A3.3 Isocost line

Thus, the isocost line represents the sum of the cost of employing K units of capital at P_K per unit and L units of labour at P_L per unit.

Figure A3.3 shows an isocost line for a given total cost and particular values for the unit cost of capital and labour.

The slope of the isocost line reflects the relative prices of the two inputs; i.e. the slope equals $(-)P_L/P_K$. Naturally, a different isocost line can be drawn for a different cost constraint and for different input prices.

Optimal combination of inputs

We can address the central question facing firms in terms of selecting the *optimal* combination of inputs. As we set out at the beginning of this appendix, this will involve:

- *either* maximising output for a given production cost;
- *or* minimising cost subject to a given level of output.

The underlying principles for both options can now easily be understood by combining the discussion above concerning isoquants and isocost lines. These are set out as follows.

Maximising output for a given production cost

Principle: to maximise output subject to a given total cost of production and given input prices for capital and labour, the firm must purchase inputs in quantities such that the marginal rate of technical substitution of capital for labour ($MRTS_{K \text{ for } L}$) is equal to the ratio of the price of labour to the price of capital (P_L/P_K).

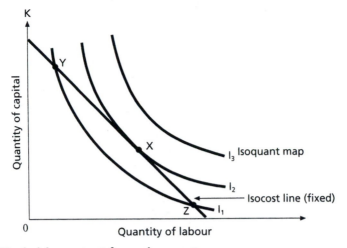

Figure A3.4 Maximising output for a given cost

Remembering that $MRTS_{K \, for \, L}$ is equal to the $(-)$ ratio of the marginal products of labour and capital (MP_L/MP_K), this principle may be written in notation form as:

$$MRTS_{KforL} = (-)\frac{MP_L}{MP_K} = (-)\frac{P_L}{P_K}$$

Thus, the optimal input combination which maximises output subject to a given total cost of production is determined when the slope of the isocost line is equal to the slope of the isoquant curve associated with the maximum possible level of output – as illustrated in Figure A3.4 this will occur when the isocost line is just tangent to an isoquant curve, I_2, at point X. Note that the firm cannot afford to produce on the higher isoquant I_3. It can afford to produce according to isoquant I_1 (employing at points Y or Z) but will not do so because this would mean a lower output for the same cost.

The optimality condition can be reorganised as:

$$\frac{MP_L}{P_L} = \frac{MP_K}{P_K}$$

This leads to the conclusion that an optimal combination of capital and labour is employed when an additional unit of money spent on any input yields the same increase in total output. Any input combination which does not meet this condition is sub-optimal since a change in input proportions could result in the same quantity of output at a lower cost.

Minimising cost subject to a given output

We will arrive at exactly the same conclusion if we view the situation from the standpoint of a firm seeking to minimise the total cost of production subject to a given level of output.

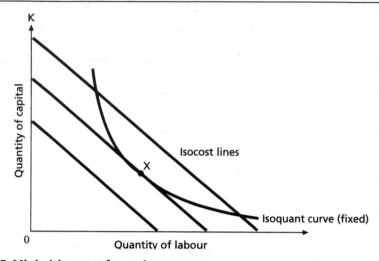

Figure A3.5 Minimising cost for a given output

In Figure A3.4, the isocost line was fixed and we sought to maximise output by moving to the isoquant curve furthest from the origin (representing a higher output level), subject to this fixed cost.

Now, the level of output is fixed (i.e., the isoquant curve is already determined) and we are seeking to minimise the total cost of producing this output level, i.e. the problem is now to move to the lowest possible isocost line. This situation is illustrated in Figure A3.5.

It will readily be appreciated that the optimal combination of inputs, at point X, is once again determined by the condition that:

$$\text{MRTS}_{\text{KforL}} = (-)\frac{\text{MP}_\text{L}}{\text{MP}_\text{K}} = (-)\frac{P_\text{L}}{P_\text{K}}$$

Or, alternatively,

$$\frac{\text{MP}_\text{L}}{P_\text{L}} = \frac{\text{MP}_\text{K}}{P_\text{K}}$$

In conclusion, the purpose of this appendix has been to examine how firms should organise production in the most efficient or economical way. This involves adjusting the quantity of factor inputs (capital and labour) employed until the marginal rate of technical substitution equals the ratio of the unit input prices – or, equivalently, adjusting input quantities until the marginal product of each input divided by its unit price is the same. When this is achieved, optimal production will take place using quantities of capital and labour denoted at point X in Figures A3.4 and A3.5.

4 Analysis of the firm's supply decision

Aims and learning outcomes

In the previous chapter we looked at the relationship between a firm's volume of production and its costs. Ultimately, the volume actually produced depends on the price which consumers are willing to pay for the good or service, which in conjunction with the costs of production determines profit. We now turn again to examine the relationship between production costs, supply and the market price before going on to discuss the concepts of the *value chain* and *transaction costs*. These concepts are important in an analysis of the boundary of the firm and in a firm's 'make or buy', or produce in-house or outsource, decision.

In Chapter 2 we dealt with the analysis of consumer demand and focused in particular on the derivation of the demand curve and the measurement and importance of the elasticity of demand.

In this chapter we cover the following aspects relating to the firm's supply decisions:

- The derivation of the firm's supply curve.
- Conditions of supply.
- Elasticity of supply.
- Supply chains and value added.
- Transaction costs and the resource-based theory of supply.
- Forms of integration of firms.
- Producer surplus.

In particular, this chapter focuses on two of the most important questions facing managers:

- How much should be produced and supplied?
- How should the supply chain be organised?

A detailed analysis of these questions provides a foundation for understanding the price and output decisions of firms within different forms of market structure covered in Chapters 6 to 9.

Learning outcomes

This chapter will help you to:

- Understand the nature of the firm's supply decision and the derivation of the firm's *supply curve*.

- Appreciate how price and non-price factors impact upon supply decisions.

- Measure the responsiveness of supply to changes in the price of the good or service in question – the *elasticity of supply*.

- Recognise the importance of *supply chains* and *value chains* in organising the supply of goods and services.

- Comprehend the significance of *transaction costs* in decisions by a firm as to whether to buy in (or *outsource*) inputs into the production process or to employ the inputs in-house.

- Distinguish between *transaction costs* and *resource-based theory* approaches to analysing the organisation of supply.

- Understand the various forms of corporate structure in terms of *vertical, horizontal* and *conglomerate integration* within the context of supply decisions.

- Identify the existence of *producer surplus*.

Deriving the firm's supply curve

For a firm in a highly competitive industry, the supply curve shows the amount that it is willing to supply at all possible market prices (just as the demand curve shows how much consumers are willing to buy at each price). In general, the higher the price the more the firm will be willing to supply, for two reasons. First, a higher price may mean more profit. Second, in many cases, especially in the short run, the marginal cost of production increases as supply rises, hence a higher price is needed to cover the additional costs. The actual extra amount supplied will depend upon the marginal cost of producing the extra output. Hence the firm's supply curve in a very competitive industry is traced out by its marginal cost curve, as illustrated in Figure 4.1. As explained in Chapter 3, in the short run a profit-maximising firm should not produce if the selling price (average revenue) is below the average variable cost of production, therefore *in the short run the firm's supply curve is the marginal cost curve lying above the firm's average variable cost curve (AVC)*. This is given by the curve AB in Figure 4.1(a), showing the output that the firm would be willing to supply at various prices, P_1, P_2, P_3, etc. In the long run a profit-maximising firm must cover *all* costs, both fixed and variable. Therefore, the supply curve will be mapped out *in the long run by the marginal cost curve which lies above the average total cost curve (ATC)* – CB in Figure 4.1(b).

It is important to note that a supply curve can only be derived from the marginal cost curve for firms operating in very competitive environments (strictly, only when competition is 'perfect' – see Chapter 6). Where competition is restricted, as in the extreme case of a single firm monopoly, the profit-maximising firm will set its price *above* its

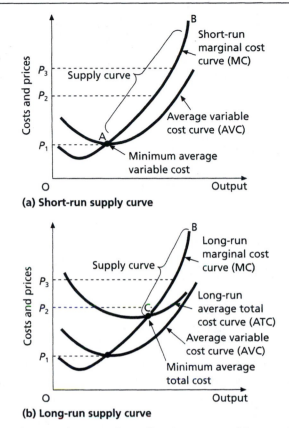

Figure 4.1 Deriving the supply curve for a firm in a competitive environment

marginal costs of production, as will be explained in Chapter 7. Therefore, in imperfectly competitive markets the concept of a 'supply curve' as defined above is inappropriate. A monopoly firm is not at the mercy of the market like a competitive firm – it does not have to take the market price as given and react to it. On the contrary, the management of a monopoly firm have the power to select the price–sales combination on their demand curve that they prefer so as to maximise profits. The monopoly firm is, therefore, a *price-maker*, not a *price-taker*. This does not mean, however, that the monopolist can increase price with no effect on demand because consumer demand will always be affected by price. The relationship between price and supply in markets where competition is highly restricted will become clearer on reading Chapter 7, which deals with monopoly. Thus, in summary:

- In the short run, a profit-maximising firm's supply curve in a (perfectly) competitive environment is mapped out by the firm's marginal cost curve (MC) lying above its average variable cost curve (AVC).
- The long-run supply curve in a (perfectly) competitive environment is the firm's marginal cost curve lying above its average total cost curve (ATC).

Conditions of supply

Of course, price is not the only factor that affects the decision to supply, even in highly competitive markets. The other factors likely to impact upon the supply decision are referred to as the *conditions of supply*. Important examples of these other factors are the following:

- **Changes in costs of production.** These include changes in the costs of labour, raw materials, capital charges and the impact of new technology on costs, all of which may impact on the balance between labour and capital intensive production and ultimately profitability. For example, when the price of oil rises sharply for prolonged periods, a number of industries dependent upon oil as a major input may be forced to retrench, and therefore reduce their production levels.

- **Prices of other products.** As the prices of other products alter, the firm may decide to switch production. For example, in farming a decline in dairy produce revenues in Europe has led to a switch by many farmers to the production of other products such as rape seed.

- **Changes in profit expectations.** Between times of boom and slump, profit expectations can change dramatically, leading to a reassessment of business strategy. For example, during the 1990s in the depressed Japanese banking and property sectors, a number of companies reduced their activities or went out of business altogether.

- **Climate.** Climate is obviously important to supply decisions in industries such as farming, construction, insurance, transport and travel.

As any of the conditions of supply change, firms will tend to supply more or less of their products at any given price. In terms of Figure 4.2, this is equivalent to a *shift* in

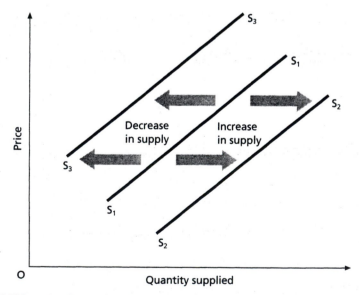

Figure 4.2 Shifting the firm's supply curve

the supply curve. A favourable change in supply conditions, such as a reduction in the costs of production, will shift the supply curve S_1S_1 to the right, to S_2S_2, as more can now be supplied profitably at any given price. In contrast, an unfavourable change in supply conditions, such as storm damage to productive capacity, will cause the supply curve to shift sharply to the left, for example to S_3S_3. One important function of management is to monitor how supply conditions are altering and are *likely to alter* in the future in relevant markets. It is important for business success, therefore, that resources are devoted to anticipating favourable and unfavourable changes that are likely to impact on production and, ultimately, the firm's profitability.

Application 4.1

Information technology industry – boom to bust?

A 'buyers' strike'

After an unprecedented boom in the 1990s, information technology companies have found themselves in the midst of an unprecedented bust at the start of the new millennium. The freeze on technology spending by many major corporate customers is being described in Silicon Valley as a 'buyers' strike' – the big question is, how long will this 'strike' last?

The 'dot.com bubble'

The tech industry's troubles stem not only from weak demand, but also from excessive optimism that it would continue to grow at breakneck speed. Tech companies have been driven forward in their expansion by a belief in the 'New Economy' – giving rise to the 'dot.com' bubble phenomenon. Companies such as Cisco Systems reported year after year revenues well in excess of forecasts. Lead times were getting too long for some products with customers having to wait up to 15 weeks for delivery in some cases. Cisco responded by ordering piles of components. But when the 'buyers' strike' emerged, Cisco was vulnerable, with sales to some major customers falling by 40% in a matter of weeks. Dot.coms began dying by the dozen, selling off their hardly used Cisco equipment at steep discount prices. Many 'old economy' companies also stopped buying new networking equipment in the face of growing uncertainty in the wider economy.

Life after death?

When will things look up again? Wall Street seems to think that technology firms are about to come out of the crisis. Some observers feel that it is too early yet to revise expectations upwards. The industry has had a roller-coaster ride over the past decade – on both the demand and the supply side of the market.

Activity

How have developments over the past decade affected the supply side of the information technology industry? With the use of an appropriate diagram or diagrams, explain how this kind of industry can go from output shortages to surpluses in a fairly short period of time and the implications for prices.

Elasticity of supply

Just as in Chapter 2 we saw that the responsiveness of consumer demand to changes in price could be measured, so we can also measure how supply responds to price changes. This gives rise to the concept of *elasticity of supply* (E_s), which is defined as:

Elasticity of supply

$$E_s = \frac{\text{Percentage change in quantity supplied}}{\text{Percentage change in price}}$$

Technically, as in the case of price elasticity of demand, elasticity of supply should be measured at a *point* on the supply curve. However, for practical purposes, estimates of the elasticity of supply are often obtained with respect to larger price changes.

The numerical value of E_s will always be positive. A figure of more than 1 suggests that the supply is relatively responsive to price changes. In other words, when a product's price rises or falls there is a more than proportional change in the amount supplied. For instance, if a 10% price rise is accompanied by a 15% increase in supply, supply in this case is said to be *elastic* – the elasticity equals 1.5. When the supply response to a price change is less than proportionate, i.e. less than 1, supply is said to be relatively *inelastic*. For example, if the price fell by 4%, but the firm chose to reduce its supply only by 1%, the supply is inelastic – the elasticity is 0.25. It is conceivable that a firm's supply might change exactly in proportion to the change in price, a situation referred to as one of *unit* or *unitary* price elasticity – for instance, a 5% increase in price which leads to a 5% increase in the quantity supplied.

The sort of factors which tend to influence the elasticity of supply include the extent to which production costs change as supply is altered; the existence of spare capacity; the extent to which the firm carries inventories; and the extent to which the firm can switch capacity from, or to, alternative production. Ultimately, the responsiveness of supply has a *time* dimension – the longer the period the firm has to adapt to the price change, then the more elastic (responsive) supply is likely to be. In the very short run, it may not be possible for a firm to change its supply at all, in which case supply is said to be perfectly inelastic (it has a zero price elasticity). Figure 4.3 gives examples of supply elasticities, showing supply curves which exhibit:

- *Relatively elastic supply* – i.e. a small percentage change in price brings about a relatively large percentage change in quantity supplied.
- *Relatively inelastic supply* – i.e. a relatively large percentage change in price results in a relatively small supply response.
- *Perfectly inelastic supply* – i.e. the quantity supplied is insensitive to any change in price.
- *Perfectly elastic supply* – i.e. the quantity supplied is so sensitive to a change in price that even a small reduction in price will lead to nothing being supplied by the firm.

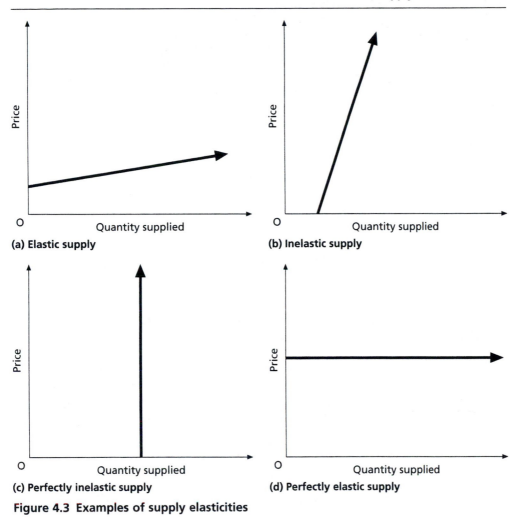

Figure 4.3 Examples of supply elasticities

It is useful to note that a *straight-line* or *linear* supply curve of any slope that starts at the origin has a unit elasticity of supply along its length. By contrast, a straight-line supply curve that cuts the vertical (price) axis is elastic in supply; whereas if it cuts the horizontal (quantity) axis it is inelastic in supply. *Non-linear* supply curves have varying elasticities along their length.

Supply and value chains

In modern economies a single firm rarely produces the entire good or service, from start to finish. For example, a manufacturing firm will tend to buy in supplies, such as raw materials and components, and sell its output to other firms that specialise in distribution and retailing. In the service sector too, firms will tend to concentrate upon

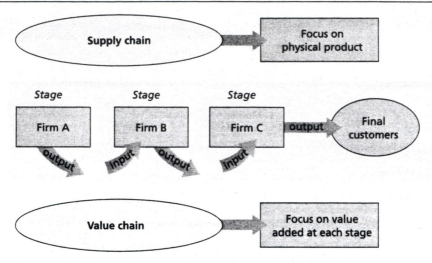

Figure 4.4 Supply chain and value added

particular parts of the *supply chain*. For instance, a retail bank may buy in or *outsource* specialised IT or legal services and will certainly resort to other suppliers for computers, telephone communications, as well as paper, pens and pencils. Also, banks tend to out-source security services (such as the provision of burglar alarm systems, money trans-portation, etc.).

Figure 4.4 illustrates a simple supply chain with different firms supplying output A, output B and output C, which is the final good sold to the consumer. The supply chain focuses on the supply of physical inputs and outputs – in other words it has a *product focus*. It is concerned with the output of A, which becomes an input to firm B; output of B that becomes an input to firm C; and so on. The supply chain can also be viewed from the perspective of *value added*. In our simple supply chain the firm producing output B takes the value incorporated in input A and *adds value* during the production process. A more valuable product is sold on to firm C. Firm C, in turn, adds value to the product by finishing it and selling it to the consumer. The figure indicates this *value added focus*. Of course, it is possible that through bad management a stage in the supply chain leads to a *loss* of value. For instance, if in our example the firm selling out-put C to the final consumers was only able to sell the product at *less* than the cost at which it purchased output B, then value would have been destroyed by that firm.

Ultimately, in competitive market economies it is the intermediate and final con-sumers in the supply chain that determine value. The higher the price at which a good or service can be sold on to consumers at the next stage of the supply chain the more likely it is that high value added will result. This is not guaranteed, however, because if the supply chain is inefficient, leading to high supply costs, then even a high price may not be sufficient to lead to value added. This conclusion leads to a focus on the *value drivers* in the *value chain*.

The value chain is concerned with identifying the value drivers or where and how value is added in the supply chain. If managers can identify the critical production

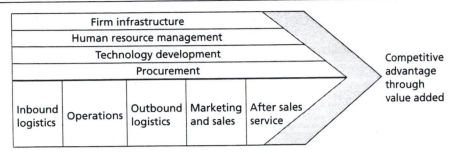

Figure 4.5 The Porter value chain

Source: Adapted with the permission of The Free Press, a Division of Simon & Schuster, Inc., from *Competitive Advantage: Creating and Sustaining Superior Performance* by Michael E. Porter. Copyright © 1985, 1998 by Michael E. Porter.

processes that add (or lose) value they can re-engineer the supply chain to maximise the value added. The value chain has been popularised by the Harvard Business School economist and strategist, Michael Porter (who we have referred to earlier, in Chapter 1, p. 18, in the context of his 'Five Forces Model' and his approach to 'generic strategies'). Figure 4.5 is based on Porter's original value chain. In this form it is most obviously applicable to a manufacturing firm. However, other formulations of this value chain exist that are more applicable to the service sector. For reasons of space we will concentrate only on the manufacturing version of Porter's value chain.

Figure 4.5 shows that value is added (or lost) along the supply chain arising from the following:

- Inbound logistics (e.g. transportation, material handling).
- Operations (e.g. the basic manufacturing processes).
- Outbound logistics (e.g. warehousing and distribution of the products).
- Marketing and sales (encouraging demand).
- After sales service (e.g. repairs, dealing with warranty claims).

All of these stages are important because the customers' satisfaction or utility from the final output will be affected by how well each of these stages in production is performed *and linked together*. For example, a customer's satisfaction with their new car depends on how well it is manufactured (which also reflects the quality of thousands of components), how well the garage treats the customer at the point of sale and later and how efficiently any warranty claims are dealt with. In Porter's value chain firm infrastructure (e.g. management accounting and legal services), human resource management, technology development and procurement provide services to each stage of the production process. Sometimes referred to as 'overheads', in principle each of these activities should also add value to the product or service produced, otherwise management attention should be paid to restructuring them or even to cutting them back.

Application 4.2

Recent changes in grocery retailing

The growth and nature of competition

The grocery trade argues that grocery retailing has experienced more competition in recent years in the UK. Competition has occurred because of the expansion of retail outlets by existing large-scale operators such as Tesco, Sainsbury, Asda and Safeway. Constant innovation in the sector in the form of in-store bakeries, faster checkout facilities, new fresh food counters, longer store opening hours and movements into providing consumer finance has added to competitive pressures. Also, some new operators have entered the market, most recently Aldi, Costco, Netto, Lidl and the US giant Wal-Mart. Wal-Mart has entered by purchasing the Asda chain. Home shopping through the TV and internet is yet to take off on such a scale as to challenge the existing retail stores, but there seems little doubt that in time it will add to competitive pressures in grocery retailing. Tesco has already established a successful internet grocery shopping business.

Retailers have striven to match their supply of produce and the ambience of their stores to the changing and diverse demands of their customers, both through product and process innovations. In particular, to remain competitive grocery retailers have been forced to seek new and more efficient ways of supplying their customers. For example, retailers have revamped their logistics and improved their methods of stocking their stores. Highly computerised stock control methods have been introduced to reduce wastage.

The arrival of Wal-Mart in the UK will almost certainly mean that there will be intensified competitive pressure to find even lower-cost ways of supplying customers. When Wal-Mart acquired two chains of hypermarkets in Germany in 1998 it priced very aggressively, by between two and seven per cent below the lowest priced competitors. Wal-Mart utilises the economies from large-scale global sourcing to drive down its costs.

Activity

Using an appropriate diagram, explain how changes in the UK grocery market are impacting on supply and price.

Transaction costs and resource-based theory

Value chain management is about managing each stage of the supply chain so as to maximise competitive advantage. Since the value chain includes inputs and outputs, it will normally be the case that managing the value chain involves controlling relationships with internal and external suppliers, distributors and retailers. This leads to a decision having to be made as to what activities should be undertaken *within* the firm and managed directly, and which are more efficiently outsourced. In other words, where is the boundary of the firm to be drawn?

In 1937 the economist Ronald Coase asked 'why do firms exist?' The competitive market is an efficient mechanism for co-ordinating demand and supply decisions, so why are not all activities undertaken in the market place (i.e. outsourced)? To answer the question, Coase identified certain circumstances when it would be more efficient to undertake activities in-house. These arise where there are benefits from directly controlling resources and where to control the resources as effectively through market contracts would be more costly. Coase's argument has been developed since the 1960s, especially by the economist Oliver Williamson.

Transaction costs

Williamson's argument is concerned with the *transaction costs* of market exchanges.

Transaction costs **in markets are the costs of negotiating, monitoring and enforcing contracts.**

All market exchanges involve some form of contracting. Purchasing a newspaper from the local newsagent involves a very simple contract, one that is negotiated and completed at one point in time. This type of contract is termed a *spot contract*. By contrast, the building of the Channel Tunnel between France and the UK involved very many and complex contracts extending over a number of years and involving great uncertainties. Such contracts tend to include terms or conditions that are triggered only by particular events. These events may be difficult to specify or predict accurately when the contract is initially negotiated. As a result, for example, major civil construction schemes, like tunnels, may contain clauses that allow for unexpected cost overruns, perhaps arising from unforeseen geological problems that raise construction costs. The contract may allow for such costs to be passed on to the client (through so-called *cost-plus contracts*). Alternatively, the contract may specify certain circumstances under which the contract or part of it takes effect or can be adjusted or renegotiated (this is an example of what are called *contingent-claim contracts*).

The more complex and uncertain the contracting environment, the higher the transaction costs are likely to be. Williamson suggests that transaction costs are raised by 'asymmetric information'; that is to say, one party to the contract at the time of contracting has superior information about the true costs and benefits of the contract than the other party. This leads to what Williamson calls 'opportunism' or 'self-seeking with guile'. An obvious example of this occurs when buying a second-hand car. Normally, the seller has superior information to that of the buyer about the history and current reliability of the vehicle. In consequence, buyers are at risk of purchasing a 'lemon' (a term associated with faulty goods).

Williamson also points to 'asset specificity' as an important cause of transaction costs. Whenever one party to a market contract has to invest in expensive assets to fulfil the contract, then that party is at risk of 'hold up'. For example, a television station that invests in studios and transmission equipment that have little or no value in any other use is vulnerable when its operating licence comes up for renewal. Without a continued operating licence, the television company will be unable to generate revenues and repay its capital costs. It is, therefore, likely to accept inferior terms at contract renewal rather than lose the contract completely (indeed, a profit maximising firm will accept a

111

contract provided that at least the variable costs of production are covered: the logic is the same as that which applies to the production decision in the short run; see p. 74 above). The inferior terms will mean lower profits than the television company might have expected when it first invested in the assets. In other words, the company might not have invested initially had it known that the contract was to be renewed on a less favourable basis.

This threat of what economists call 'hold up' at the time of re-contracting may lead companies not to invest at the outset because of the risks involved. This, incidentally, is why television transmission operating licences issued by various governments around the world often contain compensation terms if the contract is not renewed. Alternatively, the contract may require that a new company subsequently winning the licence must acquire the former company's assets at a fair value or the contractual term can be set so as to be long enough for the winner to recoup the full costs of its investments before the contract terminates.

Transaction costs alongside the firm's costs of production (discussed in Chapter 3) are a normal part of a market economy. In the case of many day-to-day purchases, e.g. a newspaper, they are negligible and can be safely ignored. In other cases, like the building of the Channel Tunnel, they can be appreciable. In such circumstances, one way of overcoming the transaction costs is to *internalise* the operations. For example, the government department issuing the television transmission operating licences could own the television companies or high-cost transmission assets. Equally, a company dependent on reliable IT systems might decide to own its own IT kit and employ its own IT staff. We can think of owning and employing resources as a means of reducing market transaction costs. The problems arising from information asymmetry should be overcome (since information is contained within the firm), as should the costs associated with asset specificity (since the risks of 'hold up' are removed by internalising transactions). Also, employees can be used flexibly within organisations without having to renegotiate contracts. Contracted labour may be limited by its contract to specific duties only; while frequent contract renegotiation raises transaction costs where resources including labour are outsourced.

The transaction cost theory approach to explaining why some activities are undertaken in-house while others are outsourced – or what is termed the 'make or buy' decision – relies upon identifying market transaction costs. These costs can then be compared with the costs of direct ownership and control of the same resources or the *vertical integration* of economic activities (owning and controlling different stages of the supply chain within a single organisation). Employing inputs directly involves its own costs in terms of management time and resources. The decision on whether to make or buy will, therefore, turn on the *relative* costs of market transacting (transaction costs) and the costs of employing and controlling the resources directly (management or 'internal' transaction costs). Williamson discusses this choice as one between procuring and controlling resources through markets or through 'hierarchies'. On the one hand, hierarchy or in-house production involves direct management control over resources, leading to more flexibility in resource use. On the other hand, markets involve the *high-powered efficiency incentives* that come from having to win and maintain contracts in a competitive environment. Unless a firm is well-managed, waste and 'slacking' by employees when activities are internalised may lead to costs that more than outweigh any market transaction costs. Where this is the case, the firm should favour a switch to market contracting.

Resource-based theory

It should be appreciated that transaction cost theory provides an important perspective on the organisation of the value chain. An alternative approach to transaction costs exists, however, as an explanation of the make-or-buy decision. This approach is associated with what is known as *resource-based theory*.

Resource-based theory **is concerned with the resources – assets, skills and knowledge – owned or controlled by the firm and hence its ability or competence to supply goods and services very competitively.**

The approach leads to the notion that firms should exploit their *core competencies* and *distinctive capabilities*, which are specific to the firm add value and are difficult for other firms to imitate. In this view, competencies and capabilities best explain why some services are supplied in-house and others are outsourced. Outsourcing stems from the fact that the firm may not have a particular capability or competence to provide a particular good or service and would therefore face excessive and possibly unacceptable costs if it tried to pursue an in-house strategy. For example, it would pay few firms to supply their own telecommunications. *Core competence theory* is dominant in much of the management literature as an explanation of the boundary for the firm, whereas *transaction cost theory* dominates the economics literature. Core competence theory is concerned mainly with explaining why some firms add more value than other firms; by contrast, transaction cost theory is concerned with the costs rather than the benefits of different ways of organising production.

These two different approaches to understanding how supply is organised can often mean that students are faced with seemingly completely separate explanations of the same phenomenon, depending on which lecture course they attend! Fortunately, however, the two approaches can be reconciled, at least in part, as explained below.

A *core competence* is something that gives a firm a distinctive competitive advantage in the market place. To be distinctive it must be difficult for other firms to imitate. To be of competitive advantage it must be valued by customers. Presumably any firm contemplating outsourcing its core competencies would need to protect its interests (assets) with very precise contracts with outside suppliers. Core competencies are an asset that need to be preserved, otherwise the firm puts at risk its competitiveness and possibly its whole existence. At the same time, it might be very difficult, and therefore very costly in terms of transaction costs, to protect the core competence from becoming available to potential competitors using a market contract. For instance, consider how a firm that owns a secret recipe in the case of a food or drink product might be reluctant to contract out the manufacturing process. How does it ensure that the recipe does not fall into the hands of other firms? Also, what happens if the supplier turns out to be a potential competitor?

In such cases, contracted-out core competencies might be protected but only by incurring very high transaction costs. The result is that core competencies will tend not be outsourced because they are more efficiently and effectively protected by producing in-house. In recent years, many firms around the world have experimented with outsourcing. In some cases it has been very successful in improving the quality of services and reducing costs. In other cases the activities have later been brought back within the firm. For instance, some firms, recognising that the management of their IT systems is crucial to their continued competitiveness, have brought IT provision back in-house.

Of course, not all supply decisions by firms involve a straight choice between 'markets' and 'hierarchies'. Today many businesses are involved in franchising, joint ventures, strategic alliances and the like. When contracting for supplies some firms do not competitively contract but use preferred supplier relationships or 'partnerships' with suppliers. *Partnership sourcing* is particularly popular in a number of industries, such as motor vehicle manufacture, both to improve the quality of components and to promote new product development. Partnerships with suppliers can mean that a company like Ford works with its suppliers to design and manufacture new models more quickly and efficiently. Partnerships and alliances are a means of controlling the organisation of supply without incurring the high transaction costs that might be associated with market contracting and without the high management costs that could result from full vertical integration.

Vertical, horizontal and conglomerate integration

Transaction cost and resource-based theories help us to understand why some supply chains are highly integrated, within one or a small number of firms, and others are not. Hierarchical forms of organising production are associated with high levels of integration. Integration can take three main forms, namely:

- Vertical integration.
- Horizontal integration.
- Conglomerate integration.

We briefly explain each of these in turn below.

Vertical integration

This form of integration occurs when firms at different stages of the supply chain merge or one takes over the other. For example, in Figure 4.4 above, the supply of input to B and outputs B and C might be owned and controlled by one firm. In which case, the supply chain is said to be completely vertically integrated. Complete vertical integration of the supply chain is rare (for example, most firms use independent retailers and all buy in *some* inputs), but it is not uncommon to find particular stages in the supply chain within one firm. For example, a company like IBM has its own manufacturing facilities and its own upstream in-house research and development capabilities.

Horizontal integration

This form of integration occurs where two or more firms at the *same* stage of production merge or are taken over: for example, the merger of Daimler and Chrysler in the motor industry. This type of integration is usually pursued to achieve economies of scale, leading to lower costs and prices. But it can have adverse effects on consumers where it leads to excessive market concentration. The result is higher prices and reduced consumer choice. The competition authorities, found in most countries, critically scrutinise horizontal mergers and will prohibit them where they decide that they are likely to result in the abuse of a monopoly position. Competition authorities will also intervene to prevent vertical and conglomerate integration if they consider such integration to be anti-competitive. Usually, however, vertical and conglomerate integration is less threatening to competition than horizontal integration because horizontal integration frequently reduces the number of independent suppliers of the same or similar products.

Conglomerate integration

This form of integration was very fashionable in the 1960s and 1970s but has been somewhat out of favour recently. Conglomerate mergers involve firms in different markets coming together. For example, a tobacco company might diversify into retailing or banking by taking over firms in these sectors. The main argument for conglomerates lies in risk spreading. If the firm operates in various markets it is less likely to suffer during an economic downturn, when some markets are more adversely affected than others. Weighed against this potential advantage, however, some conglomerates have been suspected of destroying value through poor management. It can be difficult to manage enterprises efficiently when spread across various industrial sectors. Moreover, since shareholders can spread their risks by investing in a portfolio of different companies' shares, they do not need management to do this for them through conglomerate integration. In this sense, conglomerates may be better at protecting managers from the effects of the economic cycle than they are at protecting shareholders! The resulting scepticism about the benefits of conglomerates for shareholder value and wealth creation has led investors (the risk-takers and providers of capital) to favour the break-up of a number of conglomerate organisations in recent years (such as Hanson Trust). However, some conglomerates continue to thrive. A good example is General Electric of the USA that operates in many different market sectors around the world.

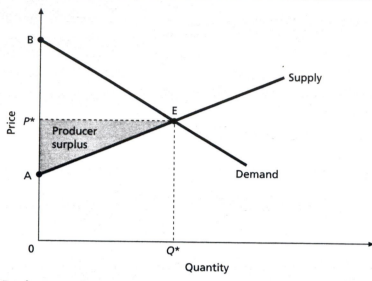

Figure 4.6 Producer surplus

Producer surplus

To complete this discussion of the firm's supply decision, we now draw attention to the subject of *producer surplus*. Producer surplus is the counterpart to consumer surplus (discussed earlier in Chapter 2, p. 31). As discussed already in this chapter, suppliers who attempt to profit maximise need an addition to revenue at least equal to the cost of producing an extra unit of production to persuade them to supply that unit. In a perfectly competitive market the supply curve is the marginal cost curve and represents the cost of producing each additional unit. In Figure 4.6 all units produced are sold at price P^*, where demand equals supply. However, all units sold other than the last unit, Q^*, earn for the firm a price in excess of their marginal costs of production. The shaded area, AP^*E, therefore represents a surplus revenue to the firm over and above the marginal costs of production. This surplus is referred to by economists as *producer surplus*. Thus:

Producer surplus **is the additional revenue that accrues to a firm when units of output are sold at a price which is in excess of the price at which the firm would have been prepared to supply, i.e. in excess of the marginal cost of production.**

Note that the area under the demand curve, bounded by the market price P^*, is the *consumer surplus* (i.e. area BP^*E).

It should be obvious that the amount of producer surplus is related to the elasticity of the supply curve, for any given demand curve. The more inelastic the supply the greater the producer surplus. If the supply curve was perfectly elastic – horizontal – then all units produced sell at a constant marginal cost and therefore no producer surplus arises.

Concluding remarks

This chapter has built on the discussion and detailed analysis of production costs set out in Chapter 3. It has been concerned with two of the most important questions facing managers:

- How much should be produced and supplied?
- How should the supply chain be organised?

In a very competitive market it is possible to determine a supply curve, which shows how much will be supplied at each price. It is also possible to determine the conditions that will lead to a new supply curve and to measure the responsiveness of supply to a change in price, i.e. the elasticity of supply. It is important to know how supply is likely to respond to price changes in order to understand behaviour in particular markets. For example, the supply of oil is likely to be more inelastic than the elasticity of supply of hairdressing services (unless there is existing excess capacity in the oil industry). This is because it takes much longer to develop new oil fields to the point of production than it takes to train new hairdressers.

The chapter also looked at supply and value chains. In supply decisions it is important for firms to understand the nature of their value chain, including where value is created (or lost). Only with a proper understanding of the value chain is it possible to organise production to ensure that the maximum value (and hence profit) is created. Sustained competitive advantage requires a full appreciation of the value chain. From the value chain it is possible to explore the nature of the boundary of the firm and to answer the important question – when should some activities be undertaken in-house and when are they best outsourced? Two broad approaches to answering this question have been put forward and discussed in this chapter, namely transaction cost and resource-based theories.

This discussion of the boundary of the firm was followed by a brief review of vertical, horizontal and conglomerate integration. All types of integration have implications for transaction costs and management costs. They also can be analysed from the perspective of maintaining and developing the firm's core competencies or capabilities so as to achieve and support an effective competitive strategy.

We have now completed, separately, the principles which underlie the demand and supply decisions in a market economy. In the next chapter we bring these principles together to demonstrate the dynamics of price determination.

Key learning points

- For a firm in a perfectly competitive industry, the **supply curve** shows the amount that it is willing to supply at all possible market prices.
- A firm's **short-run supply curve** is mapped out by the marginal cost curve lying above its average **variable** cost curve.

- A firm's **long-run supply curve** is traced out by its marginal cost curve lying above its average **total** cost curve.

- A **supply curve** can only be derived from the marginal cost curve for firms operating in very (strictly, 'perfectly') competitive environments – the concept of a 'supply curve' is particularly inappropriate when dealing with monopoly situations because a monopoly is a *price-maker, not a price-taker*, and can thus select the price–output combination on the demand curve so as to maximise profits.

- The **elasticity of supply** is defined as:

$$E_s = \frac{\text{Percentage change in quantity supplied}}{\text{Percentage change in price}}$$

- The **numerical value of** E_s will always be zero or positive, with a figure of zero indicating that supply does not respond at all to price changes; a figure of more than 1 indicating a relatively elastic response; and a figure of less than 1 a relatively inelastic response.

- The **supply chain** shows the different stages in the production and supply of outputs, e.g. in the case of a manufacturing process, the provision of materials and components, the physical production of the product, its eventual distribution and sale, and after sales service.

- The **value chain** identifies where value is created (or lost) at each stage of the supply (production and distribution) process.

- The **boundary of the firm** can be explained by *transaction cost* theory and the *resource-based* theory of the firm.

- **Transaction costs** are the costs of negotiating, monitoring and enforcing market contracts for the inputs of goods and services.

- **Resource-based theory** is concerned with the assets, skills and knowledge (i.e. core competencies and distinctive capabilities) which are (a) specific to the firm, (b) difficult to imitate and (c) are able to give the firm a distinct competitive advantage in the market place.

- **Vertical integration** is the bringing together under one ownership and control of different stages in the production of a given good or service.

- **Horizontal integration** occurs when two or more firms, at the same stage of production, integrate – usually leading to more market concentration and hence less competition in the product market.

- **Conglomerate integration** occurs when a firm enters different markets or industrial sectors.

- **Producer surplus** is the additional revenue that accrues to a firm when units of output are sold at a price which is in excess of the price at which the firm would have been willing to supply, i.e. in excess of the marginal cost of production.

Topics for discussion

1 What factors enter into the decision of a car manufacturing firm to launch a new model?

2 Using the concept of 'elasticity of supply', explain why raw material prices often tend to be less stable than manufactured goods prices.

3 Consider how a hotel owner would decide how to price hotel rooms:

   (a) when deciding whether or not to build the hotel at the outset; and
   (b) having built the hotel, so as to ensure that the maximum number of rooms is occupied each evening.

4 (a) Draw a value chain for a typical retail bank.
   (b) Discuss where most value is likely to be created and why.
   (c) Consider what are likely to be the main core competencies and distinctive capabilities that a retail bank will need to have to sustain competitive advantage.

5 On what basis might a house-building company decide whether or not to employ its own bricklayers, carpenters, plumbers, etc. rather than using subcontracting firms?

6 Give examples of firms with which you are familiar which are either

   (a) vertically integrated;
   (b) horizontally integrated; or
   (c) conglomerates.

   Consider the merits of each of these forms of organising production with reference to the firms you have listed.

7 A local radio station is about to negotiate a renewal of its operating licence. Write a report for its management setting out the approach that the management should take to the contract renewal. The current operating costs of the station are $600m per annum, the annualised capital costs are $150m, and the annual revenues from advertisers total $800m. There is no other revenue. In addition, the station pays the state licensing authority $30m per annum for an operating licence. It is rumoured that the licensing authority intends to raise the annual licence fee to $70m per annum in the next franchise period. The station and its facilities were built five years ago at a cost of $900m which is being written off on a straight-line basis over a predicted ten-year life (i.e. $90m p.a.). The annualised capital cost of $150m is composed of $90m depreciation and $60m in interest charges on loans incurred to finance the capital investment.

   In writing your report establish whether the radio station should seek a licence renewal if the rumoured new licence fee proves to be correct.

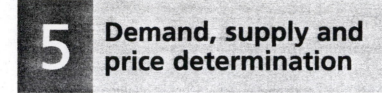

5 Demand, supply and price determination

In Chapter 2 we have seen that when the price of a good increases or decreases, the quantity demanded falls or rises respectively, with all factors remaining constant (i.e. *ceteris paribus*). Similarly in Chapter 4 we showed that in a highly competitive industry, the supply curve indicates the amount that a firm is willing to supply at all possible market prices. In general, the higher (lower) the price, the more (less) the firm will be willing to supply. We shall now build upon the analysis contained in these chapters and look in detail at how the underlying theories of demand and supply, together with the concept of elasticity, combine to determine the equilibrium price in the competitive market. In addition, the effects of taxes and subsidies on demand, supply and price are considered.

In particular, we shall analyse the following topics in this chapter:

- The price mechanism and equilibrium price.
- Changes in demand, supply and equilibrium price.
- Price and the allocation of resources.
- The effects of taxes and subsidies.
- Cobweb theory.

In a free market, the price system provides a mechanism which signals the state of demand and supply conditions to producers and consumers. These conditions will change as a result of intervention stemming, for example, from the effects of taxes and subsidies. It is important, therefore, that managers understand the fundamental principles of price determination in order to appreciate the impact of government intervention and the dynamics of the market place.

Learning outcomes

This chapter will help you to:

- Understand how *equilibrium prices* are determined in a market economy through the interaction of demand and supply forces.
- Appreciate the conditions which will lead to the establishment of an equilibrium price and why a *disequilibrium* may arise in reality.

- Grasp how changes in demand and supply *conditions* will result in the establishment of a new equilibrium price and quantity.
- Recognise the importance of relative *elasticities of demand and supply* in the establishment of a market equilibrium.
- Appreciate the functions of the price mechanism in terms of *resource allocation* and how a free market economy can result in an allocation that might not be entirely satisfactory.
- Understand the effects of the imposition of *taxes and subsidies* by governments on price and quantity equilibria.
- Grasp the meaning of the *incidence of a tax* in terms of the impact on buyers and suppliers.
- Appreciate the principles which underlie the *cobweb theory* of price determination and the conditions which are likely to give rise to *stable* and *unstable* cobweb dynamics.
- Understand the relevance of cobweb theory in the context of certain markets, such as agricultural production, and why primary *commodity prices* tend to fluctuate.

The price mechanism and equilibrium price

The *price mechanism* describes the way in which the prices charged for goods and ser-vices determine how scarce resources are allocated in a free market economy. People who want goods or services only have a limited income and so they must decide *what* to buy with the money available to them. The prices of the goods and services which they want will therefore directly affect their final buying decisions. At the same time, firms only have a limited amount of resources available with which to produce goods or services. The supply decisions of firms – *what* goods and services to supply and in *what* quantities – will be directly determined by the profits which they can make (assuming management pursues a profit-maximisation objective) and these in turn depend not only on the costs of production but also on the prices at which the goods or services can be sold in the market.

All firms do not produce the same goods or services. For example, some firms manufacture foods and beverages, others manufacture household goods or plant and machinery, others are involved in the production and distribution of newspapers. There are firms that supply financial services and restaurant and hotel services, while other firms specialise in the construction industry or in the supply of energy. The list, of course, is virtually endless. However, all of the firms that could be listed have one vital thing in common in a market economy, namely that the decisions made about what industry to operate in and what markets to produce goods or services for will be influenced by the prices obtainable. Although some firms have been established in one industry for many years, others are opening up, closing down or switching to new industries and new markets. Over time, firms in an industry increase or reduce the volume of output they sell. In the final analysis, changes in supply are directly influenced by changes in the cost of production or by changes in the selling price.

Since firms decide what goods or services they wish to supply and in what quantities (partly) on the basis of price, and since consumers decide what goods they will buy and in what quantities (partly) on the basis of price, price is a common factor influencing both demand and supply. If demand for a good or service exceeds the quantity supplied to the market, consumers will either have to stop buying what they cannot afford or they must be prepared to pay more for the good or service. At a higher price, firms should be prepared to produce and supply more of the good, given the costs of production. On the other hand, if the price of a good is such that firms want to supply more than consumers are willing to buy, production must be reduced or the price must be decreased so as to stimulate demand.

The price mechanism brings demand and supply into equilibrium such that for any good or service:

Equilibrium price is the price at which the quantity demanded by consumers and the quantity that firms are willing to supply of a good or service are the same.

The combined forces of demand and supply will determine this equilibrium price for any particular good or service.

In Figure 5.1, with the lines DD and SS representing the market demand and supply curves for a particular commodity, equilibrium is at the point E. At E, the wishes of consumers and the wishes of producers match. The equilibrium market price for the commodity will be P^* and the quantity demanded and supplied at this price will be Q^*. This equilibrium is the result of market forces in a free market, i.e. the interaction of demand and supply.

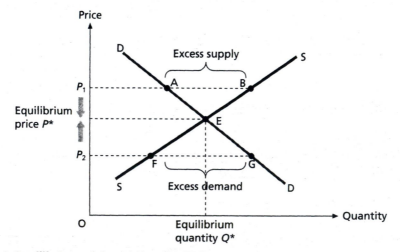

Figure 5.1 Equilibrium of demand and supply

To understand why point E is a market equilibrium, let us consider the situations which prevail at prices P_1 or P_2 in Figure 5.1. At price P_1, there is an excess quantity supplied over the quantity demanded, represented by the distance AB. The market is described as being in *disequilibrium*. In this situation, the reaction of suppliers as unsold stocks (inventories) accumulate will be to:

- lower the current level of production in order to reduce unwanted stock (i.e. de-stock); and
- reduce the selling price in order to encourage sales.

The opposite will happen at price P_2 where there will be excess demand over supply, shown by the distance FG. There will be upward pressure on price and, as a consequence, firms will want to supply more to the market.

Application 5.1

Price determination and black markets

World Cup tickets: a supply and demand fiasco!

The 1998 World Cup finals held in France will be remembered, at least by economists, for the extraordinary mismatch between the supply and demand for tickets. This led to one of the biggest 'black' (i.e. underground) markets in history operated by ticket touts, a market that was worth hundred of millions of French francs with some tickets selling at 30 or more times their face value.

In hindsight, the system of allocating tickets had serious shortcomings – with many commentators arguing that these should have been foreseen by the authorities. Tickets were allocated as follows:

- only 20% of the tickets for each game were allocated via national Football Associations to the supporters of the respective national teams;
- 60% of the tickets were available exclusively to French residents;
- the remaining 20% of tickets were allocated to corporate sponsors.

Ticket touts and the free market

The ticket touts would no doubt argue that they are merely entrepreneurs, whose role is consistent with the principles of basic neoclassical microeconomic theory, i.e. taking advantage of a profitable opportunity and providing a service consumers want at a price they are willing to pay. In other words, they are followers of the free market! This view is based on the belief that price efficiently rations out scarce goods.

Activity

What system of rationing and allocation would you have recommended for World Cup tickets? To what extent does the black market in tickets illustrate the clash between 'efficiency' and 'equity' in markets?

Thus, we are able to state that at the equilibrium price $P*$:

- The amount that producers are willing to supply is equal to the amount that customers are willing to buy.
- There will be no variation in stocks; and
- Unless something else changes, there will be no tendency for price to change.

$P*$ *is the equilibrium price*: it is the *efficient* price because at that price the market is cleared, and it is a *stable* price until the conditions of demand or supply change (in which case, there will be a shift to the left or right in the demand or supply curves).

To summarise, the forces of demand and supply therefore push a market to its equilibrium price and quantity, shown by $P*$ and $Q*$ respectively in Figure 5.1 above. We can also conclude the following:

- If there is no change in the conditions of demand and supply, the equilibrium price will rule in the market.
- If the equilibrium price does not rule, the market is in disequilibrium, but supply and demand forces will push prices towards the equilibrium price.
- Shifts in the demand or supply curves, caused by changes in the conditions of demand or supply, will change the equilibrium values of price and quantity.

Changes in demand, supply and equilibrium price

A change in either the demand or supply conditions will result in a shift in either the demand curve (DD) or the supply curve (SS) in Figure 5.1, resulting in the establishment of a new equilibrium quantity and market price. As we showed in Chapter 2, an increase in the demand for a good or service, for instance due to higher consumer income, will cause a rightward shift in the demand curve, thereby raising the equilibrium price and quantity bought and sold. This is illustrated in Figure 5.2.

The demand curve DD has shifted to the right to D_1D_1 so that, under the same supply conditions (denoted by the supply curve SS), equilibrium price rises from P to P_1 and the equilibrium quantity demanded rises from Q to Q_1. Note that while the quantity supplied increases to meet this increase in demand, supply is not perfectly elastic and hence market price rises. A perfectly elastic supply at point E (a horizontal supply curve) would mean that as the demand line moves to the right, price would remain constant at P.

Figure 5.2 also shows the effect of a decrease in demand, i.e. a leftward shift from DD to D_2D_2. The outcome is a decrease in the equilibrium price and quantity bought and sold to P_2, Q_2 respectively.

Likewise, we can show the effects of a shift in the supply curve, left or right, on the equilibrium price and quantity. These are illustrated in Figure 5.3.

A rightward shift in the supply curve SS to S_1S_1, for example due to lower input costs, decreases price from P to P_1 and increases quantity demanded from Q to Q_1. Note, however, that the demand curve is not perfectly elastic. A horizontal (perfectly elastic)

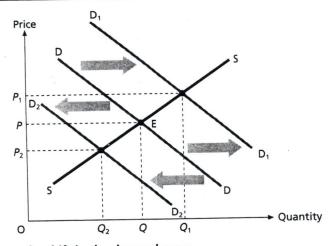

Figure 5.2 Effect of a shift in the demand curve

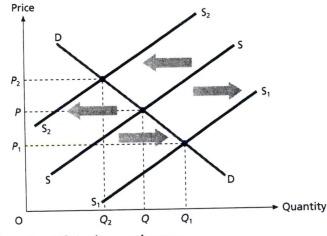

Figure 5.3 Effect of a shift in the supply curve

DD curve would mean that as the supply curve shifts rightwards, price would remain constant at P.

Likewise, a shift in the supply curve to the left, from SS to S_2S_2, increases the price from P to P_2 and reduces the quantity supplied from Q to Q_2.

In real-world markets, demand and supply will be continually changing over time. The market equilibrium is the level of price and quantity traded towards which the market will *tend to move* if demand and supply stay unchanged for some time. Shifts in demand and supply mean that the equilibrium is itself changing. It is important to appreciate that the type of equilibrium analysis outlined above freezes the market at an instant in time so as to investigate the idea of a market equilibrium. Our analysis here is *static*, yet markets are *dynamic*. The principles, however, still enable us to appreciate the fundamentals of price determination in market economies.

125

Price and the allocation of resources

The functions of the price mechanism in a free market economy are, fundamentally, to:

- Ration out scarce goods and services, so that price brings demand and supply into equilibrium.
- Indicate changes in the wants of consumers and induce suppliers to alter the quantities produced in response to changes in demand.
- Indicate changes in supply conditions, e.g. a rise in the costs of production will induce suppliers to decrease supply, while consumers will react to the resulting higher price by reducing demand for the good or service.

Prices also represent the reward for factors of production and therefore directly influence the use to which these factor inputs are put, i.e. how much of each factor is employed and how much of each good is produced. The role of prices in the employment of factor inputs (labour, capital and natural resources, including land) is discussed in detail in Chapters 13 to 15.

Thus, the price mechanism, by influencing what households will try to buy with limited incomes and what firms will try to supply with limited resources, provides a system for allocating scarce resources amongst competing users. In other words, it determines *what* goods should be produced, to *whom* they are sold and in *what* quantities.

However, left to itself in a free market economy, the price mechanism can result in an allocation of resources that might not be entirely satisfactory from a social welfare perspective. There are several reasons why this may be so relating to:

- Market imperfections.
- Incomplete or inaccurate information.
- Time lags.
- Unequal distribution of income.
- Externalities.
- Government objectives.

We comment briefly on each of these reasons for 'market failure' in turn.

Market imperfections

Some markets are imperfect and so a change in the price of a good might not result in the most *efficient* use of resources. For example, if the price of a good goes up, we would expect the quantity supplied to rise. However, if a monopoly firm controls the market, it might prevent other firms from entering the market (e.g. by claiming patent rights, or launching a strong marketing campaign with the intention of keeping customers away from new firms). If the price of the good in a monopoly market went up, the volume supplied by the monopolist would be increased, but not by as much as if the market were more competitive.

Incomplete or inaccurate information

Consumers may make bad purchasing decisions because they do not have complete and accurate information about all goods and services which are available, and their quality and ability to provide satisfaction to the buyer. Some services, such as health care, are particularly difficult for consumers to assess. Most of us, therefore, are inclined to accept the doctor's (the supplier's) diagnosis.

Time lags

It takes time for the price mechanism to work. Firms cannot suddenly enter a new market or shut down operations. The slow response of the price mechanism to changes in demand creates some inefficiency in resource allocation – for example, see the discussion of the Cobweb model below.

Unequal distribution of income

Household demand depends on household income, and if income is unevenly distributed among the population, a few rich people will demand luxury goods, whereas the many poor people might not be able to afford the basics of life. The redistribution of some wealth from the rich to the poor might be achieved by government intervention, such as through taxation of the rich to pay for government services (e.g. health, education, social welfare, police services and fire services). Government intervention in this way would be a recognition of the inability of the price mechanism to distribute resources satisfactorily so as to maximise society's well-being or social welfare.

Externalities

Some goods and services that are supplied and bought in the market place have an effect on people who do not buy them or use them. For example, cigarettes might cause discomfort to non-smokers when they are bought and used by smokers. The production of some goods damages the environment and so affect society as a whole. Alcohol consumed by car drivers endangers the lives of other road users and pedestrians. These negative outcomes of the market mechanism are examples of *externalities* and are referred to as *external costs*.

Government objectives

The price mechanism will result in a total demand for goods and services that is met by a matching total supply. This total supply might be insufficient, however, to achieve the government's objective of creating full employment within the economy, and so government might also wish to intervene to create a demand for output that would be employment-creating. Government intervention in markets might be desirable for a variety of other reasons:

- To prohibit the sale of dangerous goods, such as drugs.
- To protect a 'vital industry' such as agriculture, when current demand in the short term is low and threatening to cause an excessive contraction of the industry.
- To achieve a particular exchange rate for the domestic currency against a foreign currency.
- To reduce consumption of goods with external costs and encourage the consumption of goods with external benefits. For a fuller discussion, see Chapter 16.

The effects of taxes and subsidies

Leaving aside issues concerning the allocation of resources, governments will directly affect the equilibrium price and quantity by the imposition of taxes and subsidies.

Taxes

In the case of a *specific tax*, in which a tax is levied at a fixed rate per physical unit of the good or service, the supply curve will shift upwards by the amount of the tax. This is shown by the movement of SS to S_1S_1 in Figure 5.4, where the vertical distance AB represents the amount of the tax levied per unit. Because a specific tax has been applied, the distance AB applies at all output levels. If an *ad valorem* (by value) tax was introduced (e.g. VAT at 17.5%) then the amount of tax would rise the higher the initial price of the good. In this case the distance between the pre- and post-tax supply curves would widen the higher the pre-tax price. In other respects, however, the discussion below would still apply.

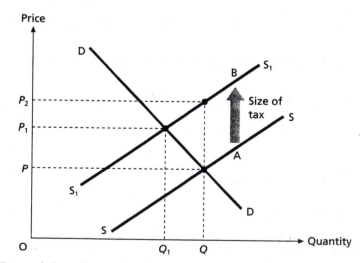

Figure 5.4 Tax and the price mechanism

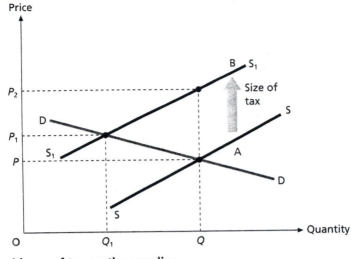

Figure 5.5 Incidence of tax on the supplier

Given the demand curve DD, the *incidence of the tax* – i.e. who bears the tax – can be examined. With an original equilibrium price of P, the after-tax new equilibrium price is P_1 and the equilibrium quantity is Q_1, given by the intersection of DD and S_1S_1. If the *whole* of the tax had been passed on to the consumer in the form of higher prices, the price would have gone up to P_2 – but of course it has not. The tax is being paid mostly by the consumer since the rise from P to P_1 represents most of the tax ($P_2 - P =$ AB) in this case. The remainder of the tax ($P_2 - P_1$) is being absorbed by the supplier. In other words, the incidence of the tax is falling mostly on the consumer, although this will not always be the case.

Figure 5.5 illustrates a situation where the incidence of the tax falls largely on the supplier. It will be seen in this example that price rises only a little from P to P_1 while the tax itself is shown again by the distance $P_2 - P$ (= AB). Note that while the equilibrium price has increased only marginally in this case, the equilibrium quantity has fallen sharply, from Q to Q_1. The key factor in determining the incidence of a tax is the slope of the demand and supply curves which, of course, is an indication of their elasticity. The more elastic demand is, the more difficult it will be to pass the tax on to the consumer and vice versa. This is not surprising since elasticity measures the responsiveness of demand to a change in price. The more elastic the demand, the more demand will contract sharply in the face of a price rise following a tax increase. Similarly, the more inelastic the supply, the less suppliers will cut supplies in response to lower prices (net of taxes); the more elastic the supply, the more suppliers will cut supplies due to a tax imposition. We can conclude, therefore, that the effect of price elasticity of demand on the distribution of the burden (incidence) of a tax is as follows:

- When demand is price inelastic, the tax ensures a large price increase and consumers bear more of the tax.

- When demand is price elastic, the tax causes a smaller price increase and producers bear more of the tax.
- When supply is price inelastic, the burden of the tax falls more heavily on suppliers because they are less able to nullify the impact of the tax by cutting output.
- When supply is price elastic, the tax falls less heavily on suppliers because they can reduce output significantly as the price they receive (net of tax) declines.

Subsidies

Let us turn now to examine the effect of subsidies on the determination of equilibrium price and quantity. In this case, a per unit subsidy provided to producers by the government will shift the supply curve downwards from SS to S_1S_1 by the amount of the subsidy – shown as the vertical distance AB in Figure 5.6 below.

Here the original price is P. After the subsidy is introduced the new price is P_1, determined as before by the intersection of DD and the new supply curve S_1S_1. If the whole of the subsidy had been passed on to the consumer, the equilibrium price would have fallen by the amount of the subsidy (i.e. $P - P_2 = AB$). In Figure 5.6, however, while most of the benefit of the subsidy has been passed on to the consumer $(P - P_1)$, some has been retained by the producer $(P_1 - P_2)$. Note also that the subsidy in this case has not increased the quantity bought and sold very much because demand is fairly price inelastic.

Figure 5.7 shows a different situation. Here, the consumer is paying a little less for the product after the subsidy is introduced (P_1 against P) but the market is much more active with quantity traded rising sharply from Q to Q_1. In this illustration the demand is relatively price elastic. The benefit of the subsidy largely rests with the producer $(P_1 - P_2)$ as a result of the impact on the quantity bought and sold.

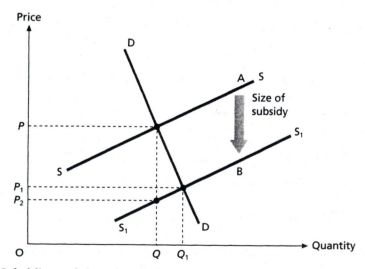

Figure 5.6 Subsidies and the price mechanism

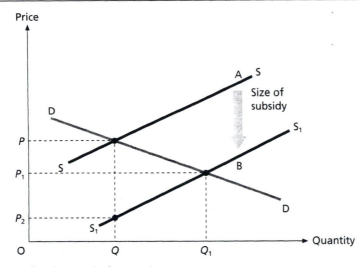

Figure 5.7 Benefit of subsidy for producer

As in the case of a tax, the precise effects of any subsidy will depend on the relative values of the price elasticities of demand and supply.

Cobweb theory

Before we end our discussion of the interaction of demand and supply, we can take the analysis of the price mechanism a stage further by looking at a simple dynamic model of price determination. So far, we have examined the market mechanism on the basis that changes in supply take place instantaneously and with a movement from one (static) equilibrium price to another (static) equilibrium price. This is known as 'static equilibrium' price analysis because the price remains unchanged until there is a change in the conditions of demand or supply. This notion of price moving smoothly and quickly from one equilibrium to another may not be a realistic assumption in a number of markets. However, by moving away from this simplistic approach we can make the theory of price determination more relevant to some markets, in particular those with time lags between price and output changes.

The quantity of a good supplied will not change immediately in response to a change in price where goods take time to be produced. For example, suppose a manufacturer aims to supply 20,000 digital cameras this year. This aim may be based on the fact that prices last year (when the firm planned its production) were assumed to support this output target. By the time the cameras are actually produced, the manufacturer may, however, discover that the prevailing price would only justify production of 15,000 cameras. Thus, the manufacturer may aim to produce only 15,000 next year, but again market conditions may have moved by then. This situation is illustrated in Figure 5.8 showing long-run demand and supply curves.

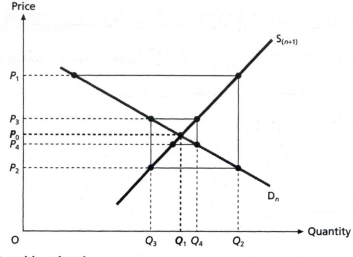

Figure 5.8 A stable cobweb

The demand curve, D_n, represents the demand for a producer in year n, the current year, while the supply curve, $S_{(n+1)}$ shows the supply of the product in the year $n + 1$. Producers decide on supply for the year $n + 1$ on the basis of price in the year n.

The market is in equilibrium at price P_0, and suppliers plan to produce Q_1 in Year 1. Suppose that a fluctuation in either demand or supply results in a price of P_1 in Year $n + 1$. Producers will set Q_2 as their output for Year 2, but at price P_1 the supply is well in excess of the demand. Stocks of unsold goods will build up which will lead to a fall in price to P_2 in Year 2. At price P_2 producers will decide to supply Q_3 in Year 3, which will result in a rise in price to P_3 because demand then exceeds supply. At price P_3 producers will wish to supply Q_4 the following year, which will mean that P_4 will actually be charged, and so on. It will be clear, therefore, that price will move around the equilibrium value, P_0, but in increasingly smaller changes until it returns to the equilibrium price P_0, when the market stabilises (until another fluctuation of demand or supply occurs).

The above explanation is based on the *cobweb theory*.

The *cobweb theory* explains the path followed in moving towards an equilibrium price and quantity in the long run where there are time tags in the adjustment of either supply or demand to changes in price.

The reason for naming this theory the cobweb should be obvious from the pattern illustrated in Figure 5.8. The pattern of price movements in Figure 5.8 is an example of a 'stable cobweb' because price tends towards stability. This assumes, of course, that the conditions of demand and supply do not change and cause a shift in either curve before the price P_0 is achieved. Note that our discussion has been based upon stable long-run demand and supply curves. In reality, producers face problems when deciding

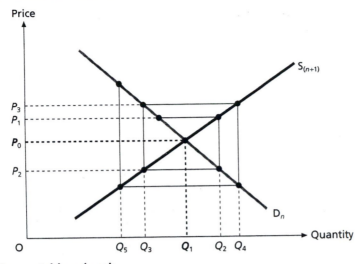

Figure 5.9 An unstable cobweb

production levels not only because of the factors emphasised in the cobweb theory, but because the conditions of demand and supply change over time. The stable cobweb is also sometimes referred to as a 'convergent cobweb' model.

Let us consider an 'unstable cobweb' situation – see Figure 5.9, also known as a 'divergent cobweb' model.

Exactly the same sequence applies here as before with price in Year n determining supply in $Year_{n+1}$ but now the price moves away from the equilibrium at P_0. Starting with price P_1, suppliers will produce output Q_2, which can only be sold at price P_2. The price P_2 leads suppliers to supply output Q_3 in the following year, leading to a higher price of P_3, and so on. This is an 'unstable cobweb' because, in theory, the escalations in price could become infinitely large.

Why in the two cobweb models above is one market stable and the other unstable in the long run? If you look at the long-run demand and supply curves in Figure 5.8 and 5.9 again, you will see that the stable market is one where demand is relatively more price elastic than supply – the demand curve is relatively flatter. The unstable market has the reverse, namely a greater relative price elasticity of supply over the elasticity of demand.

For some products, such as manufactured goods, in the *short run* the volume demanded tends to change more than the volume supplied in response to a change in price. Deficient or excess demand can be removed by a small price change, which in turn creates only a small change in supply. The change in supply does not have a big effect on price next year, and so the market heads back towards a long-run equilibrium price.

However, with staple commodities, such as wheat, supply tends to change more in response to a price change than does demand *over time*. As an example, in general the demand for wheat to make bread will be more price inelastic than the farmer's ability to supply it from year to year. If the farmer sees that the price in Year n is not going to

133

support the same production in Year $n + 1$, he can switch his resources into, say, sheep or barley in anticipation. This in turn will lead to a reduction in supply in Year $n + 2$, with a consequent price rise.

Cobweb theory was first developed in the context of certain agricultural markets (it was for some time referred to as the 'hog cycle') and helps to explain why primary commodity prices tend to fluctuate (current output is dependent upon decisions made some months or years ago and primary products cannot be easily and cheaply stockpiled when demand exceeds supply, for example the product may be perishable). If we add to this the possibility of droughts, diseases and other causes of crop failure (which shift the supply curve), we can understand why people and countries dependent upon selling agricultural goods suffer sharp fluctuations in incomes. We can also better appreciate why governments might choose to step into the market to buy up surpluses to protect prices (for example, as in the case of the European Union and its Common Agricultural Policy) and thereby attempt to stabilise supplies.

It should also be noted that a cobweb relationship could also apply if there were time lags in consumer demand responding to price changes while supply responded much more quickly. It is much harder, however, to find real world examples of where this occurs.

Application 5.2

The telecommunications industry

Massive investment in the late 1990s in the anticipation of fast growing internet and other demand for telecommunications led to a vast excess of capacity, reminiscent of other 'booms and busts' going back to the 'railway mania' of the 1840s. Investors poured billions of dollars into the construction of telecommunications networks. For example, Level 3 Communications raised US$10bn. to build a worldwide fibre optic network. This network in North America alone would have led to 1.5m miles of fibre – equivalent to circling the globe 60 times.

Demand for telecommunications services has failed to grow to anything like the same extent. In the US perhaps only 3.5% of the optical fibre laid is in use. In consequence, excess supply has led to fast falling prices for bandwidth. Falling prices will lead to increased consumer demand for telecommunications services, the extent depending upon the price elasticity. But increased demand, at least in the short term, is unlikely to remove the excess capacity. The other way the market is adjusting to the excess supply is through corporate failures. Companies that only a few months ago found banks falling over themselves to lend money are now discovering that the same banks are no longer willing to extend credit. The result will be a withdrawal of capacity from the market.

The telecommunications industry represents a good example of market adjustment in the face of the forces of demand and supply.

Activity

Why are new technology industries prone to periods of excess supply? Explain this phenomenon using appropriate demand and supply analysis.

Concluding remarks

The subject of economics is concerned with the efficient allocation of scarce resources. In market economies resources are allocated based on prices that are determined by the forces of demand and supply.

In this chapter we have reviewed how demand and supply interact in a competitive market to establish an equilibrium price. At this price unless either the demand or the supply curve shifts (that is to say, there is a change on the conditions of demand or supply) the market remains in balance with neither excess demand nor excess supply. When a shift in the demand or supply curve occurs, price adjusts so that the competitive market moves back to an equilibrium. This process of resource allocation and re-allocation was called by the eighteenth century economist Adam Smith, the 'invisible hand' of the market.

We have also seen, however, that under some circumstances the free market, the invisible hand, may fail to achieve a satisfactory outcome from a social welfare point of view. This helps to explain why governments sometimes intervene in resource allocation. The role of government in the economy is pursued in more detail in Chapter 16. In this chapter the incidence of a tax was explored. The extent to which consumers and producers bear the impact of a sales tax was shown to depend upon the elasticities of demand and supply for the good and service in question.

Finally, situations where supply does not immediately respond to changes in demand were considered using the cobweb model. In some markets producers can only respond to current demand after a time lag – this tends to be particularly the case in agricultural and other commodity markets, though some manufacturing sectors are also affected, in which case current supply is a function of an earlier price rather than the current market price. The result can be sharp fluctuations around the long-run market equilibrium. We looked at two opposite cases: (i) a stable cobweb, where price moves eventually to an equilibrium; and (ii) an unstable cobweb, where price fluctuations become more extreme over time. In practice, in both cases shifts in the demand and supply functions, which can be expected the longer the time period, would add further complexity to the analysis. The cobweb theory provides an introduction to a dynamic analysis of price changes.

In the next chapter we further our understanding of how markets and the price mechanism work by studying the operation of perfectly competitive markets.

Key learning points

- The **price mechanism** describes the way in which the prices charged for goods and services determine how scarce resources are allocated in a free market economy.
- **Equilibrium price** is the price at which the quantity demanded by consumers and the quantity that firms are willing to supply are the same.
- Changes in the **conditions of demand and supply** will lead to changes in the equilibrium values of price and quantity.

- The **functions of the price mechanism** in a free market economy are to:
  - ration out scarce resources;
  - indicate changes in consumers' wants and induce suppliers to alter production levels;
  - indicate changes in supply conditions.
- The price mechanism can result in an **allocation of resources** that may not be regarded as satisfactory arising from:
  - market imperfections;
  - incomplete or inaccurate information;
  - time lags with respect to demand and supply responses;
  - unequal distribution of income;
  - externalities;
  - government objectives.
- The **incidence of a tax** refers to the burden of taxation and in the case of a specific tax on a good or service this generally depends on the price elasticities of demand and supply.
- When **demand is price inelastic,** the imposition of a tax ensures a large price increase and consumers bear most of the tax.
- In contrast, when **demand is price elastic** the tax causes a smaller price increase and producers bear more of the tax.
- When **supply is price inelastic,** the tax burden falls more heavily on suppliers because they are less able to nullify the impact of the tax by cutting output.
- When **supply is price elastic,** the tax burden falls less heavily on suppliers because they can reduce output as the price they receive (net of tax) declines.
- As in the case of a tax, the effects of a **subsidy** will depend on the relative values of the price elasticities of demand and supply.
- **Cobweb theory** is designed to explain the path followed in moving towards an equilibrium price and output where there are time lags in the adjustment of either supply or demand to changes in prices.
- A **stable cobweb** is one which tends towards a stable equilibrium price and quantity; an **unstable cobweb** describes a situation which ripples away from the equilibrium.
- Cobweb theory was first developed in the context of certain agricultural markets and helps, in particular, to explain why **primary commodity prices** tend to fluctuate.

Topics for discussion

1 The OPEC cartel has just announced cuts in production levels which are expected to drive up the spot price of a barrel of oil by 20% in the coming weeks. Using appropriate demand and supply diagrams, examine:

   (a) The impact on the retail price of petrol.
   (b) The likely impact on the electricity supply market, bearing in mind that oil is an input into electricity generation as well as being a substitute source of energy.

2 In today's Budget Statement by the Government, a new specific tax of $2 per unit has been levied on each bottle of wine sold. Assume that before the imposition of this new tax, the sale of wine was tax-free. A newsflash on television claims that 'Tax causes wine prices to rise by $2 per bottle'. Evaluate this statement.

3 Give examples of goods or services where the incidence of a sales tax is likely to fall primarily on:

(a) consumers;

(b) producers.

4 Explain, using demand and supply analysis, why agricultural surpluses arise under the European Common Agricultural Policy in which farmers receive large subsidies linked to production levels.

5 It is often claimed that the 'free market' leads to an economically efficient allocation of resources – but is this allocation necessarily equitable from a social welfare perspective? Assess this question with reference to the domestic housing market.

6 During the past decade, microchip prices have fluctuated wildly on world markets, reflecting periods of excess demand followed by excess supply. Using appropriate diagrams, explain the impact of time lags in the production of microchips on price levels.

7 Why would you expect the wholesale price of coffee in world markets to fluctuate more than the wholesale price of daily newspapers?

6 Analysis of perfectly competitive markets

The nature of competition – an overview

As we noted in Chapter 1, the degree of competition a firm actually faces varies depending on the structure of its industry. This raises the notion of a *competitive spectrum* which illustrates the extent to which competition in the market place can range from, at one extreme, *pure monopoly* (sole supplier) to the other extreme of *perfect competition* (very large number of small suppliers selling identical products or services). Figure 6.1 shows these two extremes and the intermediary structures of *oligopoly* (relatively small number of suppliers) and *monopolistic competition* (large number of small suppliers, selling slightly differentiated products or services).

In Figure 6.1, it can be seen that firm A is in a more competitive market than firm B, which itself faces more competition than firm C. Firm C is closest to being a monopolist. At an early phase in establishing a competitive strategy it is important for management to decide where on this spectrum their businesses lie (bearing in mind that a firm may operate in various markets and therefore more than one position on the spectrum may be relevant). Note also that the degree of competition is related to the extent to which the products sold by the firms are differentiated and by the extent to which there are barriers to entry into the industry by new competing firms.

Each of the economists' market models is a theoretical construct designed as an abstraction of actual markets. Each is based on a set of restrictive assumptions and

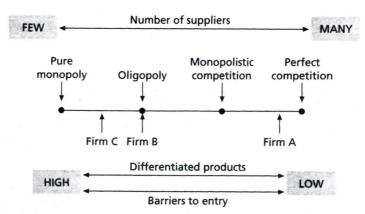

Figure 6.1 Market structures in the competitive spectrum

none is designed to *describe* a real-world market. Since every market has its own idio-syncrasies it would be impossible to provide a descriptive model for every market! Like other economists' models, they are constructed so that certain *predictions* can be made which have general application. Although abstract in nature, each of these market models provides important insights into the functioning of real-world markets. This chapter and the next three chapters deal with each of the main market structures shown in Figure 6.1, in turn. We start this chapter with an analysis of perfect competition.

Aims and learning outcomes

Markets in which competition is intense in the sense that there are very many suppliers and buyers of a particular good or service may approximate to the economists' ideal of *perfect competition*. Competition that is *perfect* requires, however, a set of very restrict-ive assumptions which are not likely to exist in their entirety in the real world. If these conditions were met then no single firm could influence the market – indeed, all firms would only be able to sell at the ruling market price determined by the interaction of supply and demand conditions in the market as a whole.

In this chapter, the following topics are covered:

- Conditions for perfect competition.
- Production in the short run and long run.
- Productive and allocative efficiency in perfectly competitive markets.

The theory of perfect competition is not intended to describe any real-world market. Rather, the purpose of studying the perfectly competitive model is to use it as a bench-mark for gaining greater insights into the economics of competition and for assessing business decision-making and outcomes in competitive markets.

Learning outcomes

This chapter will help you to:

- Appreciate the significance and usefulness of the *perfect competition model* when analysing real-world markets.
- Understand the difference between price and output outcomes in the short run and long run in perfectly competitive markets.
- Recognise the role of *supernormal profit* as an incentive for new firms to enter competitive markets, leading to a reduction in market price, and therefore the dynamics of competitive markets.
- Distinguish between *allocative* and *productive efficiency* and how these interact to ensure *economic efficiency* in perfectly competitive markets.
- Understand the meaning of *Pareto optimality* and why pareto optimal outcomes occur in perfectly competitive markets.

Conditions for perfect competition

Perfect competition is sometimes also referred to as *atomistic* competition. A perfectly competitive market is one in which there is an extremely high degree of competition. Bearing in mind that it is ultimately the consumer who defines competition, this implies a very large number of suppliers in the market between whom consumers can easily switch. Strictly, perfect competition requires the following conditions:

- **Homogeneous (identical) products** – i.e. the presence of perfect substitutes.
- **No firm with a cost advantage** – i.e. all firms have identical cost curves.
- **A very large number of suppliers** – thus no single producer by varying its output can perceptibly affect the total market output and hence the market price.
- **Free entry into and exit from the industry** – ensuring that competition is sustained over time.
- **No transport and distribution costs to distort competition.**
- **Suppliers and consumers who are fully informed about profits, prices and the characteristics of products in the market** – hence ignorance or 'incomplete information' does not distort competition.

A market which comes closest to exhibiting all of these conditions is the Stock Market. Any particular stock is homogeneous, there is plenty of readily available information (e.g. published prices), transaction costs are relatively low, buyers and sellers can readily enter and leave the market and individual buyers and sellers of stock usually have an insignificant effect on price.

Unregulated commodity markets are also highly, if not perfectly, competitive in nature. For example, in an unregulated world coffee market, the buyer might distinguish Brazilian coffee from coffee from other parts of the world but not the coffee from a particular Brazilian estate. If this is so, then from the buyer's perspective Brazilian coffee is a homogeneous product. Hence, the price of Brazilian coffee on the world market determines the price received by each of the individual Brazilian coffee growers. The individual grower is said to be a *price-taker*. The grower cannot set its price independently of the other growers. Competition drives prices down to a minimum level and if a single grower decides to raise price, buyers will switch to alternative suppliers.

Application 6.1

The law of one price

Prices in perfectly competitive markets

In the late nineteenth century Alfred Marshall enunciated the *law of one price*. Under this economic law there can be only one price in a single market for identical goods. The model of perfect competition reflects this law. In a perfectly competitive market there can be only one price at which producers sell and consumers buy.

In reality, however, it is difficult to find examples of where the law of one price holds. Undifferentiated or homogeneous goods were the ones that Marshall had in mind, but today most goods (and services) are branded and differentiated. Agricultural commodities would be very close to Marshall's ideal in the absence of state intervention in agricultural markets. One lettuce is much like another! But government policies, such as the Common Agricultural Policy in the EU, ensure that the market for agricultural goods is far from perfect. A similar argument applies to minerals, such as copper or bauxite, where producer associations, international trading agreements, and multinational mining companies influence prices. Oil is essentially a homogeneous product, but the producer cartel OPEC and taxation in consumer countries both ensure that the market is imperfect and that petrol prices vary from country to country.

The price of services generally varies enormously too. In part this is due to marketing and market positioning – for example, top 'beauty salons' are positioned well up-market from the street-corner hairdresser – and only in part is the difference in price charged due to differences in costs of production.

Activity

Explain the theoretical importance of perfect competition and the law of one price. If governments in the EU adopted the same level of taxation on a litre of petrol would prices at the pump inevitably be the same across Europe? Explain your answer.

Production in the short run and long run

In discussing the determination of price and output under conditions of perfect competition, it is necessary to distinguish between the short-run equilibrium and the long-run equilibrium. The short run and long run in production were discussed in detail in Chapter 4, pp. 103–4, and are defined as follows:

- The *short run* is the time period in which *at least one* factor input into the production process is fixed in supply – usually this will be capital or land, although in some cases this can apply to certain types of labour (e.g. highly skilled workers).

- The *long run* is the time period in which *all* factors of production become variable in supply. In the long run, progress can be made towards operating at the optimal scale of production.

We turn now to a discussion of the short-run equilibrium position before turning to look at the corresponding long-run situation under the conditions of perfect competition set out above.

Short-run equilibrium

In perfectly competitive markets because the product is homogeneous the nature of competition can only centre on price. The demand curve faced by an individual producer

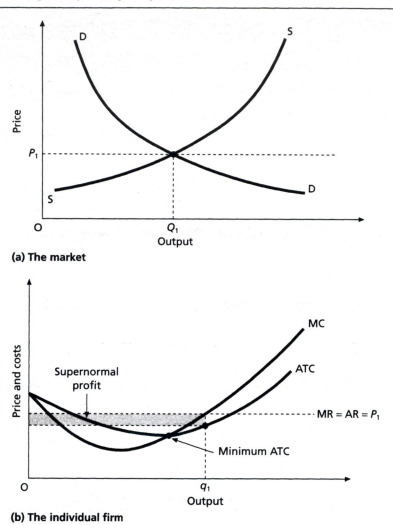

(a) The market

(b) The individual firm

Figure 6.2 Perfect competition: short-run equilibrium (profits)

is therefore horizontal or *perfectly price elastic* (see pp. 38–42 for a discussion of price elasticity). The way in which a perfectly competitive market operates can be best described with the aid of diagrams. We will stay with the Brazilian coffee example. In Figure 6.2, diagram (a) relates to the overall market and shows the demand (DD) and supply (SS) relating to Brazilian coffee. Diagram (b) shows the short-run marginal and average total cost curves (MC and ATC respectively) and marginal and average revenue curves (MR and AR respectively) for an individual coffee grower. Assuming that each grower faces the same market demand conditions for coffee and has the same cost structure, the revenue and cost curves in diagram (b) reflect the position for any of the growers.

The total supply of Brazilian coffee, Q_1, and the world demand for it sets a market price for coffee of P_1 (shown in diagram (*a*)). This means that each grower must sell at that price. The individual firm can supply varying amounts of coffee but must sell it at price P_1. Since the price and therefore the average revenue are constant, the marginal revenue is also constant and equal to the average revenue and price, i.e. $MR = AR = P_1$. Also, let us assume, as usual, that the cost curves include a *normal* profit to reflect the opportunity cost of capital (i.e. what the capital in the production activity could earn if invested in the next best alternative investment). Any additional profit above and beyond this is referred to as *supernormal profit*. To achieve maximum profit in the short run, the individual grower will aim to supply q_1 where the marginal revenue equates to the marginal cost of production, i.e. $MR = MC$ (why this is the maximum profit output was explained earlier, in Chapter 3, pp. 71–5). At this output, the pure profit earned per unit of output, q_1, is shown by the vertical distance between the AR and ATC curves – hence the total supernormal profit is the shaded area, given by the profit per unit times quantity sold.

To summarise, in the short-run equilibrium under conditions of perfect competition:

- The firm is a *price-taker*, not a price-maker.
- Marginal revenue equals average revenue and equals price; i.e. $MR = AR = P$.
- Profits are maximised where *short-run* marginal cost equates to marginal revenue (and average revenue).
- Supernormal profits can be earned given by the extent to which price (and thus average revenue) exceeds short-run average total costs at the profit-maximising output.

It should be appreciated that, by similar logic, if at the going market price average total cost *exceeds* average revenue (price), so that losses are made for each unit sold, the best that a firm can do is to minimise these losses in the short run. This is achieved by producing where marginal revenue (and average revenue) equals short-run marginal cost. This is illustrated in Figure 6.3.

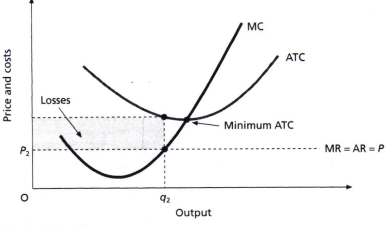

The individual firm

Figure 6.3 Perfect competition: short-run equilibrium (losses)

In a loss-making situation, the market price is set at P_2, lying below the average total cost curve. A loss is made on each unit of the quantity q_2 sold. This price may still cover the average *variable* costs of production, though not the fixed costs. If, however, price is so low that not even the average variable costs of production are covered, a loss-minimising firm can be expected to cease production immediately – see the discussion on p. 74.

Long-run equilibrium

In the long run, the existence of supernormal profit can be expected to act as an incentive for new coffee growers to enter the market. But as new suppliers enter and produce coffee, the total market supply will rise and, assuming that market demand is not also increasing, price will fall. This will continue until the supernormal profit disappears and there is no incentive for further farmers to switch to growing coffee beans. At this time, the market stabilises or reaches a *long-run equilibrium*.

This process is illustrated in Figure 6.4. The increase in the market supply of coffee is shown by a shift to the right in the supply curve in diagram (a), while the effect on the output, price and profits of each individual grower in the market is shown in diagram (b). Due to new producers entering the market, the total quantity supplied rises from Q_1 to Q_2. The amount supplied by each individual firm, however, falls from q_1 to q_2 because of the lower price in the market. The market reaches equilibrium (at a price, P_2, which is below the original price, P_1) when AR equates to long-run ATC and hence supernormal (pure) profit no longer exists. At this point supernormal profits have been competed away by new entrants to the industry and there is no longer a profit incentive for further producers to enter. Supply stabilises at S_2S_2 until such time as the conditions of demand or supply change again, triggering a movement to a new long-run equilibrium.

Turning to the case where the short-run equilibrium involves losses, then some producers can be expected to leave the industry. As they leave, the market supply will fall and in the long run the price will recover sufficiently so that normal profits are earned again. In the long run, equilibrium once more occurs where $ATC = MR_2 = AR_2$. Therefore, whenever in a perfectly competitive market firms earn more than or less than normal profits due to a change in the conditions of demand or supply, in the long run normal profit is restored through the entry and exit of suppliers.

To summarise, in the long-run equilibrium under conditions of perfect competition:

- The firm is still a *price-taker*.
- Marginal revenue still equals average revenue and price; i.e. $MR = AR = P$.
- But profits are now maximised where *long-run* marginal costs are equal to marginal revenue (and average revenue).
- Supernormal profits (or losses) earned in the short run disappear due to market entry (or exit) so that firms in perfect competition earn only normal profits in the long run ($AR = ATC$).

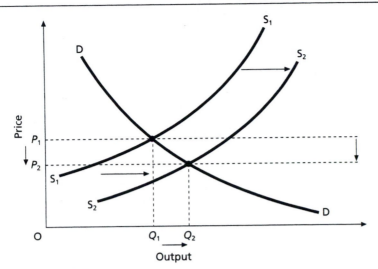

(a) The market

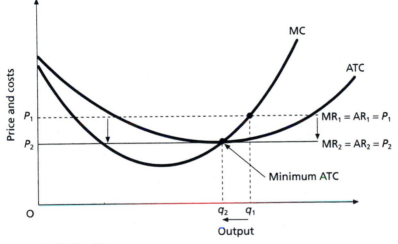

(b) The individual firm

Figure 6.4 Perfect competition: long-run equilibrium (profits)

Productive and allocative efficiency in perfectly competitive markets

It should be noted that in the short run a firm in a perfectly competitive market does *not* produce at the point where average costs are minimised, i.e. at the lowest point on the ATC curve (see, for example Figure 6.2(b) and Figure 6.3 where outputs do not occur at a level where ATC is minimised). In the long run, however, the cost minimising output is achieved – firms operate at the optimal scale of production (production

145

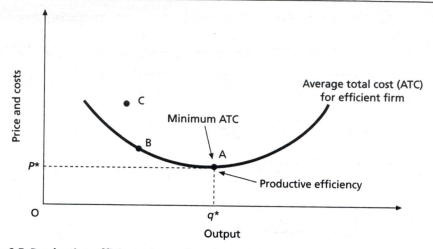

Figure 6.5 Productive efficiency in perfect competition

occurs where ATC is minimised, as in Figure 6.4(b)). Also in perfect competition there can be no X-inefficiency in the long run because firms which are not minimising their costs of production for any given output will be unable to compete at the market price (for a discussion of the meaning of X-inefficiency, see pp. 87–90).

It is because firms in perfect competition in the long run produce at optimal scale and minimise production costs that economists equate competition with *productive efficiency*.

> *Productive efficiency* occurs when a firm minimises the costs of producing any level of output, given existing technology.

The scale of output and level of average cost associated with productive efficiency is illustrated in Figure 6.5.

In Figure 6.5, productive efficiency is shown at point A on the ATC curve. Here the firm is producing at optimal scale, q^* (the lowest point of the ATC curve) and at the same time there is no X-inefficiency because the firm is producing on its (efficient) average cost curve.

By contrast, at point B, the firm is still producing efficiently but at a sub-optimal scale and therefore the average cost of production is higher than at point A. Costs will be higher still if the firm produces at, say, point C where both X-inefficiency and a sub-optimal scale of production (scale inefficiency) occur.

Productive efficiency is the result of two forces:

- *Technical efficiency* – this occurs when inputs of the factors of production are combined in the firm in the best possible way to produce the *maximum physical output*.
- *Price efficiency* – this occurs when inputs into production are optimally employed, given their prices, so as to minimise production costs.

The importance of technical price efficiencies in production decisions can be readily appreciated with reference to the analysis of isoquants and isocost lines – see the Appendix in Chapter 3 (pp. 95–100) for details.

Economists also equate perfect competition with allocative efficiency:

Allocative efficiency denotes the optimal allocation of scarce resources so as to produce the combination of outputs which best accords with consumers' demands. In other words, no other allocation of resources would produce a higher level of economic welfare, given the existing consumer demands.

Allocative efficiency is achieved when the price of a product is set at a level which equates to the marginal cost of producing it (including a normal profit). This is because price in a competitive economy reflects the marginal benefit or marginal utility to the consumer of the last unit consumed and marginal cost the cost to society of producing this last unit, in terms of economic resources used up. Therefore, if price were above marginal cost, economic welfare could be increased by producing and consuming more units until price equals marginal cost. The utility gained (reflected in the price consumers are willing to pay) exceeds the cost to society of the extra production. Conversely, where price is less than marginal cost, the utility or benefit to the consumer from the last unit(s) consumed is less than the cost to society of providing that unit(s). Therefore, economic welfare is increased by contracting the supply and transferring the production resources to other uses. Strictly, $P = MC$ is *pareto optimal* only under a number of strict conditions, for example, there should be no 'externalities' in consumption or production. But assuming these other conditions hold, when all outputs in an economy are allocated so that their price equals their marginal cost then *Pareto optimality* is said to exist (after the Italian economist Vilfredo Pareto, 1848–1923).

A *pareto optimum* is said to exist when resources cannot be reallocated so as to make one person better off without making someone else worse off.

There are three main conditions that must hold in order for a pareto optimum to be achieved.

1 Goods must be optimally distributed between consumers so that no reallocation increases economic welfare.

2 Inputs are allocated in such a way that no reallocation would increase the physical output.

3 Optimal amounts of each output are produced so that no change in output would lead to higher economic welfare.

In perfectly competitive markets, these three conditions are met in the long run. With price set equal to marginal cost (condition 1) and production cost minimised (conditions 2 and 3), this helps to explain why the perfect competition model, while abstract, is used by economists as a benchmark against which to judge actual production and the effects of actual competition.

As a final comment on the efficiency properties of perfectly competitive markets, economists define *economic efficiency* as the product of both productive and allocative efficiency. In other words, in the market an economically efficient output is one where *both* maximum allocative and productive efficiency are achieved.

Application 6.2

Competition in the vitamins industry

Vitamins are chemical products that are difficult for a producer to differentiate because they are produced to meet specified standards of purity, packaging, etc. Although the industry is dominated by a few large producers, such as BASF, Hoffmann La Roche and Aventis, a recent UK Competition Commission reports vitamins as 'commodities that are sold more or less on price only'. Some producers tried to differentiate their vitamins production by offering a wide range of products or by providing a high customer service, but the Competition Commission concluded that: 'Overall, it appears difficult to differentiate substantially the nature of the product offered, and so competition is likely to be mainly on price. All parties told us that there had been very active price competition for vitamins B2 and C since 1995. Hence, driving down production costs through maximising the efficiency of the production process is important.' From the mid-1990s on world markets, standard vitamin C prices fell by between 62% and 65%; prices for animal feed-grade vitamin B2 fell by around 70%; and prices for food-grade vitamin B2 by up to 48%.

The sharp decline in industry prices resulted from more competition between the established producers and market entry by Chinese vitamins manufacturers.

Source: Competition Commission, *BASF AG and Takeda Chemicals Industries Ltd: a report on the acquisition by BASF AG of certain assets of Takeda Chemical Industries Ltd*, Cm. 5209, July 2001, London, paragraphs 4.84–4.94.

Activity

Although far from being perfectly competitive, explain why the model of perfect competition may help us to understand price movements in the international market for vitamins. What actions might we expect vitamins producers to adopt to restrict price competition?

Concluding remarks

This chapter has set out the features of perfect competition and the implications for pricing and production decisions facing a firm in the short run and long run under conditions of perfect competition. It is important to emphasise once again that this model is intended as a theoretical benchmark for assessing the conditions and implications deriving from a range of different competitive environments in the real world of business. The abstract nature of the perfectly competitive model, however, does not diminish its importance with respect to a deeper understanding of competitive markets. The model provides a basis for determining the extent to which actual firms are able to influence price and earn above-normal (i.e. supernormal) profits. In particular, a large number of buyers and suppliers and free entry and exit of suppliers are critical to the operation of a highly competitive market.

In the next chapter we turn to look at the polar form of market structure to perfect competition, namely *monopoly*. The key difference to note between these two extremes is that individual firms in perfect competition are *price-takers* while a monopolist is a *price-maker*.

To summarise, under perfect competition:

- In the short run, until the entry or exit of sufficient firms occurs, supernormal profit or losses can exist.
- In the long run, once the process of market adjustment is complete, only a normal profit is earned.
- In the long run a Pareto optimal outcome is achieved.

Perfect competition drives profit down to a normal level and provides consumers with low-priced products and services. Also, firms in perfectly competitive markets operate at optimal scale in the long run. Economists favour the perfectly competitive model because it achieves economically efficient and, therefore, welfare maximising results.

Key learning points

- A **perfectly competitive market** is one in which there is an extremely high degree of competition with a very large number of firms selling identical products or services, with identical cost conditions, with free entry into and exit from the industry and where ignorance does not distort competition (information is complete for all producers and consumers).

- Each firm in a perfectly competitive market is a **price-taker** – it faces a perfectly elastic demand curve.

- **Short-run equilibrium** in a **perfectly competitive market** occurs when profits are maximised (or losses are minimised) and this is where the short-run marginal cost equates to price (and average revenue as well as marginal revenue: i.e. $P(= AR) = MR = MC$).

- **Long-run equilibrium** in a **perfectly competitive market** is attained where production occurs so that firms can earn a normal profit: i.e. $P(= AR) = MR = MC = ATC$. Also this will be at the output at which the long-run average cost curve is at its minimum.

- **Perfectly competitive markets** are therefore associated with both **allocative and productive efficiency**.

- **Allocative efficiency** denotes the optimal allocation of scarce resources so as to produce the combination of outputs which best accords with consumers' demands. This will be where price equals marginal cost: $P = MC$.

- **Productive efficiency** occurs when a firm minimises the cost of producing any level of output, using existing technology.

- Productive efficiency is the product of **technical efficiency** (resulting from combining inputs to achieve the maximum physical output) and **price efficiency** (achieved by minimisation of production costs given input prices).

- **Pareto optimality** exists when resources cannot be reallocated so as to make one person better off without making someone else worse off.

- **Perfect competition** is associated with **pareto optimal outcomes** and is a theoretical benchmark against which the economic welfare effects of real-world markets can be judged.

Topics for discussion

1 (a) Give examples of markets that most closely equate to perfectly competitive ones.
   (b) In what ways do they fall short of being 'perfectly' competitive?

2 If all products were sold in perfectly competitive markets, why may the allocation of resources be pareto optimal?

3 Why would managers have no discretion in setting the prices of products or services in perfectly competitive markets?

4 (a) Why is it argued that a firm operating in a perfectly competitive market will produce at the technically optimum level of production in the long run but not in the short run?
   (b) What does this imply about the efficient allocation of resources in perfectly competitive markets?

5 If a market is perfectly competitive, what would be the effect of an increase in the demand for a good or service on the output and price
   (a) in the short run?
   (b) in the long run?

6 'A firm in perfect competition makes no economic profit in the long run.' Discuss.

7 (a) Explain why a firm in a perfectly competitive market may continue to produce even when losses are being made.
   (b) Explain why such a situation cannot be sustained over a long period of time.

7 Analysis of monopoly markets

Aims and learning outcomes

Monopoly is the polar opposite of perfect competition. Economists define a monopolist as the *sole* supplier to a particular market. This should not be confused with the everyday use of the term to describe a supplier with a relatively large share of the market. Nor should it be confused with monopoly as defined in government legislation, where a monopoly may be said to exist as having less than 100% of the market. In European Union competition law, for example, a monopoly is associated with 'abuse of a dominant position in a market' with dominance occurring usually where a firm has 40% of the market or more. Like the perfect competition model, the monopoly model is designed to be an extreme case and a 100% monopoly is rarely found in practice. Commonly, state industries are described as monopolies, but though they often dominate an *industry*, they are rarely monopolies of what is strictly the *market*. In other words, it is possible to find examples of monopolistic industries, but rarely of pure monopolistic *markets*. This is a good illustration of the point that 'competition is in the eyes of the consumer'. For instance, in very many countries, the postal service has traditionally been provided by a state-owned post office. However, the provision of letter-delivery services is only one means of communication. If the market is defined as 'communication' then post offices have to compete with a wide range of other forms of service delivery – notably e-mails, faxes, telephone calls and video-conferencing. Thus, state-owned post offices do not have a monopoly of the market for communication. Similarly, one company may own a country's rail network, but the management will wrestle daily with the competition from coach services, airlines and private cars.

In this chapter we cover the following aspects of monopoly:

- The conditions for monopoly.
- Price and output decisions in monopoly markets.
- Barriers to entry and exit.
- Welfare costs of monopoly.
- Possible dynamic gains from monopoly.
- Assessing monopoly power.
- Economic rent seeking behaviour.

The principles outlined in this chapter represent the basic foundations of anti-trust legislation in modern economies. Anti-trust laws attempt to balance the economic advantages of large-scale production against the welfare costs to consumers if a firm abuses its dominance in the market place.

Learning outcomes

This chapter will help you to:

- Identify the circumstances and conditions under which a monopoly is said to exist.
- Recognise the main features of monopoly markets in terms of price and output decisions.
- Appreciate why a monopolist can be described as being a *price-maker*.
- Understand the importance and various forms of *barriers to entry* in monopoly markets as means of sustaining a position of market dominance.
- Grasp the significance of *monopoly power* and the impact on economic welfare in terms of *allocative* and *productive efficiency*.
- Assess the *degree of monopoly power* using various methods of measuring market dominance.
- Appreciate the importance of potential market entry in limiting monopoly power (referred to as *market contestability*).
- Understand the significance of *rent seeking behaviour*.

The conditions for monopoly

In economic theory, a *pure monopoly* exists when a single firm supplies the entire market for a good or service. As mentioned already, such a situation is extreme and is therefore rarely found in practice. However, some markets do have one firm that *dominates* and has considerable power over price setting in the market as a whole and the ability to deter price and non-price competition. Monopoly is associated with high barriers to entry to the market that protect the monopolist's market dominance.

Price and output decisions in monopoly markets

The monopoly model allows us to make predictions about the kind of price and output decisions we would tend to find in markets where competition is severely restricted. Since the monopoly firm is the sole supplier, *its supply is the market supply*. The demand (i.e. average revenue) curve facing the monopolist will be downward sloping, implying that more can be sold at a lower price. Thus the marginal revenue curve is also downward sloping (for an explanation of the precise relationship between the AR and MR curves, see pp. 47–8). Assuming that the objective of the monopoly firm is to

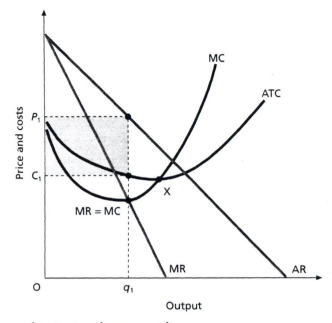

Figure 7.1 Price and output under monopoly

maximise profits when deciding how much to produce, in Figure 7.1 the firm should supply output q_1 as this is the output where profit is maximised, i.e. where MR = MC. This supply would be sold at price P_1, as indicated by the demand curve with a unit cost equal to C_1 (given by the average total cost curve, ATC). With a normal profit included in the costs of production, this price–output configuration produces a supernormal profit per unit shown by the distance between the AR and ATC curves at output q_1, i.e. $P_1 - C_1$. Hence total profit is the shaded area shown.

If this was a contestable market new entrants would enter the industry and price would fall until the supernormal profit had been competed away. True monopolists, however, are able to preserve their market because of *barriers to entry* (otherwise they would cease to be monopolists).

Barriers to entry and exit

Barriers to entry prevent competitors entering the market. Important examples are the following:

- **Patents and copyright** (e.g. the patent for instant cameras held by Polaroid which excluded competition; Microsoft's copyrights on its widely-used computer operating systems).
- **Government regulations, licences and state ownership** (e.g. the monopoly rights over certain letter deliveries held by national post offices).

- **Tariffs and non-tariff barriers** against imports.
- The existence of **natural monopolies**. Natural monopoly exists where more than one supplier leads to an appreciable rise in unit costs, e.g. in electricity transmission. This could be because of *economies of scale* in the production of one product or so-called *economies of scope*, which arise from cost savings associated with producing a range of products together (see Chapter 3, pp. 75–81).
- **Lower costs of production than competitors** because of know-how and experience economies (see the discussion of the experience curve in Chapter 3, pp. 83–4).
- **Control of necessary factors of production and materials**, e.g. a water company may monopolise extraction rights for local water supplies.
- **Control of distribution channels**, e.g. breweries owning retail outlets (bars, cafes, clubs, etc.), that is to say, outlets through which they have sole or privileged rights to sell their beer.

Even where there is no absolute barrier to entry, the monopolist may be able to deter competitors by, for example:

- **Predatory pricing** or the threat of a **price war** and other action against potential competitors.
- **Creating excess capacity**, which signals to potential suppliers that the monopolist might react to competition by increasing output and thus reducing the market price.
- **Creating brand loyalty**, including large-scale advertising expenditure.
- **High research and development expenditure**, as in the pharmaceuticals industry.
- A final barrier to entry is a **barrier to exit**. The main obvious barrier to exit facing a firm occurs where there are appreciable **sunk costs**.

> *Sunk costs* arise when there is a need for high capital investment by a potential new entrant to match the production costs of the monopolist and these are costs which cannot be recouped if the firm subsequently decides to leave the industry.

Plant and machinery may be specific to that industry and therefore cannot be used elsewhere or sold so as to recoup the book value should the firm decide to exit the industry. Sunk costs, although technically a barrier to market exit, make investing to compete with the monopolist much riskier and therefore act as an effective barrier to market entry.

The welfare costs of monopoly

As discussed in the previous chapter, perfect competition can lead to a Pareto optimum outcome in the sense that economic welfare is maximised. In this situation, no reallocation of resources will lead to an improvement in economic efficiency. The resulting output is associated with both allocative and productive efficiency (see Chapter 6, pp. 145–8).

In contrast, given the lack of competition, monopoly is associated with lower economic welfare than under perfect competition because monopolists will tend to price higher and produce a lower output (leading to *allocative inefficiency*). A monopolist may also produce output less efficiently (resulting in *productive inefficiency*), unless there are major economies of scale or scope in production as described below.

The welfare losses associated with monopoly fall into four main areas of concern. These are:

- Higher prices, higher profits and lower outputs.
- Loss of consumer surplus.
- Higher production costs.
- Loss of consumer choice.

We comment on each of these areas of concern in turn.

Higher prices, higher profits and lower outputs than under perfect competition

In a highly competitive market, price is set equal to marginal cost ($P = MC$). The monopolist, however, prices above marginal cost ($P > MC$) leading to a higher price and a smaller output. This is illustrated in Figure 7.2 where, for simplicity, constant cost production is assumed ($MC = ATC$). The profit-maximising competitive firm sets it price according to its marginal cost. The marginal cost is identical for each firm in a perfectly competitive market and the MC curve in the diagram is the summation of each

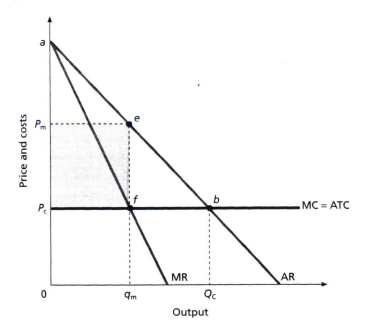

Figure 7.2 The welfare costs of monopoly

155

of the individual firms' marginal cost curves. Each firm charges a price of P_c. The total output supplied by the competitive firms is then Q_c, the MC curve representing the market supply. Each firm in perfect competition faces a horizontal demand (=AR=MR) curve at price P_c. In contrast, the profit maximising monopolist, facing a downward sloping demand curve, produces where MC = MR (<AR) and therefore produces a smaller level of output q_m which it sells at the higher price of P_m. The result is super-normal profits shown by the shaded area.

A loss of consumer surplus

Remember from Chapter 2 that the area under the demand curve can be taken to represent *consumer surplus* (utility obtained by the consumer over and above the price he or she actually pays for the product, see p. 33). With a competitive price and output the consumer surplus in the industry in Figure 7.2 is given by the triangular area aP_cb. Under monopoly, however, it is the smaller area aP_me. Part of the competitive consumer surplus has been transferred to the monopolist as supernormal profit (area P_mefP_c), while the area efb has been lost altogether and is called *deadweight loss*. In other words, monopoly has led to a net loss of welfare to society, represented by consumer surplus equal to the area efb.

Higher production costs

The profit-maximising monopolist may not produce at technically optimum scale. The minimum point on the ATC curve (point X in Figure 7.1 above) involves an output which is different from that at which profits are maximised. Also, the lack of competition may lead to waste or X-inefficiency (for an explanation of X-inefficiency see pp. 87–90), which means higher costs of production at *all* levels of output. Monopolies tend to be sleepy giants. Confirmation of this has recently come from Central and Eastern Europe where, following the collapse of communist rule, state monopolies have been forced to compete for the first time. For example, in the former East Germany the sole and state-owned travel agent, Europäisches Reisebüro, following German unification, had to face competition from over 300 newly-formed and privately-run agencies. An immediate consequence was a loss of one-quarter of its workforce and the sale of one-third of its outlets. In the United Kingdom, BT, formerly a government monopoly supplier of telecommunications, is threatened by new rival suppliers. Since the arrival of competition, BT has announced tens of thousands of redundancies and major restructuring in an effort to streamline the company.

Loss of consumer choice

In competitive markets, customers who are dissatisfied with high prices and poor services have the freedom to switch their loyalty to alternative suppliers. In monopoly markets, however, the consumer is no longer 'king' because there is only the one supplier. It is for this reason that where markets are dominated by a single supplier, prices tend to be higher, production tends to be inefficiently organised, and the quality of service tends

Application 7.1

Patents and monopoly power

Reward for innovation and risk

Many new drugs are expensive because they are patented. This grants patent holders a monopoly and allows them to reap higher profits than they would in competitive markets. The potential for high profits is the incentive for firms to innovate, making it worthwhile for pharmaceutical companies to invest the millions of dollars needed to develop and test new treatments.

Cost to society

However, patents have a cost to society. The marginal cost of producing drugs after they have been developed is usually low. If the market were truly competitive, prices would also be low – at P_c in the figure with quantity Q_c sold. The entire area above the marginal cost line, bounded by the demand curve, would be consumer surplus.

When a patent is awarded, the drug company will maximise its profits by charging a higher price, shown here as P_m, and selling a lower quantity, Q_m. Its aim is to maximise the size of the rectangular area A which represents the extra profit from being a monopolist, i.e. producer surplus.

The result is that consumer surplus is now much smaller, represented by area B. Area C goes neither to consumers nor to the producers – it represents a waste to society and is referred to by economists as a *deadweight welfare loss*.

Governments are facing a growing dilemma – how to encourage innovation and efficiency in the drug industry without the associated social welfare costs.

Activity

What recommendations would you propose to help solve this dilemma?

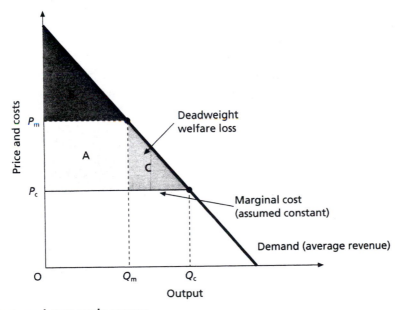

Patents and monopoly power

to be low. Managers in monopoly firms have less incentive to innovate in order to produce better products at lower cost – in this sense, monopoly is associated with an easier life than exists in the cut and thrust world of competitive markets.

Possible dynamic gains from monopoly

The allocative and productive inefficiencies associated with monopolies have led governments to legislate against the abuse of market dominance and against restrictive and concerted practices on the part of a number of firms working together and, therefore, acting like a monopolist. For a discussion of Competition Law see Chapter 16, pp. 332–4. However, it is possible to conceive of certain circumstances in which monopoly might be advantageous from an economic welfare perspective. The clearest example is where there are significant *economies of scale* or *scope*. As we saw in Chapter 3, pp. 75–6, economies of scale occur where there are major cost savings if large outputs are produced. These economies might arise in production, the financing of investment, research and development, marketing, distribution or management. Economies of scope occur when it is more efficient for a range of goods and services to be supplied by one firm. Returning to Figure 7.2, if significant economies of scale or scope existed, then the monopolist's costs could be lower at the profit-maximising output than the competitive firm's costs (imagine the MC = ATC line shifting downwards). In this case, it is possible for both the monopolist to earn higher profits and the consumer to benefit from lower prices. This could result in *more* consumer surplus than if production had occurred in a competitive industry. Competition is obviously superior to monopoly in terms of low prices to the consumer only when the production technology permits many suppliers producing at optimal cost.

Also, the profits earned by the monopolist might be ploughed back into more investment and R&D spending to the ultimate benefit of the consumer. Of course, in practice monopoly benefits can easily be frittered away by inefficient management. Nevertheless, there may be dynamic gains from monopoly which the static approach of traditional economic theory overlooks.

Note, however, that the costs of supply (the MC = ATC line in Figure 7.2) would have to decline considerably before the profit maximising output of a monopolist (q_m) exceeded the competitive industry output (Q_c). In other words, the dynamic gains stemming from economies of scale or scope would have to be very big indeed for monopoly to be superior to competition on welfare grounds. Equally, the potential dynamic efficiency gains arising from capital investment and R&D spending might prove illusory because the monopolist may lack the incentives to invest in the absence of competitive pressures.

The possibility of dynamic gains has led a number of economists in recent years to argue that, provided there are no barriers to entry into the industry, governments should not be over-concerned about the existence of monopolies. Where there are no market barriers, dominance must arise from the *superior efficiency* of the firm in meeting consumer needs. In other words, high profits are a reward for producing the right products at the right price. Another argument is that monopoly profits act as an incentive for other firms to seek out ways of competing, thus monopolies tend to be transient – a temporary first-mover advantage. As an example of this, Rank Xerox, which first developed the photocopier, earned a 41% rate of return in 1975 but by 1987 this had fallen to 13% because of increased competition.

The existing supplier may have a process patent but perhaps another, and superior, process can be found. Perhaps an alternative product can be made. If it is not possible to get bauxite to manufacture aluminium, why not make products out of steel or plastic? Moreover, provided the barriers to entry (and exit) are not significant, monopolists will be prone to 'hit and run' competition. Whenever the monopolist earns excessive profits, new competitors will enter the market. To prevent this, the monopolist will need to price the product to reduce the risks of entry. This requires prices equal to long-run average costs ($P = ATC$) and profits that are normal. Thus the monopolist may price like a competitive firm whenever its market is *contestable*.

A *contestable market* occurs where there are no barriers to the entry of firms into the market.

Also, the threat of state intervention may be a further limitation on the activities of a monopoly. Governments have legislation to control monopolies including the operation of restrictive practices. An anti-competitive restrictive practice occurs where firms that might otherwise compete in a market agree to jointly establish prices and outputs, thus acting like a monopolist. OPEC, whose members agree the outputs of oil each should produce, so as to achieve target world oil prices, is an important example of an international restrictive practice operating through a formal organisation or *cartel*. OPEC is outside the jurisdiction of national competition authorities, however.

Assessing monopoly power

If a monopoly arises from organic growth, this implies that it arose because the firm was efficient in meeting consumer needs. However, monopoly achieved by acquisitions and mergers may have been motivated by a desire to limit competition. The implications for government policy are very different. Where a firm is dominant in the market because it meets consumer needs best, arguably the state should not intervene. Instead, governments might be better advised to look to reducing those monopolies that exist because of state ownership through a programme of deregulation and privatisation (see the discussion in Chapter 16, pp. 329–31).

Government competition authorities have a number of ways in which they can assess the extent of competition in a market. Two approaches used involve an assessment of:

- Profit rates, and
- Concentration ratios.

We briefly discuss each of these in turn.

Profit rates

In a competitive market in the long run profits are competed down to a normal level. Hence, the level of profitability might be an indicator of the degree of monopolisation of the market. In practice, however, a snapshot of current profit rates tells us nothing about how profit rates are *changing* over time in the face of competition. The use of profit rates, especially short-term profit rates, may, therefore, be a misleading indicator of monopoly power. An alternative is to use what is called the *Lerner index*. Since in very competitive markets prices (P) equal marginal costs (MC), the excess of price over marginal cost can be taken to reflect the extent to which competition is imperfect. Hence, the degree of monopoly can be measured as:

$$\textbf{Lerner index} = (P - \text{MC})/P$$

Again, it will be important to look at how this index is changing over time to assess the extent to which monopoly power may be rising or falling within any business sector.

Simple concentration ratios

These ratios represent the extent of the market supplied by a given number of firms. For example, a *four-firm concentration ratio* shows the percentage of the market supplied by the four largest producers. Therefore, if the four-firm concentration ratio is 60%, this means that 60% of this market is supplied by the four largest companies. Where the four-firm concentration ratio is 100%, this means that four (or fewer) firms produce all the output and hence the industry is highly concentrated. In addition to four-firm concentration ratios, five-firm and sometimes eight-firm ratios are used by economists.

Concentration ratios including market shares

Although frequently used to assess the degree of competition in an industry, the concentration ratio does not tell us anything about the different market shares of the largest producers. For example, there may be two industries with four-firm concentration ratios of 60%, but in one industry each of the four has 15% of the market, while in the other industry three of the firms have 5% each and a dominant firm has 45% of the industry market. The amount of competition may be very different in the two markets. We might expect to see more monopolistic behaviour in the latter market, where the dominant firm may be more able to affect the market price, through, say, price leadership. An alternative approach to assessing competition is therefore needed. One measure commonly used by government competition authorities is the so-called *Herfindahl–Hirschman Index* (HHI). This index, when measuring the degree of competition in a market, takes into account both the total number of firms in the market and their *relative size distribution*. It is measured as follows:

$$Herfindahl\text{--}Hirschman\ Index\ (HHI) = \sum_{i=1}^{n} S_i^2$$

where S_i represents the market shares of each of the i firms in the market.

Hence, the index depends on the number of firms in the industry *and* their relative market shares. For example, suppose that there are 10 firms competing in a market and each firm has a 10% market share, the HHI is 1,000 (= $10^2 + 10^2 + 10^2 + 10^2 + 10^2 + 10^2 + 10^2 + 10^2 + 10^2 + 10^2$). The higher the HHI the greater the degree of market monopolisation because the figure is affected by the existence of a small number of firms and/or very unequal market shares. The HHI is a type of concentration ratio.

In a pure monopoly the HHI is 10,000 because the firm has 100% of the market ($100^2 = 10,000$). Competition authorities in the USA and UK tend to view an HHI of more than 1,800 as indicating a highly concentrated market and one of less than 1,000 as a competitive market. Therefore, a proposed merger that increases the HHI to over 1,800 is more likely to be challenged by the competition authorities in these countries.

Limitations of concentration ratios

The concentration ratios reviewed above are subject to a number of limitations and, therefore, need to be used with care. In particular, they are usually calculated based on the national market, but some goods and services are sold in regional markets. While the national market may appear competitive there may be regional monopolies. Also, concentration ratios do not measure barriers to entry. It is possible for a market to be highly concentrated but very *contestable* because of potential market entry. Hence, the incumbent firms behave as if they were in a highly competitive market. Finally, industries and markets are not necessarily the same and defining the appropriate market for competition purposes can be complex. For example, while one can readily refer to the 'paper industry' it is not easy to define a simple set of markets for paper products. Markets which use paper may be sourced by other industries, e.g. the market for disposable cups is served by both the paper and plastics industries and disposable cups are substitutes for pottery cups.

In spite of such limitations, however, concentration ratios do provide a useful input into the assessment of monopoly power, but only alongside other information about the nature and structure of the industry concerned.

Economic rent seeking behaviour

Economic rent is earnings over and above those necessary to maintain an input in its present use (or its *opportunity cost*). In production, firms must earn at least a normal profit otherwise the capital tied up in the firm would be better invested elsewhere (where it can earn at least a normal return). The monopolist, as we have seen, does better than this and earns supernormal profit and, therefore, an economic rent. In other

---

Application 7.2

Barriers to entry: branding detergents

A duopoly market

In Europe, Unilever and Procter & Gamble dominate the detergents' market. Both companies produce a range of detergent products, each separately branded and promoted, and including market leaders, Persil and Ariel.

In the detergents' market product differentiation is largely in terms of brand and marketing. Although the chemical composition of detergents can vary, few consumers are knowledgeable about chemical differences. Sometimes Unilever and Procter & Gamble will market a brand by promoting some 'new whitener' additive or by pointing to a claimed superiority in washing performance. But more importantly, marketing takes the form of promoting a brand image – of a reliable detergent, competitively priced.

Brands and market segmentation

What is the motive of the two companies in each offering a range of detergents? One motive is to capture different types of consumer – for example, a cheaper brand can be aimed at price conscious consumers; a more expensive one at consumers who expect a really white wash and are willing to pay for it! But another set of motives relates to barriers to market entry. By producing a range of detergents there is less space in the market for other companies to enter and compete. Also, research shows that consumers will not, in general, buy a washing powder unless it is heavily advertised. This means that a market entrant would have to incur large advertising costs.

Advertising is a form of non-price competition that restricts market entry in the detergents industry.

Activity

Give examples of other consumer good industries where advertising is used as an important barrier to entry. What is likely to be the impact of the growth in supermarket 'own brands' on this competitive strategy?

words, supernormal profit is an example of economic rent. *Producer surplus*, discussed earlier (p. 116), is another example of economic rent.

The term 'rent seeking behaviour' is used when economic agents attempt to earn economic rents. So when a monopolist erects and maintains barriers to market entry that is rent seeking behaviour. When firms collude rather than compete that too can be described as rent seeking.

Rent seeking behaviour is found in many areas of the economy. For example, workers who aim to earn wages above their opportunity cost by restricting entry to crafts or professions, rent seek. So do special interest groups that exhort favourable terms from governments, e.g. import controls, other regulations or subsidies, that raise profits above competitive levels. Recent government policies around the world based on privatisation, deregulation and promoting competition in the economy are intended to increase economic welfare for society as a whole by restricting the scope for rent seeking behaviour and monopoly abuse.

Concluding remarks

It is sometimes said that the biggest advantage of being a monopolist is 'a quiet life'. In this chapter we have looked at the definition of monopoly in theory and practice. We have considered how a profit maximising monopolist will set its price and output resulting in supernormal profits (economic rents) that cannot be competed away and why a monopolist is a 'price-maker' rather than a 'price-taker'.

Monopoly exists because of 'barriers to entry' into markets, which mean that, although other firms would like to set up and compete, they are unable to do so. Where there are significant barriers to entry (including sunk costs) then the market is not 'contestable' and the monopolist is able to earn supernormal profit over the long run. From society's point of view the result is *allocative inefficiency* (price is set above the marginal cost of supply: $P > MC$) and *productive inefficiency* (production does not occur at minimum average total cost). This lack of allocative and productive efficiency means that monopoly is associated with a significant economic welfare loss to society – hence explaining why governments have competition policies to prevent both an abuse of market dominance and the operation of cartels.

In this and the previous chapter we have considered the polar opposites in market economies, namely monopoly and perfect competition. The next two chapters are concerned with other, intermediary market structures – monopolistic competition and oligopoly.

Key learning points

- A **pure monopoly** exists when a single firm supplies the entire market for a good or service.

- Monopoly is associated with **supernormal profits** and with **high barriers to entry** to the market that protect the monopolist's market dominance.

- The **monopolist's demand curve** will be downward sloping, implying that more can be sold at lower price.

- Monopolists are **price-makers** and profits are maximised where marginal revenue (MR) equals marginal costs (MC).

- **Barriers to entry** prevent competitors entering the market, examples being patents and copyright, government regulations, licences and state ownership, tariffs and non-tariff barriers, natural monopolies, lower costs of production than competitors, control of necessary factors of production and control over distribution channels.

- **Sunk costs** arise when there is a need for high capital investment by a potential new entrant to match the production costs of the monopolist and these are costs which cannot be recouped if the firm subsequently decides to leave the industry.

- The **welfare losses** associated with monopoly, compared with a competitive industry, fall into four main areas of concern, namely:
  - higher prices, higher profits and lower outputs;
  - loss of consumer surplus;
  - higher production costs;
  - loss of consumer choice.

- There are, however, possible **dynamic gains** from monopoly involving:
  - economies of scale and scope;
  - increased product and process innovation through increased investment in R&D.

- A **contestable market** occurs where there are no barriers to the entry of firms into the market.

- The degree of **monopoly power** (dominance) in a market can be assessed using:
  - profit rates;
  - concentration ratios;
  - the Herfindahl–Hirschman Index.

- **Economic rent** is earnings over and above those necessary to maintain an input in its present use (or its **opportunity cost**).

- **Rent seeking behaviour** exists when economic agents attempt to earn economic rents.

Topics for discussion

1 Until the 1990s telecommunications companies such as Deutsche Telekom and France Telecom monopolised the delivery of their fixed-line telecommunications services. If these corporations had achieved maximum profit, what would this have meant in terms of allocative and productive efficiency?

2 In what ways might state ownership of a monopoly affect price and output decisions and why?

3 A firm intends to take over its only rival in the market and become the sole supplier:
   (a) give reasons why the firm may be adopting this strategy;
   (b) consider how the country's competition authority is likely to assess the consequences of the takeover;
   (c) for what reasons might the competition authority (i) prohibit, (ii) allow the takeover to proceed.

4 Mail services in most countries are provided by a single firm (which is often state-owned). Why is it important to define the market carefully before deciding whether these suppliers are monopolists in their own territories?

5 In the USA steel workers supported by their employers successfully lobby their government for import controls and other state aid. Why do some observers support the workers while others label their actions as rent seeking behaviour? What is the relationship (if any) between the behaviour of US steel workers and the behaviour of firms that collude to fix prices to consumers? Should we adopt the same analytical processes to judge both situations?

8 Analysis of monopolistically competitive markets

Aims and learning outcomes

The perfect competition and monopoly models described in the previous chapters have proved useful for predicting behaviour in markets in which there are very large numbers of suppliers or one supplier respectively. Many markets today, however, do not accord with either of these two extremes. Perfect competition assumes homogeneous products, but even where there is a large number of suppliers to a market there are often some differences between the products offered, for example, different brands serving the same market as in the case of soap and detergents. Some 'brand loyalty' on the part of consumers means that suppliers can, and do, charge different prices in the same markets; that is to say, suppliers are not necessarily complete price-takers. Examples can be readily found to varying degrees in most sectors of any economy.

Monopolistic competition refers to markets in which there is a large number of firms competing, supplying products which consumers believe are *close but not complete* (i.e. perfect) *substitutes*. Therefore, it is a market in which firms compete through slight product differentiation, and management have discretion in pricing, trading off price against quantity sold. The demand curve faced by each firm is less price elastic than under perfect competition because of product differentiation and more price elastic than under monopoly because of the existence of competition. It is assumed that there is relatively free entry into and exit from the industry and that entry and exit are stimulated by the level of profit earned.

In this chapter we deal with the following aspects of monopolistic competition:

- The conditions for monopolistic competition.
- Price and output decisions in the short run and long run.
- The implications of monopolistic competition.

The monopolistically competitive market structure is commonly associated with advertising expenditure by firms as a competitive response to promote their products. This expenditure is ultimately financed by the consumer through higher prices. It can, therefore, be argued that these higher prices (higher than in a perfectly competitive market) represent 'the price of consumer choice' and 'product information'.

Learning outcomes

This chapter will help you to:

- Identify the circumstances and conditions under which monopolistic competition is said to exist.

- Recognise the main features of monopolistically competitive markets in terms of price and output decisions.

- Appreciate the role of *product differentiation* in competitive markets and the importance of *branding* as a competitive strategy.

- Understand the economic welfare costs associated with monopolistic competition.

- Differentiate between market equilibrium under conditions of monopolistic competition in both the short run and long run.

Conditions for monopolistic competition

The growth of industrial concentration since the late nineteenth century has led economists to develop various models to assess the economic consequences associated with varying degrees of imperfect competition. Chapter 7, dealing with monopoly, looked at the most extreme example of an imperfectly competitive market – where there is only one supplier to the market. In the next chapter, we shall examine markets in which there are only a few suppliers and where there is a high degree of interdependence between them, namely oligopoly markets. In this chapter, we consider the market model known as *monopolistic competition*. The underlying theory of this market structure was developed in the 1930s to describe a market situation in which the following conditions apply:

- There is a *large number of firms* competing in the market ensuring that each firm has an insignificantly small share of the total market.

- Each firm has the *same, or very similar, costs of production.*

- There is *free entry to*, and *exit from*, the market place.

- The firms produce and sell goods or services which are *similar* (and hence they are substitutes for each other) *but not identical* to their rivals.

- Firms, therefore, compete by trying to ensure *product differentiation* for their goods or services.

The existence of product differentiation in monopolistic competition means that each firm faces a downward sloping demand curve for each of its products or services. When a firm raises its price, not all of its customers will switch to other suppliers (for example, some customers may have 'brand loyalty'). As a result, each firm does not have to sell its output at a ruling market price. This contrasts with the situation in a perfectly competitive market where each (atomistic) firm is described as a price-taker.

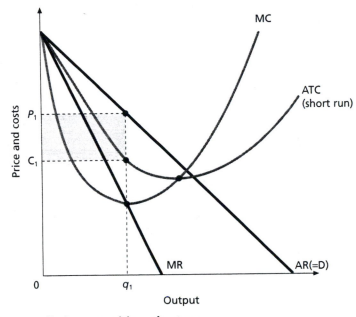

Figure 8.1 Monopolistic competition: short run

Price and output decisions in monopolistic competition

Figure 8.1 illustrates the cost and revenue curves for a typical firm in monopolistic competition in the short run. Assuming that each firm has the same costs of production and a goal of profit maximisation, the output q_1 is produced and sold at price P_1. The profit maximising output is, as usual, where marginal revenue (MR) equates to marginal cost (MC), hence the output q_1. Note that the price, P_1, is greater than the marginal cost at that output.

From the short-run average cost curve (ATC) we can see that the firm is earning a supernormal profit (an economic rent). This profit is AR – short-run ATC per unit (i.e. $P_1 - C_1$), which gives a total supernormal profit shown by the shaded area. Observant readers will have noticed that the short-run monopolistic competition diagram used here and the earlier monopoly diagram (Chapter 7) appear to be identical. In monopolistic competition, however, unlike monopoly, there are no barriers to market entry. The supernormal profit can be expected to attract new suppliers into the market. The effect of this is to reduce the demand for the output of the existing firms in the industry and to increase the price sensitivity of their products. The demand curve for each firm shifts inwards and becomes more price elastic as the market demand is shared out amongst a larger number of suppliers, competing keenly on price.

Assuming no impediments to the competitive process, new entry will continue until all of the supernormal profit represented by the shaded area in Figure 8.1 is competed away. The effect of this process is shown in Figure 8.2. The demand curve (AR curve)

167

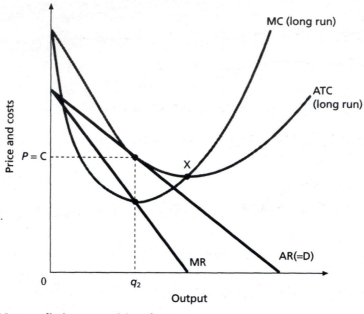

Figure 8.2 Monopolistic competition: long run

Application 8.1

Consult the *Yellow Pages*

Monopolistic competition assumes a large number of firms competing by producing and selling very similar products with identical cost structures. Market entry is unrestricted so that supernormal profits are competed away in the long run. The conditions for monopolistic competition are strict.

Nevertheless, a perusal of a *Yellow Pages* telephone directory throws up examples of markets that have similarities to monopolistic competition. For example, hairdressing firms in a locality can be expected to have similar costs, e.g. wage costs, and offer similar or identical hairdressing services. Hairdressing is also a small-scale operation – that is to say, there are no appreciable economies of scale – therefore a large number of hairdressers may exist even in a small town. Similarly, there may be a number of laundrettes and dry cleaning outlets. Fast food restaurants seem to compete side by side in the High Street offering a huge variety of products, e.g. Chinese, Indian and Italian food, and fish and chips and burgers. In these activities supernormal profits are likely to lead to the opening up of further restaurants until the supernormal profits disappear.

Monopolistic competition is, like the other market models discussed in this book, a theoretical construct. It does, nevertheless, provide important insights into the operation of markets where a large number of firms compete supplying very similar products at similar costs of production and where market entry is low cost.

Activity

Using a Yellow Pages *telephone directory identify other markets where the monopolistic competition model may have relevance.*

has shifted inwards and become more elastic until it is tangential at the profit-maximising output to the long-run average cost curve. At output q_2, the new profit maximising output MC = MR, average revenue equals long-run average cost (AR = ATC) and now only normal profit is earned. Only if a firm could either convince consumers that its product was superior – and hence worth paying more for – or obtain a cost advantage over rivals, would supernormal profits continue to be earned.

Implications of monopolistic competition

The monopolistic competition model suggests that where there is a large number of suppliers with each supplying a similar product the following will occur:

- **Competition will lower prices and profits as in a perfectly competitive market. However, the price will remain higher and the output lower than under perfect competition.** Figure 8.3 shows long-run equilibrium under perfect competition and monopolistic competition. The firm in a perfectly competitive market sets its price equal to marginal cost (P = MC). In an imperfectly competitive market price is set above marginal cost (P > MC). Since price reflects the consumer's marginal utility from the product and the marginal cost reflects the cost to society of providing it, where price exceeds marginal cost this implies a loss of economic welfare under conditions of monopolistic competition. Additional units could be supplied which would be worth more to consumers than it costs society to produce them.

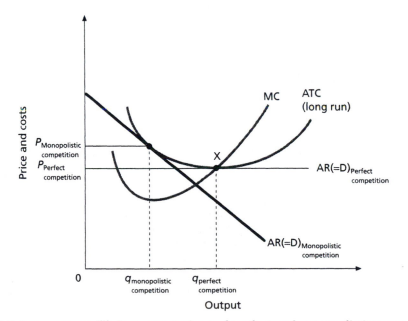

Figure 8.3 Long-run equilibrium: comparison of perfect and monopolistic competition

- **Production occurs at less than optimum scale and, as a result, there is excess capacity in the market.** From Figures 8.2 and 8.3 it is clear that production, even in the long run, occurs at an output below that at which average cost is minimised (point X). Also, because a large number of firms are competing, economies of scale are unlikely. This again implies a loss of economic welfare. Remember, by contrast, that in perfect competition in the long run production does occur at the minimum point of the average total cost curve (as shown in Figure 8.3).

- **In practice, markets that approximate to the monopolistically competitive model tend to be associated with non-price competition including branding and other efforts to differentiate the product.** This leads to expenditure on advertising, sales promotion and packaging which raises production costs. In so far as branding and advertising are *informative* they enable consumers to make better choices and therefore the expenditure enhances economic welfare. However, many large-scale sales promotions are not especially informative and might be considered wasteful of society's scarce resources. For example, advertising may try to persuade consumers that one product is better than another, even though intrinsically it is not.

It should be noted that the existence of excess capacity under conditions of monopolistic competition has led to a debate about the optimal level of consumer choice. Arguably, where consumers obtain utility from being offered a choice of differentiated products the number of such products should be allowed to increase until the marginal benefit (or utility) from an additional product equals the costs associated with producing that product. A similar approach can be adopted to assessing the economic welfare of more advertising. The role of advertising in monopolistically competitive markets is a subject of debate. It should be noted, particularly, that in monopolistically competitive markets products are very similar and this restricts the scope for competitive

---

Application 8.2

Car servicing – the need to be different

In early 2001 Mike Drake was made redundant from his job as a senior motor vehicle engineer with the Ford Motor Company in Detroit. With a major redundancy payout he decided to set up a small car servicing operation in Detroit city. During his initial meeting with his bank manager, it was pointed out by the bank that the car servicing market in the city was already extremely competitive with a very large number of small operators. The bank has expressed its concern as to how Drake will be able to thrive in this market. It has emphasised the need for a coherent and viable business plan to cover the first four years of business. In defence of his intended investment, Drake points to evidence of a recent rise in profitability in car servicing resulting from an increase in vehicle ownership. He is confident that he can succeed.

Activity

Briefly map out a business plan for Drake to support his application, highlighting the ways in which he may be able to provide a differentiated – and viable – service.

advertising (for example, advertising by one hairdresser may boost the sales of other hairdressers even though they bear none of the cost).

Concluding remarks

Monopolistic competition requires a large number of competing firms in the market place, offering goods or services that are only slightly differentiated in the eyes of consumers. The result is that, in the long run, any supernormal profits in the market are competed away. Another outcome is the existence of excess capacity in the market because the firms produce at less than optimal scale (i.e. at an output below that at which long-run average costs are minimised).

The insights provided by the monopolistic competition model for an understanding of competition are limited, however, because of its restrictive assumptions. Many real-world markets today involve a small number of larger firms in competition with each other. Therefore, attention has been paid by economists to developing models that are more appropriate to such markets – referred to as *oligopoly* markets. Indeed, much research in the field of industrial economics today focuses on behaviour in oligopoly markets. This shift in research reflects the limitations of the monopolistically competitive model in explaining behaviour in imperfectly competitive markets, especially the assumption of large numbers of firms and free entry and exit from the market. We therefore turn in the next chapter to examine the nature of competition under conditions of oligopoly.

Key learning points

- A **monopolistically competitive market** is one in which there is a high degree of competition with a large number of firms selling very similar, but not identical, products or services.

- Each firm faces a **downward sloping demand curve** because the products or services are differentiated in some way. This means that average revenue exceeds marginal revenue (i.e. AR > MR).

- The **short-run equilibrium** in a monopolistically competitive market occurs when profits are maximised. This, as always, is the output associated with the condition that marginal revenue equals marginal cost, i.e. MR = MC.

- In the short-run, **supernormal profits can exist** which act as an incentive for new firms to enter the industry supplying close substitute products or services.

- As new firms enter the market, the demand curve facing each firm shifts to the left and becomes more price elastic because of the larger number of suppliers and choice of products or services available in the market.

- In the **long-run equilibrium,** all of the supernormal profits are competed away and only normal profits now exist, determined by the condition that AR = ATC (long-run).

- Each firm in monopolistic competition produces an output, in the long run, which is lower than that at which ATC is minimised, i.e. production occurs at a sub-optimal scale resulting in **excess capacity** in the industry.

- The price paid by consumers in monopolistically competitive markets is higher than under perfect competition ($P > MC$). Thus the higher price may be interpreted as the cost to consumers of having the choice of selecting from a range of differentiated products.

Topics for discussion

1 (a) Give examples of markets that most closely equate to monopolistically competitive ones.
 (b) Describe the ways in which these markets differ from markets that are *strictly* monopolistically competitive.

2 To what extent do managers have discretion when setting prices in monopolistically competitive markets?

3 (a) Consider the role of marketing and advertising in monopolistically competitive markets.
 (b) Why will firms tend to allocate resources to the development of a brand strategy?

4 What are the economic welfare costs associated with monopolistic competition?

5 Discuss the role of product differentiation in a monopolistically competitive industry. In what sense might advertising expenditure by a particular firm in the industry be wasteful?

6 Compare and contrast the short-run and long-run equilibrium facing a firm under conditions of monopolistic competition.

Oligopoly

Aims and learning outcomes

In the previous chapter, we noted that monopolistic competition requires a large number of competitors and free market entry and exit. Many real-world markets today, however, are made up of a small number of suppliers and entry into and exit from the market are restricted. *Oligopoly* is the term used to describe such markets. Where there are only two suppliers the term *duopoly* is used. Oligopolists may supply a relatively homogeneous product, such as oil, or they may compete through differentiated products, for example as in the motor car industry. The greater the product differentiation, the greater the scope to be a *price-maker* rather than a *price-taker*.

In this chapter, we cover the following issues:

- Conditions of oligopoly.
- Theories of oligopoly behaviour, including the kinked demand curve and game theory.
- Price leadership under oligopoly.
- Collusion in oligopoly markets.

In oligopolistic markets there is a relatively small number of suppliers in the market and firms are likely to be interdependent. Therefore, competitive strategy will be based on some belief about the *reaction of rivals*, both in terms of price and non-price competition. How will competitors react to a price reduction, or a new advertising campaign, or extra investment, or development of a new product? If a firm introduces a new method of putting detergent into a washing machine, by placing a liquid inside a plastic ball, how long will it take for the firm's competitors to respond? Could the firm limit the response by patenting the process? The substance of oligopolistic competition is that each firm's price and output decision is influenced by perceptions of rivals' possible counter-moves.

Learning outcomes

This chapter will help you to:

- Identify the market conditions which lead to oligopolistic behaviour and outcomes.
- Appreciate the nature of business behaviour in oligopolistic markets where there is a small number of producers of homogeneous or, more commonly, differentiated products or services.

- Understand how the price and output decisions of one firm in an oligopolistic market may impact on the price and output decisions of rival firms.

- Recognise that interdependence and expected reactions amongst firms are central to understanding behaviour in oligopolistic markets.

- Realise the different ways in which oligopolists compete using various product differentiation strategies.

- Gain insights into two central models which attempt to identify the behaviour of firms operating in oligopolistic markets, namely the *kinked demand curve* and *game theory*.

- Appreciate why oligopolistic markets are prone to anti-competitive behaviour on the part of firms, including *price-leadership* and *collusion* of various forms.

Conditions of oligopoly

Oligopoly, like monopolistic competition situations, is a form of imperfect competition and is without doubt the most common form of market structure in developed economies. An oligopoly market is associated with the following conditions:

- **Few suppliers and many buyers.**

- **Homogeneous or, more commonly, differentiated products.**

- **Barriers to entry into the market** – allowing firms to exercise some degree of market power.

- **Mutual interdependence between firms in the industry** – such that actions on the part of one or more firms can be expected to provoke competitive reactions on the part of other firms.

- Each firm has sufficient **market power** to prevent it from being a price-taker, but at the same time there is sufficient **interfirm rivalry** to rule out the firm treating the market demand curve as identical to its own.

It is important to appreciate that with respect to the other forms of market structures analysed in the previous chapters (dealing with perfect competition, monopoly and monopolistic competition), the price and output decisions of firms are based on their own costs of production and the demand curves which they individually face. The firms do not consider any possible reactions from other suppliers to the market. In the case of an oligopolist, however, behaviour in the market will tend to be affected by the firm's own costs and demand curves as well as the possible competitive reactions by other firms in the industry. This opens up the possibility of *strategic* competitive behaviour by managers. Thus, managers take account of the impact of their behaviour on decisions in competing firms. This scenario of *action* and *reaction* lies at the heart of understanding oligopoly behaviour, highlighting the importance of understanding the meaning and implication of *strategic interdependency*.

Application 9.1

Oligopoly and supermarket price wars

Competition or consumer exploitation?

Supermarkets in the UK have embarked on a price war in recent years. This has been the result of the arrival of Wal-Mart, the largest supermarket chain in the USA, which made a successful takeover bid for Britain's Asda group. Some commentators are predicting the prospect of a 'new dawn in competition between Britain's supermarkets' and the probability of further reductions in margins. Consumers, they argue, will be the winners.

However, other observers take a different view, warning of impending 'competition casualties' with some firms being forced out of business or required to merge to ensure survival. This throws up the possibility of market concentration – with implications for government competition policy.

The figure, based on data from the late 1990s, shows the market shares of the UK's supermarket chains.

Consolidation has been at the forefront of developments in the sector over the past few years. For example, in addition to the Asda/Wal-Mart tie-up, Somerfield and Kwik-Save have merged. Somerfield also announced its desire to sell off its 'larger stores' with the intention of focusing its efforts more fully on its smaller 'convenience outlets'.

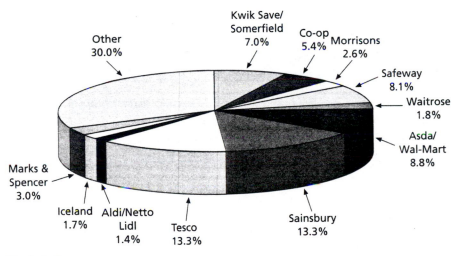

Market shares

Activity

What are the implications of consolidation in the supermarket industry for:

(a) consumers?

(b) the firms in the industry?

(c) government policy?

Justify your views.

As part of strategic decision-making in an oligopolistic environment, managers will endeavour to differentiate their goods and services from those of competitors. The more that consumers consider a good or service to be different to that offered by other suppliers, the greater the ability of the firm to exercise control over price and therefore sales, without having to consider the reactions of its competitors. *Product differentiation* may take various forms.

- **Physical differences** arising from special characteristics, design differences, packaging, product and service equality, etc.
- **Differences in consumer perception,** usually associated with brand loyalty due to advertising and effective marketing.

Theories of oligopoly behaviour

The main feature of oligopolistic markets is that each firm's price and output decisions are influenced by its management's view of the likelihood and nature of actions and reactions by competitive firms. Given the large number of possible actions and reactions, several theories of oligopoly have been developed based on different assumptions about:

(a) competitors' behaviour;

(b) the extent and form of entry and exit barriers; and

(c) the likelihood of collusion between suppliers.

All of the theories have in common, however, the uncertainty which exists in oligopolistic markets regarding outcomes. The nature and importance of rivals' reactions are captured in two central models of oligopoly behaviour, namely:

- The kinked demand curve.
- Game theory.

These are explained in turn below.

The kinked demand curve

The oligopolist faces a downward sloping demand curve, but its nature is dependent on competitors' reactions to a price change, especially where products are similar. Suppose that the current price charged by the oligopolist is P_1 and the firm is contemplating a price change to steal a competitive advantage and make more profit. Two demand curves are shown in Figure 9.1 depending on the response of the firm's competitors to the firm's price change (up or down). Demand curve DD reflects the volumes that would be sold at different prices if competitors continued to sell at their original price. Demand curve dd shows the volumes that would be sold if competitors matched the price change. The demand curve DD is, of course, the more price elastic.

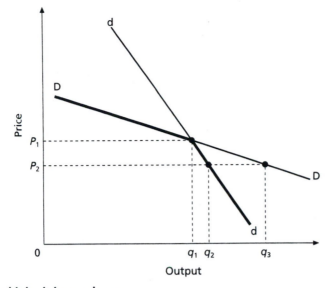

Figure 9.1 The kinked demand curve

If the firm decided to reduce its price to P_2 to steal a competitive advantage, it would hope to travel down the curve DD (selling quantity q_3) and, with demand price elastic, increase its total earnings. However, if competitors responded by *reducing their own prices*, demand would only rise to q_2, as shown by the demand curve dd. Lower prices might increase the market size, but there would only be limited switching of existing consumers away from competing suppliers to the firm in question. For this reason we might expect total earnings to rise by less than the firm expected or even to fall depending on the price elasticity of demand.

Alternatively, our firm might raise its price hoping that other firms will raise their prices too, leaving comparative prices unaffected. By charging more for each unit and expecting total sales to reduce only marginally because all firms raise their prices, total earnings will be expected to rise. This is illustrated by a movement upwards along the demand curve dd. However, if competitors *do not increase their prices* there will be a movement up the DD curve, as consumers switch to rival suppliers. If demand plummets this will lead to a large fall in the firm's total revenue.

A similar logic can be applied to changes in non-price competition: for example, reactions to a new advertising campaign or the introduction of a new product. The possibilities can be summarised as follows:

- **Optimistic scenario.** This involves a movement up the demand curve dd following a price rise (rivals also raise their price therefore there is no competitive loss) and down the demand curve DD when price is reduced (rivals do not reduce their prices and therefore a competitive advantage is achieved).

- **Pessimistic scenario.** This is based upon a movement up the demand curve DD following a price rise (rivals fail to raise their prices leading the firm to suffer a competitive disadvantage) and down the demand curve dd when price is reduced (competitors also cut their prices). This produces, in effect, a 'kink' in the demand curve at the existing price (hence the name the 'kinked demand curve' model).

The firm could attempt to place some probability weighting on the two scenarios. For example, based on past experience the firm might reckon that there is a 0.7 probability that its price reduction will spark off a similar reduction by competitors, i.e. it is 70% likely. Placing probabilities on rivals' reactions can also be applied to other competitive moves: for example, how competitors might respond to a new advertising campaign, a new investment decision, new product developments and so on. Of course, these probability weightings may in the event prove to be wrong (the past may be an unreliable guide to future reactions) and often they will be highly subjective – for a discussion of some pitfalls in business forecasting, see Chapter 17.

Introducing the firm's marginal revenue (MR) and marginal cost (MC) curves when the demand curve is 'kinked' (Dd) allows us to identify the profit-maximising output (where MR = MC). This is illustrated in Figure 9.2. It will be seen that the profit-maximising output is q_1 associated with price P_1. The MR curve in this case is discontinuous at the output q_1 because of the kink in the demand curve.

The implication of this analysis is that if the firm's own marginal cost fluctuates within the vertical gap indicated by xy, the firm will change neither its price (P_1) nor its quantity of output (q_1). The firm will only alter this price–output combination if its marginal cost fluctuates outside the xy range. This analysis may help to explain why individual firms in oligopolistic situations may not change their prices when their costs of production alter slightly (as they would in perfectly competitive, monopoly and monopolistically competitive markets). At the same time, however, large changes in a

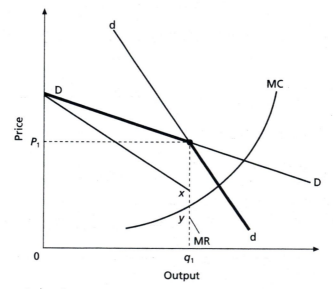

Figure 9.2 Oligopoly profit maximisation and cost changes

firm's cost structure, leading to a movement of the MC curve outside the *xy* range, can be expected to produce a price change by the firm and hence a competitive reaction by rivals.

The kinked demand curve model is said, therefore, to be associated with *sticky* prices unless production costs vary significantly (i.e. outside the *xy* range). The model also helps to explain why oligopolistic markets can be associated with periods of relative price stability, punctuated by price wars. Instability of prices is especially likely when a change in technology causes a fundamental alteration in the cost structure of a firm. A technologically-induced competitive advantage may, however, not be sustainable – with price stability returning when the competitors catch up.

Another implication of the model is that firms may prefer non-price competitive behaviour, as opposed to competition based purely on price. The above analysis suggests that, at best, price competition provides only a temporary competitive advantage until rivals respond by altering their own prices. Non-price competition, in the form of quality improvements, design features and other innovations, etc., may be much more difficult for competitors to replicate.

An obvious weakness of the kinked demand curve model is its inability to explain how the initial price (P_1 in Figures 9.1 and 9.2) is established in the first place. One possibility is that the price is originally set by some form of collusion between firms in the industry. If this price is considered to be the result of collusion between firms, then we can further develop our understanding of the impact of cost changes on prices in oligopolistic markets. As we have seen, provided that a single firm's marginal cost (MC) curve does not fall outside the *xy* range in Figure 9.2, the firm has no incentive to alter the price it charges. However, if for some reason the costs of production were to change for *all* firms, this could lead to a change in the collusive price. For example, if the marginal cost across an industry as a whole shifted upwards significantly, the collusive profit-maximising price would rise. Therefore, while a single firm's price may be 'sticky' with respect to a change in its own cost structure, cost increases affecting the whole industry (e.g. through higher taxes on inputs), tend to lead to the establishment of a new higher industry-wide price level.

Game theory

We noted that in certain circumstances it may be possible to attach some probability weightings to the likely reactions of competitors to any competitive move by one of the firms in an oligopolistic industry. The assignment of probabilities highlights the fact that competitive markets involve a degree of uncertainty as to actions and reactions – a feature of the real world!

Uncertainty about rivals' actions and reactions to competitive moves has led to the application by economists of the mathematical technique known as *game theory* to oligopolistic markets. Game theory attempts to identify the most profitable counter-moves that could be made towards one's own 'best' strategy. On the basis of the answer, defensive measures are evolved.

Game theory is concerned with *strategic behaviour*. It takes into account expected behaviour given mutual interdependence in markets. The theory is associated with the research of John von Neumann and Oskar Morgenstern in the early 1940s.

A *game* occurs when there are two or more interacting decision-takers (*players*) and each decision or combination of decisions involves a particular outcome (*pay-off*).

Applied to competition, a *game* involves one firm choosing its optimal strategy on the reasonable expectation that its competitors will choose their optimal strategies. The equilibrium of the game is when one player of the game (A) maximises its pay-off given the expected action of another player (B) or players (B, C, etc.). That is to say, A adopts its best strategy given the expected action by B, and player B adopts its best strategy given the expected action of A. This optimal strategy may be based on profit maximisation or any other management objectives, as discussed in Chapter 10.

A simple game is often illustrated using the The Prisoner's Dilemma.

The Prisoner's Dilemma

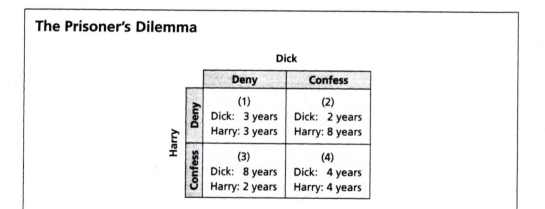

The Prisoner's Dilemma is an example of a simple game. Dick and Harry are both suspected by the police of an armed robbery. The police place each prisoner in a separate interview room.

Dick and Harry are each told that if they both confess to the crime they will receive prison sentences of 4 years each. If, however, one of them confesses and the other does not, he will receive a much shorter sentence of 2 years as a reward for co-operating with the police; while the accomplice will be given an 8-year sentence. If both deny the crime then the probable sentence is 3 years (there is a strong probability that they will be found guilty).

The issue is what is the likely outcome, or putting this another way, what are the optimal strategies for the prisoners?

Both Dick and Harry can independently work out the 'pay-offs' from confessing or not confessing based on the likely actions of the other. The above 'pay-off matrix' summarises the four possible outcomes based on confession to or denial of the crime.

The best strategy for both, and the one that *would* occur if they colluded and agreed their strategies, is joint denial and a sentence of 3 years. But each prisoner will be aware that if they deny the crime and the other confesses, he will finish up with an 8-year sentence. By contrast, each can also calculate that if he confesses and the other also confesses the sentence is 4 years; while if he confesses and the other denies then the sentence is 2 years. The best strategy for Dick is to confess since the worst outcome, if Harry denies, is a sentence of 2 years and if Harry also confesses, the outcome is 4 years in jail. By contrast, if Dick denies then the pay-off is a sentence of 3 years, provided Harry also denies, with the prospect of 8 years in jail if Harry confesses. In the same way, Harry will come to the conclusion that his *dominant strategy* (the strategy that dominates over all others) is to confess. Therefore, the 'dominant strategy equilibrium', in the absence of collusion in decision-making, is confession. If collusion were possible (the prisoners were allowed to meet privately to discuss their strategy before coming to a decision) and both Dick and Harry can then rely on each other not to cheat (the commitment is credible), the outcome will be that both will deny the crime.

The strategy of choosing the safer strategy or the one with the least bad outcome, as in the above case, is known in game theory as a **maximin** strategy. Here a player chooses an outcome that is better than the worst possible outcome. An alternative is to adopt a more optimistic approach by selecting a **maximax** strategy, which involves choosing the best possible outcome – as in the case where the prisoners collude or where a firm cuts its price in the expectation that other firms do not cut their price. A **minimax regret criterion** involves a decision rule where a player minimises the maximum opportunity loss associated with making what turns out to be a wrong decision. For example, this rule could be relevant when a firm is considering what price change to make in response to higher production costs. After the firm calculates the maximum possible losses that could result if the other firms matched each of its possible price changes, the minimax approach indicates that it should choose that price change which leads to the minimum of the range of possible losses.

The Prisoner's Dilemma involves a non-co-operation equilibrium where both players are worse off than if they were to co-operate.

The same principles which underlie the Prisoner's Dilemma can be applied to oligopolistic markets. The general idea can be demonstrated through a simple example applied to a duopoly (two-firm) industry.

For example, suppose there are two firms, A and B, deciding new expenditures on promotion of their products. Figure 9.3 shows the *pay-off matrix*, i.e. the expected profit levels given high or low promotional expenditures. If both retain low expenditures on promotion, the expected profit for each is $20 million and advertising and other marketing costs are avoided. If firm B opts for high spending but A retains low spending on promotion, B steals a competitive advantage and its profit rises to $34 million, due to much higher sales revenues that more than offset the promotion costs; while A's profit falls to $8 million. This is B's favoured outcome. Equally, if firm A spends more on promotion but B does not, then it anticipates that its profit will rise to $34 million and B's will slump to $8 million. This is A's favoured outcome. However

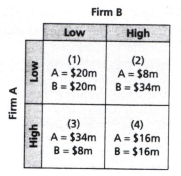

- Outcome (1) = Low promotional spending by both firms
- Outcome (2) = High promotional spending by firm B only
- Outcome (3) = High promotional spending by firm A only

⎫
⎬ Unstable since
⎪ the other firm can
⎬ increase profits
⎭ by spending more

- Outcome (4) = High promotional spending by both firms

Figure 9.3 Pay-off matrix for firms A and B with low and high promotional spending

both A and B will expect that the other firm will not allow a competitive gain in this way and hence will expect the other firm to match its promotional expenditure. Therefore, the expected outcome is high promotional spending by *both firms* leading to profits of $16 million each after the promotion costs.

The problem with this outcome is that it produces lower profits than if both firms had not increased their spending on promotion. It results from a lack of co-operation or collusion between the two firms and hence is known as a *non-co-operation equilibrium*.

An equilibrium outcome where each player analyses its best strategy given the anticipated actions of the other player is called a *Nash equilibrium*, after the Nobel prize winner, John Nash, who developed the idea in the early 1950s. In a Nash equilibrium each player maintains its current strategy given the present strategies of the other players. There is no incentive for the players to change their behaviour and hence the Nash equilibrium is self-policing. A particular type of Nash equilibrium is a *dominant strategy equilibrium*. A dominant strategy equilibrium is a Nash equilibrium (though not all Nash equilibria are dominant strategies). A dominant strategy occurs where the strategy adopted by a player is the same irrespective of the action of the other player. A dominant strategy equilibrium exists where each player in the game has a dominant strategy.

This applies in our example above. Both A and B have a dominant strategy, which is to adopt high promotional spending. Whatever the decision by the other player, A and B are better off by adopting a high promotional spending strategy compared with the alternative of low promotional spending. High promotional spending produces pay-offs of either $34m or $16m, depending on the other player's response. Whereas, low promotional spending has pay-offs of £20m or £8m. High promotional spending dominates as the desirable strategy.

In real-world markets the position will be more complex than our example. There are usually more than two suppliers and firms have to judge their competitors' actions and reactions not just to promotional spending but to all competitive activities. Nevertheless, the example does illustrate how oligopolistic outcomes can be *non-Pareto optimal* (resources can be reallocated and economic welfare improved) and why for the firms involved collusion is beneficial (in this case it would pay both firms to collude and to enter into a joint agreement not to increase promotional spending).

As in the case of the 'kinked demand curve' model, the existence of uncertainty about competitors' reactions can lead to a reluctance to change price or to be the first mover in non-price competition. Returning to our example in Figure 9.1, if the firm is uncertain which demand curve, DD or dd, will apply for any given price change, there will be an incentive not to alter price at all. Uncertainty about the likely response of competitors may produce a desire not to 'rock the boat' in the firm's markets.

We find in practice that the reaction of rivals to a price change (or to change in any competitive variable) depends upon a host of factors. For example, firms may be more likely to match rivals' price cuts to preserve their market share when they already have excess capacity. Also, high fixed costs and associated economies of scale in an industry will increase the likelihood that firms respond to a reduction in total market demand by reducing their prices or taking some other competitive action to limit the potential loss of sales. In such industries a loss of market causes a significant rise in unit costs, further worsening competitiveness. By contrast, in industries with increasing costs firms may be happy to reduce their supply to the market, perhaps as part of a longer-term strategy of withdrawal from the industry when production is unprofitable. Other factors which may impact on reactions to new competition are how profitable the market is to rivals, how fast it is growing (will one supplier's growth be at the expense of rivals?), 'switching costs' faced by consumers who wish to change suppliers, and the stage in the trade cycle. Research suggests that in the post-war period prices have tended not to be sticky in many oligopolistic markets, as predicted by the 'kinked demand curve' model; but inflation may, in part, explain this. Inflation affects the costs of all firms. It also may make consumers less resistant to rising prices.

We might also expect that when the industry is relatively new, there will be more uncertainty about rivals' reactions to both price and non-price competition and hence the age of the industry (and the stage in the product life cycle) may have a bearing on the nature of the competition in oligopolistic markets. Similarly, sudden shocks may provoke severe reactions in oligopolistic markets, precisely because they destroy existing settled positions. For example, deregulation of airline services in the 1980s in the United States led to frantic competition for passengers. Service levels were altered and prices slashed in a desperate attempt to remain competitive. Within ten years of deregulation many new airlines (e.g. People Express) had failed and the major operators were merging in an attempt to cut losses and restore order in the market. A similar competitive process is now underway in the newly liberalised telecommunications and power markets of North America and Europe. Likewise, where new firms enter the market, especially with a new and superior product, or where a strong company outside the industry buys a company in the industry to launch new competition, this also delivers a major shock to existing producers and often leads to important reactions in terms of price and non-price competition (for example, consider the impact of Japanese competition on the US automobile industry).

Therefore, nor surprisingly, oligopolistic producers tend to take actions which prevent market entry by new competitors or at least deter it. The possibilities are many. Under *entry-limit pricing* the incumbent firm sets its price at a level at which it would be unprofitable for another firm to enter the market. They might even price below average total cost, forgoing short-run profits with the objective of repelling potential rivals (firms will continue to produce in the short run provided they can cover their variable costs, see Chapter 3, pp. 73–4 above). They may also invest in additional capacity, implying increased market supply and hence lower prices and profits for new producers trying to break into the market. Or non-price factors may be used to good advantage; for instance, brand proliferation by existing suppliers limits *space* in the market for new competitors' products (e.g. the multiple brands of Unilever and Procter and Gamble in the UK detergents market). Alternatively, incumbent firms might undertake a major advertising campaign to preserve their market share. In the banking sector it is suggested that the large incumbent banks discourage their personal account holders from switching to new competitor banks (e.g. on the internet) by making the process of account switching seem slow and costly, in terms of both time and effort.

Price leadership under oligopoly

In the 'kinked demand curve' analysis there was no *price leader*. In some oligopolistic markets uncertainty in the market is reduced because one supplier may decide to take the initiative and act as the price leader. When it alters its price the competition follows suit. There are various possible types of price leadership in oligopolistic markets.

- **Dominant firm price leadership.** *A dominant firm oligopoly* exists when one of the firms has a competitive advantage over the other firms in the industry – notably a cost advantage – and produces a large part of the industry's output. The dominant firm may price like a monopolist when setting its price and output, leaving the other firms to supply the remaining market demand at the same price. These other firms price at this price otherwise there would be a disequilibrium in the market. Equally, smaller firms may fear retaliatory action by the powerful dominant firm if they were to adopt a different price.

- **Barometric price leadership.** In some markets, one 'barometer' firm (it does not have to be the dominant firm) assesses changes in demand and cost conditions and alters its price. The other firms then follow, providing this is in their interests. The barometer firm may change over time.

- **Collusive price leadership.** This exists where firms in an oligopolistic market collude on price. The collusion may be explicit or tacit.

Collusion in oligopoly markets

- *Explicit collusion* includes the creation of a restrictive practice or *cartel* between producers, where prices may be jointly set and markets shared out.
- *Tacit collusion* occurs where firms do not formally collude but nevertheless undertake actions that are likely to minimise a competitive response, e.g. avoiding price cutting or not attacking each other's market.
- *Price leadership* is a form of tacit collusion.

Collusion is easiest to achieve where prices and costs are transparent and the net benefit to each cartel member of remaining in the cartel exceeds the net benefit of cheating; in other words, the costs of being a cartel member are more than offset by the revenue advantages. Cheating behaviour includes secretly selling at a lower price than agreed so as to gain market share at the expense of the other cartel members. At the international level, a number of cartels exist to limit price competition in commodity markets. For example, the major world coffee producers have for many years operated an agreement on pricing to protect coffee-producing countries from the full effects of competition on earnings. The most well-known international cartel, however, is OPEC, the Organisation of Petroleum Exporting Countries, though cartels have existed in a wide range of other industries, including civil engineering and pharmaceuticals. For example, in the early to mid-1990s the leading European vitamin producers (e.g. Hoffmann La Roche and BASF) operated a secret price-fixing cartel in the supply of certain vitamins on world markets. Most developed economies have legislation which makes such 'restrictive trade practices' illegal and subject to fines or even imprisonment. When the vitamins cartel was discovered, the companies involved faced large financial penalties imposed by competition authorities in a number of countries and some executives were imprisoned in the United States. The cartel was exposed when one of the cartel members revealed to the US competition authorities the existence of the cartel in return for more favourable treatment at the hands of the authorities. Other reasons cartels break down include high prices, that encourage alternative suppliers outside the cartel to increase production (e.g. the vitamins cartel was being undermined by the mid-1990s by increasing Chinese vitamin exports) and production-quota busting by cartel members, also keen to cash in on high prices.

In real-world markets 'cheating' might be a dominant strategy in other circumstances. In particular, 'one-off' transactions, such as the purchase of a second-hand car may lead the seller to disguise the true state of the vehicle from a buyer. However, where there are repeated transactions, firms may value their 'reputation' for fair dealing. Firms attempt to build up 'trust' with consumers and input suppliers. In 'repeated non-finite games', i.e. where the game is repeatedly played for an indefinite period, each player can reward or punish the other player for its previous actions. One form of response is 'tit-for-tat'. A tit-for-tat strategy involves a player co-operating in one period if the other player co-operated in the previous period or cheating in the current period if the other player cheated in the previous period. This may lead both players to co-operate because of the

Firm B

		Cheat	Co-operate
Firm A	**Cheat**	(1) A = 0 B = 0	(2) A = 6.0 B = −2.0
	Co-operate	(3) A = −2.0 B = 6.0	(4) A = 3.0 B = 3.0

Figure 9.4 Duopoly: cheating as the dominant strategy

fear that cheating will be punished in the next round. Another strategy, more extreme, is a 'trigger strategy', where if at any stage co-operation breaks down and cheating occurs, the other player adopts its Nash equilibrium strategy permanently; that is to say, it adopts its own best strategy given the action of the other player. In some circumstances there may be no dominant strategy and then the result is games involving more complex strategies.

The following is an example of a duopoly game involving the scope for both collusion and cheating. Figure 9.4 sets out the pay-offs of the two firms assuming that they either co-operate in the cartel, agreeing common prices, or cheat by reneging on the agreed common price. Acting in common they can set price as a monopolist and each earn supernormal profits of 3.0 (quadrant 4 of the pay-off matrix). If, however, either firm were to cheat and set a lower price, whilst the other firm continued to set the monopoly price, it would gain market share and profit at the expense of the other firm. For example, if A cheats while B co-operates, A's supernormal profit is 6.0 and B's 'profit' collapses to a loss of −2.0 (quadrant 2); if B cheats while A co-operates the outcome is reversed (quadrant 3); if both cheat, prices fall and supernormal profit is competed away (quadrant 1). Now consider the Nash equilibrium. A will reason as follows, 'Suppose B cheats and I do not, I make a loss of −2.0; whereas, if I also cheat my supernormal profit is 0. If we both co-operate I earn supernormal profit of 3.0. However, suppose B co-operates and I cheat, my supernormal profit is 6.0.' It should quickly become apparent to A that its dominant strategy is to cheat, regardless of whether B cheats or co-operates. By the same logic, cheating is the dominant strategy for firm B. The outcome is that both firms will cheat and the cartel collapses. This outcome is, of course, sensitive to the pay-offs for cheating and co-operating. A different set of pay-offs could make co-operation the dominant strategy, as in Figure 9.5 below.

In the game summarised in Figure 9.5 a strategy of cheating provides a pay-off to each firm of −1.0 or 3.0, depending upon whether the other firm cheats or co-operates. By contrast, a strategy of co-operation provides pay-offs of 0 or 4.0. Both firms will therefore, independently, select the strategy of co-operation. If, for example, firm A chose a cheating strategy its possible loss is −1.0 and possible gain 3.0, depending upon B's strategy, whereas choosing co-operation produces pay-offs of 0 or 4.0, which are superior. The same applies to firm B.

Figure 9.5 Duopoly: co-operation as the dominant strategy

Oligopoly and market dominance

Market structure – the 'Big Three' iron ore companies

In 2001, Brazil's Companhia Vale do Rio Doce (CVRD), the world's largest iron ore mining company, announced two purchases of local competitors worth a total of US$980m. The company had already agreed to pay Thyssen–Krupp, the German steel group, $697m for Ferteco, and had bought a 50% stake in Caemi from Japan's Mitsui for $280m.

The export market for iron ore was already dominated by just three corporations – CVRD, and Rio Tinto and BHP-Billiton, the UK and Australian-listed groups. By some calculations, their combined share of global trade was set to rise to between 75% and

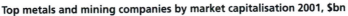

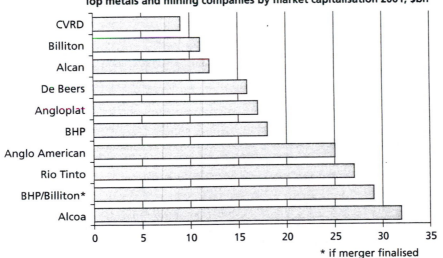

Top metals and mining companies by market capitalisation 2001, $bn

* if merger finalised

Oligopoly and market dominance

80%, with Rio Tinto and BHP-Billiton dominating markets in Asia and CVRD leading in Europe.

Concerns about competition

The European Commission (EC) expressed concerns about these developments. When the Commission conducted an initial review of BHP's planned purchase of Caemi, earlier in 2001, it decided to launch an investigation 'over fears that the deal would have reduced competition in the European Union market for iron ore'. However, that investigation did not go ahead because BHP withdrew when Mitsui, which already owned 40% of Caemi, decided to exercise its pre-emptive right to acquire the remainder of the shares.

Most industry experts expected the CVRD deal to go ahead eventually, even if the company had to offer some concessions. CVRD was expected to argue that calculations suggesting that its share of the European market would be more than 50% assumed that it exercised full control over some of its joint ventures; that the iron ore market should be looked at on a global, rather than a regional basis; and that due attention should be paid to the weighty 'buyer power' of the steel industry.

It could also point out that when the EC decided in 2000 not to oppose Rio Tinto's acquisition of North, an Australian iron ore miner, Brussels noted that 'the geographic market for iron ore is worldwide'.

However, at the time of the abortive BHP/Caemi deal earlier in 2001, the European Commission appeared concerned by the prospects of a reduction in the number of big groups in the sector.

Activity

(a) *Should the European Commission be concerned about these developments? Why?*

(b) *Why do you think the European Commission appeared interested in the reduction in the number of big groups in the sector?*

Concluding remarks

This chapter has dealt with one of the most common forms of market competition in modern economies. Oligopoly involves competition amongst a small number of firms, sometimes producing homogeneous but, more commonly, differentiated products. The behaviour of oligopolists is not confined to any one particular model of price and output decisions. There are a number of models which seek to explain the behaviour of firms in oligopoly markets. In this chapter we have considered two of them in detail: namely the *kinked demand curve* and *game theory*. Common to all of the oligopoly models is the notion of *interdependence* amongst the firms in the market. The price and output *actions* of one firm are likely to provoke *reactions* on the part of competitors.

Oligopoly markets are often associated with dominant pricing by one firm – giving rise to *price leadership* behaviour. At the same time, such markets are also prone to the formation of cartels leading to *collusive pricing* – behaviour that is likely to attract the attention of competition authorities. Oligopoly firms have an incentive to collude so as to reduce the uncertainty which exists in markets where the actions of one firm may spark off price cutting or other competitive responses, leading to sharp reductions in profits for all concerned.

In the next chapter we look in detail at the objectives which managers may pursue when deciding on their competitive strategy in various types of market structure including oligopoly.

Key learning points

- **Oligopoly** is the term used to describe markets where a small number of firms compete, supplying relatively homogeneous or differentiated products.

- **Duopoly** refers to an oligopolistic market where there are only two firms competing.

- There is a high degree of **mutual interdependence** between firms in oligopoly markets and the *actions* of one firm are likely to lead to competitive *reactions* by the other firms.

- Each firm has sufficient **market power** to prevent it from being a price-taker, although interfirm rivalry will prevent each firm from treating the market demand curve as identical to its own.

- Several **theories of oligopoly** have been developed, each having in common the uncertainty which exists regarding outcomes.

- The **kinked demand curve** theory is concerned with the reactions of firms to an increase or reduction in the price charged by one of the firms in the market. This model is associated with *price rigidity* ('sticky' prices).

- **Game theory** explores more complex oligopoly situations based on interacting decision-takers (players) and different outcomes (pay-offs) associated with different competitive strategies.

- The results of *game theory* are assessed using a *pay-off matrix* and an equilibrium outcome, where each player chooses his best strategy given the actions of the other players, is called a **Nash equilibrium**.

- A **maximin** strategy involves a player choosing the best possible outcome from among the set of worst possible outcomes.

- A **maximax** approach involves choosing the strategy that has the best possible outcome.

- A **minimax** strategy involves a player minimising the maximum opportunity loss associated with what might turn out to be a wrong decision.

- A **dominant strategy** occurs where the same behaviour is suggested by different strategies by other players.

- The **Prisoner's Dilemma** highlights how two or more players, acting in their best personal interest, may choose an inferior outcome than if they had colluded. This analysis neatly illustrates why firms have incentives to form cartels.

- Oligopoly markets are associated with **price leadership**, involving **dominant, collusive** and **barometric** pricing behaviour.

Topics for discussion

1 Ollipolly is a company producing business magazines, which has one main rival in the market, Polliolly. Ollipolly has 45% of the market and Polliolly, 55%.

  (a) What type of market does Ollipolly operate in?
  (b) What competitive strategy would you suggest to the board of Ollipolly to improve (i) its market share; (ii) its profitability?
  (c) Would it be in the interests of the two companies to merge or for one to acquire the other?

2 With reference to the Prisoner's Dilemma, explain why collusion is often a feature of oligopoly markets.

3 Identify two oligopolistic industries and compare and contrast the ways in which the firms in these industries compete. Explain the reasons for any differences in competitive behaviour that you identify.

4 Using the kinked demand curve model, identify why oligopoly markets may be subject to relative price stability, interspersed with periods of aggressive price wars.

5 Explain why non-price competition is often found in oligopolistic markets.

6 Joe and David own the only two restaurants in a village. They have reached a secret agreement that they will each serve smaller portions of food in order to increase their profit margins. Under what circumstances is this cartel agreement likely to:

  (a) hold
  (b) break down?

7 Assume that hotel Y is considering four possible strategies to increase its occupancy rate. These strategies are:

  (a) to reduce price overall by 10%
  (b) to increase advertising expenditure by 30%
  (c) to offer enhanced facilities to its guests
  (d) to enter into a new agency agreement with a travel promotion company.

The hotel considers that it is very likely that its competitors will respond with similar deals. The pay-off matrix below represents hotel Y's estimates of the effects on its profits corresponding to each of its four alternative strategies and four likely responses (1, 2, 3, 4) of its competitors.

		Rivals' reactions			
		1	2	3	4
	a	25	20	70	−5
Hotel Y	b	70	120	−10	90
strategies	c	10	18	50	30
	d	30	0	5	10

   (i)   Which of the four strategies should hotel Y adopt if it follows a *maximax* rule?

   (ii) Which of the four strategies should hotel Y adopt if it follows a *maximin* rule?

   (iii) Under what circumstances is the hotel management likely to adopt a maximin over a maximax strategy?

8 How should competition authorities react to the announcement of a cartel arrangement between a country's largest breweries to maintain beer prices and allocate regional markets amongst them? Would your answer be different if the national breweries faced intense competitive pressure from imported beers?

10 Managerial objectives and the firm

Aims and learning outcomes

In the previous chapters we assumed that the firm's primary objective is to maximise profits. This assumption underlies the competitive environment which we mapped out using the frameworks of the perfect competition (Chapter 6), monopoly (Chapter 7), monopolistic competition (Chapter 8) and oligopoly market models (Chapter 9), and which allowed us to establish benchmarks for the analysis and comparison of price–output decisions under different market structures. This approach, often referred to as the traditional (or 'neoclassical') approach, is sometimes criticised, however, on the grounds that it does not provide a satisfactory explanation of real-world production and pricing decisions. By assuming away many complexities, the simplistic assumption of profit maximisation enables us to make very clear-cut predictions about the firm's behaviour. However, it is one thing to make predictions, but another to say how realistic they are or how accurate they are. The traditional theory of the firm seems to be at its best when analysing behaviour in perfectly competitive and monopoly market structures. In practice, these theoretical extremes are rarely to be found – in reality most firms are confronted with market conditions which are more readily described as imperfectly competitive with oligopoly being the dominant market form in some industries. This is not to say that we should dismiss the analysis presented in the previous chapters – on the contrary, it is essential to the development of a deeper understanding of the fundamental relationships between pricing and production decisions.

Most economists sympathise with the defence of the profit maximisation assumption, recognising its usefulness as a mental, theoretical link to explaining how one gets from the 'cause to the effect'. The models reviewed in the previous chapters were developed to *predict*, not to describe, behaviour in markets. In more recent times, however, a collection of new, alternative theories of corporate behaviour has been put forward. The purpose of this chapter is to review these theories and to assess their merits in terms of the insights they provide into business behaviour alongside the traditional approach. We shall consider these new theories under the following three basic headings:

- Principal–agent theory.
- Managerial theories.
- Behavioural theories.

A fourth area of development has already been discussed, in Chapter 9, in the study of oligopoly. There we introduced the concept of 'game theory' which represents a major development in the understanding of real-world corporate behaviour in ologopolistic industries.

In this chapter we also consider the relationship between management objectives and business ethics. This is an area of growing importance in today's business environment and involves concerns about the impact on the environment and society in general from the actions and behaviour of firms.

Learning outcomes

This chapter will help you to:

- Analyse the different objectives firms may choose when deciding on their production and pricing decisions.

- Appreciate the meaning and significance of *principal–agent theory* and its relationship to business objectives and corporate governance.

- Recognise the nature of different managerial theories of the firm, namely *sales revenue maximisation, utility maximisation* and *corporate growth maximisation* models.

- Distinguish between managerial and behavioural theories of the firm and the contrast between *maximising* and *satisficing* strategies.

- Understand the importance of *business ethics* within the framework of managerial decisions in today's business environment.

Challenging the traditional assumptions

The new theories of corporate behaviour which we shall discuss below stem, in the main, from abandoning one or both of the following assumptions which are central to the traditional approach, namely that:

- Decisions are made under conditions of perfect knowledge.
- The objective of the firm is to maximise profits.

There are five main reasons which can be offered as justification for abandoning these two assumptions. These relate to the following:

- The growth in oligopoly.
- The growth of managerial capitalism.
- Difficulties surrounding profit maximisation in practice.
- The organisational complexity of firms.
- Recognition that real life decisions are often made in the face of imperfect or incomplete information.

Before examining the alternative theories of corporate behaviour listed above we shall briefly discuss the significance of each of these developments in turn.

The growth in oligopoly

As mentioned earlier, oligopoly is the most common form of market structure in reality and yet it is the structure to which the traditional assumptions fit least well. Empirical evidence of the growing importance of oligopoly can be found by measuring the degree of concentration across industries using one of the methods outlined in Chapter 7 (pp. 159–61). When an industry is concentrated, but not a monopoly, it displays the characteristics of oligopoly. Empirical studies of a number of countries have shown a general trend across many industries towards this type of market structure.

There are two main reasons why the traditional theory of the firm, based on the assumptions of perfect knowledge and profit-maximising behaviour, fails to provide a satisfactory explanation of market behaviour under oligopoly. These concern:

● The extent to which firms are *interdependent*.
● The degree of *uncertainty* that exists in oligopolistic markets.

These issues have already been discussed in Chapter 9. Briefly, mutual interdependence arises in oligopoly because each firm produces a sufficiently large proportion of the industry's total output for its behaviour to significantly affect the market share of its competitors. Uncertainty arises because the behaviour of one firm is conditioned not just by what its rivals are doing but also by what it *thinks* its rivals *might* do in response to any initiative of its own. Uncertainty and interdependence can be tackled through a game theory approach to market behaviour.

The growth of managerial capitalism

The traditional assumption of profit maximisation implies that the 'firm' somehow has a mind of its own, capable of arriving at independent, rational decisions. In reality, of course, firms do not make decisions – it is entrepreneurs, managers and employees (i.e. individuals) who make business decisions. A 'firm' is nothing more than an abstract concept covering owners, managers and employees.

Over time, the relationship between *ownership* and *control* in firms has changed substantially. In their earliest form, business units or firms were owned and managed by the same people, therefore the assumption of profit maximisation did not seem unreasonable. Over time, however, with the growth of large corporations and the dominance of public joint-stock companies, there has emerged a separation of ownership from control in many businesses. Ownership is in the hands of shareholders, who may or may not exercise their voting rights at company annual general meetings. Control, however, is largely in the hands of the senior managers and executive directors of the firm. This situation is described as *managerial capitalism* and has given rise to 'managerial theories' to explain the behaviour of firms. With managers in control it is easy to question the validity of the profit maximisation assumption of the traditional theory. Some managers may seek to keep shareholders happy by reporting a certain level of profit, while leaving themselves the flexibility to achieve, perhaps personal, objectives (such as business growth, diversification, salary, etc.). Even if profit maximisation is stated as the key objective of the firm as a whole, it is unlikely that every individual within the firm, even within senior management, will be pursuing this objective consistently.

There appears, in particular, to be a potential division between the goals of shareholders (principals) and the goals of management (agents). Recently this issue, related to who governs or controls the goals of joint-stock companies, has been approached through *principal–agent theory*. Principal–agent theory is concerned with analysing the problems that can arise for *corporate governance* where ownership and control are divorced. The form of corporate governance may well affect the objectives which companies and other organisations pursue, in particular profit and growth.

Difficulties surrounding profit maximisation

In practice, businesses may have insufficient accurate information about demand and cost conditions to be able to use the concepts of marginal revenue and marginal cost as the basis for determining the profit-maximising output. As a result, pricing policies may be determined by other methods, such as on the basis of a mark-up over average unit costs subject to the achievement of a 'required' profit margin (see Chapter 12, pp. 242–4). As much of the output as possible will then be sold on the market at this price.

Other price guidelines may be followed for different firms in different industries. For example, over the years two basic pricing guidelines for state industries in market economies have emerged: *marginal-cost pricing*, and *mark-up pricing* to achieve a target rate of return. Full details of these and other pricing policies are given in Chapter 12. The key point to note here is that the traditional theory of the firm does not provide a particularly useful framework for analysing the behaviour of state and 'not-for-profit' firms (such as charities and co-operatives).

The organisational complexity of firms

A further reason for questioning the validity of the traditional approach to understanding the behaviour of firms relates to the changing organisational structure of firms. As with the growth of managerial capitalism, this reflects the fact that as firms have increased in size, so too they have become much more complex in terms of their organisational structure. The result may be different parts of the organisation having different goals. The structure will incorporate the sometimes conflicting views of owners, managers and workers. Within each grouping there could be still more complex structures: perhaps reflecting different categories of shareholders with different share holdings who are interested in different objectives (short-term versus long-term profits perhaps); different managers at different levels with different aims and aspirations; blue-collar workers and white-collar workers with different career expectations and reward packages, perhaps represented by different unions. Finally, there will often be different groups of consumers to be satisfied (such as the one-off customer versus the long-term, loyal customer).

Given the degree of complexity of organisational structures today, some economists argue that it is unlikely that a useful theory of business decisions can be based on a *single* objective such as profit maximisation and that instead the subject should be approached through a study of the behaviour of individuals or groups within the firm. Also, it is sometimes held that such an approach should start from the position that people in firms, including managers, do not aim to maximise anything – they simply aim to 'satisfy' a range of objectives. This 'behavioural' approach to the firm will be discussed later in the chapter.

Incomplete information

Decisions in firms are made in the face of complex, often conflicting advice and other information. Indeed, if business decisions were made given perfect or complete information, then outcomes could be perfectly planned and there would never be failures or disappointments. Management would simply be a matter of routine – as it is in the perfect competition, monopolistic competition, monopoly and some oligopoly models, where production and pricing decisions are simply based on equating known marginal costs and marginal revenues.

In reality, incomplete information is the norm in business, leading to notions of 'management ability' and 'management judgement'! Recognition of the existence of incomplete information leads to much more interesting and varied approaches to the study of business decision-making.

In summary, therefore, the traditional theory of profit maximisation featured in previous chapters may be criticised because:

- It may not be readily applicable to oligopoly markets.
- It takes inadequate account of the need to gather and utilise information.
- It is no longer appropriate in today's environment, where managerial capitalism has taken over from entrepreneurial capitalism and where control of businesses has become divorced from their ownership in many industries.
- Pricing policies in practice may bear little obvious resemblance to those suggested by the MR = MC principle.
- The complexity of organisational structures today calls into question some of the basic assumptions of the traditional theory and draws attention to the *process* of decision-making.

We turn now to discuss some developments that have taken place in the analysis of the behaviour of firms, starting with the concept of *principal–agent theory*, referred to already. This theory recognises the growth in managerial capitalism and the complexity of modern organisational structures.

Principal–agent theory

In many areas of economic activity, people and organisations carry out transactions on behalf of others. That is to say, *principals* appoint *agents* to undertake economic transactions on their behalf.

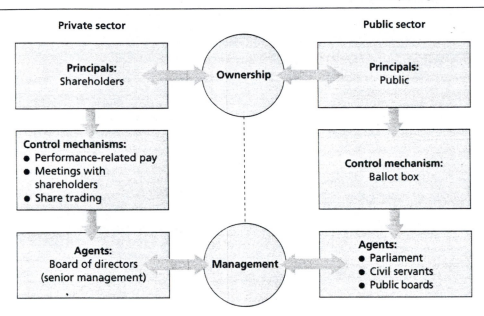

Figure 10.1 The principal–agent relationship: private v public sector

The broad thrust of agency theory as a basis for understanding the behaviour of firms is summarised in Figure 10.1 above, which shows the *principal–agent* relationships that exist in the private and public sectors. In the private sector, the *principals* are those who ultimately have the rights to the net assets of the firm if it is liquidated or who 'own' the firm (while recognising that in some legal systems the shareholders' ownership rights are restricted). In joint-stock companies these are the shareholders and they appoint directors as *agents* to manage these assets on their behalf. In theory, the directors should manage the assets in the interests of the principals but in practice this cannot be guaranteed. In practice, agents may lack incentives or motivation to pursue the goals of their principals and the principal–agent relationship may involve costs in terms of lower efficiency. At the root of the problem lies the fact that the principals face costs, not least in terms of the time and effort involved, in monitoring the work of their agents.

There are, however, 'control mechanisms' in the *private* sector. Managers may be incentivised to pursue shareholder value through performance-related pay and stock options. Also, shareholders may attend meetings with management and, in particular, company annual general meetings to question and, if necessary, replace the directors. Perhaps more importantly, the shareholders can exercise their right to sell their share holdings altogether. Many economists argue that the existence of such a control mechanism acts as a major constraint on private sector management. If management pursue a quiet life or other objectives which reduce profitability, then shareholders can react by disposing of their shares. This will tend to drive down the share price, making the company more vulnerable to a takeover by new management.

By contrast, however, some economists question the significance of shareholder power, arguing instead that shareholders are fairly inert to management performance

Application 10.1

Daewoo: an alternative approach

Although Daewoo had a market share of only 1.5% of UK new car registrations in 1999, it provides an interesting example of an alternative approach to the distribution and servicing of cars. Daewoo entered the UK car market in April 1995 with a target of achieving a 1% market share as quickly as possible. After studying the performance of recent entrants into the market, its management decided that the conventional retail system, using franchised dealers, could not achieve the target level of sales quickly enough.

Daewoo consequently developed a different approach that gave it direct control over its interaction with customers. This is based on wholly-owned sales outlets that sell at fixed prices direct to end-users. Daewoo's personnel are directly employed and do not receive sales-related commissions. In October 1999, it had three types of outlets:

(a) Wholly-owned sales outlets that concentrate exclusively on selling new cars, including:
   (i) eleven large flagship units in retail parks that display up to 16 cars; and
   (ii) three smaller outlets, which each display one car, in leased shop units located at three of Sainsbury's Savacentre hypermarkets.

(b) Twenty-one wholly-owned sites that sell cars, provide service support and retail used cars.

(c) Ninety-five service sites, 91 of which are located in Halfords garages servicing superstores but staffed by a mixture of Daewoo customer support personnel and Halfords technicians. Twenty-eight of these sites have been upgraded to include new car display areas. Four stand-alone service sites owned by Daewoo have recently supplemented these service sites.

Source: Competition Commission, *New Cars: A report on the supply of new motor cars within the UK*, Cm 4660, 2000, paragraphs 6.141–6.142.

Activity

With reference to principal–agent theory, discuss the merits of this method of vehicle selling adopted by Daewoo in the UK. What other reasons may have driven Daewoo to adopt this method of retailing its cars?

unless it is clearly poor. Most shareholders rarely attend annual general meetings and the existence of transactions costs and capital gains taxation may reinforce a tendency to hold onto shares in the hope that things will get better. If, following some share sellings, things do get better, those who have held on to their shares benefit and this produces a 'free rider' problem in the sense that these shareholders benefit from the action of other shareholders disposing of their holdings. In these circumstances, all shareholders may be reluctant to sell, hoping that other shareholders do sell. Further, it is not obvious that it is necessarily the less profitable firms which succumb to a takeover bid. Sometimes what appear to be profitable, well-managed firms face hostile bids.

Figure 10.1 also illustrates the principal–agent relationship which exists in the *public* sector. In this case, civil servants and public boards manage industries and services on behalf of the public. Since there are no shares to sell or annual general meetings to attend, the public are unable to indicate, directly, dissatisfaction with management performance. Voters can express their views on government performance through the ballot box, but this is a crude indicator of satisfaction and dissatisfaction with particular state activities (such as the postal service, police, education, etc.). Votes at elections reflect broad manifesto pledges and party loyalties and not, usually, views about the quality of service of one particular public industry or state sector. For this reason, there appears to be greater scope for managerial discretionary behaviour by management in the public sector compared with much of the private sector. Consequently, there may be a tendency for production costs in the public sector to be higher than in the private sector. This has been an important rationale for privatisation programmes around the world.

A further constraint on managerial discretionary behaviour relates to the *product market*. Firms, whether private or public sector (unless backed by considerable taxpayers' funds), must be *efficient* to survive in competitive markets. Under conditions of competition any inefficiency which leads to higher prices will be penalised through a loss of market share and eventual bankruptcy. This constraint is illustrated in Figure 10.2, which shows two average cost curves. Assume that the curve AC_1 applies to the firm when it is fully efficient and that AC_2, being higher, reflects X-inefficiency (for an explanation of X-inefficiency see pp. 87–90). If the firm was earning only normal profits when operating on the curve AC_1, then when costs rise to AC_2 losses will be incurred. As a general rule we can conclude, therefore, that non-profit goals which raise costs are likely to be more prevalent in firms operating where product market competition is imperfect (because if the market was perfectly competitive the firm would not be able to survive in the face of non-profit goals which raised costs).

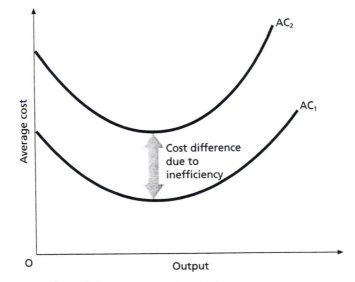

Figure 10.2 Impact of inefficiency on average cost

Managerial theories

Once we acknowledge that managers in the private and perhaps more especially in the public sector are able, to some degree, to pursue their own goals rather than that of profit maximisation, especially where competition is imperfect, the question arises as to what are these goals and what is their effect on prices and outputs. We consider the following three possible goals:

- Sales revenue maximisation.
- Managerial utility maximisation.
- Corporate growth maximisation.

The common feature of the underlying models concerned with these is that they each reject the simple profit-maximisation assumption, replacing it with an alternative goal which management aims to achieve. These goals stem from the study of what motivates different managers where there is a separation of the ownership from the management (control) function, i.e. a principal–agent relationship, which leaves managers with some degree of freedom to pursue non-profit goals, at least in the short term.

Sales revenue maximisation

The idea of sales revenue maximisation as a management goal was first put forward by William Baumol. The argument is based on Baumol's own research into managerial behaviour and is couched in terms of oligopolistic industry and in which there is a divorce of ownership and management of resources. Baumol argues that managers are likely to attach a great deal of importance to achieving high sales revenues for the following reasons:

- High and expanding sales revenues help to attract external finance to the firm – larger firms generally find it easier to raise capital, while financial institutions may be less willing to deal with a firm suffering from declining sales.
- High sales assist the distribution and retailing of products – resulting in economies from selling in bulk.
- Consumers may view a firm with falling sales in a less favourable light – this may deter consumers from buying and reduce sales even further.
- The distributive trade may be less co-operative, for example in extending credit lines, when a firm's sales are declining.
- Falling sales may result in reductions in staffing levels, including managerial staff, as costs are cut.
- Last, but not least, managers' salaries may depend on a fast growth of sales revenues – managers are often rewarded for expanding the business.

Baumol's theory does not ignore profit altogether but is presented in terms of *sales revenue maximisation subject to* a *minimum profit constraint*. As long as this constraint

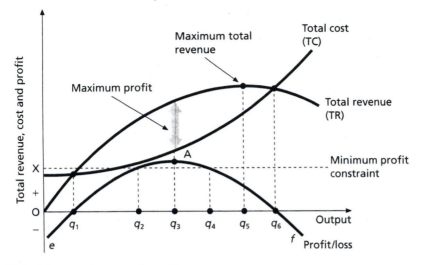

Figure 10.3 Sales revenue maximisation

is met, based on the assumption that this will be sufficient to satisfy shareholders, the firm's management will aim to maximise sales revenues. The needs of shareholders cannot be ignored, but the minimum profit constraint will usually be less than the maximum profit feasible. Presumably this will especially hold true where shareholders do not know what is the maximum profit that could conceivably be achieved. Lack of information on the part of shareholders may lead them to accept the annual reported profit. We might expect this to be most prevalent where there are no competitor firms reporting profits to facilitate comparisons.

Figure 10.3 illustrates the principles of the sales revenue maximisation model where the total revenue (TR) and total cost (TC) curves are drawn for a typical firm. The curve ef shows the total profit or loss and is derived from the TR and TC curves for each level of sales. It will be seen that the output which maximises profit is q_3, i.e. where the vertical distance between TR and TC is at its greatest. At outputs q_1 and q_6 TR = TC and therefore profit is zero. To the left of q_1 and to the right of q_6, TR is less than TC and therefore losses are made.

In the absence of a minimum profit constraint, management could pursue sales revenues by expanding output to q_5 where TR is at its maximum (the firm's management would presumably not wish to increase output beyond this point because total revenue would fall). With the imposition of a minimum profit constraint, such as level X in Figure 10.3, sales can now only be expanded up to q_4. Expansion beyond this point would lead to a reduction in total profits below the minimum level considered acceptable to shareholders (note that the profit constraint is also met at output q_2 but since output q_4 provides a higher level of sales revenue, a sales revenue-maximising management would not choose q_2 over q_4).

With the pursuit of sales revenue constrained by the required profit level to satisfy shareholders, any increase in this level (shifting the profit constraint line at X upwards)

201

will lead to a reduction in output, whereas any reduction in the required profit will lead to an expansion in output. Note that only if the profit constraint line passes through point *A* would production be at the level to maximise profits. From this model we can conclude that, in contrast to management which attempts to profit-maximise, a sales revenue-maximising management will tend to:

- Produce at a higher output level.
- Set prices lower (because, given a normal downward sloping demand curve, a higher output can only be sold at a lower price).
- Invest more heavily in measures that boost demand, such as advertising (to increase demand without reducing price and therefore profits).

In later formulations of his model Baumol substituted as the objective of management the maximisation of the *growth* of the firm for the maximisation of sales revenue. The two goals are, of course, related, though growth maximisation is a more dynamic concept because it relates to production over time. Also, whereas in the sales revenue maximisation model the profit constraint could be at any level (whatever keeps the shareholders happy), in the growth model it is set by the 'means for obtaining capital needed to finance expansion plans', i.e. by the need of management to attract finance from investors for investment to grow the firm. The 'optimal profit stream' is that which is consistent with raising adequate investment funds to achieve the highest rate of growth of output *over the firm's lifetime*.

Managerial utility maximisation

Baumol's model outlined above implies that management has some choice in the trade-off between profit and sales revenue in business decision-making. This recognition has led to the development of other models which explain firms' behaviour in terms of *managerial discretion*. One important approach has been developed by the American economist Oliver Williamson, who argues that managers in large firms may have enough discretion to pursue those policies which give them personally most satisfaction. Whereas it can be reasonably assumed that shareholders equate their level of satisfaction (i.e. utility) with profit (since the higher the profit the higher the share dividends and share price, *ceteris paribus*), management is considered to have a utility function which includes a number of personal goals and personal measures of 'well-being'. These goals may include the achievement of a plush office, a large company car, a high salary, etc. In this approach to managerial objectives the goal of sales revenue maximisation could be interpreted as a special case, where that single goal dominates all other managerial goals or is the means by which the other managerial goals are realised.

Williamson's model makes allowance for markets not being perfectly competitive and for the principal–agent relationship in firms, described by Figure 10.1. He suggests that managers' self-interest focuses on the achievement of goals in four particular areas, namely:

- **High salaries.** This includes not just take-home pay but also all other forms of monetary income such as bonuses and share options. The desire for large salaries reflects a desire by managers for a high standard of living and a high status.

- **Staff under their control.** This refers to both the number and quality of subordinate staff as a measure of status and a measure of power within the firm (reflecting the 'I hire them, I fire them' type of management philosophy).

- **Discretionary investment expenditure.** This does not refer to investment that is essential for the success of the firm but rather to any investment over and above this amount. This includes any pet projects of the management that are excused as necessary to the general development of the firm (such as sponsorship, say, of Formula 1 motor racing in the case of a petrol company). The manager may be able to further his or her own personal interests and hobbies (sponsoring staff golf outings, for example). The extent of the manager's authority over discretionary expenditure may also be taken as an indication of his or her status within the firm.

- **Fringe benefits.** Managers might strive for an expense account, a lavishly furnished office, a company car, free club memberships, etc. These perks may be part of the 'slack' in the organisation, i.e. non-essential expenditures that force up the firm's costs.

Williamson expresses these goals in terms of a *managerial utility function*. Believing that the first two goals (concerning salaries and staff) are closely related, he combines them under the symbol S. Discretionary investment is represented by I_d while M represents expenditure on management perks. Using U to denote utility which the manager seeks to maximise, Williamson's argument can be presented using the following managerial utility function:

$$U = f(S, I_d, M)$$

Profits are not ignored by Williamson. Like Baumol, he recognises that a certain profit must be paid to shareholders, to placate them, but argues that managers will strive to increase their utility as long as this profit constraint is satisfied. Equally, however, it is possible to conceive of management desiring higher profits because they derive satisfaction from business achievement. Profitability is a measure of business success and buoyant profits provide a fertile environment in which managers can then pursue their other goals.

Corporate growth maximisation

The third and final variation of the managerial theory of firms' behaviour, which we present here, also sees managerial motivation in terms of striving to maximise a target. This time the target is the firm's growth. The model is associated with the work of the economist Robin Marris. Again, competition is assumed to be limited, with a principal–agent relationship so that there is scope for managerial discretionary behaviour. The theory stems from Marris's view of the institutional framework and organisation of the modern corporation. He sees the firm as typically a bureaucratic organisation – a self-perpetuating structure where corporate growth and the security that it brings is seen as a desirable end in itself. Managers are expected to see a relationship between the growth of the company and hence profits ploughed back into investment, and their own personal goals (such as increased status, power and salary). At the same time, managers are expected to balance investing in the firm's growth against the impact on current profits and dividends – especially, they must beware of the danger of low dividends depressing share prices which may leave the firm vulnerable to a hostile takeover bid. Therefore, growth and security compete as management objectives and each requires a different approach to risk in terms of investment and capital raising.

There may be a trade-off between securing profits to pay dividends and taking risks when investing to increase the growth of the firm. At the same time, while profits provide the retained earnings to help finance new investment which leads to growth, excessive company liquidity may attract predators. Cash-rich companies attract take-over bids. In the Marris's model this conflict is summarised as management seeking the *optimal dividend-to-profit retention ratio*. This is explained below with respect to the *valuation ratio*.

The *valuation ratio* for any company is its current share price multiplied by the number of its issued shares divided by the net book value (assets less liabilities) of the company.

The ratio is important because it acts as an indicator of the firm's vulnerability to a takeover bid. In particular, firms which have a valuation ratio of less than one are clearly vulnerable. The value of their net assets is greater than the cost of purchasing their shares. Therefore, in principle, profit can be made by buying the issued shares, taking control of the company and then selling the assets (assuming that the net book value of the company has been correctly measured). The higher the valuation ratio that management must achieve to ward off a takeover bid, the higher in this model dividend payments must be to keep the share price buoyant and hence the lower the retained earnings to finance growth.

At first an increasing growth rate may have a beneficial effect upon the valuation ratio because lower dividends resulting from the implied higher rate of retained earnings are balanced by the prospect of higher future dividends resulting from the firm's growth. If this is so the share price remains buoyant and there is no trade-off between growth and the valuation ratio. Eventually, however, for shareholders the future dividend expectations do not offset the forgone current dividends and a faster growth rate can only be obtained by accepting a lower valuation ratio.

This is illustrated in Figure 10.4 as a *valuation curve* with a maximum at point X, which gives a valuation ratio of V_1 and a growth rate of G_1. Also in this diagram are a number of indifference curves U_1 to U_n each showing different combinations of the valuation ratio and the firm's growth rate between which management is indifferent (for an explanation of indifference curves see Chapter 2, pp. 53–60). Each higher

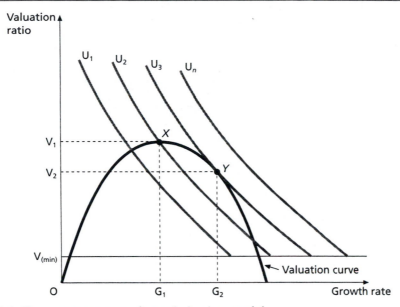

Figure 10.4 The corporate growth maximisation model

indifference curve implies a higher level of total utility to management but management is constrained from moving to U_n (and beyond) by the valuation curve. Note that the indifference curves terminate at $V_{(min)}$. This limit is set by the lowest level of the valuation ratio which management will accept given the constant threat of a takeover.

In Figure 10.4 the highest utility feasible is represented by the indifference curve U_3, which is tangential to the valuation curve at Y. This gives a growth rate of G_2, and a valuation ratio of V_2. Notice that point Y is to the right of the maximum point of the valuation curve, X. This means that the growth rate is higher than that compatible with a maximum valuation ratio ($G_2 > G_1 : V_2 < V_1$). Given that shareholders can be assumed to prefer the highest possible share price and hence a higher valuation ratio (V_1), Marris's growth model implies that there is a bias in firms with a division between ownership and control towards having a growth rate in excess of that desired by the shareholders.

Application 10.2

Transforming the Japanese Company

Corporate objectives – market share versus profitability

A pervasive weakness in the Japanese approach to competition is its disregard of the role of industry structure in deciding both where to compete and how. Profitability is influenced not only by a company's own competitive position but also by the structure of its industry. Japanese companies regularly flock to 'high-tech', 'sunrise', or growing industries without fully understanding that none of these things guarantees industry

▶

attractiveness. As a result, they end up crowding into unattractive businesses or under-mining the structure of what could be attractive industries by transferring power to customers, reducing barriers to entry, and driving the basis of rivalry toward price. Then they wonder why profits are poor or non-existent. The Japanese corporate model derives, in large part, from the goals set by companies. Lifetime employment makes expansion an imperative. The stigma attached to laying people off, even during an economic downturn, has meant Japanese companies have consistently opted for product proliferation and entry into risky new growth areas.

This was possible because shareholders are seen as secondary and exert little or no influence on management. In most large Japanese companies 60% to 70% of shares are held by stable and friendly shareholders such as banks, insurance companies, and affiliated companies for relationship purposes. Not sensitive to profits, these controlling shareholders have rarely sold their shares. Such an ownership structure encourages top managers to focus not on near-term profits but on growth, which creates more business for affiliated companies. Also, most top managers of large Japanese companies hold solely salaried positions, so they have little incentive to pursue profitability.

Not surprisingly, then, the metrics used by Japanese companies to measure performance are market share and growth. It is notable that market share data are more available in Japan than anywhere else in the world, yet profitability data are scarce and unreliable. There is no line of business reporting that allows comparisons of profitability in particular businesses.

Japanese companies have a near obsession with market share, pursuing it at the expense of profitability. For example, in 1996, when Toyota's domestic market share dropped below the 40% mark for the first time in fifteen years, the company shifted into crisis mode and pulled out all the stops to reverse the decline. If market share remained below 40%, President Hiroshi Okuda said 'It will have a negative impact on morale'.

In Japan, employees become emotionally charged about winning or losing market share points *vis-à-vis* an arch rival. In Sony's General Audio Division, for example, employees make constant reference to 'BMW', which stands for 'Beat Matsushita Whatever'. Such rivalry is a good thing when it is channeled into proper strategic focus and oriented to improving profit performance. However, there is a danger in pursuing market share for its own sake.

The preoccupation with market share drives imitation and competitive convergence. Instead of concentrating on certain products or groups of customers, Japanese companies succumb to the temptation of pursuing broadly-based strategies. They resist making trade-offs because they fear this will constrain growth. By doing everything, though, Japanese companies become unique at nothing.

Source: Edited extract from by Porter, M., Takenchiaad, H. and Sakakibara, M. (2000) *Can Japan Compete?* Macmillan Press, Basingstoke, pp. 169–70.

Activity

Consider the implications for prices and outputs if Japanese industrialists were to focus much more on profitability and less on market share. Use an appropriate diagram or diagrams to illustrate your answer.

Behavioural theories

The approaches to managerial goals considered so far go well beyond the simple notion of profit maximisation. However, they still cling to the idea that management endeavours to maximise *something*, whether it be sales revenue, utility or the firm's growth. But, in a world of uncertainty and large organisations it could be argued that maximising behaviour of any kind is not relevant. A radically different approach, which is adopted by so-called *behaviouralists*, rejects the whole notion of maximisation in favour of a less strong goal of 'satisficing'. Whereas the traditional profit-maximising model and the alternatives reviewed so far have been more concerned with how firms *should* behave to maximise profits, sales revenue, etc., the behaviouralist approach is more concerned with exploring how firms *actually* behave with attention focused on the internal decision-making structure of the firm. The aim is to understand the decision-making process, stressing the nature of large companies as complex organisations, beset by problems of goal conflict and imperfect communications problems. Behavioural theories look at the inherent conflict which exists in such organisations between the goals of individuals and sub-groups. They suggest that organisational objectives stem from the interaction among these individuals and sub-groups (such as between a firm's departments). Such theories of the firm contrast sharply with the maximising analysis lying behind profit maximisation and the other theories of managerial behaviour discussed above.

The idea of 'satisficing' was initially introduced by Professor H.A. Simon. He argues that, faced with incomplete information and uncertainty, individuals are more likely to be content to achieve a *satisfactory* level of something rather than to strive to *maximise* goals, and that this level will be revised continuously in the light of experience. This notion has been developed further by R.M. Cyert and J.G. March who have established a behaviouralist model of the firm. In this approach the *process* of decision-making, ignored in the other models of the firm discussed earlier, is of critical importance. According to Cyert and March, the firm can be thought of as a *coalition* of various interest groups: different departments, different levels of management, different groups of workers, suppliers and consumers, shareholders, etc. Hence, from a behviouralist perspective, a complex process of bargaining takes place between these various groups within the firm to determine their *collective* goals. Some of the goals could be related to the following with the determination of the 'satisfactory' level the subject of internal debate and perhaps conflict:

- **Production.** A goal that output must lie within a certain satisfactory range.
- **Sales.** A goal that there must be a satisfactory level of sales however defined.
- **Market share.** A goal indicating a satisfactory size of market share as a measure of comparative success as well as of the growth of the firm.
- **Profit.** Still an important goal, but one amongst a number rather than necessarily the goal of overriding importance.

Consequently, there is no single objective of the firm; instead, there are multiple goals which emerge from the potential for conflict amongst interest groups within the firm. In addition, these goals can be expected to alter over time as circumstances change. Different managers from different departments and sections of the organisation will have a strong affiliation for targets in their own areas. For example, sales personnel will tend to identify with the goals of the marketing and sales departments, while accountants will tend to identify with the financial outcomes and the interests of the finance department. There is no necessity that the goals of these different groups should be the same or easily reconcilable. In these circumstances, the objectives of the firm are eventually determined by factors such as the following:

- *Bargaining* between groups and the relationship between groups within the firm.
- The *power* and influence of different groups within the firm.
- The method by which objectives are *formulated* within the organisation.
- How groups and, therefore, the 'firm' react to *experiences* and make *adjustments*.

The various goals set by different departments and sections of the organisation may well conflict and it may arise that senior managers are prepared to sacrifice some profit to achieve a compromise. The way in which such conflicts are resolved in Cyert and March's behaviouralist model (and more refined versions of it that have since been published) draws attention to the process of *decision-making* within organisations.

The goals that are pursued may be inconsistent, but it is possible to see how they can be reconciled if we introduce the idea of *satisficing* in the place of maximising behaviour. The aim will be to achieve a *satisfactory* performance for each of the goals. For example, sales staff might accept what they regard as a satisfactory level of sales growth to maintain an agreed profitability, while finance staff agree to the firm forgoing some immediate profit by raising spending on advertising. To facilitate such compromises being made within the organisation, Cyert and March argue that different groupings are bought off by 'side payments' when their particular goals are not being met. These side payments can take pecuniary or non-pecuniary forms, such as higher pay for a section of staff or plusher offices for certain managers. Similarly, disgruntled shareholders might be bought off by a rise in this year's dividends per share. Normally, there will be groups who are able to exert a greater influence on objectives from time to time. In this behaviouralist approach to the firm psychology plays a key role in the management of the firm because people's actions and reactions are to a degree a result of their aspirations, which in turn stem from their perception of how well they feel they ought to be treated within the firm.

In summary, the essence of the behaviouralist approach lies in the study of human beings in terms of their relationship with their organisation. Within the complex environment of the firm, behaviour can be seen as a compromise between conflicting views and interests. In achieving a compromise so that the firm can function, it is the view of many behaviouralists that it is unlikely that any single goal could ever be maximised at the expense of other favoured goals, at least for long.

Business ethics

A study of managerial objectives and behaviour within firms would not be complete today without reference to the subject of *business ethics*. While corporate governance is concerned with the relationship between principals and agents or owners (e.g. shareholders) and managers (e.g. directors), business ethics focuses on the way in which firms behave and what objectives firms should pursue in the interests of *all* of their stakeholders – their staff, customers, suppliers, local community, etc., as well as their shareholders.

Today, companies increasingly recognise that their corporate reputation and hence their long-term profitability depend upon meeting the needs of different stakeholder groups. In particular, firms now recognise the importance of issues such as:

- The public's growing interest and concern about *environmental challenges*, involving pollution, the use of non-renewable resources, energy efficiency, etc. – leading to the so-called 'greening of business'.
- The *rights of workers and human rights* in general, supporting the development of fair pay, equal opportunities, health and safety at work, etc.
- *Ethical marketing* involving limitations on the selling of products such as tobacco and alcohol that may damage public health and general well-being.

There are many examples around the world today of companies which, at face value at least, actively embrace such ethical issues in formulating their corporate strategies. Examples include Body Shop, Shell, Benetton and Volkswagen – it is interesting to note that the latter's cars are designed and manufactured in such a way as to maximise the number of recyclable parts. Body Shop does not support animal testing of its body-care products. Benetton is known for its strong stance against the exploitation of low-paid labour in less-developed countries. Shell's corporate strategy has been developed around a number of economic, financial and social goals within an ethical framework. Shell explicitly states that it has a responsibility to all of its stakeholders, including society at large.

Sound business ethics can make economic sense because the costs associated with environmental damage, including the loss of consumer goodwill, may be substantial. For instance, when the oil tanker *Exxon Valdes* went aground in Alaska with devastating long-term effects on local wildlife, there was a global outcry about Exxon's failure to ensure the safe transportation of oil cargoes. This episode cost the company dearly both in terms of the immediate clean-up costs and its international reputation and brand image.

The pursuit of sound business ethics does, however, create dilemmas for management. For example, should a pharmaceutical company bring to market a life-saving drug when its safety to humans can only be ascertained after pre-testing on animals? Should firms close plants and create unemployment in areas of already high unemployment to maintain financial viability? Should firms 'exploit' labour market conditions in poorer countries and pay 'poverty wages' to compete successfully in world markets? Another question concerns the extent to which 'green' and other ethically-based objectives should be pursued, even at the expense of destroying value for shareholders (i.e. resulting in reduced long-term profitability). Nevertheless, whatever one's personal answer to such complex questions, it is clear that a full appreciation of the firm's supply decision cannot be entirely separated from the subject of business ethics in the modern era.

Concluding remarks

The behaviouralist approach to the firm has won many adherents because it appears to be the most descriptively realistic. Rather than simply assuming some maximisation objective (profits, sales, growth, etc.), it seeks to explore the internal decision-making of the firm and the process by which the organisation's goals emerge. It allows for and copes with conflicting and changing goals, an issue which the other theories reviewed in this chapter avoid directly discussing. Also, it is concerned with *how* firms reach decisions and *why*. Its main weakness, however, lies in its lack of generality and thus *predictive ability*. Clearly, maximisation of something is easier to model than satisficing behaviour and because every firm is different, there may be a different behavioural outcome for each firm and for the same firm over time. Economists prefer economic models which are generally applicable and which have general predictive ability even when this is gained at the expense of descriptive reality. Hence, the continued preference in economics for the assumption of profit maximisation. Although perhaps descriptively unrealistic (at least in some circumstances), profit maximisation does have the advantage of providing the basis for developing predictive models of firm behaviour.

The other approaches to the firm discussed in this chapter provide interesting variations on the traditional profit-maximising assumption, recognising the existence of principal–agent relationships, where ownership and control are divorced. In the sense that these other approaches highlight managerial discretionary behaviour, the choice of goals, goal conflict and the constraints upon management decisions, they have considerable value. However, most economists regard them as supplements to the profit-maximising model, at least in relation to much of the private sector; in the state sector and other not-for-profit organisations where there is no dominant profit goal, they may be more appropriate.

Even within the alternative models of the firm discussed in this chapter, profit exists as an important constraint upon management. Also, it remains the case that the profit-maximising model serves us well in predicting *how* price and output will change when, for example, product taxes are raised, costs of production increase or market price is lowered. Moreover, some economists stress that profit maximisation and the other models of the firms can be reconciled through a more careful definition of profit maximisation which stipulates the time period concerned. Sales revenue growth, for example, may be a short-run target management set in order to achieve a greater market share with a view to maximising profits for shareholders in the longer term.

The importance of the different theories reviewed in this chapter arises from the insight that they provide into the impact of different managerial objectives on the behaviour of firms and, more specifically, price and output decisions. Determination of the firm's goal or goals is a crucial first step in developing an effective competitive strategy. Only once we clearly define where we want to go can we begin to decide how to get there.

Also, a discussion of the firm's objectives cannot be divorced, today, from the contentious issue of business ethics. Business ethics is concerned with the objectives that some argue firms *should* pursue from a social welfare perspective. In other words, it is concerned with what some believe is the necessary standard of behaviour by firms which is compatible with the growing concerns of society in general about environmental and ethical issues. Business ethics may constrain management's pursuit of its goals (e.g. profit maximisation); but to date the study of business ethics is not well integrated into the study of firms' pricing and output decisions in economic theory.

Chapter 12 focuses on the different pricing policies which can be adopted by firms. The precise policy chosen will, amongst other things, reflect the precise objectives which management decide to pursue. But first we turn to a detailed review of competitive strategy, in the next chapter.

Key learning points

- The **traditional theory of the firm,** based on the assumptions of perfect knowledge and profit-maximising behaviour, may not be readily applicable, given the complexity of markets and organisational structures today.

- **Principal–agent theory** recognises the growth in managerial capitalism and the complexity of modern organisational structures based on a *growing separation* between the owners of the firm (the principals) and the firm's senior management or directors (the agents). This theory leads to a focus on **corporate governance** arrangements.

- Baumol concludes that management which attempt to **maximise sales revenue** will tend to produce at a higher output level, set lower prices and invest more heavily in measures that boost demand than management which attempt to maximise profits.

- Williamson's **managerial utility maximisation model** argues that managers seek to maximise their own self-interest based on the achievement of goals such as high salaries, authority over staffing, discretionary investment expenditure decisions and fringe benefits.

- Marris's **corporate growth maximisation model** suggests that management seek to maximise the growth of the firm subject to an optimal dividend-to-profit retention ratio, in order to safeguard the firm from a hostile takeover bid.

- The **satisficing** explanation of managerial behaviour is associated with **behaviouralist theory** and argues that there is no single objective of the firm; instead, there are multiple goals. These emerge from the potential for conflict amongst interest groups within the firm, such that the aim will be to achieve a satisfactory performance for each of the goals without necessarily any single, maximisation objective.

- **Business ethics** is concerned with the social responsibility of management towards the firm's major stakeholders, the environment and society in general. There is a growing belief that ethical and 'green' business are linked to improved business performance over time because of increased public concern for human rights and the world environment. Business ethics extends to treating all stakeholders 'fairly'; hence the growing emphasis on health and safety issues, 'good' working practices and the like in business decision-making.

Topics for discussion

1 Is 'profit maximisation' a satisfactory assumption when modelling the behaviour of firms? Explain your answer.

2 What do you understand by the term 'the growth of managerial capitalism'?

3 Give examples of 'principal–agent' relationships in economic transactions and discuss their importance when analysing business decisions.

4 Using an appropriate diagram, show the effect of a higher minimum profit constraint on a sales revenue-maximising firm. To what extent will the competitiveness of the capital market affect where the minimum profit constraint lies?

5 In what circumstances is Williamson's managerial theory of the firm likely to be most applicable? In what principal–agent relationships is it likely to be found?

6 To what extent do 'behavioural theories' of the firm provide a more useful insight into the behaviour of firms than the other theories reviewed in this chapter? Consider the argument that whilst the behavioural approach is descriptively attractive, it does not lend itself to predicting accurately pricing and output decisions.

7 Distinguish between corporate governance and business ethics.

8 Discuss whether or not a firm interested in maximising shareholder value should be concerned with ethical issues.

9 Identify a company which argues that it pursues an ethically-based corporate strategy.
   (a) What are the ethically-based aspects of this strategy?
   (b) What are the costs and benefits to the company arising from this strategy?
   (c) What are the costs and benefits to other stakeholder groups, including society in general, arising from the strategy?
   (d) To what extent could it be argued that this ethical strategy is merely marketing hype?

11 Understanding competitive strategy

Aims and learning outcomes

The previous chapters have set out the principles underlying the nature of competition within various forms of market structure. A detailed understanding of the nature of competition is essential in order to appreciate the meaning of *competitive strategy* because only then does it become clear what level and type of competition exists. For example, there is no point in the management of BMW shaping their strategy until it is clear *who* are the competitors and what is the precise *nature and scope* of the competition. We now turn to provide an introduction to competitive strategy, drawing upon the principles of business economics detailed in this book.

The following topics relating to competitive strategy are set out in this chapter:

- The meaning of *competitive strategy*.
- Mission and objectives of the firm.
- Levels of competitive strategy.
- Environmental scanning.
- Industry analysis.
- Strategic positioning.
- Formulation and implementation of competitive strategy.
- Resource-based theory and the value chain.
- Change management and force-field analysis.
- Competitive strategy and globalisation.

At the outset, it is important to appreciate that competitive strategy and strategic choice are completely constrained in perfectly competitive markets. As products are homogenous in such markets, each firm has identical costs and technologies and every firm is a *price-taker* (see Chapter 6 for details). There are no strategic decisions for managers to take other than to follow the very same decisions as every other firm in the industry. In reality, very few firms are pure price-takers and often firms have a number of cost structures and technologies available to satisfy consumer demand. In other words, competitive advantage depends upon managers formulating and implementing appropriate corporate and business-level strategies.

Learning outcomes

This chapter will help you to:

- Appreciate the meaning of *competitive strategy* and *competitive advantage*.

- Recognise the different levels of strategy within a firm, namely *corporate*, *strategic business unit* (SBU) and *functional levels*.

- Understand the importance of effective *environmental scanning*, at both the macro and micro levels, in the pursuit of competitive advantage.

- Identify how competitive advantage can be achieved through effective industry analysis using Porter's *five forces model*.

- Grasp the importance of *strategic positioning* in terms of cost and differentiation strategies.

- Understand how competitive strategies are formulated and implemented based on the *classical* (*traditional*) approach to strategic decision-making.

- Recognise other approaches to strategic decision-making including the notion of *emergent strategies*.

- Appreciate the nature of the *resource-based approach* to strategic decision-making with its emphasis on the firm's *core competencies* and *distinctive capabilities*.

- Identify the role of the *value chain* in the determination of competitive advantage.

- Grasp the importance of *change management* and the usefulness of *force-field mapping* as a means of determining the key drivers and restrainers relevant to the achievement of change within the firm.

- Comprehend the importance of *globalisation* in competitive strategy.

- Identify the significance of *Porter's diamond* in exploring competitive advantage at the international level.

- Recognise the limitations of the traditional *structure–conduct–performance paradigm* in the context of achieving competitive advantage.

The meaning of competitive strategy

Competitive strategy is concerned with how management formulate and implement strategies to maximise the firm's competitive advantage in the competitive environment. More formally:

Competitive strategy is defined as the search for appropriate corporate-level and business-level strategies to achieved *sustained competitive advantage*.

Note the emphasis in this definition on 'sustained' competitive advantage. Many firms are able to achieve a temporary competitive advantage by, for example, cutting costs or launching a new product but, eventually, the advantage gained is eroded as competitors react or the market changes.

Competitive strategy is, in essence, concerned with the nature of competition within the market place. To understand the meaning of competitive strategy requires management to address three fundamental questions, namely:

- *Where* should the firm compete?
- *What* products and services should the firm compete with in the market?
- *How* can the firm gain sustainable competitive advantage?

It is vital that management have answers to these questions in order to ensure that a clear competitive strategy is developed and that the strategy is effectively implemented and integrated across the various *functional strategies* of the firm, involving marketing, finance, personnel, information technology, etc.

Mission and objectives of the firm

The starting point in designing an appropriate competitive strategy is to identify the firm's *mission and objectives*.

- The *mission* – a similar concept is the *vision* – of the firm encapsulates the firm's overall values and general aspirations.
- *Objectives* set out precisely the quantitative or qualitative goals through which the firm's mission is to be achieved.

For example, the firm's mission may be to become the global market leader in its industry. The objectives might include, first, becoming the major supplier in the domestic market by a particular date, then second, becoming the dominant player in the North American market and, finally, achieving global dominance by a specified future date. Objectives might also be set in terms of profitability, productivity levels, quality of service and customer satisfaction targets, etc. – all of which may be necessary to achieve global competitive advantage.

Firms often have *mission statements* setting out their overall values and aspirations. They may also publish some details of their short-term, medium-term and long-term objectives. Such information is published both for internal and external consumption. Internally, it is important to convey such information to motivate and direct staff at all levels. Externally, the information provides a statement of intent to the firm's external stakeholders, notably shareholders, lenders and suppliers. These statements also send signals to the firm's competitors and potential competitors and customers.

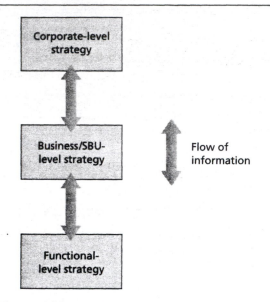

Figure 11.1 Levels of competitive strategy

Levels of competitive strategy

Strategy is formulated and implemented at three main levels within larger organisations, as illustrated in Figure 11.1.

Corporate-level strategy is concerned with the development of strategy for the entire organisation, including all of its operational subsidiaries and divisions. Responsibility for strategy at this level rests with the main corporate-level board.

Each separate business within the organisation will have its own specific strategic decisions to be made in order to achieve specific objectives relating to each part of the overall business. Such parts of the organisation are often referred to as 'strategic business units' (SBUs). An SBU may be concerned with supplying a particular product or range of products, employing a particular technology, or supplying a particular market segment or markets. *Business-level (SBU) strategy* should, of course, follow from and be consistent with the overall corporate-level strategy. For example, if the corporate-level strategy is focused on delivering high-quality customer service and satisfaction then a business level (SBU) strategy which failed to achieve high customer satisfaction would be inappropriate.

Functional-level strategy deals with decision-making at the operational level of the organisation involving the various departments of marketing, finance, personnel, operations, R&D, etc. Once again, the strategies at this level should be complementary to the strategies at the business level and at the corporate level, otherwise the strategic direction of the organisation is likely to become confused leading to reduced competitive advantage.

Environmental scanning

In designing appropriate competitive strategies at the corporate, business and functional levels it is essential that managers pay full attention to the external environment facing the firm. This requires what is referred to as *environmental scanning*.

Environmental scanning involves identifying and evaluating external drivers of change affecting the business at both macro and micro levels.

- *Macro-environmental analysis* is concerned with identifying external trends relating to political, economic, social and technological developments which are likely to impact on the firm.
- *Micro-environmental analysis* focuses on the nature of the competitive environment of the firm at the industry or market level.

Macro-environmental analysis is usually carried out using a *PEST analysis* – reviewing the main *p*olitical, *e*conomic, *s*ocial and *t*echnological factors which are currently impacting on the firm and which are likely to do so in the foreseeable future. Once this has been undertaken, managers can assess the *opportunities* and *threats* facing the firm and evaluate the firm's *strengths* and *weaknesses* in this context – giving rise to a so-called *SWOT analysis*.

By contrast, micro-environmental analysis is concerned with the firm's positioning within its own industry (or industries) and markets in order to assess the factors which determine profitability. This level of analysis is often undertaken using what is known as the Five Forces Model, as developed by Michael Porter of Harvard University.

PEST analysis is discussed more fully elsewhere within this book (see pp. 319–20). Although we introduced the concept of the Five Forces Model in Chapter 1, it is now dealt with in more detail, under the heading of *industry analysis*.

Industry analysis

Figure 11.2 highlights the Five Forces which impact upon profitability within an industry. Each of these forces must be assessed in some considerable detail if a firm is to be in a position to develop an effective competitive strategy. To give management some guidance in conducting a Five Forces analysis, Michael Porter has provided sets of questions under the headings of each force which should be addressed. The checklists set out below have been developed and revised on the basis of Porter's original questions.

The bargaining power of buyers

This force is concerned with understanding how much leverage a firm's buyers (customers) have in determining the price of the product or service offered for sale. The checklist of questions may be grouped under three sub-headings:

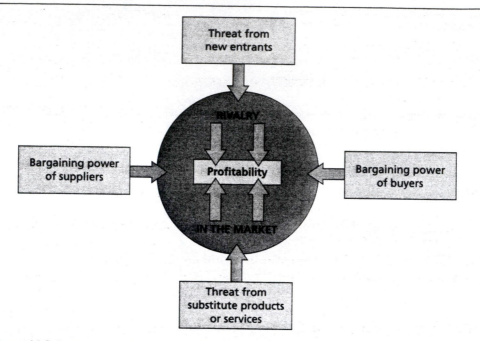

Figure 11.2 Porter's Five Forces Model

Source: Adapted with the permission of The Free Press, a Division of Simon & Schuster, Inc., from *Competitive Strategy: Techniques for Analyzing Industries and Competitors* by Michael E. Porter. Copyright © 1980, 1998 by The Free Press.

(a) Intrinsic leverage

- How many buyers are there in the market?
- Has buyer concentration been increasing or decreasing?
- How well informed are buyers about the firm's costs?
- What substitute products or services exist which buyers can or could consider using?
- Is there evidence of buyers operating together (e.g. buyer groups or associations)?

(b) Price sensitivity

- How large are buyers' purchases of a particular product or service compared to their total spend?
- Is there any brand or company loyalty?
- How different are competing products or services?
- How does product or service quality affect buyer performance?
- How profitable are buyers from the viewpoint of the firm?
- Do buyers need to receive any incentives to buy?

(c) Buyer purchase criteria

- What are the buyer purchase criteria (BPCs)? Why will customers choose one particular product or service rather than another?

- Are there 'minimum' standards or requirements that need to be met?
- Can the BPCs be ranked (high, medium, low)?

The bargaining power of suppliers

This force is concerned with the degree of competition amongst input suppliers which determines the availability and price of inputs to the firm. Key questions here are:

- What are the main purchased inputs?
- What percentage of total costs does each input account for?
- How many suppliers are there?
- How differentiated are suppliers?
- How easily can the firm switch from one supplier to another?
- How often does the firm switch suppliers?
- Can the firm backward integrate (i.e. take ownership of suppliers)?

The threat from potential new entrants into the market

This force is concerned with the degree of 'market contestability' or the extent to which firms are able to enter the market and compete for customers. Key questions concern:

- How much does it cost a new entrant to get into the industry in terms of:
  - capital?
  - access to inputs, e.g. staff?
  - advertising?
  - experience or learning curve?
- How important are economies of scale?
- How easy is it to access distribution?
- How easily or how often do customers switch?
- Have there been any new entrants recently into the industry?
- Is retaliation likely against new entrants (by existing players)?
- How differentiated are competitors?

The threat from substitute products or services

This force is concerned with the extent to which existing products or services can be substituted by new product or service innovation and focuses on issues concerning:

- What substitutes exist or may be introduced which could replace existing products or services?
- What is the relative cost or benefit to users of each product or service?
- What are the costs of switching from existing to new products or services?

- What are the current trends in usage for existing products or services which might determine the potential for customers to switch?
- What is driving current usage and substitution trends?

The degree of competition (rivalry) in the market

This force is concerned with understanding the nature and impact of rivalry amongst *existing* firms in the market place. Key questions which arise are:

- What is the industry growth rate?
- Who are the main players in the market?
- What are the market shares of existing firms in the market?
- What percentage of the market is controlled by the top 2, 5, 10 firms?
- How have market shares been changing over time?
- How committed is each player to the business based on:
  - core business (yes or no)?
  - percentage of revenue and profits?
  - historical reasons for commitment to the business?
  - personal attitudes of senior management?
  - current actions or signals?
- How diverse or similar are competitors?
- What is the role and importance of branding?
- Is there over-capacity in the industry?
- What is the ratio of fixed to variable costs?
- What exit barriers exist?
- How differentiated are the competitors?
- How much brand or company loyalty exists?
- How easily can buyers switch from one firm to another?
- What product or market strategies are competitors following in terms of:
  - product or service design?
  - image?
  - market position?
- Is there evidence of price competition?

Porter's Five Forces Model produces a useful framework for assessing the firm's positioning in the market place. It allows managers to formulate views about the relative power and importance of buyers, suppliers, rivals, new entrants and new products or services. A clear appreciation of the impact of each force on overall profitability is critical in order for managers to focus attention on the most important determinants of competitive advantage. It also leads to an appropriate assessment of the firm's *strategic positioning* in the market place.

Strategic positioning

Strategic positioning involves the firm in identifying what competitive stance it should take in the market. Today, most firms operate in a number of different markets. An electrical goods supplier such as Sony supplies computers, televisions, video recorders, DVDs and camcorders, to name but some of its major products, and to related but different markets. Therefore it is a major abstraction to talk about a *firm* and *its market*. Firms are usually made up of a number of business units with different products aimed at different markets. Equally the notion of an industry runs into similar difficulties when analysing competition. It can be difficult to define the *boundaries* of an industry. Mercedes and Daewoo are operators in the world car industry, but they are not necessarily direct competitors in any meaningful sense. Competition is ultimately defined by consumers' perceptions – does the consumer see the firms' products as substitutes when making expenditure decisions? A substitute is something the consumer perceives as meeting the same need.

Substitution is the key to competition and one way of expressing this, as we saw in Chapter 2, is in terms of *cross-price elasticity*. Cross-price elasticity of demand relates to the proportionate change in demand for one product to a given proportionate change in the price of another product. Where products are readily substitutable by consumers, there will be a relatively *high* and *positive* cross-price elasticity. For example, the prosperity of a glass bottle manufacturer may be affected less by other members of the glass industry (companies in the industry which do not manufacture bottles are of no significance) and more by producers of alternative drinks containers, namely metal can and plastic bottle suppliers.

Only after the nature of the competition is defined and the market clarified can a worthwhile *competitive strategy* be developed, because only then can it become clear what level and type of competition exists and how competitive advantage can be achieved.

Porter has suggested that there are two *generic strategies* for gaining competitive advantage, as was initially discussed in Chapter 1:

- *Low-cost producer.* A firm can aim to be the *low-cost producer* thereby earning higher profits to reinvest in the business or to undercut the competition on price.
- *Product differentiation.* A firm can develop *differentiated products* (through innovation and marketing) and possibly charge premium prices.

In the case of a low-cost strategy, it is important that the consumer does not perceive the product or service to be of such a low quality that it is no longer attractive to purchase. Also, firms competing solely on cost remain exposed to even lower-cost producers who in time entice customers away with lower priced or higher-quality substitutes.

Both low-cost and product differentiation strategies can be associated with narrow or broad product areas or markets. This determines the degree of low-cost or product differentiation *focus* adopted by the firm. In general terms, it should be noted that a product-differentiation focus is likely to protect a firm from competition more

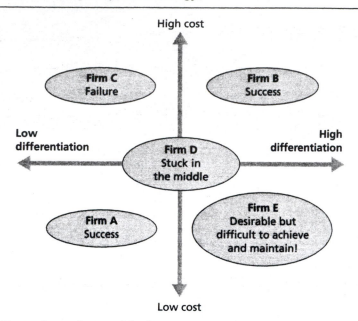

Figure 11.3 Strategic product positioning

successfully than a low-cost focus. This is because, while other firms might successfully compete on cost, they may find it much more difficult to compete in terms of product differentiation. For example, no other car producer can differentiate in the market place by adopting the brand name Mercedes.

According to Michael Porter, failure in competitive markets is often associated with being 'stuck in the middle' achieving neither low cost nor differentiation. In Figure 11.3, Firm A, despite an undifferentiated product, has competitive advantage because of low production costs, while Firm B also has competitive advantage despite high production costs because of product differentiation. Firm C, however, is almost certainly destined for failure because it provides a product which is undifferentiated and is produced at high cost. Firm D is 'stuck in the middle' without a clear focus on cost or differentiation and hence lacks a clear competitive position in the market place.

Finally, a positioning with high differentiation and low cost production would clearly provide very significant competitive advantage, shown by the position of Firm E in Figure 11.3. This position is, however, very difficult to achieve and maintain because there tend to be inevitable costs associated with high product differentiation (e.g. branding, advertising, R&D, etc.), leading to higher-cost production.

Study of a number of markets suggests that the above analysis of low-cost and product-differentiation focus strategies is reasonably robust, although some economists object to the idea that these are either/or strategies. In the past, Japanese manufacturers gained competitive advantage *both* by raising the quality of their goods and at the same time by driving down their costs of production. Even the most highly differentiated producers must keep an eye on costs, especially when they do not appear to add value to the consumer.

Competitive strategy and the banking industry

Forces driving change

The UK economic environment today is very different from that which prevailed in previous decades. Industry of all kinds is in the process of restructuring, and financial services is no exception.

The 1980s saw rapid and, at times, undisciplined expansion of business in all areas of financial services as a result of widespread deregulation. A race for growth in market share was at the top of the agenda for many institutions, resulting, for example, in major acquisitions of estate agency chains and attempts at expansion into Europe by a number of key players. However, following this expansionary climate, the 1990s heralded extensive consolidation and rationalisation, with profitability rather than critical mass the dominant strategic issue facing all organisations in the industry.

Impact of change – restructuring of the industry

As a consequence, the start of the new century is seeing more dramatic changes in the structure of the financial system than there have been in decades. The inevitable outcome is that banks, building societies and insurance companies will be transformed to such an extent that they will cease to be identifiable as separate institutions, with merger and takeover activity remaining at the forefront of the plans of many organisations.

The most visible result will be a continuation of the contraction in the number of retail branches, particularly in the banking sector, due to factors such as continued growth in the use of plastic cards and automated banking facilities, telephone and home banking services, and so on. This downward trend in the number of branches in the UK is clear from the figure below.

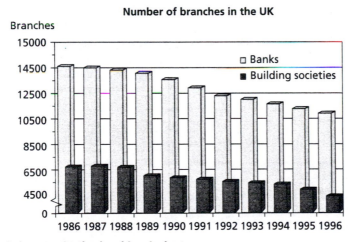

Number of branches in the UK

Branches

☐ Banks
■ Building societies

1986 1987 1988 1989 1990 1991 1992 1993 1994 1995 1996

Structural changes in the banking industry

Source: Annual Abstract of Banking Statistics, British Bankers' Association, London

223

This has already led to considerable rationalisation of staffing levels in the banking sector since the boom years of the late 1980s. It is likely that further rationalisation will take place until an appropriate mix of skills is achieved to complement the seemingly unceasing explosion of new technology and the growing demands of customers for more personalised and competitively priced services.

Today we are seeing the impact of this in many organisations already, as the traditional roles of branches and staff are being modified to take into account the move away from reliance on profits generated from transactional business (lending and depositing) to greater fee-generating activity.

No part of the financial services industry will be immune from the challenges of such changes in the new millennium.

Source: Edited extract from: Joseph G. Nellis (1998) 'Strategies for staying ahead' in *Chartered Banker*, Vol. 4, No. 6, June.

Activity

(a) Conduct a PEST analysis, identifying the key developments and trends in the wider business environment which will impact upon the financial services sector during the next decade.

(b) Using the Five Forces Model, assess the competitive pressures that are likely to arise within the financial services industry, highlighting the strategic implications.

Whatever product positioning strategy the firm decides to adopt, the strategy will need to be both properly formulated and effectively implemented. We now turn to some of the key principles involved in formulating and implementing strategies.

Formulation and implementation of competitive strategy

Competitive strategies need to be appropriately planned and careful attention must be given to ensure successful implementation. Competitive strategies can fail either because they are badly formulated or thought out or because, while the strategy may be appropriate, it is inefficiently or poorly implemented within the firm.

A *classical* (i.e. *traditional*) approach to strategy analysis involves the key steps set out in Figure 11.4. Essentially, this approach views strategy as a process of clear stages between setting the mission and goals of the firm and achieving this mission and the goals. Since the process is a series of progressive steps, it is sometimes referred to as a 'linear' approach to strategy.

However, it is more fashionable today to see strategic decision-making as a much more complex and less linear process and incremental rather than totally planned. In this view of strategy, strategic outcomes are the product of both purposeful formulation and implementation and unintended and emergent stages. This more modern approach is summarised in Figure 11.5, which is based upon the writings of Henry Mintzberg.

Mintzberg's approach, which is often referred to as a *processualist* view of strategy, recognises that some elements of a planned strategy are abandoned or disregarded as

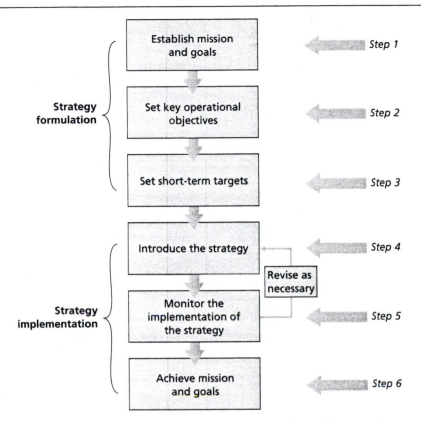

Figure 11.4 Strategy formulation and implementation – classical approach

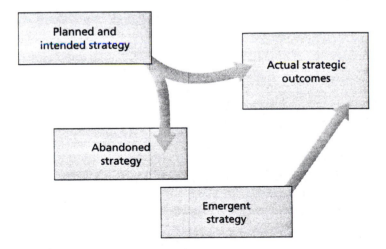

Figure 11.5 Mintzberg's emergent strategy

the external environment of the firm changes or because of changes within the internal management of the firm, e.g. changes in the relative power and influence of groups of managers. At the same time, some elements of a firm's strategy emerge or evolve in response to these environmental changes and due to changes in the internal 'politics' of the firm (depending on whose view counts within the management hierarchy!). As a result, strategic outcomes are the product of, in part, planned and intended strategy and, in part, the emerging strategy over time.

Other approaches to strategy formulation and implementation emphasise the importance or role of social and cultural values in strategic decision-making. For example, the strategy process in firms in South East Asia may be very different to the strategy process in North American firms because of differences in social and cultural values (e.g. regarding the importance of profit-making as a business objective versus family and corporate loyalty). Cultural differences can also help to explain differences in strategic decision-making in highly structured and bureaucratic firms (e.g. General Motors) and smaller and flatter businesses, between the public and private sectors and between 'for profit' and 'not-for-profit' firms, e.g. charities. Culture – or 'the way we do things around here' – is therefore important at the national and firm levels.

Resource-based theory and the value chain

Whatever particular approach to strategy is adopted, necessary attention must be paid to the internal resources of the firm. The competitive strategy adopted will be constrained by the firm's *core competencies* and *distinctive capabilities* (see pp. 113–14). In other words, a resource-based approach to strategy requires the matching of internal capabilities to the needs of the external environment. For example, management may recognise the advantages of investing and producing in China as part of a globalisation strategy, but may lack the necessary resources to operate successfully in this complex market. In such circumstances, the firm would need either to adopt a different strategy altogether and abandon its aspirations to produce there or to acquire the necessary resources (e.g. through takeovers, mergers or joint ventures).

Figure 11.6 illustrates how the internal resources of the firm lead to organisational capabilities that feed into strategic decision-making in order to achieve sustained competitive advantage. The resources of the firm can be categorised as:

- *Tangible* – financial or physical resources.
- *Intangible* – technology, reputation and culture of the firm.
- *Human* – specialised skills and knowledge, motivation and personal interaction.

It is the task of management to identify the valuable resources within the firm and to combine them successfully to achieve maximum competitiveness. In doing so, it is necessary for management to understand the firm's *value chain*.

When a firm considers its core competencies and distinctive capabilities it should pay attention to the nature and form of its *value chain*. Porter's value chain was set out in Chapter 4. This analysis is concerned with the different stages of the production of a

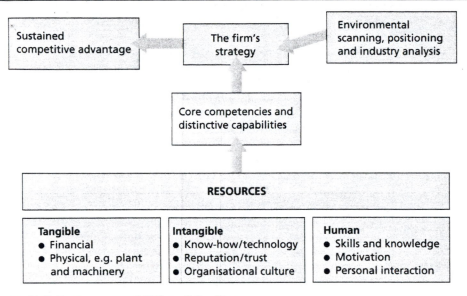

Figure 11.6 Resource capabilities of the firm

good from initial inputs to after-sales service. At each of the stages in the production process, value should be created rather than destroyed. It is ultimately out of surplus value that profits are derived. Therefore, appropriate attention to maximising value and minimising costs in the value chain is a key consideration in achieving sustained competitive advantage, alongside issues of strategic positioning and the resource base.

Change management and force-field analysis

One of the most important issues in strategy implementation is the achievement of changes in *strategic direction* – often referred to as *change management*. Existing technologies, traditions within the firm and the firm's culture (values, customs and practices) all reinforce the existing ways of working. This makes implementing significant strategic change costly and time consuming. Although managers readily accept the need for organisational change, the forces against change *within* organisations can be formidable. The forces *for* and *against* change within any organisation can be analysed using a *force-field mapping*. An example of a force-field mapping is provided in Figure 11.7, showing a number of typical forces for and against change within an organisation.

The purpose of the exercise is to identify the blockages to change and to identify how the desired change may best be achieved. Force-field mapping requires the adoption of an effective process within the organisation to identify the most important *forces for change* ('drivers' of change) and *forces against change* ('restrainers'). A change management strategy is more likely to be successful in achieving the firm's objectives if procedures are put in place which seek to maximise the drivers and minimise (or eradicate altogether) some or all of the restrainers.

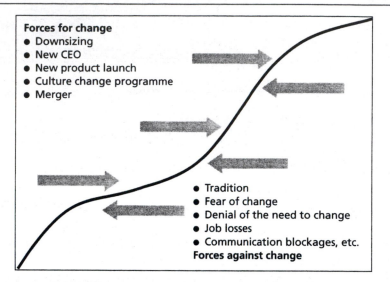

Figure 11.7 Force-field analysis

Competitive strategy and globalisation

For many firms today the competitive environment that they face extends beyond domestic and regional markets to the global market place. Many firms export and import and some have major markets overseas. In other words, their competitive strategies must reflect the global environment in which they operate if sustained competitive advantage is to be achieved.

Globalisation is concerned with the development of competition on a worldwide basis, involving large flows of products and services and international capital across national boundaries. In 1990 Michael Porter extended his analysis of the competitive advantage of firms to an explanation of the competitive advantage of nations. He asked why some countries had performed well (notably Japan), sweeping the competition aside, while others appeared to have lost out in world markets (notably the United Kingdom and the United States). Although the 1990s were associated with a sharp slowdown in Japan's economic development and a speeding up of economic activity in the USA, Porter's analysis is still of great interest. Porter argued that four broad attributes of a nation determined its economic success. These are illustrated in Figure 11.8 (the figure is often referred to as Porter's 'diamond'). This 'diamond' shapes the economic environment faced by firms and either promotes or impedes the creation of competitive advantage. The four attributes are as follows:

- The *quantity* and *quality of factors of production* (e.g. skilled and educated labour force and the economic infrastructure) – i.e. factor conditions.

- The *nature of the demand for products* (especially a demand for high-quality goods which requires domestic producers to improve quality) – i.e. demand conditions.

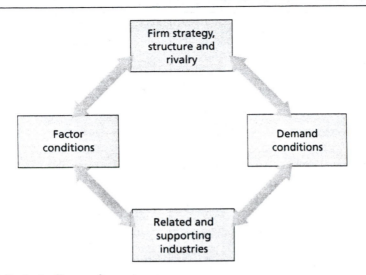

Figure 11.8 Porter's diamond

Source: The Competitive Advantage of Nations by Michael E. Porter. Copyright © 1990 The Palgrave Press, London.

- The *existence of related and supporting industries* which are internationally competitive and help reduce production costs.
- *Firm strategy, structure* and *rivalry*.

While all four attributes are important, the last one is of particular interest in the context of this chapter on competitive strategy and competitive advantage. Porter's central message is that tough domestic rivalry (competition) breeds international success. Although the current fashion is to talk about firms operating 'globally', this does not rule out domestic competition. Indeed, Porter argued that Japan's success in international markets from the 1960s onwards lay in having not one dominant supplier in an industry, but numerous competing suppliers of high quality products. By the late 1980s there were nine car manufacturers, fifteen TV manufacturers, twenty-five suppliers of audio equipment and fifteen camera producers in Japan. Porter argued that the force of domestic competition and the battle to survive in the home market generated the search for high-quality products at low cost in Japan. Competition was also the spur in Japan and elsewhere which lay behind the rapid technological change of recent decades.

In certain circumstances competitors may gain through joint R&D projects and in some industries only one domestic supplier may be able to operate close to minimum efficient scale (e.g. aircraft manufacture). Therefore, Porter's analysis does not rule out altogether industry consolidation through mergers and takeovers or firm alliances such as joint ventures. It does, however, serve as a timely reminder of the importance of successful competition for economic success and counsels against hasty mergers and alliances aimed at defending the domestic market. The central message of Porter's analysis is that with globalisation the successful domestic producer is one that is also successful in world markets.

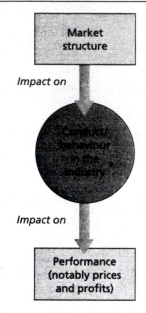

Figure 11.9 The structure–conduct–performance paradigm

Concluding remarks

Much of the approach to competition in the economic literature is still based on the *structure–conduct–performance* paradigm – see Figure 11.9. This is based on the idea that the structure of the market (namely, the number of suppliers and their market shares) determines the conduct or behaviour of management, and that this in turn affects the performance of the industry in terms of prices, profits, etc.

This approach to decision-making implies that managerial conduct is simply a function of market structure. The principles set out in this chapter have gone beyond this limited approach by recognising that sustained competitive advantage requires appropriate competitive strategies and that management choose from the range of strategies available.

Once the nature of the competitive environment in which the business operates is determined, an appropriate competitive strategy has to be formulated so as to win over the customer. This strategy should be based on a 'competitive analysis', which involves a consideration of customer demands, product developments, the firm's core competencies and capabilities and the strengths and weaknesses of competitors, alongside their likely response to any competitive move (for a discussion of competitive moves see Chapter 9, which deals with strategic decisions in oligopoly markets). Ultimately, as we have seen, two broad product positioning strategies usually exist – competing on *cost* (a lowest-cost approach) or a *differentiation focus* – though they are not necessarily mutually exclusive. Also, since products go through life cycles and industries change, it is important to appreciate that what is the most appropriate strategy in any one period may not be the best for another. This places the emphasis on effective *change management* so as to keep the firm's strategy aligned with the needs of the changing external environment.

Overall, strategy formulation and implementation will rarely, if ever, simply be a routine matter. It will normally involve complex judgements, alongside economic analyses of the firm's external environment and internal resource capabilities.

In the next chapter we provide a fuller discussion of the different pricing strategies that a firm might adopt as part of its competitive positioning. This aspect of strategy is dealt with separately because appropriate pricing is fundamental to the long-term survival of the business and encapsulates many of the most critical aspects of competitive strategy.

Key learning points

- **Competitive strategy** is concerned with a search for appropriate corporate-level and business-level strategies to achieve sustained competitive advantage.
- A competitive strategy should address three fundamental questions:
  - **Where** should the firm compete?
  - **What** products and services should the firm compete with in the market?
  - **How** can the firm gain sustainable competitive advantage?
- The **mission** encapsulates the firm's overall values and general aspirations usually captured within a formal **mission statement**.
- The **objectives of the firm** can be distinguished from the mission because they are usually a more precise set of goals that can be measured quantitatively or qualitatively.
- Competitive strategy is usually formulated and implemented at three levels within large organisations: **corporate, business (SBU)** and **functional levels**
- **Environmental scanning** involves analysing the firm's external environment and is often undertaken using a **PEST** framework.
- **PEST analysis** is concerned with detailing the main political, economic, social and technological factors impacting or likely to impact on the firm.
- A **SWOT analysis** looks at the firm's internal strengths and weaknesses in the context of the external analysis of the opportunities and threats which it faces.
- Determining an appropriate competitive strategy requires managers to understand the nature of the industry and markets in which the firm operates – often achieved using **Porter's Five Forces Model** as the framework for analysis.
- The **Five Forces Model** helps us to identify the impact on profitability of:
  - the power of buyers;
  - the power of suppliers;
  - rivalry in the market place;
  - the threat from new entrants;
  - the threat from substitute products or services.

- **Strategic positioning** involves the firm identifying what competitive stance it should take in the market place – two generic positioning strategies are usually recognised, namely being the **low-cost producer** or pursuing **product differentiation**.

- Successful **strategy formulation** and **implementation** involve a number of steps ranging from clearly establishing the mission and goals of the firm to successful implementation of the strategy.

- Approaches to competitive strategy formulation and implementation range from the **classical approach,** based around formal planning and rational analysis, to approaches which more clearly recognise that strategy decision-making is less predictable and more incremental and are based, for example, on the culture and values of the firm, internal decision-making processes as well as responses to continuous changes in the external environment – leading to the notion of an **emergent strategy**.

- A **resource-based theory** of the firm identifies the critical importance of the firm's internal resources in determining competitive scenarios, including the firm's **core competencies** and **distinctive capabilities**.

- **Value chain analysis** centres on a study of the different stages in the production process and the extent to which value is created at each of these stages.

- Sustainable competitive advantage requires the firm to adapt to changes in the external environment – **change management** is concerned with bringing about this adaptation and managing the forces for and against change within any organisation (perhaps analysed using a **force-field mapping**).

- **Competitive advantage** today is concerned with assessing and adapting to dynamic forces in the global economy – **Porter's diamond** is a useful mechanism for assessing competitive advantage under conditions of globalisation.

- The traditional **structure–conduct–performance paradigm** in business economics suggests that market structure determines the conduct and behaviour of management and, in turn, industry performance. The study of competitive strategy in this chapter emphasises a much more complex set of factors that impact upon and underpin the behaviour of management when formulating and implementing strategy.

Topics for discussion

1 Select an organisation with which you are familiar and prepare a detailed report to help the management establish an appropriate competitive strategy for the next few years.

2 Conduct a Five Forces analysis of the retail food industry in your home country. Assess the impact of each of the Five Forces on the industry's profitability over the next five years.

3 What do you understand by the term 'Porter's generic strategies'? Critically appraise Porter's arguments concerning generic strategies.

4 To what extent is strategic change within firms determined more by the organisation's internal culture and politics than by the external environment?

5 What political, economic, social and technological factors are most likely to cause turbulence in the external environments of the following industries:

(a) International passenger airline travel?
(b) Oil exploration?
(c) Global management consultancy?
(d) Global telecommunications?

6 Undertake a force-field mapping for a firm with which you are familiar, detailing the key internal drivers and restrainers which it is likely to face in the context of management's attempts to increase profitability.

7 Consider the limitations of the classical approach to strategy. To what extent does the idea of emergent strategies improve our understanding of the competitive strategy process?

8 It is often said that the 'dot.com' bubble burst at the start of this millennium. Using the tools and concepts set out in this chapter, prepare some reasoned arguments to explain why the strategies of many 'dot.com' companies were misconceived.

9 Critically appraise Porter's 'diamond' as an explanation of competitive advantage in the global economy.

10 Why may the 'structure–conduct–performance' model be inadequate as a tool for determining the level of profitability across industries?

12 Understanding pricing strategies

Aims and learning outcomes

Choosing the appropriate price to charge for a good or service is one of the most important challenges facing management. Set the price too low and the result will be overwhelming demand and frustrated customers, much as existed in the former Communist bloc countries where governments kept prices low for social and political reasons. Set the price too high and there will be stockpiles of unsold goods and a probable cash flow crisis. Determining the right price to sell all of the production profitably and to leave no unsatisfied customers – that is to say, customers who want to buy at that price – is like trying to balance a set of kitchen scales – too much weight on either side will cause the scales to tilt. Not surprisingly, therefore, economists call the price which exactly matches the supply and demand for a particular good or service, the *equilibrium price*.

This chapter considers the various approaches to pricing that managers might adopt. In particular, we examine the following topics:

- Price determination and managerial objectives.
- Generic pricing strategies.
- Pricing and the competitive environment.
- The marketing mix and the product life cycle.
- The economics of price discrimination.
- Pricing in multi-plant and multi-product firms.
- Peak-load pricing.
- Two-part tariffs.
- Pricing policy and the role of government.

In practice, the 'best' or 'correct' price to charge must remain uncertain ahead of actual production and sale. Market conditions are in a constant state of flux which produces uncertainty and therefore pricing decisions are inevitably subject to a margin of error. However, so that the basic techniques of optimal pricing strategies can be fully analysed, the assumption is made in this chapter that pricing decisions are being made with full or complete information available to managers about consumer demand, competitors' reactions, supply costs, etc. – in which case there can be no margin of error. This is highly unrealistic but it provides a useful starting point for an understanding of best-practice pricing.

Learning outcomes

This chapter will help you to:

- Understand that price serves three functions: (a) as the basis on which firms generate revenue; (b) as a rationing device in markets; and (c) as a signal to producers to alter supply.

- Identify how price is determined in a competitive market economy through the interaction of demand and supply.

- Realise that pricing decisions are driven by particular managerial objectives (such as profit maximisation, sales revenue maximisation, etc.).

- Distinguish between different generic pricing strategies adopted by firms, namely: *marginal cost pricing, incremental pricing, breakeven pricing* and *mark-up pricing*.

- Appreciate the nature of various *pricing strategies* in markets with differing degrees of competition.

- Recognise that pricing strategies require the integration of pricing decisions into a wider *marketing mix*, taking into account non-price as well as price factors that affect demand.

- Appreciate how pricing decisions may vary over the *life cycle* of a product or service in the market.

- Understand the economics of *price discrimination*.

- Grasp the complexities introduced into pricing decisions where *multi-plant* or *multi-product* production occurs and the nature of *transfer pricing*.

- Identify when *peak-load pricing* and *two-part tariff pricing* may be appropriate.

- Recognise the ways in which *government affects prices* in market economies today.

Price determination and managerial objectives

Prices serve three broad functions.

- Prices raise revenue for the firm.
- Prices act as a rationing device.
- Prices indicate changes in the wants of consumers and induce suppliers to alter product accordingly.

All managers will be familiar with the first of these functions. Price (*P*) multiplied by the quantity sold (*Q*) determines the firm's total revenue (TR) and, depending on production costs, ultimately the firm's profitability.

$$TR = P \times Q = PQ$$

The second broad function is of equal importance in market economies. Price rations out the available production amongst consumers on the basis of their ability and willingness to pay. Chapter 2 contained a detailed discussion of consumer demand, in which the importance of the demand relationship and of price elasticity was emphasised. At any given time consumers are likely to buy more of a good or service only if its price is reduced (assuming the other conditions of demand such as income and tastes stay unchanged). Later in the chapter we will consider factors other than price that may influence buying decisions, in a discussion of the 'marketing mix'.

The third role of prices is to send a signal to producers that consumer demand is changing, thereby inducing producers to change their levels of output to reflect new consumer preferences.

Since price is an important determinant of the amount sold, it follows that it also determines the amount supplied. When demand rises and price increases, the firm will attempt to cash in by increasing supply, *ceteris paribus*. In turn this means that investment projects are directly dependent on the expected prices of the product concerned. In deciding whether to invest, some judgement must be made regarding likely prices over the lifetime of the investment project (or at least over the period in which cash flows are being discounted to present values – see Chapter 14). Once the decision has been taken to produce and the investment has been installed, pricing is more tightly constrained. Hence, the greatest freedom in choosing a pricing strategy comes at the *planning stage*. It should, therefore, be an integral part of investment planning. In general terms, the higher the expected price, the bigger the output the firm will want to supply and hence the larger the investment in capacity that the firm will be willing to make. Just as demand is a function of price, so too is supply, as we saw earlier, in Chapter 4.

Price determination

As we discussed in detail in Chapter 6, in a competitive market economy price is determined by the forces of demand and supply.

A good example is the market for colour TVs, where there are a number of suppliers – Sony, Hitachi, National Panasonic, Philips, Toshiba, etc. – each attempting to sell to consumers. The consumer may, of course, not buy on the basis of price alone (though no doubt many do), but for the present we shall concentrate on price as the principal determinant. Figure 12.1 illustrates the general market situation for one of these suppliers, e.g. Sony. The demand curve for Sony TVs will be downward sloping, implying that more sets will be sold as the retail price is reduced (for simplicity we talk about the demand and supply of Sony TVs, but in reality there will be different demand and supply curves for different models of Sony TVs reflecting different consumer perceptions and different supply costs). The demand curve has also been drawn to suggest that the demand for Sony TVs is price elastic (price sensitive) around price P_1. In practice, Sony's marketing will be aimed at creating 'brand loyalty', but we shall assume that many consumers will still switch to competitors' products if the relative price of a Sony TV is increased. Therefore, when Sony raises its prices, say from P_1 to P_2, and competitors' prices are unaltered, the expectation is that the demand for Sony TVs will fall sharply from q_1 to q_2, confirming a high price-elasticity. Equally, if Sony reduces the price of its

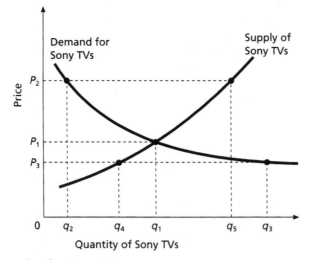

Figure 12.1 The market for Sony TVs

sets, say from P_1 to P_3, and its competitors do not follow suit, the demand will rise sharply from q_1 to q_3 again showing that demand is price-elastic in this price range.

The supply curve in Figure 12.1 shows how many TVs Sony will be willing to supply at each price (for an explanation see Chapter 4). Provided that price is set at P_1 the market will be cleared – hence P_1 is the equilibrium price. All consumers wanting to buy Sony TVs at that price are able to obtain them and Sony is left with neither unsatisfied demand nor unsold stocks. Clearly, if the price is established above P_1, Sony will want to sell more TV sets as it is now more profitable to do so, but consumers will be less willing to buy them. The result is unsold sets (i.e. stocks). Equally, if Sony reduces the price below P_1, demand will expand, but given that supplying is now less profitable, output will contract, leaving unsatisfied customers. For example, the unsatisfied demand at price P_3 will be quantity shown by the distance q_4q_3. The amount of unsold stocks at price P_2 will be the distance q_2q_5.

In practice, the conditions of demand, such as consumer perceptions of the product or competitors' prices, and the conditions of supply, notably costs of production and technology, are likely to change regularly if not continuously. This means that an equilibrium price is likely to be short-lived. Equally, producers usually lack adequate information about the market to predict the equilibrium price precisely. Nevertheless, we can usefully view the competitive market as an evolving process in which firms attempt to position their products and set their prices so as to sell their outputs profitably and expand their businesses. Any changes in the conditions of demand and supply must lead to a new equilibrium price in the market – see Chapter 5. The firms most successful at responding to price changes are those most likely to succeed over the long term; they carry fewer stocks of unsold products and do not alienate consumers by a failure to supply.

Price and managerial objectives

Pricing is driven by managerial objectives. The precise objectives pursued by management ultimately determine the kind of pricing strategy that is adopted. As we saw in Chapter 10, management might pursue profit maximisation, corporate growth maximisation, sales revenue maximisation, or they might attempt to maximise their own sense of economic welfare (perhaps subject to a minimum profit requirement to keep shareholders contented). Equally, firms may not maximise anything, preferring instead to achieve a satisfactory outcome to a range of objectives (a 'satisficing' policy). In some industries, notably where there are state-run firms, the target could be breakeven or perhaps involve a negative mark-up. That is to say, the price is set so as to produce a politically acceptable rate of loss, the burden of which is borne by taxpayers. Equally, private sector firms may from time to time adopt for short periods a pricing policy which leads to no profits or even losses, perhaps to win market share or to protect a brand during a cyclical downturn in the economy or to fight off a competitor in the market place. Occasionally, products may be used as 'loss leaders' (for instance, to attract consumers into the store, some goods could be priced very low and displayed in the shop window). Firms also need to keep a wary eye on important considerations in the market, such as the state of current demand, the market growth rate, the stage in the product's life cycle, its price elasticity, and the prices set by competitors.

Whatever objective is pursued will have implications for pricing. The firm which endeavours to maximise its profits will adopt a different price to one which is more concerned with maximising its market share or sales (see Chapter 10). This follows from the fact that, in general, firms face downward sloping demand curves. The lower the price the larger the volume of sales and hence the greater the likely market share. By contrast, the more profit-orientated firm will restrict its output to where marginal cost equals marginal revenue, and by so doing maximise the difference between its sales revenue and supply costs.

Generic pricing strategies

In this section we consider the generic pricing strategies that firms might adopt. It is possible to conceive of firms adopting different pricing strategies as competition in the market alters over time, or for different products. The implications for pricing of competition, the product life cycle and multi-product firms are considered later in the chapter.

Four generic pricing strategies are discussed here, namely:

- Marginal cost pricing.
- Incremental pricing.
- Breakeven pricing.
- Mark-up pricing.

Marginal cost pricing

Marginal cost pricing involves setting prices, and therefore determining the amount produced, according to the marginal costs of production, and is normally associated with a profit-maximising objective.

A firm maximises its profits when the difference between total sales revenue and total supply costs is at its greatest. This is equivalent to the output level where marginal cost (MC) equals marginal revenue (MR), as explained earlier in Chapter 3, pp. 71–5.

In a highly competitive market the price charged by a firm in the industry must be identical to the prices charged by the large number of competitors. Hence, the firm faces a perfectly elastic demand curve in the sense that any attempt to price above the market price, even by a very small margin, will result in a total collapse of the firm's sales. This means that when price is set at the market price, the marginal revenue is constant and equal to this price. Therefore, the profit-maximising condition MR = MC results in price being set equal to marginal cost – see Chapter 6, pp. 141–5, for a more detailed explanation. This is the essence of a marginal cost-pricing strategy in highly competitive markets.

In an imperfectly competitive market where products are differentiated sufficiently so that firms can charge different prices (e.g. as in the colour TV market), the demand curve faced by the individual firm is downward sloping, as is the marginal revenue curve. The condition of MR = MC still determines the profit-maximising output but now price is set above marginal cost (see Chapters 7, 8 and 9 which deal with pricing in monopoly, monopolistically competitive and oligopoly markets respectively). In such markets price is *set above* marginal cost rather than *equal* to it.

Incremental pricing

Marginal cost is the change in total cost from expanding output by *one* unit, while marginal revenue is the incremental revenue arising from the sale of this extra unit. However, because of indivisibilities in many industries' outputs it is not realistic to talk about one unit output changes. Instead, the issue is whether to produce a further batch of output or open another shop or bank branch, etc. Also, in many instances the firm's demand and cost conditions at the margin may not be known precisely and they may be too costly to discover. In such cases, a form of marginal cost pricing called *incremental (cost) pricing* might be adopted.

Incremental pricing deals with the relationship between *larger changes* in revenues and costs associated with managerial decisions. Proper use of incremental analysis requires a wide-ranging examination of the *total* effect of any decision rather than simply the effect at the margin.

It will be appreciated that fixed costs are irrelevant to both marginal cost and incremental pricing in the short run since these costs are 'sunk' and therefore do not change with output (unless the firm is already working at full capacity and therefore output can only be increased by investing, i.e. by incurring more fixed costs). The decision to supply then simply reflects whether the change in total revenue (TR) is greater or less than the change in the variable costs (i.e. the marginal or incremental costs from raising output).

An example of incremental pricing would involve, say, an airline which has to decide whether to add to or cancel flights according to whether the increase in TR from a flight covers the incremental cost of the flight. If fixed costs (the aircraft, management overheads, etc.) are ignored and the costs of keeping a plane parked at an airport are reflected in the opportunity costs of not flying, it may make sense to fly a route even where losses result. In other words, it makes sense to fly when a *smaller* loss will result from flying than not flying. Hence, in such a situation, the airline's operating rule would be, in effect, 'does the flight at least cover its marginal or incremental costs?' Where a flight more than covers these costs, though it still operates at an overall loss, it will make a useful contribution towards the fixed costs.

This example raises the related subject of the allocation of (fixed) *joint* or *common costs*. Joint costs arise when by-products are produced in fixed proportions (see p. 257). In this case all costs of production are common and there is no economically sound method of cost allocation between the products. Common costs, by contrast, are expenses that relate to management overheads and the like and should be apportioned across the products produced on an economically sound basis according to their contribution to the production of each output. In modern accounting, rules exist for allocating common costs (notably through methods such as *activity-based costing* that attempt to apportion common costs across goods and services according to their contribution to production) so as to minimise distortion of resource allocation. Nevertheless, some firms still cling to broader brush rules, such as allocating overheads according to a product's share in total revenue or total output. This is not simply an academic issue. The extent to which a product bears fixed costs affects its total costs and hence its viability. Loading higher common costs onto high-revenue earners or high-volume products (successful products!), produces smaller margins for these products, and may even lead to their eventual withdrawal from the market. Once these products no longer exist, the common costs must then be allocated to the remaining products, putting their viability in jeopardy. The lesson is that all of the pricing strategies detailed in this chapter rely for their success on sound internal accounting and costing systems.

Breakeven pricing

Breakeven pricing requires that the price of the product is set so that total revenue earned equals the total costs of production.

Using simple arithmetic, we can calculate the breakeven output. For instance, if we are told that the unit sale price of a good is $20 per item and that the variable costs are $9 per unit with fixed costs of $330,000, the breakeven sales level is:

At breakeven:

total revenue (TR) = total costs (TC)

total revenue (TR) = fixed costs (FC) + variable costs (VC)

Therefore:

$$\$20 \times \text{quantity } (q) = \$330,000 + \$9 \times q$$
$$20q = 330,000 + 9q$$

Hence:

$$11q = 330,000$$

$$\therefore \quad q = \frac{330,000}{11}$$

$$\therefore \quad q = 30,000 \text{ units}$$

Two breakeven points are illustrated in Figure 12.2. The breakeven output, q_1, (where TR = TC) is lower than that at which profit is maximised, i.e. q^*, while breakeven output, q_2 involves a higher level of output. (Note: since MC is the slope of the TC curve, profit maximisation is where the slopes of the TC and TR curves are the same, i.e. where MC = MR.) If the managerial objective is to maximise sales revenue subject to a breakeven constraint, then we would expect output q_2 to be chosen rather than q_1.

Like marginal cost pricing, breakeven pricing requires knowledge of the firm's cost and demand conditions. It should also be noted that breakeven analysis is much more complicated for multi-product firms, a subject to which we turn later in the chapter.

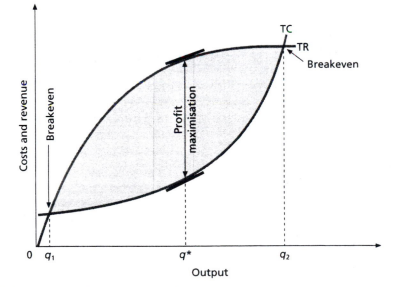

Figure 12.2 Pricing strategies compared

Mark-up pricing

Mark-up pricing is similar to breakeven pricing, except that a desired rate of profit is built into the price (hence this pricing is associated with terms such as cost-plus pricing, full-cost pricing and target-profit pricing).

The particular mark-up will be what management consider appropriate or necessary to achieve a profit which satisfies their shareholders. This might be equivalent to what the capital could earn if employed elsewhere in its next best alternative use (i.e. a 'normal' profit). For example, if the next best use generates a rate of return of 8% and the investments are of equal risk, then the capital would have to earn at least 8% in its current use or it would pay to invest elsewhere. It should be appreciated that mark-up pricing tends to lead to stable prices when costs are not changing much and to price increases at times of inflation, when nominal (money) costs are rising.

When following a mark-up pricing strategy, a firm needs to estimate the average variable cost of producing and marketing the product. This requires some view as to the level of output. It is common practice to take an assumed level of output based on an expected capacity working, such as 80%. On the basis of this output, variable costs can be calculated. The average variable cost is then added to the average fixed cost to calculate the average total cost. A mark-up figure is then added which represents the required profit margin.

In notation:

$$m = (P - AC)/AC$$

where m is the mark-up, AC is the average total cost, and $P - AC$ is the profit margin.

The price, P, is then given by:

$$P = AC(1 + m)$$

For example, assuming a desired mark-up of 25%, the average variable cost per unit at $10 and the fixed cost per unit at $6, such that AC = $16, the selling price, P, is equal to $16(1 + 0.25) = $20.

A strategy of mark-up pricing tends to be simpler to implement than marginal cost pricing because management do not need to know the relevant marginal revenues and costs. Also, to the unwary it appears to guarantee the desired profit! However, it is unlikely to generate *optimal* profit-maximising prices since this pricing strategy ignores demand completely. There is no guarantee that the output produced will all be sold at the particular mark-up price or even that the output is sufficient to satisfy demand. This highlights the risk associated with pricing based on an arbitrary profit margin rule. Prices may not necessarily clear the market and there is the further danger that the price set may be undercut by the competition. Like all cost-based pricing strategies, it could be argued that mark-up pricing starts at the wrong point. It will usually make more

Pricing strategies in different sectors

Choice of pricing strategy

An effective pricing strategy is essential to the achievement of a firm's objectives. Firms adopt a whole range of pricing strategies with the choice in any time period dependent on the particular circumstances facing the firm. Many variables affect pricing strategy, which itself has to be integrated with other strategies (marketing, human resources, finance, operations management, etc.) to achieve the firm's changing objectives.

The table below illustrates that there are notable differences in pricing strategies between different sectors. Most of the terms used in the table have been defined in this chapter, but there are two exceptions: *complementary* and *psychological pricing*. Complementary pricing arises when a new product is launched alongside the existing ranges with the new addition priced as part of a 'bargain package'. The whole range is now priced slightly cheaper to encourage consumers to buy and become loyal to the now extended range. Psychological pricing refers to the common practice in the UK, Denmark, Germany and elsewhere of using 9s and 4s in prices (e.g. £2.99 and €6.49).

The key points to note from the table are:

● Competitive and cost-plus pricing are the dominant strategies across all sectors.

● Psychological and complementary pricing are more popular in the retailing sector than in the other sectors.

● Breakeven pricing is most commonly found in the manufacturing sector.

● Loss-leading is most common in the services sector.

Activity

With reference to the table, provide possible explanations as to why different sectors adopt different pricing strategies.

Percentage of companies adopting each of the following pricing strategies

Strategies	Services	Manufacturing	Retailing	All Sectors
Competitive	84	93	80	84.7
Cost-plus	59	85	63	63.9
Penetration	25	13	23	22.7
Complementary	14	6	28	15.3
Profit maximisation	9	6	23	11.1
Loss leading	12	6	0	8.8
Psychological	4	0	30	8.1
Breakeven	8	11	0	7.0
Skimming	9	0	6	7.0
Other	7	3	0	5.1

Note: Many firms adopt three or four different pricing strategies at any given time. Research took 100 firms at random. There were 65 firms in the service sector, 16 in manufacturing and 18 retailers. The one primary sector company was disregarded as statistically unreliable.

Source: G. Nichols, 'How do firms "really" price their products?', *Economics Today*, Vol. 6, No. 4, March 1999.

sense for management first to discover the maximum price at which the product could be sold (the price set by competitors?) and then work backwards, determining what costs are permissible to leave an adequate profit margin *at that price* (this is known as 'backward cost pricing').

In practice, most firms which claim to use a mark-up pricing policy also consider the implications for demand. If they didn't they would not survive for long! Although mark-up pricing is still widely used, there is evidence that firms are becoming much more flexible in their pricing strategies. In an increasingly competitive environment, mark-ups are being varied to reflect demand conditions. This leads to prices which are closer to those which would be determined by marginal cost pricing. Where firms apply higher mark-ups to products which are less price sensitive (i.e. less price elastic), mark-up pricing approximates to the profit-maximising rule.

Pricing and the competitive environment

The nature of the market in which the product is sold will have a major influence on the pricing policy adopted. As we saw earlier markets can be conveniently divided into four broad kinds:

- Perfectly competitive markets.
- Monopoly markets.
- Monopolistically competitive markets.
- Oligopoly markets.

We discuss briefly below the appropriate approach to pricing in each of these market forms.

Pricing in perfectly competitive markets

*In perfectly competitive markets the firm is a **price-taker**.*

That is to say, each firm's product is indistinguishable from the products of all other competitive firms and therefore the consumer buys only on the basis of price. Commodity markets come closest to this type; for instance, tin producers tend to have to accept the going world price for their tin, otherwise they are undercut by other suppliers. Where perfect competition exists, management has no discretion regarding the individual firm's pricing strategy. Survival decrees that the output must be sold at the market price, which is the price charged by competitors.

Pricing in monopoly markets

*In a monopoly situation, the firm is a **price-maker**.*

As markets become less competitive, i.e. as the degree of monopoly power of the firm increases, suppliers have more discretion when setting prices. Raising the price will reduce demand but not completely destroy it. Price elasticity of demand now becomes an important consideration in price setting. The less price elastic (i.e. the more insensitive) the demand for the product, the greater will be the firm's market power and the greater the management's freedom to set prices. Hence, the monopolist has more freedom than a firm in a competitive market to determine its price. The actual price set by the monopolist will depend upon what objective is being pursued. For example, a sales maximisation strategy, perhaps to preserve the monopoly position by deterring new competitors, implies a lower price than a short-term profit maximisation goal. One type of pricing strategy is commonly referred to as *entry-limit pricing*. This form of entry deterrence involves setting a low price to ward off possible market entrants. For example, a firm may, in the short run, set its price to cover only its variable costs, its fixed costs being sunk; while firms considering market entry will take into account their total costs (variable plus fixed costs) when deciding whether to enter the market.

Pricing in monopolistically competitive markets

Perfectly competitive and pure monopoly markets are rarely found – most firms are subject to some competition but to a lesser extent than would arise under perfect competition. Some firms are faced with a large number of competitors producing highly substitutable products, such that an attempt to achieve product differentiation is a dominant feature of the market place. This situation, referred to as monopolistic competition (see Chapter 8), means that firms cannot sell all they want at a fixed price, nor would they lose all their sales if they raised prices slightly. In other words, these firms face downward sloping demand curves.

In monopolistically competitive markets, firms put considerable marketing effort into segmenting their markets in an effort to reduce price competition.

Pricing in oligopoly markets

In some circumstances firms may make pricing decisions without explicitly taking into consideration competitive reactions. While this may be appropriate for some industries, it is not applicable in an oligopoly market where an individual firm's actions are very likely to provoke a competitive response.

In oligopoly markets it is crucial to know how competitors are likely to react to a price change. Will they follow suit or not? Or will they react in some other way, for example with an extensive advertising budget to preserve their market share? Oligopoly markets, therefore, reflect various competitive strategies in which price may or may not be the critical variable. As observed in Chapter 9, oligopoly markets are also prone to *collusion* and the formation of cartels (if firms co-operated in setting their prices uncertainty faced by firms would be reduced) and to *price leadership*. In markets where there is a price leader, pricing policy involves one firm establishing the market price which the other firms use as a benchmark when setting their prices.

Oligopoly markets are imperfectly competitive and price leadership is but one possibility in pricing strategy. For example, when Ford raises the price of its popular Focus range of cars, it knows that demand will be affected but it can also be confident that because of brand loyalty sales will not totally collapse even if its competitors do not raise their prices. Also, firms in oligopolistic industries may price to forestall new entrants. For instance, if Ford suspects that competitors will only be able to supply the Focus-type market at a unit cost of $12,000 because of their level of production costs, the price of the Ford Focus may be set lower to deter entry (this is a form of entry-limit pricing).

The marketing mix and the product life cycle

The marketing mix

Pricing strategies require the integration of pricing into a wider *marketing mix*, which takes into account other factors than price that may determine demand. Some firms may be reluctant to change price because of the uncertain effects on rivals' actions, so the other marketing variables take on added importance. At the same time, research suggests that consumers may only have a vague idea of the price of some products they buy, which appears to relegate the importance of price in demand, though it does not remove it altogether. At the very least, pricing should complement the other factors in the marketing mix.

In developing an effective marketing strategy, marketing professionals draw attention to the importance of the following 'four Ps':

● Product.
● Place.
● Promotion.
● Price.

Together the four Ps determine what is called the 'offer' to the consumer.

Product

The product raises the issue of consumers' perceptions of the product's characteristics. The perceived value or utility to the consumer rather than the supplier's costs of provision becomes the key to pricing strategy, with non-price factors used to increase the perceived value. Whereas breakeven and mark-up pricing emphasise costs as the basis of price, attention to the marketing mix places the emphasis more squarely on demand, with products perceived to be of higher quality or status than the nearest competition attracting 'premium prices'. When the founder of Revlon cosmetics proclaimed that, 'In the factory we make cosmetics, in the store we sell hope!', he was well aware that his marketing success had opened the road to high profit margins.

The economist Kelvin Lancaster has argued that it is the *characteristics* or attributes of a product (or brand) which give utility to the consumer and not the product itself.

For example, different cars are similar in many respects but each model has unique characteristics, such as fuel economy, acceleration, internal space, etc. Lancaster's approach to consumer demand suggests that the consumer's choice between products is best analysed in terms of the utility derived from the individual characteristics the products possess, rather than in terms of the products themselves. This approach is also often referred to as the 'hedonic approach' to demand (stemming from the Greek word *hedone*, meaning 'pleasure').

Place

Place relates to the distribution of the product. How well a product is distributed is important to its success. Hence, successful suppliers put considerable time and resources into distributing the product effectively. Can the product be moved quickly from warehouse stores to retail outlets? Is the product best displayed in supermarkets? Are distribution costs controlled to enable competitive pricing? A complicating factor for producers of a consumer good lies in the growing power of the retailer. A market trend has been the manufacturer's loss of control over his or her own product's marketing at the point of sale.

Promotion

Brands are an important way of differentiating products in the market place and promotion is used to support an effective branding strategy. Product promotion involves effective marketing including the provision of adequate credit (a very important consideration especially for consumer durables) and advertising. Brands with intrinsically average quality but high advertising budgets may achieve premium prices. Advertising shapes consumers' perceptions of the product and if successful increases consumer demand at all prices. Thus more can be sold at a constant price or the same amount at a higher price, leading to healthier margins (i.e. there is scope for *margin management*). There is also some evidence that successful branding and advertising by increasing market segmentation reduce price elasticity. They therefore enable suppliers to gain a *differential advantage* by distinguishing themselves from the competition. In effect, the firm gains a 'quasi-monopoly' position. Market segmentation and differential advantage involve aspects of *product positioning* in the market place, in which price is just one variable contributing to that positioning.

Price

Product, place and promotion all leave their mark on both a firm's demand and cost relationships. Price has to fit with the remainder of the marketing plan because together they determine the product's positioning. For instance, Mercedes and Daewoo both produce cars but if their cars were perceived to be the same by consumers, competition between the two marques would centre on price and Daewoo would gain market share at the expense of Mercedes. The fact that this does not occur is in part a tribute to the marketing of Mercedes cars. Mercedes is popularly perceived to produce cars of high quality and high status and this is supported by the company's skilful marketing. By contrast, the Daewoo is judged to be a mass-produced, functional vehicle and hence it sells more on price. There are no prizes for guessing where the highest profit margin is earned. Over the years, Mercedes has successfully cultivated an image which gives it 'brand loyalty'. The brand loyalty relating to Daewoo is almost certainly much smaller and more vulnerable to competition. Daewoo distributors therefore face a threat from *brand switching* and must price very competitively in order to retain customers.

In the motor industry, price has become a leading indicator to consumers of supposed quality. This is also especially true for services, where what is being bought cannot be easily inspected before purchase. For example, in the marketing of management training courses, high-priced courses are positioned by their providers as high-quality, elitist events. Consumers believe that it is more worthwhile to participate in a highly priced course provided by a leading business school than a cheaper alternative at the local technical college – rightly or wrongly!

To the usual four Ps of marketing can be added three further Ps relevant to the marketing of services (as opposed to physical products). They are: customer *perceptions* (based on staff uniforms, company logo, ambiance in restaurants, etc.), *people* (the attitude and quality of the personnel who provide the service) and *processes* (efficiency of service delivery, lack of queuing, ease of payment, etc.). The positioning of a good or service in the market has major implications for pricing policy. There is no point in marketing a high-quality product and then selling it at a down-market price. Equally, a product perceived to be of low value must be priced accordingly. Where a firm is competing for consumers and wants to earn high profit margins, it must try to ensure that its and its competitors' 'offers' as far as possible are not compared on price alone. Figure 12.3, which is a reformulation of Figure 11.3 presented earlier, illustrates the trade-off between quality and price when marketing goods and services. Firms can trade successfully in quadrant A (high perceived quality and high price) or in quadrant B (lower perceived quality matched by low price). Both represent sustainable competitive positions because price is appropriate given the quality of the product or service offered (and assuming the positioning strategy is supported by appropriate marketing). Quadrant C (high perceived quality and low price) is difficult to achieve because maintaining high quality usually involves more costly production methods and higher marketing costs. In contrast, quadrant D (low perceived quality and high price) is most

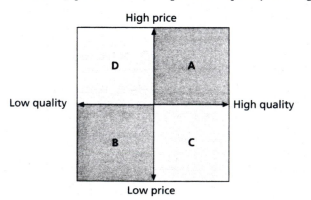

Figure 12.3 Product positioning and customers' perceptions

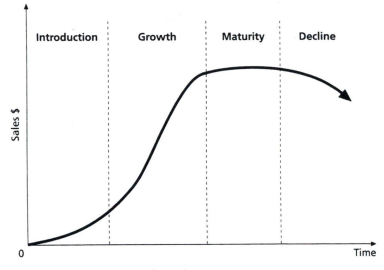

Figure 12.4 Phases of the product life cycle

likely to be associated with business failure. For example, in the 1960s, the British motorcycle industry collapsed in the face of competition from cheaper and higher quality (more reliable) Japanese motorcycles.

The product life cycle

A further important factor in designing a pricing strategy is the *product life cycle*. Products usually undergo life cycles covering the period from their inception in the market to their eventual withdrawal. A typical life cycle is illustrated in Figure 12.4.

The notion of the product life cycle raises important issues for pricing since it implies that there may be a case for adopting different strategies at each stage of the cycle. Notably, when a product is launched the following two broad pricing strategies may be adopted, (1) 'promotional pricing' and (2) a 'price skimming policy'.

(1) 'Promotional' or 'penetration pricing' occurs when the price is set low to enter the market against existing competitors, attract consumers to the new product and gain market share.

There is, therefore, a more rapid diffusion of the product in the market and as output rises unit costs fall. Penetration pricing makes most sense where unit costs fall dramatically and quickly as output rises due to economies of scale and experience curve effects.

At the early, introduction phase of the product life cycle initial losses from pricing low might be financed in multi-product firms by mature cash-generating products ('cash cows'). In single-product firms the strategy requires, however, sympathetic and strong-nerved investors and bankers willing to finance the launch of the new product.

249

By contrast, in the growth phase of the product life cycle, price may have ceased to be a primary consideration for consumers, other aspects of the marketing mix having taken over in promoting the product. In the maturity phase, there is less point in pricing to gain market and the emphasis instead is likely to be on *profit contribution*. Lastly, in the final phase of the product life cycle, as the product declines in popularity, prices may have to be cut to maintain demand and hence margins shrink.

(2) A 'skimming policy' arises when price is set high initially to earn high profits before competition arrives or to cover large unit costs in the early stage of the product life.

This policy will be attractive where a new product has a monopoly position in the market for a short period. Producers attempt to maximise the present value of the future profit stream by charging a monopoly price in the early years of the product's life and a lower price later once competitive pressures begin to emerge. The high initial price under a skimming policy implies a lower rate of growth of sales than under a penetration pricing strategy. Hence, it will be more appropriate where unit production costs do not decline significantly as output rises. A skimming pricing strategy is also associated with industries that have high product development costs, such as in the pharmaceutical industry where high research and development costs are incurred before a product can be sold in the market.

Whichever pricing strategy is adopted for a new product, it is important to recognise that the price set at the outset will have implications for longer-term pricing, especially in the case of consumer products. Consumers may relate their perceptions of the product to the initial price. It may be difficult to alter price significantly once consumers associate the product or service with a particular price level.

In the same way as there are product life cycles, there are also *market-power life cycles* with a firm's ability to price high varying over time depending upon its competitive position in the market for its entire production range. When a firm is fighting to survive, prices will reflect this and will be aimed at increasing immediate cash flow. This may also be so in the recession period of a trade cycle.

The economics of price discrimination

Many producers sell their products at different prices to different customer groups for various reasons. For example, quantity discounts may be given for bulk purchases or to retain a valued customer. Prices may reflect differences in transport costs to different markets. Also, where demand fluctuates with the seasons or time of day, marginal supply costs may justify some form of peak-load pricing (considered fully later in the chapter). In all these cases price varies essentially because the costs of supplying different consumers vary or the nature and cost of the product varies. However, economists reserve the term *price discrimination* specifically to identify only those circumstances where costs of supplying different consumers do not vary but different consumers do exhibit different responses to prices; i.e. where there are different price elasticities. Such a situation justifies differential pricing for the *same product*.

Definition of price discrimination

Price discrimination represents the practice of charging different prices for various units of a single product when the price differences are not justified by differences in production/supply costs.

The critical factor for successful price discrimination is the ability of the firm to control its own prices. In other words, there must be imperfect competition such that an effective barrier exists to stop consumers from being able to buy the product at a low price and to on-sell at a higher price (hence the reason why low-priced airline tickets are usually non-transferable). Also, there must be different price elasticities of demand in the various markets. These differing elasticities may reflect different preferences, information and perceptions of the product, and incomes and tastes. Where different price elasticities exist there is scope for price discrimination. An obvious example is the pricing of seats on public transport. The cost of transporting a child is the same as transporting an adult but the demand elasticities are likely to differ.

Price discrimination, in practice, is a matter of degree. Thus, three possible strategies may be identified. These are referred to as:

- First-degree price discrimination.
- Second-degree price discrimination.
- Third-degree price discrimination.

We examine the underlying principles of each of these below.

First-degree price discrimination

At the extreme, it is possible to conceive of a producer who sells each unit of output separately, charging a different price for each unit according to each consumer's demand function. Imagine a situation where, if a consumer is willing to pay $1.50 for a chocolate bar then that is what he or she is charged. Another consumer willing to pay only $1 would be charged that amount, and so on. Since all consumers pay for each unit of consumption a price which just reflects the marginal utility (i.e. satisfaction) they get from the product, the result is the transfer of all of the *consumer surplus* to the producer (for an explanation of consumer surplus see p. 31). Although attractive to the producer, price discrimination of this intensity would require the producer to have a very detailed knowledge of each consumer's demand function. In practice, consumers will be very reluctant to reveal the maximum amount they are willing to pay. At the same time, the transaction costs of administering a perfectly discriminatory pricing policy (i.e. setting individual prices for individual consumers) are likely to be prohibitive. Most companies therefore settle for charging, say, two or three prices in their tariff schedules as rough

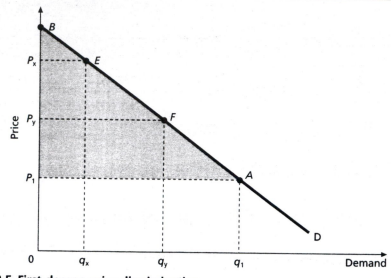

Figure 12.5 First-degree price discrimination

approximations to differences in consumer demand across their range of customers (see below).

To further illustrate the nature of first-degree price discrimination, Figure 12.5 represents the demand for a firm levying charges for a toll road. If all travellers using the road are charged a standard price, P_1, the firm earns a total revenue equal to the area $0P_1Aq_1$. At this price, the consumer surplus is represented by the shaded area P_1AB. By charging each traveller the maximum amount that each is individually willing to pay to use the road, this consumer surplus is converted into *producer surplus* of the firm. For instance, traveller q_x will be charged P_x, traveller q_y will be charged P_y, etc.

Second-degree price discrimination

Second-degree price discrimination involves charging a uniform price per unit for a specific quantity or block of output sold to each consumer. This policy extracts part but not all of the consumer surplus and is found where demand can be metered, as in the pricing of gas, water and electricity, or usage monitored, for example where computer processing time or photocopying machines are rented. For example, in Figure 12.5 setting a price of P_x for consumers on the demand curve from B to E; price P_y for consumers on the demand curve from E to F; and price P_1 for consumers on the demand curve from F to A, allows the firm to extract some, though not all, of the consumer surplus.

Third-degree price discrimination

Most frequently found is *third-degree price discrimination*, which simply involves charging different prices for the same product in different segments of the market.

The markets may be separated in the following ways:

- *By geography* – as when an exporter charges a different price overseas than at home.
- *By type of demand* – as in the market for, say, butter where demand by households differs from the bulk purchase demand of large catering firms.
- *By time* – with a lower price charged for off-peak periods (as in the case of seasonal charges for hotel rooms).
- *By the nature of the product* – as with private dental care with differential pricing, where if one patient is treated he or she is unable to resell that treatment to someone else.

By charging differential prices to the various market segments for the same product, the so-called *price discriminator* will be able to increase total profits above the level that would have existed in the case of uniform pricing. This is because the price discriminator is soaking up as much consumer surplus as possible given the third-degree price discrimination strategy (and hence transforming it into *producer surplus* – i.e. supernormal profits).

The economics of third-degree price discrimination are illustrated in Figure 12.6. Here, two sub-markets for a product are shown, market A and market B. For convenience, the demand curves are shown as straight lines. The demand elasticities are different in the two markets. If the firm wishes to profit-maximise, then it will sell each unit of output it produces in that sub-market where the revenue added (the marginal revenue) is greatest. In other words, it will allocate its output between the sub-markets until the marginal revenue earned in both is equal. There is then no further incentive to reallocate production between the sub-markets.

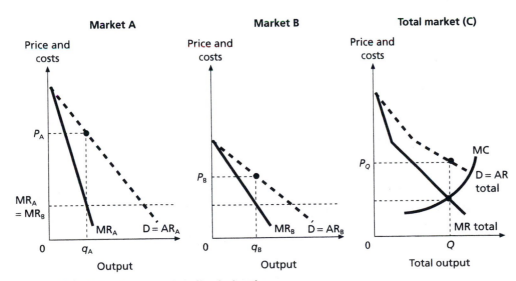

Figure 12.6 Third-degree price discrimination

Application 12.2

E-commerce and price discrimination

The growth of e-commerce

The business-to-consumer (familiarly referred to as B2C) e-commerce market is estimated to be growing at a rate of 200% per year. More than three quarters of retailers are selling online with online revenues accounting for around 10% of total sales and over 7% of manufacturers' revenues in the USA. Business is expected to rise sharply in the coming years with the increased use of new web-based technologies.

Implication for price discrimination

The emergence of e-commerce markets is expected to have important implications for discrimination in pricing structures in the future. This is highlighted by a report in the *Washington Post* newspaper that Amazon (one of the largest internet-based retailers) charged different customers different prices for identical DVD players. It was suggested in the report that regular visitors to the Amazon site were charged up to a fifth more than new users (we take no view on whether this was true or not).

The arrival of consumer e-commerce, coupled with the vast amount of consumer-specific information now available to retailers and marketing companies, increases the likelihood of first degree price discrimination. Consumers will increasingly be offered the products they want at prices which they are likely to be willing to pay. There are two key reasons to support this prediction:

● Online consumer shopping catalogues can be personalised to match the buying patterns of individuals.

● Online 'menu costs' (or price list changes) are practically zero, hence online retailers can quickly adjust their prices cheaply and efficiently to match consumers' willingness to pay.

Activity

Do you believe that first-degree price discrimination will become a widespread phenomenon in the consumer e-commerce market? Explain your answer and consider reasons for continuing barriers to such discrimination.

The combined marginal revenues in the two sub-markets are shown in segment C of the figure, along with the marginal cost curve, which relates to the production of the total output, and the total market demand curve. As usual, profit is maximised where MR = MC, which in this case is at an output $Q(= q_A + q_B)$. This output is allocated across the sub-markets so that the marginal revenue is equal in both. Hence, q_A is sold in market A at a price P_A per unit and q_B is sold in market B at a price P_B per unit. No other allocation of the total output between the sub-markets will achieve a higher profit than that which is earned here.

For all forms of price discrimination to be successful it is essential that arbitrage cannot occur. Otherwise, consumers buying the product at a lower price could capitalise by selling it in the higher-priced market. This would boost the supply in this market and reduce prices until they were eventually equal in the two markets and the scope for arbitrage ceased to exist. For example, if consumers in market B were able to buy the product at price P_B and resell it in market A at price P_A, they would make a tidy profit. This profit would continue until the extra supply in market A through reselling reduced price in market A and the lower supply left in market B raised prices there. Eventually, if there were no costs associated with this arbitrage operation (e.g. transport costs), prices in the two markets would equalise, at price P_Q, with price lowered in market A and raised in market B. We can now understand why car manufacturers are keen to prevent the re-import of cars sent to foreign markets for sale at lower prices!

Before adopting a price discrimination policy it is important to consider wider effects. The practice of British motor manufacturers selling cars more cheaply elsewhere in the EU than in the UK has led to consumer resentment and a recent investigation by the UK's Competition Commission. Firms contemplating price discrimination need to consider not only whether it is technically feasible, but also its wider impact on both their image with consumers and the threat of state intervention.

Pricing in multi-plant and multi-product firms

So far we have been primarily concerned with the pricing of one product by a firm which appears to produce its output in one location. In practice, however, most firms of any real size produce a range of products and on more than one site. This raises interesting questions for pricing and for the resulting distribution of production across the firm. The existence of more than one production point also facilitates price discrimination between different geographic areas served. This will be especially so where the production occurs in different countries and national markets are protected by import controls.

The multi-plant firm

> Where a firm's output of the *same* product is produced on more than one site, the profit-maximising output rule that marginal supply costs must equal marginal revenue, is unchanged, but in this case this marginal cost is the *sum* of the separate plants' marginal costs and production must be allocated between the plants so that the marginal supply cost at each plant is identical.

This situation is illustrated in Figure 12.7, where the firm is assumed to have two plants, A and B, which both produce an identical product. Profit maximisation occurs where the firm's total output Q_T is divided between the two plants in the proportions q_A in plant A and q_B in plant B. This follows since profit maximisation requires cost minimisation and if MC_A did not equal MC_B costs could be further reduced by shifting some

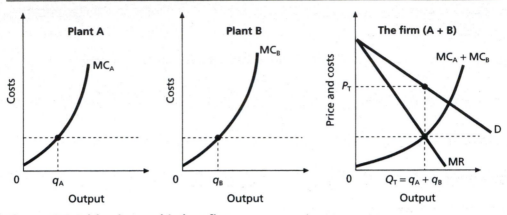

Figure 12.7 Pricing in a multi-plant firm

output from the higher-cost to the lower-cost plant. The output of the two plants is sold into the market at price P_T.

Where the firm produces multi-products on different sites the production and pricing problem is more complicated.

The multi-product firm

When producing and pricing a product, the multi-product firm has to take into consideration not only the impact on the demand for that product of a price change (its own price elasticity of demand) but the impact on the demand for the other products in the firm's product range (the relevant cross-price elasticities). In other words, pricing now involves obtaining maximum profits from the full product range rather than from the individual products.

Such *full-range pricing* means that the firm may be content to earn little or no profit on certain products, preferring to use them as 'loss leaders' to attract consumers who will then (they hope) buy the higher-profit items. This has long been the strategy of some supermarkets. They may decide to make very slim margins on basic goods such as bread and potatoes, which because they are widely sold in other shops have a relatively high price elasticity, making their profits on higher-margin (i.e. lower-demand elasticity) goods, such as items sold at the delicatessen counter. Contrast this with the attitude to pricing in the former British motorcycle industry where the objective was to earn healthy profits from each model, and the price was set accordingly. The British industry's market disappeared within a decade as Japanese competitors undercut the UK producers' prices. The Japanese goal initially was market share and longer-term profits from selling a full product range.

In multi-product firms the products can be complementary, such as Kodak which sells cameras and film, or substitutes, such as Procter & Gamble's detergents. In both cases demand for the products is interrelated. This means that profit maximisation requires that the output levels and prices of the products produced are determined *jointly* (in some firms the marketing departments of the various products may compete to increase efficiency and drive down costs, but this risks ignoring the high cross-price elasticities with damaging results for overall profitability).

In addition to demand interdependencies, multi-product firms may have production interdependencies. The most obvious example relates to the production of by-products. In such cases, complex 'joint-costing' rules must be introduced and *economies of scope* recognised (i.e. cost reductions resulting from supplying together two or more products). Products can be produced jointly in fixed or variable proportions. The classic example of production in fixed proportions is beef and hides which are produced equally. Hence, the costs of supply cannot be meaningfully apportioned between the two outputs – the costs are truly joint. In some other forms of production the different products (e.g. different bank accounts) are produced together but their output can be varied (more savings accounts, fewer cheque accounts). In this case, there needs to be some formula for allocating *common costs* (e.g. head office and branch costs). Various accounting methods exist for allocating common costs, as referred to earlier (see p. 240).

Where products can be produced in variable proportions joint and common costs must be apportioned. Following an appropriate apportionment, the profit maximisation rule requires that the marginal revenue from each output is equated with its own marginal cost, but with due recognition also given to any demand interdependencies.

Transfer pricing

Large-scale multi-product, multinational firms are often decentralised by being split into semi-autonomous divisions, with each responsible for its own price and output decisions as well as profit performance. However, decentralisation brings with it problems of internal resource allocation, one aspect of which is the pricing of products which are transferred between divisions. This gives rise to the need for *transfer pricing* and the problem of determining the transfer price which maximises overall company profits. For example, it may be possible for one division to raise its own reported profits by raising the transfer price but this may be at the expense of profits made by the receiving division. In such situations the general answer to the transfer-pricing problem is that the products being transferred between divisions should be priced at their marginal cost of production. Therefore, the intra-corporation pricing rule mimics that pricing rule appropriate to a competitive market place leading to a similarly efficient allocation of (internal) resources.

It should be noted, however, that multinational corporations may for tax reasons adopt a different internal pricing strategy. When divisions are located in different countries with different tax systems, transfer pricing can be used to redistribute profits between countries in order to minimise the overall tax liability. This could be achieved, for example, in situations where one country, A, has a high profits tax relative to another country, B. By setting the transfer price artificially low in country A, the profits can be realised in country B. It should be noted, however, that under fiscal regulations such arrangements are usually illegal – though they are also difficult for national tax authorities to police.

Peak-load pricing

Where the demand for a product varies over time it can pay to introduce a form of discriminatory pricing called *peak-load pricing*. In this case, the major factor leading to differentiated prices is the differences in supply costs over time, i.e. the marginal cost of supplying the product or service is much lower at off-peak times when there is spare capacity, and much higher at peak times when the capacity is fully utilised leading to congestion. The higher peak-time costs may be due to several factors, as follows:

- **Diminishing returns** and hence higher short-run marginal costs.
- The need to use **more expensive inputs** to satisfy peak-time demand.
- The whole of the **capital costs** of the additional capacity needed to satisfy peak-time demand being attributable to the peak users.
- **Externalities**: for example, rush-hour traffic congestion imposes external costs on other travellers such that the marginal cost to *society* as a whole rises.

Peak-load pricing is used extensively not only in public transport, but in electricity and gas supply, the postal system and telecommunications, and by airlines and hotels that charge more during times of high demand.

When differentiated pricing is introduced in this way some consumers will alter their demand pattern. For example, they may change to travelling off-peak or they might install an off-peak gas or electricity meter. This is desirable as it smoothes out demand thus increasing capital utilisation when there is available capacity and reducing congestion and the need for additional capital investment in peak periods. However, if peak-load pricing causes a large shift in consumer demand, a previous off-peak period could become a peak period. In such cases, prices would need further tuning, perhaps leading to less differentiated pricing and with all users bearing some of the capital costs incurred to meet peak demand.

Figure 12.8 illustrates a simple case where peak-load pricing would be appropriate. Here it is assumed, for simplicity, that the short-run marginal cost (MC) of production is constant at C until the system's capacity is exhausted, at output q^* (with no further output then possible). Two demands are shown – D (off-peak) and D (peak). In the off-peak period there is under-utilisation of capacity and price is therefore equated with marginal cost (= C). In the peak period, however, supply is capacity constrained. At a price equal to marginal cost demand would exceed supply. To ration the available system capacity price should be set at price P (peak). The result is two prices: a lower one set according to short-run MC and a higher one to equate demand to capacity at the time of peak demand. In the long run capacity may be increased, financed by the higher charges on the peak users.

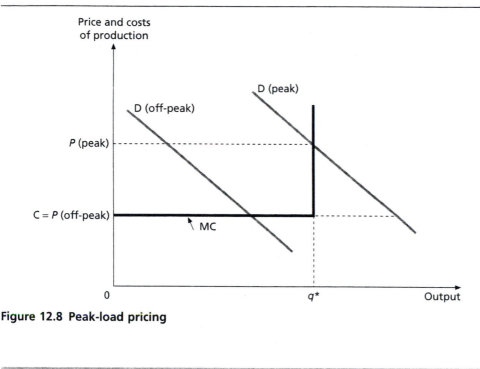

Figure 12.8 Peak-load pricing

Two-part tariffs

Another form of pricing involves a *two-part tariff*.

> A *two-part tariff* is concerned with levying a charge according to the number or volume of the units consumed, plus a fixed charge to cover fixed joint or common costs, usually on a quarterly or annual basis.

This form of charging is common for public utility services such as gas, electricity, water, etc. The volume element of the charge can be established according to the short-run marginal cost of providing additional units of the good or service to the consumer. The fixed element of the charge, which does not vary with consumption, can be set to provide the additional revenues needed so that the firm can cover its total costs of supply (variable plus fixed).

Public utility industries are associated with significant economies of scale and therefore declining long-run marginal costs (LRMC) and long-run average costs (LRAC) – see Figure 12.9. If the volume charge is set according to marginal cost, then the firm would incur a loss; for example, in Figure 12.9, a loss per unit for output at Q_1 and price P_1 shown by the distance X. The fixed charge is calculated to offset such a loss. It should be noted, however, that in practice public utilities often set their fixed and volume charges according to other principles, including the social and political goals of government. For instance, government may decide that high fixed charges and low volume charges are unfair to low users of a service such as pensioners. For this reason,

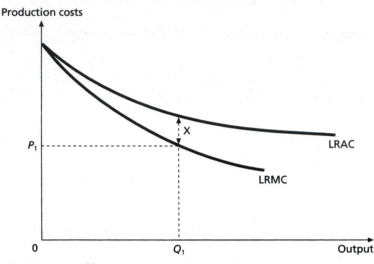

Figure 12.9 Two-part tariffs

the operation of two-part tariffs by state-owned or state-regulated utilities may not even loosely follow the theoretical principles outlined here.

It should also be noted that a more detailed analysis of the economics of two-part tariffs would take into account the effect on resource allocation of levying equal fixed charges on consumers. Such charges might lead some consumers (e.g. poorer users) to disconnect from the system. For this reason economists tend to prefer levying fixed charges according to consumers' elasticities of demand. The so-called *inverse price elasticity rule* suggests that consumers with the more price inelastic demands should bear a higher proportion of fixed charges than consumers with a higher price elasticity of demand. This rule is also sometimes referred to as *Ramsey pricing* after the economist who first proposed it. The rule means that the quantity demanded is least affected by the imposition of the fixed charge. This pricing rule may not, however, be compatible with wider social goals. It does not necessarily follow that those with the higher price elasticity are necessarily the poorer or more needy sections of society.

Pricing policy and the role of government

All market economies have some state intervention in pricing in the form of taxation and subsidies, and direct controls, such as regulations and licensing. Also, in many countries state-owned industries exist at central and local government levels and some decision must be taken on the pricing of their outputs.

Taxes and subsidies

In a private market the price consumers are willing to pay reflects the benefits they receive from marginal consumption. However, in some cases the price consumers are willing to pay may not accurately reflect the true *social* benefits and costs of the consumption, i.e. there are *externalities* (see pp. 321–4), in which case the price could be altered through taxes and subsidies. For example, coal-fired power generation causes major pollution, so it could be discouraged by imposing a pollution tax (based on the principle that the polluter should pay). Equally, in so far as public transport has wider social benefits by reducing congestion on the roads, demand for it can be encouraged by state subsidies to keep prices low.

It is important to appreciate, however, that only some forms of taxation have an effect on the pricing decision. For example, for a profit-maximising monopoly a tax on corporate profits should not affect price or output because neither marginal revenue nor marginal cost is affected. The tax simply removes some of the monopolist's super-normal or excess profits.

Taxes on products do affect prices and outputs. The price to the consumer is raised, which will affect demand depending on the price elasticity of the product. A subsidy has the opposite effect and the price is reduced, though not necessarily by the full amount of the subsidy. Just as the supplier may have to absorb some of the tax to retain demand, so the producer might absorb some of the subsidy (see pp. 128–31).

Direct price controls

Government direct controls on pricing arise out of prices and incomes policies, anti-monopoly and restrictive practices legislation, and other forms of regulation and licensing. The latter have grown in importance in a number of countries in recent years following the privatisation of major public utilities, namely, telecommunications, gas, electricity, water and rail industries in some countries. The monopoly suppliers now operate under authorisations or licences granted by the state and, to prevent the abuse of monopoly power, prices are regulated by the state. Two common methods of economic regulation are:

- Rate-of-return regulation.
- Price-cap regulation.

Rate-of-return regulation involves the state setting a maximum price that the firm can charge consumers according to the firm's costs of production and after allowing for a normal rate of return on investment (it is therefore sometimes alternatively referred to as *cost of service regulation*).

Price-cap regulation sets the firm's maximum price according to the economy's rate of inflation less an amount to reflect anticipated efficiency gains by the firm. This means that the *real* price is adjusted by the efficiency targets set by the regulator. Unlike under *rate-of-return* regulation, the firm now has an incentive to pursue further efficiency gains, over and above the targets set, because, during the life of the price cap, there is no limit on profitability. By contrast, rate-of-return regulation may provide little incentive for management to reduce production costs because costs are passed through to consumers in higher prices. Also, because the allowed rate of return is based on the capital stock, rate of return regulation is prone to over-investment (higher investment increases the capital stock and hence the firm's total profitability provided the rate of return is above the cost of financing the investment).

Rate-of-return regulation is ultimately an indirect form of price regulation because the price charged is an important variable in determining profits; whereas the price cap is a direct form of price regulation. Whether the price is directly or indirectly regulated, regulation tends to distort competition away from price competition to some other aspect of the marketing mix. In the airline industry, for example, where prices in the past have been heavily regulated, competition has often focused on the level of service, in-flight catering and movies, speed of the check-in desk, and who flies the most modern aircraft and at the peak demand times. It is generally considered that government price controls distort the operation of normal competitive markets and therefore should be kept to a minimum.

Pricing in the public sector

Although many of the issues raised so far, notably peak-load pricing, are relevant to the public sector, pricing in the public sector raises certain unique issues. To begin with, the public sector may well have different objectives since it is concerned with the wider *public interest* rather than profits. If this is so, state enterprises should set their prices with an eye to the *marginal social benefits* (MSB) from the additional output and the *marginal social costs* (MSC) of producing that output. The MSB reflects the benefits to the immediate consumer plus any external benefits (wider social gains) and the MSC is calculated to reflect not only the normal marginal costs – wages, raw material costs, etc. – but any external (social) costs, such as environmental effects. By pricing in this way, a public utility maximises the difference between the social benefits of production from the output and the social costs of producing that output. The result, however, may be losses which have to be met out of taxation, which in turn may distort employment, investment and spending decisions. Also, subsidies imply a welfare transfer between payers of taxes and the recipients of subsidised services. Why should all taxpayers subsidise rail users? Is the implied income redistribution equitable?

On the basis of the 'public interest' rule, the public sector should invest and expand output when the marginal social benefits of expanding output exceed the marginal social costs (MSB > MSC), and should contract production when the marginal social costs exceed the marginal social benefits (MSC > MSB). But such pursuit of the 'public interest' depends upon government correctly assessing the public interest (rather than pursuing a short-term political goal) and pursuing it relentlessly. In practice, politicians have tended to interfere with the prices set by state-owned industries even when it has been difficult to perceive a public interest objective. To critics the result has been higher inefficiency in the public sector and lowered managerial morale. A key argument for privatisation of state industries has been the removal of damaging political control and the restoration of commercial pricing. Taxes and subsidies levied by governments may well reflect political goals rather than the pursuit of maximum economic welfare (i.e. production occurs where MSB ≠ MSC).

The fact that prices may reflect political considerations rather than true marginal social benefits and costs is a major weakness of state intervention in pricing. This is likely to be an especially acute problem for government services such as social security, education, health and defence. In such services, usually no price is charged, or it is a nominal charge and all or most funding comes from taxation. For example, in the United Kingdom most medical care is free to the user within the National Health Service (NHS).

Concluding remarks

This chapter has been concerned with pricing policies under differing market conditions. As we have seen, optimal economic pricing requires a full consideration of both demand and cost conditions. Prices based solely on supply costs (with a fixed profit margin) are unlikely to reflect sufficiently the state of consumer demand and hence are likely to lead either to over-supply and thus a build-up of unsold inventories, or excess demand and unsatisfied consumers. We have also seen that there is a case for a more flexible approach to pricing where markets with different price elasticities are supplied or where a peak-load problem exists. The pricing formula also becomes more complex in multi-plant and multi-product firms and where separate charges need to be levied to cover both the marginal cost of the volume supplied and the fixed joint or common costs of providing the service (through so-called *two-part tariffs*). In addition, pricing in the public sector raises its own peculiar problems, associated with the inevitable political pressures that government and public sector managers face. Nevertheless, one common theme has run through the chapter – successful firms in a market economy are those which gain and retain competitive advantage and price remains an important variable in achieving this advantage. In the next three chapters we turn to consider another set of crucial factors in competition, namely the appropriate employment of factor inputs. We start by looking at the underlying principles of the labour market.

Key learning points

- **Equilibrium pricing** is likely to be short-lived since the conditions of demand and supply are likely to change regularly if not continuously. In addition, producers may lack adequate information about the market to predict the equilibrium price precisely.
- **Pricing**, in practice, is driven by managerial objectives relating to factors such as profitability, corporate growth, sales revenue, managerial satisfaction, etc.
- **Generic pricing strategies** may be based on marginal cost, incremental cost, break-even or mark-up pricing.
- **Marginal cost pricing** involves setting prices, and therefore determining the amount produced, according to the marginal costs of production, and is normally associated with a profit-maximising objective.
- **Incremental pricing** deals with the relationship between larger changes in revenues and costs associated with managerial decisions.

- **Breakeven pricing** requires that the price of the product is set so that total revenue earned equals the total costs of production.

- **Mark-up pricing** is similar to breakeven pricing, except that a desired rate of profit is built into the price (therefore this pricing is also sometimes referred to as cost-plus, full-cost or target-profit pricing).

- In **perfectly competitive** markets, the supplier is a price-taker.

- In a **monopoly** situation, the firm is a price-maker.

- In developing an effective **marketing strategy**, marketing professionals draw attention to the importance of the four Ps: product, place, promotion and price.

- With respect to the **product life cycle, promotional or penetration pricing** sets the price low to enter the market against existing competitors and in order to attract customers to the new product and gain market share.

- A **skimming policy** arises when price is initially set high perhaps to cover large unit costs (e.g. R&D costs) in the early stage of the product life cycle or to make higher profits before competitors can respond.

- **Price discrimination** represents the practice of charging different prices for various units of a single product when the price differences are not justified by differences in production/supply costs. Successful price discrimination requires an absence of arbitrage opportunities and differing elasticities of demand in the various markets.

- **First-degree price discrimination** arises in the case of a producer selling each unit of output separately, charging a different price for each unit according to the consumer's demand function. This results in the transfer of all **consumer surplus** to the producer.

- **Second-degree price discrimination** involves charging a uniform price per unit for a specific quantity or block of output sold to each consumer.

- **Third-degree price discrimination** involves charging different prices for the same product in different segments of the market. The market may be segmented by geography, by type of demand, by time, or by the nature of the product itself.

- In the case of a product produced by a **multi-plant firm**, the profit-maximising output rule ($MR = MC$) is unchanged, but in this case the marginal cost is the sum of the separate plants' marginal costs and production should be allocated between the plants so that the marginal supply cost at each plant is identical.

- The **multi-product firm** has to take into consideration not only the impact of a price change on the demand for the product, but also the impact on the demand for the other products in the firm's product range. Pricing policy, therefore, involves obtaining the desired rate of return from the full product range rather than from individual products.

- Decentralisation of large firms brings with it problems of internal resource allocation, one aspect of which is the pricing of products which are transferred between the firm's divisions. This gives rise to the need for an appropriate **transfer pricing** policy and the problem of determining the transfer price so as to maximise overall company profits.

- **Peak-load pricing** involves differentiated pricing which reflects differences in supply costs, given variations in demand for the product over time.

- A **two-part tariff** is concerned with levying a charge per unit according to units consumed *plus* a charge to reflect fixed joint or common costs.

- The **inverse price elasticity rule**, sometimes referred to as Ramsey pricing, suggests that consumers with the more price inelastic demands should bear a higher proportion of fixed charges than consumers with a higher price elasticity of demand.

- On the basis of a **public interest** or **economic welfare maximation rule**, state enterprises should set prices in order to reflect the marginal social benefits from the additional output and the marginal social costs of producing that output.

- **Taxes and subsidies** should be set so as to minimise the damage to resource allocation in the economy. In practice, state policies are determined by a mixture of political, social and economic criteria so economic welfare maximisation is far from guaranteed.

Topics for discussion

1 What are the three main functions of price in a market economy?

2 Citibank has appointed you as a consultant to help in its reconsideration of its charging policy for current (cheque) accounts. You are required to set out the principles of the different approaches to pricing that the bank might adopt.

3 Tophols Travel Company has decided to preserve its profit margin on the holidays it sells by passing on to consumers the full cost of a rise in the air fares it pays. Every holiday will bear an equal mark-up to cover the extra air fare costs. Advise the company on the possible impact of this policy.

4 When DVD players were first launched in the market in the 1990s they were priced much higher than today. How do you explain this? Does it always make sense to price a new product initially at a high price and reduce the price later?

5 Explain why: (a) an electricity generator may charge a lower price for units of electricity after 11pm at night and before 7am in the morning; (b) an airline charges substantially more to fly 'first class' and 'business class' compared to 'economy class'.

6 A water company is currently operating at a loss. It calculates that one way of removing the loss is to raise both its charge per cubic metre for water consumed and its fixed connection charge by 30%. Consider the case for adopting equal or different increases in the volume and connection charges.

7 Give three examples of third-degree price discrimination, highlighting in each case the reasons why price discrimination is possible and the degree to which it is sustainable.

8 Why does it remain possible for European motor manufacturers to sell their car models at different prices in different European countries?

13 Understanding the market for labour

Aims and learning outcomes

In many firms the cost of labour represents a significant proportion of overall production costs. This chapter deals with the factors which determine the amount of labour employed in a firm and the wages paid. The key issue to bear in mind is that the demand for labour, like other factors of production, is essentially a *derived demand*. People are employed for the output they produce.

The principle of marginal analysis, developed in earlier chapters, can be usefully applied to the labour market. Most firms aim to make and sell goods and services for profit, although as we saw in Chapter 10, managers may also pursue other objectives. Obviously, a profit-maximising firm will not want to pay its employees (including on-costs such as pension provisions and national insurance) more than they add to the value of production. In other words, they will not want to employ someone if the marginal cost of employment to the firm exceeds the marginal revenue generated by the additional employee through more sales. Therefore, firms wishing to maximise profits will employ more people until the marginal cost of employing them equals the marginal revenue that can be earned by selling the output they produce – where there are other variable costs related to employment these will also need to be taken into account when calculating the employment costs. Even where firms do not aim to profit maximise, the principles of marginal analysis are still valuable when discussing the employment decision. They help managers to answer such questions as, 'What are the consequences of expanding or reducing our labour force?'

A discussion of employment, especially in economies with highly institutionalised labour markets (e.g. Sweden) cannot, of course, afford to neglect the role of collective bargaining. After a detailed explanation of what economists call *marginal revenue product theory*, the chapter includes, therefore, a consideration of the impact of unions on wages and employment.

In this chapter, we cover the following aspects of the market for labour:

- The demand for labour and the concept of the *marginal revenue product*.
- The supply of labour and the concept of the *elasticity of labour supply*.
- The *determination of wages* in the labour market.
- The impact of *collective bargaining* and trade unions on wages and employment.

- Discrimination in labour markets.
- Minimum wage legislation.
- Taxation and the incentive to work.
- The importance of education and training.

It is important to understand that throughout this chapter 'an increase in wages' means an increase in the *real* wage, not simply an increase to offset inflation. It is an increase in the real wage which affects the price of one kind of labour in relation to other types of labour and substitute factors of production, such as labour-saving capital equipment.

Learning outcomes

This chapter will help you to:

- Understand how wages and employment levels are determined in *competitive labour markets*.
- Grasp what is meant by the *marginal product of labour* and the important role that it plays in explaining the demand for labour in market economies.
- Identify those factors which influence the *supply of labour* and the effect of the willingness to work on wages and employment levels.
- Appreciate the effects of *labour market imperfections* on wages and employment levels.
- Recognise the ways in which *trade unions* affect labour markets in terms of their impact on the demand for and supply of labour.
- Realise the significance of both *negative* and *positive* discrimination in modern labour markets and the resultant economic consequences.
- Understand the likely impact of *minimum wage legislation* on wages and employment.
- Recognise the role of *taxation* in explaining the incentive to work and the implications for the labour market.
- Appreciate the importance of *education and training*, and therefore investment in *human capital*, in determining real wages and employment in all economies.

The demand for labour

For competitive markets, economists link the demand for labour by the individual firm to the *marginal value product* (MVP) of labour. The marginal value product is the value added to production by employing one more person. More formally it can be calculated as follows:

$$MVP = MPP \times P$$

where
   MVP is the marginal value product;
   MPP is the marginal physical product, i.e. the *volume* of output added by employing one more person; and
   P is the price at which the output sells in the market place.

For example, assume a perfectly competitive market where the firm sells all of its output at a constant (market) price of $30 per unit. If the twentieth person employed increased the volume of total output in the firm by 5 units per week, then the MVP of the twentieth employee is $5 \times \$30 = \$150$. Provided that the weekly cost of employment is less than that amount and there are no other costs associated with the additional output, the employment is profitable from the firm's viewpoint. If the cost exceeds $150, then it is costing more to employ the twentieth person than he or she is contributing to the value of production.

At first, as a firm employs more people, the value that each extra person adds to production may rise. This may be because as employment rises people are able to specialise in tasks, so increasing the productivity of the total labour force. However, we tend to find that there will come a point at which, as more and more are employed, unless we increase the amount of capital equipment including factory and office space, *diminishing returns* set in. In other words, once a certain employment level is achieved for any given assembly line, shop or office or agricultural land, any further increase in employment leads to a decline in the marginal physical product of labour (MPP). For example, consider a computer department of a firm which currently has twenty employees. The employment of a twenty-first person may lead to a lower MPP. In other words, that person adds less to the volume of production than the twentieth person. Adding a further person, a twenty-second employee, may be associated with a lower MPP than the twenty-first employee and so on. If the firm foolishly carries on employing more and more people eventually the last person taken on might not be able to find any work to do and therefore the MPP would be zero. If employment continued beyond this point the office might become grossly overcrowded and the *total* volume of production would fall. Now the MPP has become negative.

Table 13.1 shows an example of the relationship between MVP and the number employed. Thus we note that the MVP of the twelfth worker employed equals $1,500, that for the thirteenth worker is $1,800, for the fourteenth worker $1,500 and so on. The table illustrates the MPP rising at first, then falling as output is increased. The MVP curve derived from the data in Table 13.1 is illustrated in Figure 13.1. It will be seen that when the employment level reaches thirteen people, the MVP curve begins to decline. If we now assume that all employees are employed at the same wage of $900 per month, and that there are no other employment costs other than wages, it will clearly pay the firm to employ sixteen people. To employ beyond this number would mean that the marginal cost of employment (the wage) exceeds the value added to production (the MVP). On the basis of this analysis it should be apparent that managers

Table 13.1 Calculation of marginal value product (firm in perfect competition) ($)

Quantity produced (units)	Number of workers employed	Marginal physical product (MPP)	×	Price (per unit)	=	Marginal value product (MVP)
550	11	–		–		–
600	12	50	×	30	=	1,500
660	13	60	×	30	=	1,800
710	14	50	×	30	=	1,500
750	15	40	×	30	=	1,200
780	16	30	×	30	=	900
800	17	20	×	30	=	600
810	18	10	×	30	=	300

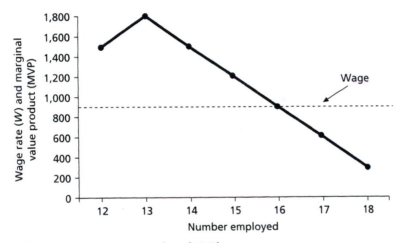

Figure 13.1 The marginal value product (MVP) curve

wishing to maximise profits should employ labour (including managers!) only if the cost of employing them does not exceed their MVP.

When deciding the level of employment, management should be concerned not solely with the volume of output added by the marginal employee, but also with the price at which that output is sold. In real-world markets (i.e. markets that are less than perfectly competitive), the firm may well have to reduce the price of its product to sell an increased output. In this case, the marginal revenue (MR) will be less than the price (average revenue). To distinguish the employment result in imperfectly competitive markets from the result under conditions of perfect competition, it is usual to refer to the *marginal revenue product* (MRP), rather than the marginal value product:

Marginal Revenue Product (MRP) = Marginal Physical Product (MPP)
× Marginal Revenue (MR)

= MPP × MR

269

Table 13.2 Calculation of marginal revenue product

Quantity produced (units)	Number of workers employed	Marginal physical product (MPP)	×	Price (per unit) $	=	Marginal revenue product (MRP) ($)
550	11	–		–		–
600	12	50	×	30	=	1,500
660	13	60	×	29	=	1,740
710	14	50	×	28	=	1,400
750	15	40	×	27	=	1,080
780	16	30	×	26	=	780
800	17	20	×	25	=	500
810	18	10	×	24	=	240

If the firm cannot sell all of its original output at a constant price, the MRP will decline more swiftly than the MPP (and MVP). This follows since MRP = MPP × MR. As output rises and a firm has to reduce its selling price to sell the additional production, the MRP falls because of both a decline in MPP (due to diminishing returns) and because the firm must accept a lower price for its product (due to a downward sloping demand curve), leading to a lower MR.

Table 13.2 shows the calculation of the MRP of labour. It will be seen that this table is very similar to Table 13.1 except that the price per unit of output falls as the quantity produced and sold increases with the additional employment of labour. Now with a wage of $900 per month, it will not be efficient to employ more than fifteen workers. If sixteen workers were employed, the sixteenth worker would have an MRP of $780, which is less than the wage being paid to this employee.

Figure 13.2 shows the corresponding MRP curve derived from the data in Table 13.2. It will be seen that, as before, the curve rises and then falls but with the decline

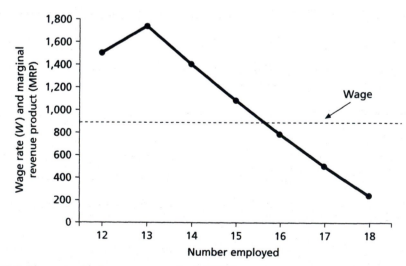

Figure 13.2 The marginal revenue product (MRP) curve

occurring due to both diminishing returns and the fall in selling price as employment and output increases. Accordingly, the MRP declines more quickly than the MVP curve in Figure 13.1. It should be noted that the firm's employment decision will always be based on the declining part of the MRP curve. When MRP is rising, it will *always* pay to employ more workers at a common wage because the next worker employed has a higher MRP than the last one employed. For this reason, it is normal practice to ignore the upward sloping section of the MRP curve when discussing employment and marginal revenue product theory. Hence, the remaining diagrams in this chapter, which illustrate the MRP curves, follow this convention. In addition, for simplicity, we illustrate the demand (MRP curves) and supply curves for labour as straight lines, although in practice they may well be non-linear.

We can conceive of an MRP for each type of labour employed from low manual to the highest levels of management. It should be apparent that a way to increase employment and/or wages is to increase either the productivity of labour (MPP) or the price of the product produced (P) or both. The effect in both cases is to raise the MRP of labour. This is illustrated in Figure 13.3 by a shift in the MRP curve to the right. With a given wage of W_1, N_1N_2 more workers can be profitably employed because the value added to production is increased. Alternatively, N_1 could still be employed but at the higher wage of W_2, or some combination of a higher wage and higher employment, identified along the stretch of the MRP_2 line between X and Y, could be chosen.

The extent to which the demand for labour (i.e. the responsiveness of employment) might be affected by a change in wages is determined by the *elasticity of demand for labour*.

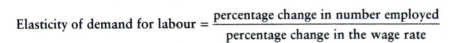

$$\text{Elasticity of demand for labour} = \frac{\text{percentage change in number employed}}{\text{percentage change in the wage rate}}$$

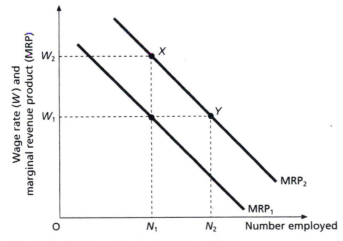

Figure 13.3 Raising labour's marginal revenue product

In some cases a wage change may have a significant effect on the demand for labour. In other cases the effect may be much less significant. The extent to which the demand for labour changes in response to a wage change will depend upon such factors as the following:

- The extent to which the labour can be easily replaced by either other labour or capital equipment.

- The extent to which the firm can pass on increased wage costs to the consumer without appreciably affecting sales of its product. This in turn depends upon the product's *price elasticity of demand*.

- The proportion of labour costs in total costs. Wage demands can be most easily accommodated where wages make up only a small part of the firm's total costs (for example, in capital intensive industries such as chemicals).

Using the above formula we can say that the demand for labour is *elastic* when the resulting figure is greater than 1 and *inelastic* when it is less than 1. The procedure for calculation of the elasticity is identical to that for a product's price elasticity (see Chapter 2, pp. 38–42) and again the negative sign, by convention, is ignored.

So far we have been concerned with what is the optimal number of people to employ at a given wage rate. To determine *how the wage rate is derived* we also need to consider the supply of labour.

The supply of labour

At its most basic, the supply of labour is determined by the following:

- **Demographic factors.** The birth and death rate, immigration and emigration, and the participation ratio (the proportion of those of working age who make themselves available for work) are all important in determining the size of the national labour force.

- **The wage rate and other employment inducements, e.g. status, perks, etc.** These factors determine the supply of labour to a particular occupation or firm. Higher wage rates, perks, etc., attract more people to a job or occupation.

- **Barriers to entry into different occupations.** Such barriers may be social or cultural, legal restrictions or prohibitions (e.g. on women working in coal mines), trade union entry restrictions (such as the pre-entry closed shop), or involve the need for particular qualifications (e.g. graduate-only employment or professional examinations). In addition, ignorance can often be a very potent barrier to labour mobility both between occupations and geographically. Workers may be unaware of job opportunities elsewhere. Barriers to entry and other such restrictions on the supply of labour move the labour supply curve to the left and make it less 'supply elastic' (see below) thus raising the wage (as illustrated in Figure 13.4). Note that employment discrimination against particular groups (on grounds of gender, race, creed, disability, etc.) alters the *demand for labour* and is discussed separately below.

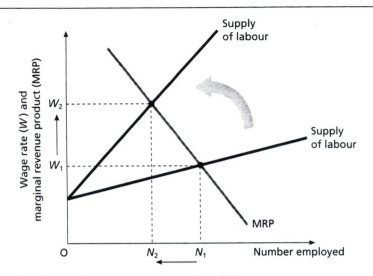

Figure 13.4 The effect of restricting the supply of labour

- **Labour mobility.** In a perfect labour market, people would move swiftly and freely from one occupation to another and from one geographic area to another. However, educational and skill requirements limit occupational mobility. Manual labourers cannot readily be accountants (although if necessary accountants could become manual labourers!). Equally, there could be unemployed accountants in one area of the country and a shortage of accountants in another area. Thus we often have in an economy shortages of certain skilled labour alongside a pool of unemployed and great regional variations in employment opportunities. The answer, of course, is to train the unemployed and to adopt a regional policy to level out job opportunities nationally, but both take time and resources. They also require accurate forecasting by government of future job shortages.

Wage determination in the labour market

Leaving aside the other factors which may affect the supply of labour to concentrate upon the wage paid, suppose that the firm is small and when it increases its demand for a type of labour it does not have to increase the wage offered. In other words, the wage is determined in the industry's labour market as a whole and the firm pays the going wage rate. In effect the firm then faces a perfectly elastic supply curve of labour. This is illustrated in Figure 13.5, where in a highly competitive labour market the supply curve is horizontal at a wage rate equal to W. Ignoring any other costs of employment, the average costs (AC) and marginal costs (MC) of employing labour are constant at that wage. Hence, the firm will employ N amount of labour, i.e. where MC = MRP.

In a less competitive situation where a firm may be so large that when it increases its demand for labour it has to pay a higher wage to attract additional employees, the wage paid to the marginal employee will exceed the average wage bill. In other words, the

273

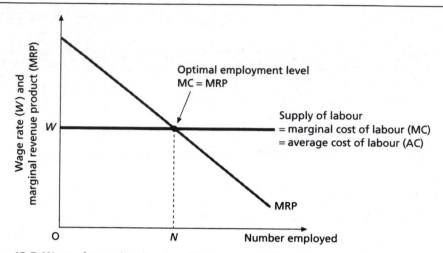

Figure 13.5 Wage determination in a highly competitive labour market

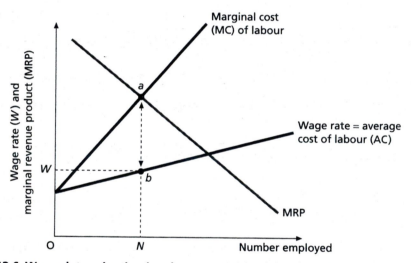

Figure 13.6 Wage determination in a less competitive labour market

marginal cost of labour rises more quickly than the average cost of employment. Again it will pay the firm to employ labour to the point where the marginal cost of employment equals the value added to sales by the marginal employee, i.e. N workers, given where MC = MRP, as illustrated in Figure 13.6. Here W represents the average wage bill to the entire workforce and hence the employees as a whole are paid less than the marginal revenue product (the shortfall is represented by the distance ab).

In a few cases an employer may be the sole purchaser of a type of labour, in which case the employer is a *monopsonist* (meaning single buyer) and the analysis in Figure 13.6 applies.

The extent to which a firm's supply of labour rises or falls in response to a wage change can be expressed in terms of labour's *elasticity of supply*. The *elasticity of supply of labour* is a measure of the responsiveness of the supply of labour to a change in the wage paid.

The elasticity of supply tends to be lower where there are labour shortages and for more highly skilled jobs, for example, dentists. In contrast, the elasticity of supply tends to be high in relatively unskilled jobs, where there is surplus labour and where it is relatively easy to move into the occupation, for example office cleaning. This helps to explain why a senior executive with skills in short supply earns a lot more than a manual labourer in a market economy, even ignoring any differences in their MRP. The supply of senior executives with the right background is very limited, hence the supply is relatively inelastic. By contrast, there is usually a large pool of manual labour which forces down wage levels in the manual labour sector.

The elasticity of labour supply is measured as follows:

$$\text{Elasticity of labour supply} = \frac{\text{percentage change in supply of labour}}{\text{percentage change in the wage rate}}$$

Restrictions on the supply of labour into an occupation tend to make the supply less responsive to wage changes and hence more *inelastic*.

The discussion so far has been concerned with the marginal productivity theory of wage determination in which the demand for labour is a reflection of the marginal revenue product of labour. This approach is obviously most relevant to firms operating in industries where wages are freely negotiated between the employer and employee and therefore in firms which are non-unionised. In some industries, however, wages and the conditions of work may be set by collective bargaining, involving a trial of strength between a *monopoly seller* of labour (the union) and a *monopsony or single buyer* of labour (e.g. an employers' federation). In this case, does the above analysis have any relevance?

Collective bargaining

In 1979, 12 million people in the United Kingdom were in trade unions. Ten years later, as a result of unemployment and anti-union legislation, this number had fallen by a third to 8 million. There have been similar trends in a number of other countries. Nevertheless, at the start of the twenty-first century, unions are still a major feature of the labour market in most economies.

A *bargaining theory* of wages suggests that wage determination is a matter of 'negotiation' between 'determined' unions on the one hand and 'intransigent' employers on the other. To managers and union representatives directly involved in wage bargaining this may seem so. Wages are simply the product of a power struggle. However, below the surface of collective bargaining in a market economy the principles of marginal productivity theory still apply. The forces of demand and supply in the labour market are still important. In particular, in the long run it is unlikely that unions can raise wages substantially without causing unemployment unless there is a matching increase in the marginal revenue product of labour. As we have already observed, profit-maximising firms will make redundant any labour which costs more to employ than it contributes in added value. In certain circumstances a firm might be willing to absorb a wage increase out of profits, and may have to in the short term, but over the longer term the firm will have an incentive to cut costs, for example by substituting capital for labour.

From our earlier discussion we can deduce that unions will tend to be at their strongest in wage bargaining if:

- The firm currently makes more than a normal profit so higher wages can be paid out of the higher profits.
- The employer is a monopsonist and currently the average wage paid is less than the MRP (as in Figure 13.6).
- The employer has limited scope to introduce further labour savings.
- Labour costs are only a small part of total costs so that a wage rise can be more easily absorbed.
- Firms can more easily pass on some or all of a wage increase to consumers through higher prices. This will occur when either the demand for the product is rising (e.g. because incomes are rising) or where consumer choice is restricted and the price elasticity of demand of the product is, therefore, low (e.g. in a monopolistic industry such as water supply).
- In state enterprises where wage increases for state employees are funded from compulsory tax payments – unless there is strong public opposition to taxation.
- The employer, although not a monopsonist, is currently paying a wage which is less than the MRP of labour (for example, as illustrated in Figure 13.6).

Trade unions can adopt two broad strategies to maintain increased wage rates for their members:

- Restrict the supply of labour in the market.
- Raise the demand for labour.

The supply of labour can be restricted by trade union closed-shop agreements (i.e. requiring all employees to be members of the union) or by the imposition of entry qualifications (such as lengthy apprenticeship periods). Turning to the demand for labour, this can be raised, for example, by unions co-operating with employers in productivity deals. Raising productivity increases the MRP of labour so that higher wages can be paid without lower profits and a loss of jobs. The impact of trade unions on the supply and demand for labour is illustrated in Figure 13.7. Assume that in a competitive labour market the MRP curve and therefore the demand for labour curve is D_A and the supply curve for labour is S_A. A trade union could raise the wage rate paid to its members from the competitive equilibrium level of W_1 to W_2 by restricting the supply of labour. The supply curve will shift from S_A to S_B but the number of workers employed will fall from N_1 to N_2, leading to some unemployment. This fall in employment levels can be avoided, however, by increasing instead the demand for labour, i.e. to MRP_B, or

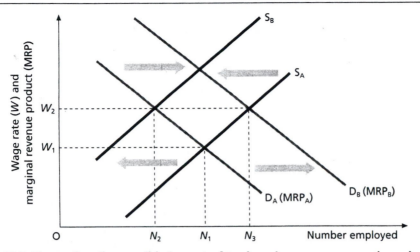

Figure 13.7 Illustrating the possible impact of trade unions on wages and employment

from D_A to D_B. Increasing the demand for labour requires the union to co-operate in increasing the MRP of labour, for example through productivity deals and more flexible working methods. In Figure 13.7 the demand for labour shifts to the right sufficiently for the higher wage rate not to cause any fall in the employment level – indeed employment rises to N_3.

In collective bargaining, employers' organisations act like monopsony (i.e. dominant) buyers of labour. By co-operating rather than competing for labour in the market, employers' federations can work to minimise wage rises. The disadvantage as far as firms are concerned lies in the inflexibility introduced by national wage deals. National agreements fail to reflect local demand and supply conditions leading to localised labour shortages. Hence, they are often supplemented by wage deals at the firm or plant level. In such circumstances the national deal can become largely irrelevant, or worse it can become the 'going rate' on which inflationary local deals are based.

Application 13.1

De-industrialisation and trade unions

Do trade unions have a future?

Trade unions were created during the Industrial Revolution of the nineteenth century to fight poverty and poor working conditions. But one hundred and fifty years on, do they still have a role?

Certainly trade unionists have declined as a proportion of the labour force in almost all of the major industrial economies, suggesting that forces are at work that are reducing the attractiveness of joining unions. In France today only 9.1% of the workforce are in unions, in Japan it is 24%, in Germany 28.9% and in the UK slightly under 33%. The figure below shows that Sweden is something of an exception with over 90% of the labour force unionised and the proportion has actually risen since the mid-1980s.

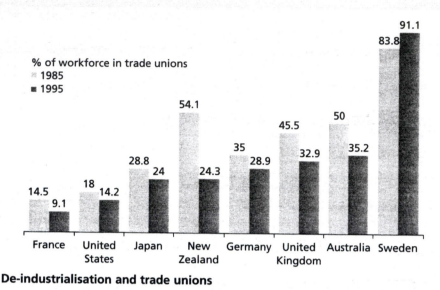

De-industrialisation and trade unions

Pressures on trade union membership

What are these forces that are at work? The most obvious is de-industrialisation. As economies mature comparative advantage lies in producing services rather than bulk manufactured goods. In the last fifty years production of commodities such as steel, toys, textiles and more recently motor vehicles has switched to the developing economies. Much of this production is labour intensive and these countries have cheaper labour. This is a problem for unions because unionisation has traditionally been greater in manufacturing than in private services.

Another factor has been privatisation and controls on public spending. In the UK under 20% of workers in the private sector are in unions. The proportion is much larger in the public sector. With cuts in employment in state industries and services the number in unions inevitably declines.

Lastly, recent years have seen social changes unfavourable to unions, such as higher structural unemployment and an increased emphasis on 'individualism'. New technologies require more highly educated labour that may be less inclined to join a union. Flatter management structures, outsourcing and part-time working are also unfavourable to unionisation.

What can the unions do? Some are fighting back by reinventing themselves as associations offering customer services such as credit cards and health insurance. Others are canvassing co-operation with employers to raise productivity. What is clear is that the economic forces that led to mass unionisation in the past have changed.

Activity

Assess the likely impacts of the developments outlined above on the determination of wages in the labour market.

Further issues in the labour market

In addition to the impact of trade unions and the role of collective bargaining in affecting the wage rate and employment levels of labour, we consider in this last section a number of other issues concerning the labour market which are the subject of much debate leading to government legislation in many economies. The following topics are analysed here:

- Discrimination.
- Minimum wage legislation.
- Taxation and the incentive to work.
- The importance of education and training.

Discrimination

Unfortunately, some individuals and groups in society suffer from discrimination in the labour market. Discrimination may occur on grounds of race, sex, creed and physical disability, etc. The result of discrimination is to reduce the employer's perception of an individual's marginal revenue product below the actual (true) level. Alternatively, the employer may recognise the correct MRP pertaining to an individual but refuses to offer employment – in effect, leading to a reduction in the demand for labour for the group being discriminated against.

The impact of discrimination is illustrated in Figure 13.8 below where, in the absence of discrimination, N_1 workers would be employed at wage W_1. The effect of discrimination is to shift the perceived MRP (i.e. demand for labour) curve to the left, leading to a lower level of employment, N_2, and a lower wage of W_2. This figure highlights the impact of *negative discrimination*.

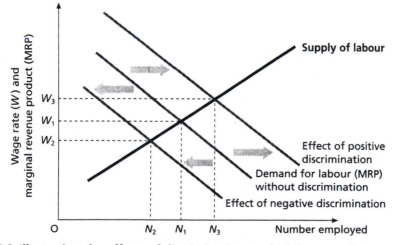

Figure 13.8 Illustrating the effects of discrimination on the labour market

By contrast, if an employer (either voluntarily or as a result of government legislation) adopts *positive discrimination*, and thereby favours the employment of particular individuals or groups in society, the result, in effect, will be to shift the demand curve for these individuals or groups to the right. The outcome is higher employment and higher wages – this is illustrated by a shift in the perceived MRP curve rightwards in Figure 13.8 with the new employment level at N_3 and wages of W_3.

Application 13.2

Discrimination in the labour market

Exploitation of women?

As shown in Table 1 below, women form the majority of employees in three major occupational groups in the UK – clerical and secretarial (75%), personal and protective services (66%) and selling (62%). These three groups account for over a half of women in employment.

But in these occupations, as elsewhere, women tend to be crowded into the lower-level jobs in terms of experience and pay. On average, females earn around 25–30% less than male employees. In part this is explained by the level at which women are employed. For example, in education women make up the vast bulk of primary school teachers but very few university professors are female. Most secretarial posts in organisations are filled by women, while at board level men dominate.

Table 2 on p. 281 shows the female to male earnings ratio for Great Britain between 1886 and 1998. What stands out is how little the ratio has changed despite the political emancipation of women and equal opportunities legislation.

What might explain this continued sharp difference in rewards to men and women in the workforce? One explanation is simple prejudice on the part of employers. Other explanations include lower productivity amongst women workers because of lower education and skills and interruptions to careers caused by child rearing. Some women work shorter hours to coincide with their children's school day and term times. The supply of labour to particular occupations also impacts on male–female wage differentials.

Table 1 Occupation distribution of males and females, 1997

Sector	Female %	Male %	Women as % of all employees
Clerical and secretarial	25.10	6.78	74.6
Personal and protective services	16.02	6.41	66.4
Managerial	11.7	19.4	32.4
Science, health and teaching	11.5	9.11	49.9
Selling	11.3	5.47	62.0
Professional and related	9.23	10.92	40.1
Miscellaneous	8.36	7.23	47.8
Plant and machinery	4.00	13.65	19.0
Craft related	2.42	20.67	8.5

Table 2 Female to male earnings ratio for Great Britain 1886–1998

	1886	1960	1970	1987	1998
Weekly earnings (manual)	0.515	0.514	0.499	0.611	0.643
Hourly earnings:					
Manual	n/a	0.605	0.601	0.695	0.724
Non-manual	n/a	n/a	0.525	0.621	0.687
All	n/a	n/a	0.637	0.741	0.801

Note: Figures are a ratio of female-to-male earnings. A figure of 1 would mean equal pay.
n/a = not available.

Activity

Using appropriate labour demand and supply curves explore why earnings differ for women and men workers. What is the likely economic impact of government equal pay legislation?

Minimum wage legislation

A number of countries have legislation which establishes a minimum wage for workers. This means that employers are not permitted to pay workers a wage rate below this level. Minimum wage legislation is controversial because, on the one hand, workers are protected from poverty-level wages. On the other hand, minimum wage legislation interferes with the operation of the labour market and may lead to unemployment. Unemployment can be expected to result if the wage rate is set at a level which is above the market clearing rate.

In Figure 13.9 the competitive market equilibrium is determined by the forces of demand and supply in the labour market. The result is a wage rate of W_e and employment of N_e. Suppose that a minimum wage is introduced by the government at the level W_m. This leads to a decline in demand for labour, as shown by the demand curve, to N_d. At the same time, the higher wage rate causes more people to want employment, as shown by the supply of labour curve. The supply of labour rises to N_s – representing an increase in the willingness to work given the higher wage. However, not everyone willing to work will be offered a job. The distance N_d to N_s represents unemployment resulting from the introduction of the minimum wage. The extent to which unemployment occurs will depend upon the extent to which the minimum wage, W_m, is set above the competitive equilibrium wage, W_e. Any minimum wage set below the competitive equilibrium rate would be ineffective and, therefore, need not be considered further.

It should be noted that the above discussion is based on the existence of a competitive labour market. Where there are labour market imperfections leading to some workers being paid less than their marginal revenue product, a minimum wage need not

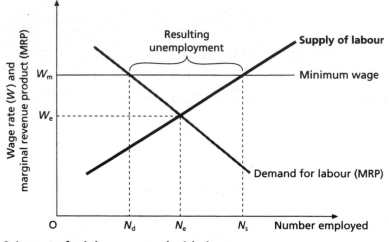

Figure 13.9 Impact of minimum wage legislation

lead to unemployment. Also, if a minimum wage leads to a more motivated and better managed workforce then the MRP of labour should rise, shifting the demand curve for lower paid workers to the right and thereby avoiding unemployment. The impact of minimum wage legislation is, therefore, uncertain. Studies of countries that have adopted statutory minimum wages have produced conflicting results – some studies suggesting reduced employment amongst lower-paid workers and others suggesting no effects, negligible effects, or in a few cases positive effects! Much appears to turn on the extent to which the legislation raises wages. The larger the increase, the more likely it is that unemployment will result. This conclusion is consistent with the approach to employment and wages set out in this chapter – in other words, it is consistent with marginal revenue product theory.

Taxation and the incentive to work

As we have seen earlier in this chapter, in market economies the employment of labour is determined by demand and supply in the labour market. In practice, however, governments affect employment through the imposition of taxes on employees. The main taxes are income tax and social security contributions (the latter are usually paid by both employers on behalf of their employees and by employees directly).

In Figure 13.10 the competitive equilibrium employment level in the absence of taxation is N_1 and the wage rate established is W_1. The imposition of a tax shifts the supply of labour curve to the left, to S + tax. This results in a rise in the before-tax wages (i.e. gross wages) while after-tax wages fall. It will be seen that the number of workers employed falls from N_1 to N_2 as a result of taxation.

In Figure 13.10, at the new after-tax employment level, N_2, the tax levied is equivalent to the vertical distance between W_2 and W_3. Although the gross wage paid by

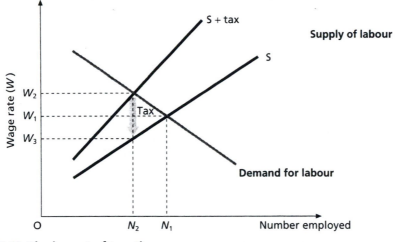

Figure 13.10 The impact of taxation

employers is W_2, tax equal to $W_2 - W_3$ is paid over to the government, leaving the employee with a net wage equivalent to W_3.

It should be noted that the labour supply curve after the imposition of tax becomes less elastic – see S + tax in the figure. Drawn in this way, the diagram shows that the amount of tax paid increases progressively with the level of wages, i.e. this illustrates the nature and impact of a *progressive* tax system in which more tax is paid as wages rise. It also highlights the extent to which progressive taxes create a disincentive to work and hence reduce the supply of labour and thus affect the levels of employment and unemployment.

It follows from the above discussion that the greater the tax burden on employment, the greater the negative impact of taxation in the competitive labour market.

Education and training

Today's industries require high levels of well educated and highly trained labour. In other words, managers today are concerned not only with the quantity of labour that they can employ but its quality. This places a growing emphasis on what economists call *human capital*, alongside the traditional emphasis on physical capital (e.g. plant and machinery).

High levels of education and training lead to a workforce that is more productive and, consequently, one that has a higher marginal revenue product. This results in an increased demand for labour alongside higher real wages. In effect, education and training are an investment in human capital that causes the MRP curves in labour markets to shift to the right – as shown in Figure 13.11 with wages rising from W_1 to W_2 and employment rising from N_1 to N_2.

It is also important to note that educational qualifications are considered by many economists as *screening devices* in modern labour markets. Employers often have a

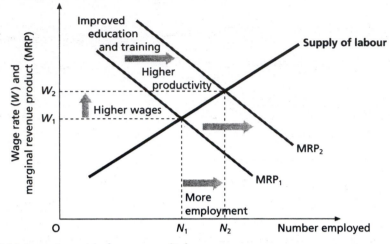

Figure 13.11 Investment in human capital

potentially large pool of labour from which to choose their employees. Educational qualifications help to reduce the cost to employers of seeking out suitable employees – referred to by economists as *search costs*. For example, an employer may advertise for managers who hold an MBA qualification, thereby reducing the number of applicants to those who can be expected to have the necessary skills and experience. Of course, it does not necessarily follow that MBA graduates make the best managers, but many employers find this qualification a useful screening device to limit the number of applicants to be processed prior to final selection.

Concluding remarks

A major objection to the marginal productivity approach to employment and wage determination lies in the in-built assumption that the firm can exactly (or closely) measure the MRP of its employees. Often managers will be faced with imperfect information about an employee's productivity (and especially a potential employee's productivity) and sometimes even about the full employment costs. The fact that the MRP of labour can only be measured if all other factors of production are held constant complicates the picture. It may prove impossible to separate out exactly the MRP of an individual worker in an integrated production process, especially where employees operate together as teams. Moreover, in some state activities such as the police, where no revenue is earned directly from the work provided, the concept of an MRP does not appear to be particularly useful.

Nevertheless, marginal productivity theory is valuable for the general insight it gives economists and managers into the roles of demand and supply in the labour market in determining employment and wages. The analysis in this chapter underlines the importance of carefully monitoring, even if only in general terms, the value added by the extra labour employed. Over-manning, especially in expanding firms, where people are taken on in the anticipation of work that does not materialise, can quickly, and sometimes disastrously, escalate costs and remove competitive advantage. Indeed, the root of many business failures lies in insufficient attention to labour's MRP. As this chapter has stressed, employment should add *net value* to the firm – labour should be an asset not a liability!

This chapter has also helped us to appreciate the potential impact of trade unions in the labour market, along with the importance of discrimination, minimum wage legislation, taxes on employment and education and training (i.e. human capital). In the next chapter we turn to look at the market for another very important factor of production in modern economies – the market for capital.

Key learning points

- The **demand for labour** is a derived demand, i.e. people are employed for the output they produce.

- The **marginal value product of labour** (MVP) under conditions of perfect competition is the value added to production by employing one more person and is calculated as follows:

$$MVP = MPP \times P$$

where MPP is the marginal physical product (i.e. the volume of output added by employing one more person) and P is the constant price at which the output sells.

- Under conditions of imperfect competition the **marginal revenue product of labour** (MRP) is affected by MPP and changes in price (i.e. MR), so that

$$MRP = MPP \times MR$$

- Managers seeking **to maximise profits** should employ more labour only if the marginal revenue product exceeds or is equal to the marginal cost of employment.

- The **elasticity of demand for labour** measures the responsiveness of employment to a change in wages, calculated as:

$$\frac{\text{Percentage change in number employed}}{\text{Percentage change in the wage rate}}$$

- The **supply of labour** is determined by demographic factors, the wage rate and other employment inducements, barriers to entry into different occupations and labour mobility.

- In a **highly competitive labour market,** the supply curve for labour is horizontal at the industry wage rate W; the average and marginal costs of employing labour are therefore constant at that wage, so that the optimal level of employment will correspond to the point where MC = MRP.

- In a **less competitive labour market,** the marginal cost of labour rises more quickly than the average cost of employment. While the profit-maximising condition MC = MRP still holds, the average wage rate will be less than the value of the marginal revenue product.

- The **elasticity of supply of labour** is a measure of the responsiveness of the supply of labour to a change in the wage paid, calculated as:

$$\frac{\text{Percentage change in supply of labour}}{\text{Percentage change in the wage rate}}$$

- **Collective bargaining** refers to arrangements between employers and trade unions regarding the setting of wages and conditions of work.

- Where **trade unions** are powerful they are able to raise wages above the levels that would otherwise exist but this may occur at the expense of the number employed – resulting in **unemployment.**

- Trade unions can impact on the labour market by both reducing the supply of labour and raising the demand for labour.

- **Negative discrimination** can occur in labour markets, for example on grounds of race, sex, creed, physical disabilities, etc., leading to a lower demand for labour from these groups.

- **Positive discrimination** can also occur leading to increased demand for labour from particular groups in society.

- A number of countries have introduced **minimum wage legislation,** preventing employers from 'exploiting' workers by offering wages at levels which society may consider to be unacceptable – the result may, however, be higher unemployment.

- **Taxation** can reduce the incentive (willingness) to work and, in effect, shift the supply curve of labour leftwards, resulting in lower employment levels.

- Higher levels of **education and training** are an investment that lead to improved human capital with a consequent increase in the marginal revenue product of labour and therefore higher real wages and more employment.

- **Educational qualifications** also act as a screening device in the labour market, thereby reducing the cost imposed on employers in searching for suitably skilled labour to fill job vacancies.

Topics for discussion

1 What do you understand by the terms 'the marginal value product' of labour and 'the marginal revenue product' of labour?

2 How does the calculation of MVP and MRP differ?

3 Using marginal productivity theory, explain why a profit-maximising firm will employ fewer people when the wage that has to be paid rises, everything else being equal.

4 How can an understanding of the elasticity of supply of labour help a manager to determine wages and other terms of employment?

5 Under what circumstances are trade unions most likely to be able to obtain wage increases?

6 Consider the impact on employment of adopting a 'national minimum wage' which exceeds the competitive market equilibrium wage rate.

7 Why might an employer and an employee be willing to share the costs associated with the employee studying for a professional qualification such as the MBA?

8 What are the likely implications of labour immigration on wage rates and employment levels? Consider these implications with respect to the immigration of highly educated and skilled labour in contrast to those with minimal education and skill levels.

9 The government has just announced a 5% decrease in tax for all employees. Using an appropriate diagram, consider the impact of this tax change on the labour market, particularly with respect to those on low wages compared with those at the top end of the pay scale.

10 **Jubilee Products**

Number of employees	Total output of products	Price per unit ($) of products in the market
100	5,000	8.00
101	5,100	6.50
102	5,250	5.70
103	5,350	5.50
104	5,400	5.45
105	5,420	5.43
106	5,430	5.42

The wage rate paid is $550 per week (there are no other employment costs)

From the above data determine using marginal revenue product theory the number of workers that the firm, Jubilee Products, should employ at the going wage rate.

14 Understanding the market for capital

Aims and learning outcomes

In the previous chapter we discussed the market for labour as a factor of production. We concluded that from the viewpoint of a profit-maximising firm, labour should be employed until the marginal revenue product of labour equals the marginal cost of employing the labour. In this chapter, we turn to examine the market for capital and we apply the same principles. Like labour, the demand for capital is a derived demand. Capital is employed by firms to assist in the production of goods and services and to expand the firm's productive capacity. Unlike employing labour, however, the employment of capital often involves a lengthy time period between the initial decision to invest in new capacity and the resulting increase in capacity. This means that *expectations* of future returns on investment are of vital importance to capital investment decisions.

In this chapter, the following topics are covered:

- Capital as a resource of the firm.
- Capital and profit maximisation.
- The investment decision-making process.
- Estimating and ranking capital investment projects.
- Calculating the cost of capital.
- Understanding cost benefit analysis.

Capital expenditures impact upon the scale, efficiency and structure of a firm and they are therefore of central importance to strategic management decisions. For example, a well planned series of investment outlays can transform the nature and fortunes of a company. Successful investment decisions can turn around a declining firm into a successful business, while foolish investments can rapidly sink a firm that might otherwise have remained healthy.

Learning outcomes

This chapter will help you to:

- Understand the basis upon which *capital investment decisions* are made by firms.
- Identify the level of capital investment which will be undertaken by a profit maximising firm.

- Distinguish between the *stock of capital* and the *flow of new capital* (i.e. investment in the capital stock).
- Identify the various stages involved in the capital investment decision-making process.
- Grasp the importance of estimating the cash flows from a planned capital investment project.
- Distinguish between three different methods for evaluating and ranking capital investment projects, namely the *payback method*, the *discounted cash flow method* and the *internal rate of return method*.
- Appreciate the role of the cost of capital in capital investment decisions and why a *weighted average cost of capital* is calculated when a range of sources of finance is used.
- Understand the principles and stages involved in undertaking a *cost benefit analysis* – CBA takes into account the usual financial returns on an investment and the cost of capital but also the impact of the investment decision on the wider economy (the *external* or *social costs and benefits* of the investment).

Capital as a resource of the firm

Economists define *capital* as a factor of production which includes all physical, manufactured products that are used in the production of other goods and services. Examples of capital employed by firms include a wide range of items such as industrial and commercial buildings, plant and machinery, computers, business fixtures and fittings, etc. It is the services provided by such capital items that enter into the production process.

The price of capital as a factor of production is directly linked to the value of the service derived from the use of the capital. Therefore, the more productive a machine, the higher its market price is likely to be. It is important, however, to distinguish between the *price of capital*, say the price of a machine, and the *income* or *return* that the capital produces. For example, a machine may cost $5m to buy and produces an income stream of $500,000 per annum. The income stream is referred to as the return on the initial capital investment – the *return on capital employed*. Alternatively, rather than buying the machine, a firm may decide to rent it from its owner. In effect, the rent paid per time period represents a *return* to the machine's owner.

It is also important in the concept of capital to distinguish between a *stock* and a *flow*.

- The *stock of capital* is the quantity or value of the total capital invested within the firm, i.e. the total value of buildings, machines, equipment, etc. that are available within the firm.
- The *flow of capital* is the increase or reduction in the stock of capital over a given time period, i.e. the net addition to the capital stock arising from purchasing new machines. Investment is the term used for additional capital expenditure that creates new assets.

The net addition to the capital stock will, of course, also depend on the rate at which existing machines are wearing out (depreciating).

Capital, as discussed in this chapter, needs to be clearly distinguished from the 'capital' or funds invested in a business and funds invested in financial institutions (e.g. banks or the stock market). Although the accountant may refer to financial capital as 'capital', economists prefer to distinguish financial assets from physical wealth-producing assets. Financial capital represents a sum of money on which interest or dividends are paid. This financial investment could well be used at some stage to purchase physical capital for use within a business. It is, however, only when physical capital is bought and employed in the business that capital investment, as discussed within this chapter, occurs. Financial capital and financial investment represent a stock and flow of savings, respectively. Unless these funds are used to purchase plant and machinery etc., tangible capital creation does not occur.

Capital in the form of physical, manufactured products that are employed to produce other goods and services, also needs to be distinguished from human capital. *Human capital* is concerned with the skills, talents and abilities of the labour force and which leads to a higher marginal physical product of labour. Human capital was discussed in the previous chapter and is important in a discussion of wages.

Capital and profit maximisation

As in the case of the firm's decision to employ labour, the profit-maximising firm will consider both the cost and benefit from employing additional units of capital. More specifically, the firm will demand additional capital (K) up to the point where the marginal cost of capital (MC_K) equals its marginal revenue product (MRP_K).

Employment of capital to maximise profits requires that:

$$MC_K = MRP_K$$

This applies irrespective of whether the firm buys or hires its capital inputs.

This profit-maximising rule can be applied in two broad sets of factor market conditions, namely:

- Where the firm is a *price-taker*, in the sense that its demand for capital is so small that it buys or hires at the going market price for the capital. This would occur most obviously in a *perfectly competitive capital market.*

- Where the firm is a *price-maker*, in the sense that it is a dominant buyer or hirer of the capital and the price paid for the capital will therefore vary with the amount employed. This would obviously occur if the firm were a *monopsony buyer* of a particular type of capital equipment.

Note that the market price of capital, whether for purchase or hire, will depend upon the total demand for capital and the total supply of capital in the market place. In

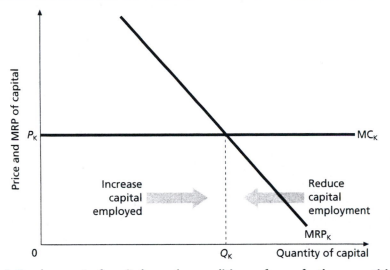

Figure 14.1 Employment of capital – under conditions of a perfectly competitive factor market

competitive markets, the market price will be determined by the interaction of demand and supply in the usual way. If, however, a firm supplying a particular type of capital equipment has *monopoly power* – being a monopoly seller as opposed to a monopsony buyer of capital – it will be able to restrict supply and force up the market price.

Figure 14.1 illustrates the case of a perfectly competitive factor market. Being a price-taker, the firm can employ differing levels of capital all at the same unit price P_K $(= MC_K)$. The demand for capital is a derived demand reflecting the marginal revenue product of capital (MRP_K). The MRP_K is downward sloping because of the law of diminishing returns – in other words, employing additional capital to a given stock of other factor inputs leads to lower marginal returns to capital.

If the firm increases the amount of capital employed, while holding other factor inputs such as labour constant, diminishing returns to capital will occur. In Figure 14.1 profit maximisation requires that capital is employed at the level Q_K. To the left of Q_K, $MRP_K > MC_K$ $(= P_K)$ and therefore it will be profitable for the firm to employ more units of capital. Conversely, to the right of Q_K, $MC_K > MRP_K$ and therefore it will pay the firm to reduce the amount of capital employed.

Figure 14.2 shows the contrasting case of a monopsony buyer or hirer of capital. As the firm is the dominant or, more technically, the sole buyer of the capital, the price it pays will vary with the amount it uses. In this case, the $MRP_K = MC_K$ rule still applies but note that the MC_K is not constant – in this case it rises as more units of capital are demanded and employed by the firm. The firm now employs Q_K^* and pays a unit price of P_K^*, as shown by the average cost of capital (AC_K) curve. This average cost curve is effectively the capital supply curve. It is possible, however, that a dominant (monopsony) buyer of capital could use its bargaining power to drive down the price at which it buys additional units of capital, in which case Figure 14.2 would not apply.

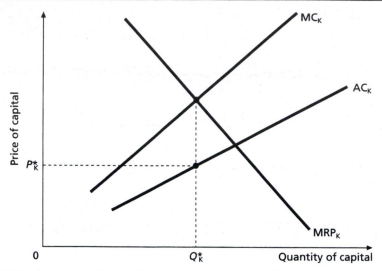

Figure 14.2 Employment of capital – a monopsony factor market

For example, a large volume buyer of personal computers may be able to obtain a lower price per unit than a small buyer. As a result, the MC_K and AC_K curves would be downward sloping, as long as each additional unit could be purchased or hired at a lower price.

As we have already noted, physical capital may be bought or hired. Where the capital is hired, the MC_K is the extra rental expense incurred by the firm over a given period of time (e.g. a year) while the MRP_K is the extra revenue earned by employing the hired capital over the same time period. The situation is a little more complex, however, when the capital is purchased. In this case, the MC_K is best interpreted as being the extra expense incurred when buying the unit of capital, e.g. the cost of a machine; while the MRP_K is best interpreted as the revenue produced by that unit of capital over its entire life. In this case, because the returns are being measured over a lengthy period of time – the life of the machine – the annual revenue stream will need to be *discounted* to provide figures to be compared with the MC_K at the time of purchase. The choice of an appropriate discounting method is discussed below in the context of the investment decision-making process.

The investment decision-making process

So far the discussion in this chapter has centred on capital investment and the profit-maximisation rule. Usually firms will be faced with a range of possible capital investment projects – for example, the purchase of machine X or machine Y, locating a new factory in region A or region B, etc. We turn now to look at how the firm may choose a particular investment project from a range of projects which are available to it. This choice involves a five-step investment decision process:

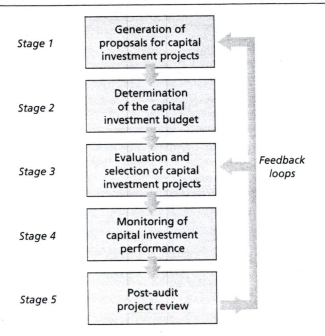

Figure 14.3 The investment decision process

- Step 1: Generation of capital investment proposals.
- Step 2: Determination of the capital investment budget.
- Step 3: Evaluation and selection of capital investment projects.
- Step 4: Monitoring of capital investment performance.
- Step 5: Post-audit project review.

This process is illustrated in Figure 14.3. We comment on each stage briefly.

- **Step 1: Generation of capital investment proposals.** This is perhaps the most important step in the investment selection process. Without investment ideas, perhaps backed by appropriate research and development, firms are likely to wither and die. The generation of investment ideas represents the seed corn for future growth and prosperity in all businesses. In terms of strategic planning, it is vital that management develop a creative and stimulating environment within the organisation which encourages profitable investment proposals.

- **Step 2: Determination of the capital investment budget.** Often investment is budget constrained, in the sense that not all of the generated proposals can be financed. In some cases the budget for capital investment may be determined by a process of consultation or it may be rigidly imposed on the management team from above, as in the case of a holding company determining the budget of a subsidiary. Budgetary control, therefore fulfils a central role in capital investment selection.

Application 14.1

Investment failure – the case of Swissair

In July 2001 Swissair and the Belgian government came to a compromise agreement to limit the corporation's exposure to liabilities arising from its partial acquisition of the Belgian state-owned airline, Sabena. Swissair's purchase of 49.5% of Sabena in the 1990s proved to be a serious financial blunder. Sabena has continued to haemorrhage money in the increasingly competitive, international air travel market. Once a successful airline with an enviable quality of service reputation, by 2000 Swissair was fighting for survival in the face of losses totalling US$1.7bn and debts equivalent to six times its equity value.

Swissair's share price (in Swiss Francs)

Sabena was one of a series of ill-fated investments in the 1990s by the management of Swissair. Stakes were bought in a number of European airlines in addition to Sabena, at a cost of over US$1bn. Stakes were taken in three small French airlines, LOT the Polish airline, LTU in Germany and TAP of Portugal. In addition, Swissair invested heavily in developing its catering operations and in global alliances between airlines – alliances that were later abandoned.

This disastrous investment strategy was reversed through business disposals and by downsizing of many of the remaining operations. Even so, Swissair continued to walk a tightrope between commercial success and failure. Its share price in mid-2001 languished at a fifth of its peak level. In late 2001 Swissair collapsed.

Activity

Consider how the proper use of the investment appraisal techniques set out in this chapter might have prevented some of Swissair's later financial problems. Why is having debts totalling around six times the equity value a problem?

- **Step 3: Evaluation and selection of capital investment projects.** All relevant information concerning the possible capital projects should be quantified in order to estimate their expected cash flows. Various techniques are available to do this, taking into account the degree of uncertainty which may be attached to each project. On the basis of estimated cash flows and associated risk and uncertainty, management can evaluate and select what appear to be the most appropriate projects for implementation given the capital budget.

- **Step 4: Monitoring of capital investment performance.** Once a project is selected and then implemented it is important to monitor its performance on an on-going basis. This monitoring may be in terms of production flows, control of costs and the generation of the revenues, all of which will be under the domain of the relevant managerial functions, e.g. production, finance, sales, etc. Firms should, of course, monitor project performance on a regular time basis, the actual time period being dependent on the nature of the investment. It is important that if problems are arising, such as cost escalation, appropriate corrective action is taken.

- **Step 5: Post-audit project review.** Once a project is well established, it is advisable, perhaps after a year or so, to examine in finer detail its performance in the light of initial expectations concerning cash flow, risk, performance, etc. This should ensure a greater likelihood of success when making future capital investments through a learning process, thus enhancing corporate profitability in the long run. There are, therefore, important feedback loops from Step 5 into the generation of proposals (Step 1) and into the evaluation and selection procedures (Step 3). An *ex post* evaluation may reveal new opportunities to increase profits further. In addition, post-auditing of investments is likely to enhance the overall quality of decision-making and planning. It should also help to tighten internal control systems and ultimately improve the management of future projects.

The above is a simplified representation of the investment decision-making process, but it helps to highlight some of the most important steps and the relationships that are involved between them.

Estimating capital investment cash flows

Capital is durable and produces a flow of income or returns over time. For each proposed capital investment project it is therefore necessary to estimate the corresponding cash flows over the expected life of the project. This is not an easy task since the future is never certain. In addition, some projects may be implemented solely on the basis of the personal objectives of management, as discussed in Chapter 10, in which case the five-step process just discussed and the estimating of cash flows may not be of decisive importance. Good investment appraisal, however, ensures that all cost and revenue estimates are reviewed carefully in order to minimise any bias. In the context of capital investment, the term cash flow is used to represent the net income stream generated by a given investment decision.

The following three points should be borne in mind when estimating cash flows:

- *Incremental analysis.* Cash flows for a project should be estimated on an incremental basis, i.e. the difference between the business cash flow with or without the project. For example, if the firm does not install new equipment to produce outputs of sufficient quality which match competitors' products it may end up losing much of its market altogether.

- *The role of tax.* Companies and other businesses pay tax on their profits and hence cash flows should be calculated on an after-tax basis, based on the appropriate marginal tax rate.

- *Spillover effects.* In calculating the cash inflows and outflows for a particular project, it is important to take account of the extent to which these are sensitive to indirect or what economists call 'spillover' effects. These effects reflect the consequences, both positive and negative, that a particular activity may have on other parts of the business. It may at first sight appear profitable for a firm to introduce a new product line, but it is important that consideration is given to the impact that this may have on other products sold by the firm. Similarly, the capital investment may have spillover or external effects in the wider economy. Such spillover effects from investment are commented upon in the discussion of cost–benefit analysis below.

Figure 14.4 shows a typical cash flow profile. In the initial stages of a capital investment project implementation cash flow is negative. Once sales expand sufficiently, this situation is reversed, though it may be some time after the actual introduction of the product to the market before cash revenues more than offset additional cash outlays. Throughout this cash flow cycle it is important that management continuously monitor the performance of the capital investment and take corrective action as required.

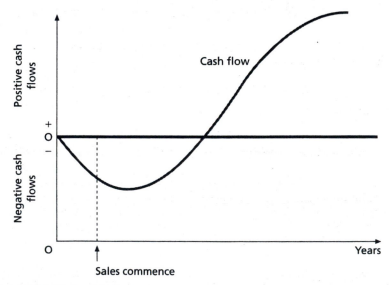

Figure 14.4 Estimating cash flows

At the planning stage, after cash flow projections have been arrived at for a particular capital investment, an evaluation of the project should be carried out (a) to determine its expected total worth to the firm over its lifetime, and (b) to enable management to rank and select which investments should be undertaken. There is a variety of methods for doing this, the most important of which we discuss below.

Evaluating and ranking capital investment projects

As part of the capital investment decision-making process it is important both to evaluate effectively and rank the various possible investment projects that could be undertaken by the firm. Three main methods exist for evaluation and ranking purposes, namely:

- Payback method.
- Net present value method.
- Internal rate of return method.

The net present value and internal rate of return methods, unlike the payback method, take into consideration the returns over the entire life of a project. Both these methods for evaluating and ranking investment projects are based on the concept of *discounted cash flows* (DCF) from capital investments, whereby expected cash flows are discounted back to the present day so as to obtain their *net present value* (NPV).

The formula for doing this is given by the equation:

$$\text{NPV} = \sum_{t=1}^{n} \frac{s}{(1+r)^t}$$

where
  s is the future sum or, more correctly, the incremental after-tax net cash flow in each year;
  t represents each year in the life of the investment from the present ($t = 1$) up to a certain number of n years in the future;
  r is the discount rate; and
  Σ denotes summation over the time period concerned.

Payback method

The simplest approach to evaluating an investment is the *payback method*. Although considered to be less satisfactory than the other methods discussed here, it is, nevertheless, still widely used by businesses worldwide. Under the payback method investments are judged in terms of how quickly they generate sufficient net returns (income less operating costs) to cover the initial investment outlay on the capital project. Projects which, for example, repay within three years are considered preferable to those which take longer to pay back. The major drawback of this method lies in the fact that it neglects net returns accruing in later years. The project taking, say, five years to pay back may be more profitable over its life than the project paying back within three years, but under the payback method the latter investment project would be the one preferred.

Net present value method

Before calculating the net present value (NPV) of a project the firm must decide the value of the appropriate *discount rate* which is to be used in the above formula for calculating discounted cash flows (DCF). The appropriate discount rate should represent the opportunity cost of capital to the firm and the ways in which this can be computed are discussed in a subsequent section of this chapter. For now we just take the discount rate (r) as given.

If the capital outlays for a project all occur in the current year, the NPV of the stream of future cash flows arising from the project is given by the following:

$$NPV = \sum_{t=1}^{n} \frac{s_t}{(1 + r)^t} - I$$

where s, t and r are as defined in the earlier net present value formula, and I is the initial investment outlay for the project. Where the investment outlay occurs over more than the current year the value of I would also need discounting.

The decision about whether capital investment in a project should be undertaken rests on whether or not its NPV is greater than zero. If the NPV is positive the investment has a positive net return in present value terms and should be accepted; if the NPV is negative it should be rejected, *ceteris paribus*. Using this simple rule, management are able to choose between a range of capital investment proposals for implementation. Of course, there may be circumstances where an investment would still be undertaken even with a negative NPV, for example where it is an essential part of a project which overall has a positive NPV.

It should be noted that some capital investments will have a residual value at the end of their planned lives (e.g. scrap value), in which case this residual value should be included as part of the expected cash flow for the final year of the project in the above NPV calculation. The same approach to residual value is adopted when calculating the internal rate of return.

Internal rate of return method

Another measure of the expected profitability of an investment project is referred to as the *internal rate of return method* (IRR). The IRR is defined as the rate of interest that equates the present value of a project's net cash flow to the cost of the initial capital investment outlay. To calculate its value we simply set the NPV for the project equal to zero, i.e.:

$$\text{NPV} = \sum_{t=1}^{n} \frac{S_t}{(1 + \text{IRR})^t} - I = 0$$

The problem therefore is to solve the equation for the value of IRR which produces a zero NPV. This interest rate or discount rate is the one that equates the present value of the net cash flows to the investment outlay (I), i.e. it is the project's internal rate of return.

Calculation of the IRR can be achieved on the basis of a trial and error procedure. First, an arbitrary rate of interest is chosen, and based on this value, NPV is calculated. If the NPV is positive, this interest rate must be lower than the true IRR so a higher rate is then tried. If the NPV is then negative, then a lower rate must be used. This procedure occurs until the correct discount rate, which produces a zero NPV, is found. At first sight this procedure seems laborious and it is! However, computer programs are available to calculate the IRR quickly.

Managers might be inclined to adopt a 'belt and braces' approach and use both the NPV and IRR methods when evaluating and ranking investment projects. While using the NPV and IRR methods will often result in the same decision to accept or reject a project, they can result in different decisions, in particular where cash flows are both negative and positive over a project's life. In general the NPV approach is to be preferred.

A firm with an unlimited capital budget would carry out all the investment projects with a positive NPV since each of these investments adds to shareholders' wealth (presuming, of course, that the expected cash flows materialise!). A problem arises, however, where a firm faces a number of projects, some of which may be interdependent and which cannot all be undertaken because the amount of capital available is limited or 'rationed'. In a perfect capital market it would be possible to borrow funds to finance any project with a positive NPV, after discounting using the cost of raising capital as the discount rate. But sometimes firms may rely on internal resources to fund investments, rather than resort to an external capital market. In some countries, external capital markets are not well developed. In such cases projects have to be ranked in order to distribute the firm's limited investment funds amongst the opportunities available. The problem of capital rationing has to be solved. Various solutions to this problem exist which revolve around attempting to maximise the NPVs from the entire investment programme given the limited budget. A discussion of these methods, however, is outside the scope of this book.

Calculating the cost of capital

Earlier we noted that the discount rate used in the NPV calculation should represent the opportunity cost of capital to the firm taking the investment decision. The cost of capital has to be measured and this raises a number of issues.

In essence the cost of capital is related to the source of the funds used for the investment. A firm may raise funds in a number of ways, including the following:

- Loan capital, e.g. bank loans and debenture (fixed interest) stock.
- Retained earnings.
- New equity issues (issuing shares or stock on which dividends are paid out of profits earned).

If a firm uses its own retained earnings or profits to finance a capital investment, no actual interest is paid for these funds by the firm, but the firm does incur an opportunity cost; that is to say, the interest that would have been earned if the funds had been invested elsewhere, e.g. in a bank account. In such a case, the cost of capital is the opportunity cost of the retained earnings. If only equity finance is used, the return to equity will be the same as the cost of capital. In contrast, if a project is financed entirely by a loan, the cost of capital is the cost (the interest rate) on the loan. Where various sources of finance are used then calculating the cost of capital becomes more complex. Now the cost of capital must be calculated as a weighted average of the costs of retained earnings, loans and equity finance, known as the *weighted average cost of capital* (WACC).

Illustration: calculating the weighted average cost of capital (WACC)

In the simplest of cases and ignoring taxation effects, the WACC is calculated by weighting the cost of raising finance for capital investment from the different sources available. Suppose that the opportunity cost of retained earnings to a firm is 8%, that it can borrow funds at 10% and raise equity financing in the stock market at an effective rate of 9% (all rates are per annum). Also, assume that the capital project costs $1 million and is funded as follows:

$800,000 from new loans
$100,000 from retained earnings
$100,000 from a new equity issue.

The WACC will be given as follows:

$$\left(10\% \times \frac{100,000}{1,000,000}\right) + \left(8\% \times \frac{800,000}{1,000,000}\right) + \left(9\% \times \frac{100,000}{1,000,000}\right) = 1\% + 6.4\% + 0.9\% = 8.3\%$$

Where loan finance is used to fund capital investments, issues arise concerning the impact of *leverage* or the *gearing ratio* (the proportion of debt to equity finance) on the weighted average cost of capital. Different tax treatments of equity and loan finance further complicate the issue. In the United Kingdom, for example, business loan interest is tax deductible, but dividends on equity are not. This often makes debt financing more attractive than equity financing, especially on a post-tax basis. This will be so provided that the financial markets believe that the amount of debt financing (the gearing ratio) is acceptable. If the financial markets decide that further borrowing will lead to an increased risk of business failure, then they will require a higher interest rate on loans to compensate for the higher risk. Unlike dividends on ordinary shares, interest on debt has to be paid each year and even in a serious economic recession when the firm may be suffering losses. Also, a high gearing ratio can raise the cost of equity financing because

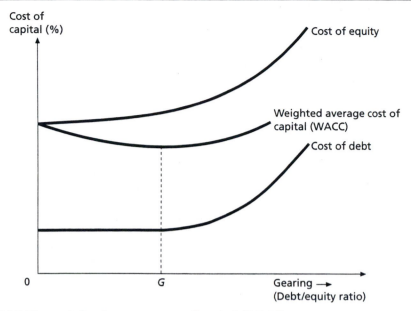

Figure 14.5 The weighted average cost of capital (WACC)

shareholders may fear that the firm will not have sufficient funds to pay dividends after making the interest payments. Where shareholders fear that dividends may not be paid, equity financing becomes more expensive, reflecting what is termed the 'equity risk premium'. It is for the above reasons that gearing rates can become an important consideration when calculating the WACC. Figure 14.5 provides examples of the cost of equity finance and the cost of debt finance with both rising, especially the latter, as the ratio of debt to equity (gearing) rises. The WACC line reflects the combined costs of debt and equity and falls initially as (cheaper) debt financing occurs to supplement equity financing. It then rises when the firm becomes more highly geared and both loan creditors and shareholders require compensation for the higher risk of business failure.

Application 14.2

Gearing and the cost of capital

The choice of capital structure

The extent to which capital structure affects the cost of capital is a subject of much debate in the financial economics literature. Modigliani and Miller in 1958 demonstrated that under certain conditions the firm's market value was independent of its capital structure. In the most simple of terms, they reasoned that while debt financing was usually cheaper than equity financing, a higher level of debt to equity raised the risk of business failure and therefore raised the cost of capital. This suggested that whether investment was financed by debt or equity, *the weighted average cost of capital* (debt and equity weighted by their relative shares in total financing) could be unaffected.

This finding depends upon a number of strict assumptions that in reality do not hold. In particular, taxation does not tend to be neutral between debt and equity. Usually interest on debt can be deducted from profits before profit taxes are paid, whereas dividends are paid out of taxable profits. Consequently, many textbooks deal with the choice of capital structure as a trade-off between the tax advantages of debt financing and the extra risk of financial distress that higher debt gearing (or leverage) may bring.

At the same time, some studies have suggested that firms may be indifferent between debt and equity financing over a wide range of gearing, provided that the tax advantage of debt is small. Other studies have pointed to big differences in debt to equity ratios across firms even within the same industry, which suggests that management retains considerable discretion when choosing its gearing ratio. It does seem that the weighted average cost of capital may be quite flat over a range of moderate levels of gearing.

The focus in the financial economics literature seems to have shifted today from studying what is the 'optimal' capital structure, to the *process* by which managers decide how to finance their investments. In other words, how do managers decide on their method of financing? It is also important to recognise that in most cases how successfully companies manage their capital investments will be far more important to their ultimate economic success than the manner in which the investments are financed.

Activity

Consider the relative merits of debt and equity financing of a large capital project. What will be the impact of taxation on your decision? Why might the cost of capital be relatively less important than other factors in determining the level of corporate investment?

It will be seen that the overall cost of capital is minimised at a level of gearing given by the point G. This point will vary from firm to firm reflecting the perceived business risk on the part of financiers.

Undertaking a cost–benefit analysis

So far our discussion has been concerned with appraising investment in terms of the resulting net returns to the firm. Today, however, more and more private sector firms are conscious of a need to take into account the wider effects of their capital investments on society, while in the public sector there is a long tradition of what is known as *cost–benefit analysis* (CBA). CBA is concerned with identifying and evaluating both the internal and external consequences of an investment. The internal consequences are the cash flow effects to the firm. The external consequences, or *externalities*, relate to the wider social implications of a capital investment both in terms of costs and benefits.

Cost–benefit analysis is a method for assessing capital projects where it is important to take into account all of the impacts of the investment decision, including the effects on other people, other firms, regions and so on. This involves accounting for the total *social costs and benefits* of a capital investment project.

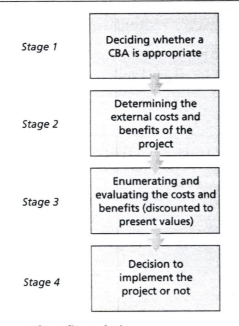

Figure 14.6 Stages of a cost–benefit analysis

Cost–benefit analysis involves four main stages, as shown in Figure 14.6.

Stage 1 is concerned with when a CBA is appropriate. It will, of course, be most appropriate where there are likely to be appreciable externalities from a capital investment project. **Stage 2** is more tricky and requires identifying all of the relevant external costs and benefits. Many of these may be intangible, such as 'noise' and 'beauty'. Evaluating and enumerating these externalities is undertaken in **Stage 3**. The intangible externalities may be particularly difficult to deal with; for example, how do we place a value on someone's loss of peace and quiet? In road improvement schemes, what value do we put on a human life? This stage can require tricky evaluation and sometimes the results may be highly controversial. Once all of the benefits and costs over the life of the project are enumerated, they must be discounted to present values, in the same manner as for private investments as detailed earlier. Lastly, in **Stage 4**, a decision must be reached as to whether or not to proceed with the capital investment. Especially in the public sector, the decision is likely to be influenced not only by the figures produced in Stage 3, but by political considerations. The conclusions of public sector CBA studies are sometimes overturned following political pressure from those likely to be most inconvenienced by the investment, for example those whose homes would be the most affected by a new motorway link or an airport runway extension. It should be noted, nevertheless, that CBA is particularly appropriate as a method for evaluating public sector capital programmes because they tend to be associated with externalities.

Although CBA has been associated predominantly with investment decision-making in the public sector, concerns about environmental issues (see pp. 312–16) have led some private sector firms to adopt a similar investment decision-making process. Such a process takes into account important externalities, as well as the usual financial costs and benefits associated with a capital project and that directly impact on the firm. For example, an oil company may take into account the impact on the natural environment of drilling for oil. A property company might decide to undertake a CBA of the impact of a new out-of-town shopping complex that it intends to develop – the results may be valuable when lobbying the planning authorities for their agreement!

Concluding remarks

This chapter has been concerned with the market for capital and investment appraisal. Profitable investment is a key factor in the long-term success of any enterprise. Hence it is important that all capital investments are carefully evaluated. We have seen that the profit-maximising firm (with no capital rationing) should adopt capital investment projects until the marginal revenue product of capital is equal to the marginal cost of capital. We have also examined a number of methods for appraising investments with particular attention given to the use of discounted cash flow techniques. DCF recognises the significance of the timing of revenues and expenses over the life of a project, whereas the main alternative frequently used in investment appraisal, the payback method, places a premium on the net returns in the early years of the investment.

This chapter has also considered the basic principles of how the cost of capital or the cost of raising finance for capital investment projects should be estimated. Where different sources of finance are used the appropriate measure is the weighted average cost of capital (WACC).

Whichever precise method of investment appraisal and selection is adopted, it is important to include all of the relevant costs and benefits. A profit-maximising firm may be concerned only with the costs to itself of undertaking and financing the investment and the revenues the project generates. In contrast, firms that have become more socially and environmentally aware will take into account the wider effects of their investments on the community. Cost–benefit analysis is a way of evaluating investments by taking into account *all* of the costs and benefits of a project to the firm and to society. Although initially developed for use in the public sector, it is now playing a greater role in private sector decision-making because of growing environmental awareness. Environmental issues are also important in the study of the market for natural resources, which is the subject of the next chapter.

Key learning points

- **Capital** is a factor of production which includes all physical, manufactured goods that are used in the production of other goods and services – for example, plant, machinery, buildings and business fixtures and fittings.
- The **stock of capital** is the quantity or value of the total capital invested with the firm.

- The **flow of capital** is the increase in the stock of capital over a given time period resulting from new capital investment.

- **Employment of capital** to maximise profits requires that the marginal cost of capital (MC_K) equals the marginal revenue product of capital (MRP_K), i.e.

$$MC_K = MRP_K$$

- The **marginal cost of capital** reflects the cost of financing investment and will vary depending upon the degree of competition for funds in the capital market.

- There are five steps in the **investment decision-making process**: generation of capital investment proposals, determination of the capital investment budget, evaluation and selection of capital investment projects, monitoring of capital investment performance, and post-audit project review.

- The **payback method** for evaluation of an investment project is based on an assessment of how quickly the investment can generate sufficient net cash returns to cover the initial investment outlay.

- The **net present value** and **internal rate of return** methods for evaluating and ranking investment projects are based on the concept of discounting expected cash flows back to the present day so as to obtain their net present value (PV).

- **Net present value (NPV)** is given by the formula:

$$NPV = \sum_{t=1}^{n} \frac{s_t}{(1 + r)^t}$$

where s is the incremental after-tax cash flow in each year t of the life of the project and r is the discount rate.

- If all of the capital outlays for a project occur in the current year, the **net present value (NPV)** of the stream of future cash flows arising from the project is given by:

$$NPV = \sum_{t=1}^{n} \frac{s_t}{(1 + r)^t} - I$$

where I is the initial investment outlay for the project. In general terms, if the NPV is positive the investment has a positive net return in present value terms and should be accepted; if NPV is negative it should be rejected.

- Another measure of the expected profitability of an investment is based on the **internal rate of return** (IRR) method where the IRR is defined as the rate of interest that equates the present value of a project's net cash flow to the initial investment outlay. To calculate its value we set the NPV for the project equal to zero and solve the equation below for the value of IRR which produces a zero NPV:

$$NPV = \sum_{t=1}^{n} \frac{s_t}{(1 + IRR)^t} - I = 0$$

- The **weighted average cost of capital** (WACC) is given by the weighted average of the cost of raising the funds for the capital investment project.

- If only **retained earnings** are used, the cost of capital is equal to the return that could have been earned if the internal funds were invested elsewhere (their opportunity cost).
- If only **equity finance** is used, the return to equity will be the same as the cost of capital.
- If a project is financed entirely by a **loan**, the cost of capital is the rate of interest paid on the loan.
- In practice, projects are often financed by a mixture of **debt and equity capital**. In this case, the calculation of the cost of capital raises issues concerning the impact of **leverage** or the **gearing ratio** (the proportion of debt to equity finance) on the overall WACC.

Topics for discussion

1 Using an appropriate diagram, explain how a profit-maximising firm should decide on the level of its capital investment when the firm:
   (a) is in a perfectly competitive capital market;
   (b) has monopsony power in the buying or hiring of capital equipment.

2 Strong Steels is deciding whether or not to invest in a new strip rolling mill. Advise on the approach the firm should adopt in appraising the possible investment.

3 After considering your report, Strong Steels has decided not to invest in the new mill because the payback period is 7 years. The company has a policy of investing only when the payback is 4 years or less. The strip rolling mill would have an expected life of at least 15 years. Comment on this decision.

4 Explain the difference between the 'net present value' and the 'internal rate of return' methods of investment appraisal.

5 How should the discount rate be set when a firm appraises its investments using the DCF method?

6 Suppose an investment project is expected to yield net cash over the next five years of $100m (year 1), $95m (year 2), $75m (year 3), $50m (year 4) and $80m (year 5). The initial cost of the project is $250m. A the end of the fifth year the investment has no residual value.
   (a) What is the payback period?
   (b) Calculate the NPV (assume a discount rate of 10%).
   (c) Calculate the internal rate of return.

7 How should a firm decide upon its weighted average cost of capital (WACC) and how does the WACC enter into NPV calculations?

8 The government is deciding whether to build a new rail link between two expanding regions. The aim is to move traffic from the roads, but building the link will mean demolishing 200 homes at a cost of $120m and will cost a total of $1.2bn to complete. Public works schemes have a discount rate of 10%. Expected rail receipts are put at $100m per annum over the next 10 years (the assumed life of the investment before major reinvestment will be needed). It would appear that the investment is not worthwhile. Do you agree?

9 Does cost–benefit analysis have any part to play in private-sector investment decisions? Explain your answer.

15 Understanding the market for natural resources

Aims and learning outcomes

The previous two chapters have dealt with two important factors of production, namely labour (Chapter 13) and capital (Chapter 14). In this chapter we now turn to the study of a further factor of production – natural resources, including land and minerals. A discussion of this factor of production also requires consideration of the importance of the natural environment (involving exploitation of finite resources) and the impact on long-term economic activity of degrading the quality of the natural environment (e.g. through industrial pollution). The importance of this topic to business decisions and government policy has increased significantly in recent years as a result of the debate concerning global warming and the sustainability of economic growth. Below we identify the key principles which underlie the market for natural resources.

In this chapter, the following concepts are covered:

- The market for natural resources.
- Economic rent verses quasi-economic rent.
- Environmental issues.

This subject clearly has implications for future social welfare. The environmental costs arising from the production of goods and services not only impact on current firms and society at large but also pose considerable challenges for future generations.

Learning outcomes

This chapter will help you to:

- Understand the role of *land and other natural resources* in the production of goods and services.
- Appreciate how the prices of land and other natural resources are determined by the interaction of demand and supply.
- Identify how a resource in finite supply (e.g. land) may earn *economic rent* or a payment above its *transfer earnings*.
- Distinguish between economic rent and *quasi-economic rent*.
- Grasp the importance of *environmental* issues in the production process.
- Appreciate the implications for *social welfare* of environmental costs arising from the production of goods and services and how these may be best tackled.
- Understand the meaning and importance of *property rights* in a discussion of environmental issues.

The market for natural resources

Businesses combine labour, capital and natural resources to produce goods and services. An obvious natural resource is land which, unlike the other two factors of production, is generally fixed in total supply. This means that in total land has more or less a perfectly inelastic supply and, therefore, the price of land (sometimes referred to as its *rental rate*) may be thought to depend solely or very largely on the level of the demand for land. This is so for geographic reasons. Although some land reclamation does occur each year – and some land slips back into the sea – the total supply of all land varies very little from year to year.

Figure 15.1 below illustrates the case where land is perfectly inelastic in supply and only the level of demand determines its price (rental rate). When the demand for land increases from DD to D_1D_1, the price rises from P_1 to P_2 for the fixed quantity Q.

In practice, of course, land has alternative uses and the economic value is directly determined by the level of demand relating to each possible use. In other words, while the total amount of land is more or less in fixed supply, this is not the case for land for particular uses. For example, agricultural land can sometimes be switched to land used for building or leisure purposes.

However, suppose that there was only one possible use for land and that the supply available for this use was Q (as in Figure 15.1). In such a case, given that the land has no alternative use, the opportunity cost (i.e. the benefit forgone in the next best alternative use) is zero. This means that all of the revenue from the land is *economic rent*.

Economic rent **represents the earnings to a factor of production over and above its opportunity cost or the minimum payment needed to keep it in its present use, known as the** *transfer earnings***.**

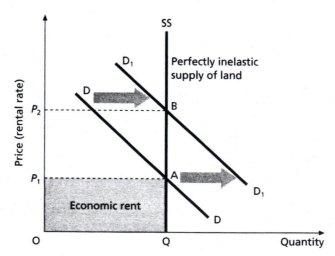

Figure 15.1 The market for land – perfectly inelastic supply

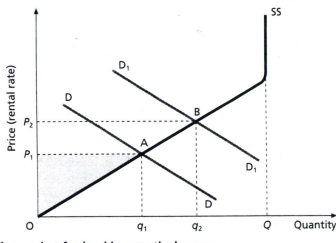

Figure 15.2 The market for land in a particular use

In Figure 15.1, with the level of demand DD, the economic rent is equivalent to the shaded area, OP_1AQ. The higher the demand for the land, the higher the economic rent. For example, if demand rose from DD to D_1D_1, the total economic rent would increase to OP_2BQ. It should be obvious, therefore, that provided the demand for land is greater than the supply, OQ, economic rent will be earned. Another implication is that economic rent could be taxed by government and there would be no effect on the quantity of land supplied. Only if the owner of the land suffered a tax on its use that attempted to remove more than the economic rent earned would supply be affected – in which case it would pay the owner of the land not to offer the land for productive use.

As is noted above, land normally has a number of alternative uses. In which case, the supply is not perfectly inelastic, as shown in Figure 15.1. Figure 15.2 shows the more normal case where, although the total amount of land available is still fixed at OQ, it has alternative uses. Here, when demand increases from DD to D_1D_1, more land is made available to satisfy the demand related to this particular use. The supply for this use, therefore, increases from Oq_1 to Oq_2 and the price rises from P_1 to P_2 – a rise in price which is less than would have occurred if the supply of land had been perfectly inelastic with respect to this particular use. Given that the land has alternative uses, its availability for one particular use implies a positive opportunity cost. This opportunity cost is represented by the area under supply curve SS. For example, at price P_1, the opportunity cost is given by the area OAq_1. The economic rent is the payment over and above the opportunity cost and is now represented by the shaded area OP_1A. In other words, where land has an alternative use, the economic rent is smaller than where it has only one use.

It should be noted, incidentally, that the same principle concerning economic rent and the elasticity of supply applies to any factor of production. For instance, an individual world-class professional footballer is in fixed supply and consequently earns substantial economic rent, represented by the income earned over and above what the player could have earned in his alternative employment – referred to as the *transfer earnings*.

Returning to Figure 15.2, the increase in demand from DD to D_1D_1, leads to greater economic rent, given by the area OP_2B. Should demand continue to increase and eventually exceed the maximum that can be supplied, namely OQ, then all further earnings will represent pure economic rent, as in the case shown in Figure 15.1.

When demand for land increases with respect to a particular use, some land is switched away from other uses to satisfy this demand. Similarly, if the demand for land in a particular use falls, it will pay landowners to switch some of the land to alternative uses. Indeed, in a competitive market for land, switching between alternative uses will occur until such times as the price (rental rate) of land in each use is the same. If this were not the case, it would be profitable for the landowner to continue to switch land from a lower priced to a higher priced usage.

A similar argument applies in relation to other natural resources that are in finite supply. The price of iron ore or bauxite on world commodity markets will fluctuate according to the current level of demand. This means that producers at times of high demand can earn substantial economic rents. Economic rents also arise in the housing market. At times when there is an acute shortage of suitable building land, land prices tend to rise sharply, creating economic rents for landowners. This leads to a common error of blaming high new house prices on the high prices demanded by landowners to release land for building purposes. This is mistaken because, like other factors of production, land has what is called a *derived demand* – it is demanded for the services it provides.

As David Ricardo pointed out in the early nineteenth century, the price of land reflects the demand for its services. In the housing market high land prices arise when there is a high consumer demand for new residential accommodation. In other words, the blame for high house prices lies with the market for housing and not with the greed of landowners. Landowners can only obtain a high price for their land if there is a high demand for it. This explains why the price of building land fluctuates substantially, reflecting booms and slumps in the domestic housing market. Again, this explanation of volatile prices applies to all markets for natural resources, whose supply tends to be fixed or fairly fixed in supply, at least in the short run.

Economic rent versus quasi-economic rent

The above discussion has highlighted why a large economic rent can be earned by a factor of production which is perfectly inelastic (fixed) in supply or where there is a relatively fixed supply (a highly inelastic supply). This applies particularly to land and other natural resources that are in finite supply.

In some market situations a factor of production may be in inelastic supply leading to economic rents for some significant period of time. In the longer run, however, the supply can be varied. For example, exploration for new mineral resources occurs when their market prices are high because of the opportunities to make large profits by supplying more resources to the market. Eventually, therefore, new mines, oil fields, etc. start production leading, *ceteris paribus*, to lower prices in the market. In such cases

Regional housing markets

Regional house price inflation in 1999

The bar chart shows regional house price inflation in the UK in 1999. Across the UK as a whole house prices rose by around 7%, but in some regions house price inflation was much higher. In London prices rose by over 16%. By contrast, those areas of the UK that were less economically buoyant that year, such as the West Midlands and Scotland, saw much lower price increases.

Determination of house prices

House prices are driven by demand and supply. The demand for housing is related to incomes. Households with higher incomes tend to 'trade up' in the market by buying larger and more expensive properties. The demand for housing is also linked to mortgage rates (the rate of interest on property loans) and expectations of future house prices. When house prices are rising people may well accelerate their search for a new property in anticipation of having to pay more for the same quality of property at a later date.

The supply of housing depends upon the existing stock of housing, the willingness of owners to put their properties on the market, and the rate of new house building. At times of rising house prices land prices are bid up therefore increasing the cost to house builders of constructing new properties. Major beneficiaries of a housing boom are those who are already in the housing market, and who see an appreciation in the value of their properties (a kind of 'windfall' gain) and landowners. Land released for house building fetches much higher prices at a time of fast increasing property values.

Activity

With reference to the bar chart discuss, using appropriate demand and supply diagrams, the reasons for differences in house price inflation in different parts of the UK. What are the implications for the economic rents earned by house owners and landowners in different regions?

economic rents may prove to be temporary. Temporary economic rents are referred to as *quasi-economic rents*.

Quasi-economic rents occur when a factor of production earns economic rents that are competed away in the long run as the supply of the factor of production is increased.

Quasi-economic rents are common in market economies and act as an incentive for producers to compete in markets. For example, suppose that there was a large increase in the demand for rapeseed oil. Farmers who had already planted and were now harvesting rapeseed would earn higher than expected prices for their crops. These prices would presumably exceed the opportunity cost (transfer earnings) of the land used for growing rapeseed, leading to the farmers earning economic rents. These rents from rapeseed growing would, however, lead farmers to switch land from other uses (e.g. growing wheat or dairy farming) to growing rapeseed. The result would be a much larger supply of rapeseed at the next harvest and, *ceteris paribus*, a fall in the price of rapeseed oil. Therefore, the economic rent is competed away. This is an example of how, in competitive markets, economic rents tend to be temporary or *quasi-rents*. It should be remembered that in the discussion of competitive markets earlier in this book, supernormal profits – a type of economic rent – were similarly removed by competition, in the long run. Supernormal profit in the short run, therefore, is a quasi-economic rent in perfect competition and monopolistic competition (see Chapters 6 and 8). It disappears in the long run. By contrast, under conditions of monopoly, supernormal profit is an economic rent that because of barriers to market entry cannot be competed away (Chapter 7).

Environmental issues

An important issue for business today is the growing public concern about a perceived deterioration in the quality of the physical environment. In particular, problems involving pollution, depletion of non-renewable resources, over-fishing of the seas, etc. are receiving growing media attention. In response, businesses are having to demonstrate a greater concern for the impact of their decisions on the environment and governments are having to respond to these so-called 'green issues'.

Environmental issues may be discussed under the two broad headings of:

- Social welfare.
- Property rights.

Social welfare relates to the well-being of society and reflects both private (internal) and public (external) costs and benefits stemming from the production of goods and services. Social welfare can therefore be affected by those activities which damage the environment. Activities which are the focus of much of the debate today concerning the impact on the environment include road usage, energy generation, use of finite natural resources, over-fishing, etc.

The Kuznets curve

Environmental damage and economic growth

The environmental Kuznets curve relates the level of environmental degradation to the level of economic development. It suggests that at first there is a direct relationship between environmental damage and GDP per capita. This seems borne out by the USA. The USA has one of the highest incomes per head and accounts for around 25% of all of the world's greenhouse gases.

The Kuznets curve, however, is an inverted-U shape. It suggests that beyond a certain level of economic development public pressure mounts for environmental legislation and consumers become more environmentally aware. The richer we become the more resources we consume and the more environmental degradation tends to occur, but the Kuznets curve suggests that the environment is, in effect, a good with a high income elasticity of demand. The richer consumers are the more concerns they have for the environment. The result is a growing willingness to invest larger amounts in environmental schemes such as energy saving, emission purification schemes, recycling, etc. The Kuznets curve may help us to understand why the quality of the air in a major European city such as Paris is much superior to the quality of the air in a developing-economy city such as Bangkok.

The Kuznets curve is criticised, however. For instance it puts an emphasis on the benefits of economic growth, whereas some environmentalists would argue that economic growth is the problem rather than the solution. For some it also glosses over why the inverted-U really occurs. One possibility is that as countries develop they transfer their dirtier and more unpleasant, heavy industries to lower income economies. Cleaner rivers in the UK today result in part from de-industrialisation. Finally, some would suggest that environmental degradation actually damages the prospects for future economic growth.

Activity

Explore the relationship between economic development and environmental damage. To what extent is environmental degradation 'a problem' or simply a reflection of consumer preference?

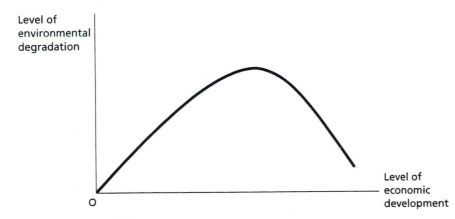

The environmental Kuznets curve

Property rights in the context of environmental issues are concerned with assets that are over-used because their ownership is not clearly defined or protected in law.

Social welfare

Pollution, noise and other undesirable environmental effects are examples of *external* economic costs associated with business activity. When consumers use more electricity, the price they pay for this additional supply reflects generation, transmission and other supply costs incurred by the electricity producers and suppliers. There may, however, be other costs incurred by society in general, that are not reflected in these (private or internal) costs of supply. An obvious example of an external cost in the case of electricity generation is the pollution resulting from power station emissions. The costs associated with this pollution (such as health risks and global warming) are not borne by the generating company directly but by the public in general – giving rise to *social costs* and a reduction in *social welfare*.

Figure 15.3 illustrates the difference between private costs and social costs and implications for social welfare. The MC curve represents the private marginal costs associated with increasing production (the cost to the electricity generating and supplying firms of producing and supplying each unit of electricity). By contrast the MSC curve represents the *marginal social costs* of producing extra units. This curve lies above the MC reflecting the fact that the external costs to society of producing more electricity are now included. The vertical distance between the two curves is a measure of the external costs, which in this case are assumed to rise as electricity production rises (hence the distance between the MC and MSC curves increases with output).

The MSB curve represents the *marginal social benefit* associated with the consumption of each extra unit of the good. Assuming that there are no external benefits from consuming the good, then the MSB curve is also the product's demand curve. In other words, only the consumers of electricity benefit from (or obtain *utility* from) electricity generation and supply.

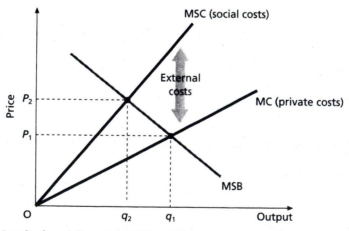

Figure 15.3 Marginal social costs and benefits

In the absence of government intervention the output supplied would be where private marginal costs are equal to marginal social benefits, i.e. the output q_1 in Figure 15.3. This output would be sold in the market for price P_1. At output q_1, however, marginal social costs exceed marginal social benefits from the production, implying a social welfare loss. Social welfare is maximised at output q_2 (where MSC = MSB).

Output could be reduced by government from q_1 to q_2 in one of the following ways:

- **Taxation.** A tax could be levied on each unit produced and sold thereby raising the price from P_1 to P_2 (for more detail of how taxes affect prices and outputs see the discussion of the incidence of a tax, pp. 128–30).

- **Prohibition or regulation.** Government could prohibit or regulate electricity output to ensure that it does not rise above output q_2.

- **Pollution permits.** Permits to produce and thereby cause some pollution could be sold by government and perhaps traded between producers. Producers would have an incentive to curb pollution voluntarily because they could then sell some, or all of their permits to pollute to other companies. In effect the pollution permit becomes an asset of the firm to be used and traded like any other valuable asset.

In general, economists tend to prefer market solutions to economic problems. State prohibitions and regulations may distort production leading to economic loss. For example, new efficient producers may be unable to enter the industry because of government restrictions on the industry's total output. In recent years tradable pollution permits have gained in popularity amongst economists as a solution to external costs, such as industrial pollution, because the resulting market in the permits should lead to them being allocated efficiently. Efficient, low-cost producers are likely to be willing to pay more for the permits, and thereby obtain more of them, than higher cost, lower profit producers.

To summarise the above discussion concerning the social welfare implications associated with production and the environment:

- If MSB *is less than* MSC, output should be reduced.
- If MSB *equals* MSC, output is at the appropriate level to maximise social welfare.
- If MSB *exceeds* MSC, increased output should be encouraged.

Property rights

Property rights are concerned with the rights to benefit from, utilise and transfer property. Most assets in modern economies have clearly defined property rights. For instance, the owner of a retail store will own the freehold or the lease of the shop, will own the stock, and will have full rights to benefit from the economic activities of the store. Some property in society has, however, much less clearly defined property rights. The air and the seas are good examples. It can be argued that the reason that the air is polluted by emissions is that no one has clear property rights over the air around us. If the air was owned by someone them presumably that person would expect to be paid by polluters for adversely affecting their 'property'! Similarly, over-fishing is a serious problem in our seas and arguably occurs because the seas, and the fish in them, are considered to be owned in common. If fish in a sector of the seas were privately owned the owner would have a clear incentive to protect fish stocks just as any property owner has an incentive to protect his or her property. Over-fishing, leading to asset depletion, would eventually lead to serious economic loss to the owner.

In other words, economists often argue that it is the lack of clear property rights that leads to externalities, over-production and lower social welfare. In which case the answer is to allocate and enforce property rights. Governments have claimed rights to fishing in coastal waters for their country's fishing fleets. This may help to preserve fish stocks. International waters are, however, open to all countries to fish unless particular agreements are reached, e.g. the EU's fisheries policy. By its very nature, property rights over the use of the air are also problematic, though international agreements do cover such matters as airspace for aircraft and the allocation of frequencies for radio and TV broadcasting.

Concluding remarks

Production in market economies results from combining the inputs of factors of production to produce the output demanded by consumers. Previous chapters looked at the markets for labour and capital while this chapter has been concerned with the market for natural resources, and especially land.

Natural resources are ultimately finite in supply. Land, in particular, in total is more or less perfectly inelastic in supply, although it has a more elastic supply when considered in terms of the uses to which it can be put. Any factor of production in high demand is likely to receive earnings over and above what could be earned in the factor's next best alternative use. This gives rise to the concepts of economic rent and transfer earnings. As land has an inelastic supply, when the demand for land for a particular use rises, landowners are likely to receive economic rents. Where these rents are merely temporary, for example until more land is made available and the price of land then falls, these rents are referred to as quasi-economic rents.

In recent years, there has been growing concern in society about the over-exploitation of the world's natural resources and the environmental damage caused by the production of goods and services. This has moved the discussion of environmental costs higher up the agenda of many businesses and governments. From a social welfare perspective, production should occur at the level of output where marginal social costs (private and external costs) are equal to the marginal social benefits (private and external benefits) from consuming the output. The socially efficient level of production will, therefore, be lower in the presence of external costs (and higher in the presence of external benefits) than would result in the free market. This introduces a possible role for intervention by government in market transactions; in the case of environmental costs to reduce production and consumption through taxation, prohibition, regulation, or production permits.

A discussion of environmental issues also draws attention to the role and importance of property rights in society. Where property rights are not clearly defined and are poorly protected, then resources are likely to be subject to over-use.

In the next chapter, the subject of external costs and benefits is further developed in a discussion of the role of government in business.

Key learning points

- **Natural resources** including the supply of land are an important input into the production process, alongside labour and capital.

- Natural resources ultimately tend to be **finite in supply**, although there may be many competing alternative uses to which they can be put.

- **Economic rent** represents the earnings to a factor of production over and above its opportunity cost or the minimum payment needed to keep the factor of production in its present use, known as its **transfer earnings.**

- Economic rent tends to arise when a factor of production is **inelastic in supply** such as land, and the demand for the factor of production increases.

- **Quasi-economic rents** occur when the supply of the factor of production can be increased in the long run and the economic rents are therefore competed away.

- From the viewpoint of **social welfare**, natural resources should be used in productive activities up to the point where the marginal social benefit from their use is equal to the marginal social cost arising from their use; i.e. MSB = MSC represents the condition for a socially efficient level of production.

- Governments may become involved in the market process to limit production and consumption where there are appreciable **external costs**, such as pollution, through taxation, prohibition, regulation and pollution permits.

- Where there is no clear ownership or **property rights** over natural resources (e.g. fish in the sea) then over-production and over-consumption are likely to arise.

Topics for discussion

1 'House price rises are caused by greedy landowners.' Discuss.

2 Consider the case for the imposition of a development land tax by government. (Development land tax is a tax on the value of land used for development, e.g. housebuilding or industrial use.)

3 Will taxation of economic rents affect the allocation of resources?

4 Discuss the case for using pollution permits rather than prohibitions on new production to limit the environmental damage from the production of goods and services.

5 What issues are likely to be considered when an environmental audit is conducted by:

   (a) government;
   (b) a profit-maximising firm?

6 Consider the role of property rights in a discussion of environmental issues.

16 Government and business

Aims and learning outcomes

This book is primarily concerned with the firm and its relationship with the markets in which it sells its products and buys its inputs. In this chapter, however, we turn to consider the impact of government on managerial decision-making. In most of the advanced economies today the state has a major role with government expenditure and taxation usually accounting for over 40% of total gross domestic product. The role of government extends beyond the provision of social and economic services, such as education and health care, to establishing and policing property rights, limiting business activities (e.g. to protect the environment), maintaining the infrastructure (e.g. roads and airports), and to providing a safety net in the shape of unemployment, sickness and disability benefits.

This chapter covers the following aspects of the impact of government on the business environment and managerial decision-making:

- Analysis of the business environment.
- The principles of state intervention.
- Macroeconomic policy.
- Industrial policy.
- Competition law.
- Regional policy.

It will be appreciated that the potential scope of this chapter is very wide. Governments intervene in market economies in many ways. Also, the form the intervention takes varies from country to country and from time to time. Inevitably, therefore, we are only able to provide a very broad overview of the key principles of government policy that impact on businesses and their wider environment.

Learning outcomes

This chapter will help you to:

- Appreciate the importance of the wider business environment in the context of developing a business strategy, based on a *PEST analysis.*
- Understand the meaning of *market failure* and the distinction between *public goods* and *private goods.*

- Recognise the importance and role of government in *market intervention*.
- Identify the *drivers of economic activity* and the role of government in influencing the level of economic activity through various policy options.
- Appreciate the impact of *industrial policy* on the development of particular industries, sectors of the economy, or firms.
- Grasp the fundamental principles of *competition law* and the reasons for regulating monopolies and prohibiting restrictive practices.
- Understand the role of *regional policy* in the reversal of regional decline and in the limitation of regional expansion.

Analysis of the business environment

A common approach in management when evolving a business strategy is to undertake an analysis of the wider, changing, business environment (we addressed the importance of this briefly in Chapter 1). The study of the wider environment is commonly referred to as a PEST analysis.

A PEST analysis is concerned with identifying and evaluating the *Political, Economic, Social* and *Technological* factors likely to impact on the business in the time period under study (Figure 16.1).

For example, a PEST study for the German telecommunications industry in 2001 might have revealed the following factors (the list is far from exhaustive):

- **Political.** Expansion of the European Union to include new member states, licensing regimes.
- **Economic.** European integration, EU telecommunications liberalisation directives, introduction of the euro, 3G licences and development of national regulatory authorities.

Figure 16.1 A PEST analysis

- **Social**. Universal service obligation and concern for the environment.
- **Technological**. Fast technological change, development of new mobile communications, optical fibre systems and convergence of telecommunications and broadcasting.

By identifying and evaluating the relevant factors likely to impact on the industry through a PEST analysis, management can formulate an appropriate strategy to take advantage of expected opportunities and minimise the impact of anticipated threats.

Obviously, government economic policy will usually be central to a PEST study. Changes in government policy have a major impact not only on the political environment but on the economic, social and technological future that an industry faces. For example, higher interest rates can be expected to slow down economic activity (economic), lead to higher unemployment (social), reduce political support for the government (political), and affect the level of investment in new technology and R&D (technological change). An understanding of the nature of government economic policy is therefore crucial to successful managerial decision-making (for a full treatment of government policy at the macroeconomic level, see our companion volume, *Principles of Macroeconomics*).

In the rest of this chapter we consider the principles underpinning state intervention before moving on to look at the following four key areas of state involvement in the market:

- Macroeconomic policy.
- Industrial policy.
- Competition law.
- Regional policy.

It is important to appreciate the growing significance of European Union (EU) legislation for businesses operating in or trading with the EU. In the past, a discussion of the impact of government on business was likely to have centred upon the role of national governments. French managers were primarily affected by the nature and scope of French state intervention in the economy, German managers with German economic policy and so on. Nowadays, however, the EU is playing an increasing role in the economies of member states. This extends to the macroeconomy where the introduction of a common currency, the euro, has reduced the freedom of national governments to pursue independent monetary and fiscal policies, and to the microeconomy where the EU is developing European industrial and social policies. At the same time, the 1986 Single European Act introduced a new momentum into European integration, helping to sweep away a number of the remaining barriers to free trade and free movement of factors of production in the EU. Frontier checks have been simplified, public procurement programmes liberalised, trade-distorting taxes and subsidies simplified and technical standards levelled. Similarly, in North and South America and the Far East trading agreements, such as NAFTA, Mercosur, APEC, etc., are leading to the development of alternative trading blocs.

The principles of state intervention

Economists usually argue that the market is an efficient allocator of resources because it is based on consumer choice. There may be certain circumstances, however, where this is not true and the free market cannot be relied upon to provide an optimal allocation of resources resulting in *market failure*. This is most likely to occur where there is monopoly or where there are appreciable *externalities*.

'Market failure' occurs where the market price fails to reflect the true *social benefit* of consuming a good or service and the marginal cost fails to reflect the true *social cost* of providing the good or service. A normal or *private good* has no appreciable social costs and benefits. By contrast, a *public good* is one where such externalities are pervasive. More correctly, a *public good* is non-excludable and non-rival.

- *Non-excludable*: it is not possible (or possible without prohibitive cost) to exclude non-payers from benefiting from consumption of the good; e.g. those who choose not to be vaccinated against a disease may still benefit because provided others are vaccinated they are less likely to contract the disease.
- *Non-rival*: there is little or no social advantage from excluding non-payers from consuming the good or service because consumption by one person does not reduce the amount that can be consumed by others (the good or service is 'non-rival'); e.g. defending an additional person or persons in a locality adds no additional cost to the national defence budget.

Private goods are excludable and rival and non-payers do not benefit from their provision. Goods or services that are true 'public goods' are subject to a 'free rider' problem, namely as non-payers benefit alongside payers, there is no incentive for any individual to reveal their preference for the good. The result is that the free market records a lower than optimal demand for the public good or service leading to under-provision. In such circumstances state provision and compulsory payment through taxation may make sense.

We have already had cause to refer to externalities in Chapters 1 and 15. The term refers to benefits and costs which are not reflected in the prices paid by the consumers of the immediate product. Where there are appreciable external costs or benefits, state intervention may take one or other of the following two forms with the objective of encouraging or discouraging consumption:

- Subsidy or taxation of products.
- Prohibiting, licensing or regulating suppliers.

Presuming that government has the objective of maximising social well-being, consumption should be encouraged of those products which are believed to have significant

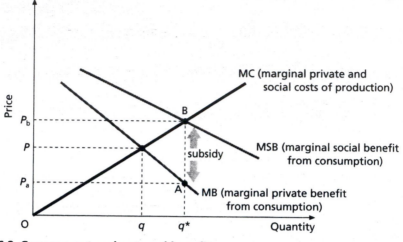

Figure 16.2 Government and external benefits

external benefits (e.g. education and health care), while the consumption of products with external costs should be discouraged (e.g. leaded petrol and noisy aircraft). Therefore, today most governments are involved in one form or another in encouraging the supply of health and education services, usually through provision or regulation and direct or indirect subsidies, and discouraging pollution and noise, through regulations, licensing and taxes. Figure 16.2 illustrates how government can improve social welfare by increasing consumption using a price subsidy. Assume that the (private) marginal cost (MC) of production also represents the marginal *social* costs of production; in other words there are no external costs in this example. There are, however, external benefits from consumption; hence the MB curve represents the (private) marginal benefits that consumers receive by consuming the good or service and the MSB curve represents the marginal *social* benefits. The vertical difference between the MB and MSB curves reflects the degree of external benefits from consumption. In this diagram the gap between the two curves widens as output and consumption rise, implying larger external benefits from increased consumption (e.g. the larger the number of people who purchase immunisation from a disease, the more the remainder of society is protected from infection). Without government subsidy or other state intervention output q will be produced and consumed and the market price will be at level P (where MB = MC). To increase production and consumption to the socially desirable level q^* (where MSB = MC) the state could introduce a subsidy equivalent to the distance AB. Producers will now receive the price P_b, which they require to cover the higher marginal costs of producing output q^*, and consumers purchase the output at price P_a. This illustrates how government can use subsidies to stimulate production and consumption to reflect external benefits. Note also that government can also intervene in the market using taxes to reduce production and consumption in the presence of external costs (this case was discussed in detail in Chapter 15, pp. 314–15).

In addition to encouraging or discouraging consumption where there are appreciable external benefits or external costs respectively, governments also intervene in markets for the following reasons:

- **To regulate the level of economic activity.** Since the Great Depression of the 1930s, governments have tended to believe that the level of economic activity cannot be safely left to market forces. This has applied to both right-of-centre and left-of-centre governments. In newly developing economies governments have 'planned' investment, often using powerful state companies. In the developed economies measures have been adopted to influence investment and consumption with a view to minimising unemployment while avoiding damaging inflation and balance-of-payments problems.

- **To protect consumers and employees.** Although the consumer is considered to be sovereign in market economies, many governments have introduced laws to prevent undesirable trading. Consumer protection law covers such issues as prohibiting anti-competitive practices and provision of safety standards. Most countries also have laws to protect the small investor. In the United Kingdom advertising is self-regulated through the Advertising Standards Authority, though if the 'voluntary' code failed government would no doubt intervene directly to prevent misleading advertisements. Governments also have a number of laws relating to the labour market covering the operation of collective bargaining, health and safety at work, equal opportunities, hours of work and statutory minimum wages. Initially, these laws were motivated by a desire to protect workers considered to be at risk of exploitation by unscrupulous employers.

- **To alter the free market distribution of income and wealth.** Decisions about the 'right' income and wealth distribution are largely social and political, reflecting the values held by society at the time. In this century, democratic governments through progressive taxation and state welfare benefits have become involved in redistributing incomes and wealth from the richer to the poorer sections of the community. During the 1980s the pattern of income distribution was reversed in a number of countries, such as the United Kingdom and the United States, because of worries about the impact of high taxes and generous welfare benefits on incentives to work, save and invest. To what extent this is a temporary change remains to be seen. Also, governments have intervened in the location of businesses through regional policy with a view to redistributing income and wealth spatially.

In the pursuit of these goals governments have introduced a range of policies, the details of which are summarised below. But before turning to the policies it is important to note that while the market can 'fail', in the sense of providing a sub-optimal allocation of resources, so can the state. 'State failure' is the term used to refer to the economic distortions caused by wasteful public spending, taxation disincentives and economically damaging regulation. The state may worsen rather than improve economic welfare because of information and incentive problems.

- **Information.** The market co-ordinates the decisions of millions of consumers and producers every minute of every day. It is inconceivable that a state bureaucrat or planning committee could gather and process a similar amount of information. The result is that consumer demands and resource costs may well be incorrectly evaluated by the state, leading to economic waste.

- **Incentives**. Even if the state could gather and process the appropriate information about consumer wants and production costs, there is by no means any guarantee that politicians and state officials would then allocate resources accordingly. Politicians and civil servants could be prone to pursuing their own utility (salaries, plush offices, tenure, etc.) rather than the public's utility or pursuing the ends of groups that have particular power within the political process (e.g. captains of industry and trade union officials).

Information and incentive costs can be expected to be pervasive within government. There can be no guarantee, therefore, that state intervention will improve upon an (imperfect) market allocation. Modern economies suffer from both market and state failure and whichever is the greater problem at any particular time needs careful evaluation.

Macroeconomic policy

Government macroeconomic policy is concerned with regulation of the level of economic activity. It therefore impacts directly on businesses by affecting the level of consumer demand and the cost of raising capital. Economies are complex and to many managers fluctuations in economic activity must seem hard to explain or predict. However, managers need to have some understanding of the nature of macroeconomic policy if they are to anticipate successfully the consequences for their trades of policy changes, e.g. a rise in interest rates. It is important to appreciate *why* authorities alter interest rates, taxes and spending and *how* the level of economic activity and hence consumer demand are likely to respond. Firms that ignore the macroeconomic environment are likely to be wrong-footed by policy changes.

In essence, we can usefully liken an economy to a water barrel, as illustrated in Figure 16.3. The level of water in the barrel represents the level of economic activity. When the water level is constant this is equivalent to a stable level of economic activity. When it rises too quickly and begins to overflow the top of the barrel, this is equivalent to inflation caused by an excessive level of economic activity which pushes up costs and prices and leads to a deterioration in the balance of payments (due to too much demand relative to the domestic supply of goods and services). If the water level falls sharply then this represents a decline in economic activity, which usually leads to unemployment and bankruptcies (due to too little demand relative to supply). Although this is a simple representation of the workings of an economy, the central message is clear – the key to good government policy lies in keeping economic activity at a level where the economy is fully employed without inflation. In Figure 16.3 this is the level FE which, it should be noted, is below the top of the barrel. Economies need some unemployed

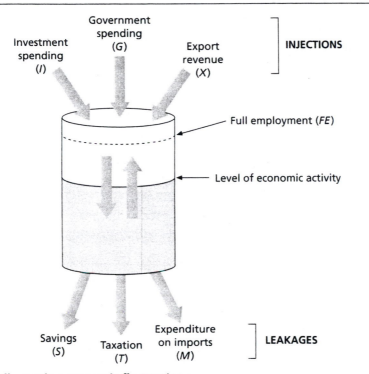

Figure 16.3 Illustrating economic fluctuations

resources – it would be unwise to attempt to achieve 0% unemployment because a dynamic economy is associated with some unemployment as people move from declining to expanding activities and from one job to another. Putting this another way, operating with a completely full barrel risks a 'spillage' of demand leading to inflation and balance-of-payments difficulties.

You will notice from the figure that there are a number of inflows and outflows from an economy. The 'leakages' are savings (S), taxation (T) and expenditure on imports (M). The 'injections' are investment (I), government spending (G) and revenue from exports (X). In an economy, savings, taxation and spending on imports all reduce the level of economic activity, in the sense that there is less income left over to continue circulating around the economy in the form of demand for the goods and services produced. For example, if households save more and spend less, retail sales in the high street decline, leading to fewer factory orders and so on. In contrast, investment spending, government spending and export sales increase the level of economic activity by adding to total domestic income. For example, new investment in office buildings leads to more orders for the construction industry, more employment in this industry and ultimately more spending in the shops. We can therefore say that just as the level of water in the barrel will vary depending upon the relative size of the inflows and outflows of water, so the level of economic activity is affected by the relative size of the *injections into* and *leakages out* of the economy at any given time. It follows therefore that:

If

$$I + G + X \text{ equals } S + T + M$$

then the level of economic activity stays constant.

If

$$I + G + X \text{ exceeds } S + T + M$$

then the level of economic activity will *rise*.

If

$$I + G + X \text{ is less than } S + T + M$$

then the level of economic activity will *fall*.

From this analysis we can better understand the nature and form of macroeconomic policy. Since 1945, Western governments, notably in the United Kingdom and the United States, have tended to pursue active measures aimed at maintaining the level of economic activity, so if it appeared that the level of economic activity was declining, action was taken to reduce the leakages and increase the injections. For example, in terms of monetary policy interest rates might be cut both to act as a disincentive to save and as an incentive to invest. Alternatively, in terms of fiscal policy government could reduce taxation and increase its own spending (G). If the level of economic activity appeared to be rising too quickly, leading to inflation, then these policies could be reversed.

In more recent years some governments have questioned the value of such intervention and have preferred to rely more on market forces to restore the full employment income level. Government policy has, therefore, been aimed at removing impediments to free-market forces, for example by reducing trade union powers, removing government regulations and lowering tax rates. This policy stance involves reducing the restrictions on supply in the economy and is therefore broadly described as *supply side policy*, in contrast to *demand side* economic management. In particular, questions have been raised about the desirability of using public spending and taxation as a means of regulating the economic injections and leakages. Critics have argued that such demand-side interventionist policies are often mis-timed, leading to an unfavourable impact on economic activity, and that governments vying for votes through more public spending create higher and higher inflation.

Increasingly, macroeconomic policy in the EU is constrained by economic and monetary union. The introduction of the euro and replacement of national currencies limits the freedom of member governments to pursue independent monetary policies. Interest rates in the EU are now set by the European Central Bank (ECB) and have to be set with an eye to maintaining macroeconomic stability across the EU rather than in any individual member state. Also, in the absence of the possibility of devaluing their currency, member states can maintain price competitiveness in international trade only by ensuring that national inflation is not out of line with the rate in other member countries. This in turn requires more co-ordination in the EU of tax and government spending, thus further reducing the scope for independent reflationary policies. In the future, if the power of the major EU political bodies (the European Parliament and the Council of Ministers) and of the European civil service (the European Commission) over macroeconomic policy increases, the role of national governments will further diminish. Macroeconomic management will be shaped increasingly on a European scale. The same applies to industrial policy.

Industrial policy

All economic policies have some effect on business, but industrial policy is concerned with those policies which are intentionally adopted by governments with a view to influencing the development of particular industries, sectors of the economy, or firms. Industrial policy impacts on business structure and business restructuring.

A market economy is naturally associated with constant change resulting, in particular, from changes in consumer demand and new technologies. Consequently, at any given time some industries and businesses will be expanding while others are contracting. A problem can arise, however, in terms of *adjustment costs*. The decline of an industry can mean high unemployment and social deprivation, especially when it has been concentrated in particular regions of the economy, for example as in the cases of coal mining and shipbuilding. The rise of a new industry might be held back by inadequate risk capital or labour shortages. For these and related reasons, governments have felt the need to introduce industrial policies to speed up or slow down economic change.

Accelerative industrial policies are designed to speed up the adjustment process, for example by providing 'soft loans', tax allowances, state subsidies and restructuring grants. By contrast, *decelerative* policies are intended to slow down the pace of change, usually through financial aid, and are usually directed at industries in serious decline. In both cases the state intervention may either be aimed at one firm or selected firms or spread across an industry or business sector.

The matrix in Figure 16.4 offers a convenient means of analysing the various types of industrial policy in relation to the precise focus and whether the policy is intended to be accelerative or decelerative. In box 1 lies the 'national champion' strategy. Here the state attempts through sponsoring mergers and financial aid to build up a major and internationally competitive enterprise. This sort of initiative was especially fashionable in the 1960s in Europe and led, for example, to the rise of the electrical giant Thomson

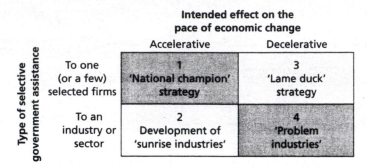

Figure 16.4 Basic types of industrial policy
Source: Based on J. Burton (1991) 'Industrial Policy: the European Context', *Business Studies*, October, p. 6.

in France and the motor goliath British Leyland in the United Kingdom. Many economists now argue that this policy, which involves the state in 'picking winners', is a high-risk strategy. British Leyland, despite continued doses of taxpayer funding through the 1970s and 1980s, by the late 1990s (renamed Rover) had shrunk to being a very minor player in the European car market.

Box 2 includes industrial policy aimed at developing 'sunrise industries', usually taking advantage of new technologies, for example in computing, biotechnology and telecommunications. Once again it relies upon the ability of government to recognise where competitive advantage in the future will lie. The downside risk is the development of industries which can never compete against more efficient foreign rivals without state aid.

Turning to decelerative programmes, box 3 is the typical 'lame duck' strategy. An example might be the subsidies given in the 1990s to the French national airline, Air France, and to the Spanish state-owned airline, IBERIA, when they were faced with financial difficulties. In so far as the aim of a decelerative programme is to slow down for economic and social reasons the *pace of decline*, the policy might be defended, provided it does not impede necessary long-term restructuring.

Lastly, box 4 is concerned with 'sunset industries'. In Europe and North America since the 1970s large amounts of state aid in the form of subsidies or protection from imports have been directed at industries such as shipbuilding, steel, textiles and coal that are in long-term decline. As a result, the decline of these industries has been slowed down, though rarely reversed. State funding and restrictions on imports tend to create a dependence on continued protection against market forces. Too often decelerative industrial policies mask continued inefficiencies in the industry at a long-term cost to the public in terms of higher prices and slower economic growth. For example, 'temporary' taxpayer funding can turn into permanent protection as governments capitulate to the demands of politicians, whose constituencies would be adversely affected by industrial closures, and self-interested pressure groups, notably trade unions with members in the industries.

On the basis of this discussion, we can summarise the problems faced by industrial policy as follows:

- **Picking winners.** This is fraught with difficulty. Who in the 1970s accurately predicted the rise of microcomputers or the success of home video recorders and the compact disc player? In the main these products were developed by enterprises operating in highly competitive product markets and not by state-protected firms. Even when governments accurately pinpoint market opportunities, there is a danger that state aid will cushion inefficiencies in firms. Where this occurs development is fatally slowed down and costs of production are raised so that the firm can never be a major player in the world market.

- **Supporting losers.** Decelerative industrial policies may bring economic and social benefits to hard-pressed industries and regions, but past experience of this policy suggests that governments find it difficult to remove taxpayer support once granted. This has two effects. First, it slows to a trickle industrial restructuring. Resources remain tied up in lame duck firms and industries, when they could earn a higher return elsewhere. As a consequence, economic growth is reduced. Secondly, it stimulates governments in other countries to protect their industries. For example, if cars exported from Malaysia benefit from state largesse to Malaysian manufacturers, they undermine the competitiveness of car producers in other countries. This leads to demands in those countries for matching state aid. The result is a 'beggar my neighbour' policy with taxpayers and car buyers the major losers.

Disillusionment with the longer-term economic effects of both accelerative and decelerative industrial policies led many governments in the 1980s and 1990s to pursue a different type of industrial policy. Instead of state interference with market forces, governments introduced programmes aimed at reducing state subsidies and controls, while re-introducing market competition into areas of the economy served by sleepy state and private monopolies. The main features of such programmes have been the following:

- **Liberalisation of markets.** For example, deregulating and opening up telecommunications, electricity supply and airlines to competition in Europe.

- **Privatisation.** The sale of state-owned industries to the private sector. The objective of privatisation is to raise economic efficiency (both allocative and productive efficiency) by replacing state ownership with private ownership. Private owners are believed to have more incentive to police how efficiently their investments are being managed than does the public in the case of state ownership. This is an example of substituting a more efficient for a less efficient principal–agent relationship, leading to higher economic welfare (for a fuller discussion of principal–agent theory see pp. 196–9).

- **Competitive tendering.** Opening up certain state-supplied services, such as refuse collection and hospital cleaning, to private firms and introducing more competition in other areas of public procurement, notably defence contracts.

- **Reducing state subsidies.** The reduction or ending of state financing of both sunrise industries and lame duck firms.

- **Enterprise initiatives.** The redirection of state funding and other support towards retraining programmes and assisting the start-up of small enterprises with venture capital.

As a result of these programmes, the nature of industrial intervention has been substantially altered away from a dependence upon state aid towards a much greater reliance on market forces. This has been adopted in a number of countries, both in the developed and developing world, and accords with the idea of a 'level playing field' for producers to compete internationally, not least in Europe. The purpose of the EU is to provide a free trade area in Europe in which competition will not be distorted by state subsidies, tariffs, preferential procurement policies and the like. Today, government policy in Europe emphasises competition over state protection.

Application 16.1

International privatisation

The former UK Prime Minister, Mrs Thatcher is remembered for privatising telecommunications, gas, electricity, water, British Airways, British Aerospace, Rolls Royce, and much more. In total, over £60bn of industrial assets were transferred from the state to the private sector under the Conservative Governments of Margaret Thatcher and her successor John Major.

More recently, privatisation activity in the UK has slowed down. In part this is because of the election of a Labour Government in 1997, and in part because there is relatively little state enterprise left to sell. In spite of Labour's traditional hostility to privatisation there are plans, however, to introduce private capital into the London Underground.

Outside of the UK, privatisation activity continues to grow. The year 2000 may have seen the largest value of privatisation sales so far, breaking the previous record of US$160bn worth of asset disposals. In Europe there have been major share sales in telecommunications (e.g. in Telia of Sweden and Deutsche Telekom). In Portugal, a very active market exists for 'public private partnerships' (PPPs) in the financing, operation and maintenance of roads, rail and water services. Other countries are also experimenting with PPPs, particularly the UK, to finance roads, schools, hospitals and other public infrastructure.

As the top pie chart on p. 331 shows, telecoms dominate international privatisation, accounting for around 36% of all sell-offs. Both the costs of financing modern telecommunications and the opportunity to make telecommunications markets more competitive and raise efficiency are driving governments across the globe to privatise. Similar forces are causing governments to sell state enterprises in the power, oil and gas, financial and transport sectors.

To date over one-half of all privatisations by value have occurred in Western Europe (see the lower pie chart). But as privatisation continues to grow in popularity, it is to be expected that the balance will shift in favour of the other regions. So far privatisation has made very little impact on the economies of the Middle East and Africa, in spite of the need for considerable industrial restructuring in these countries.

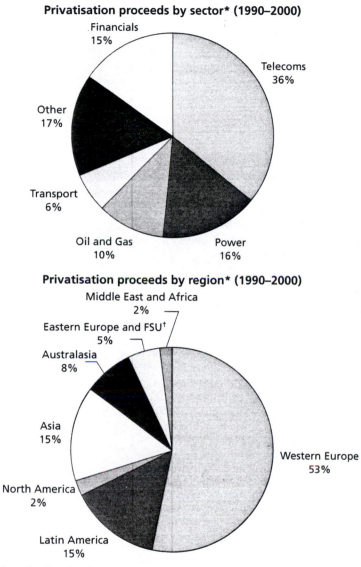

Privatisation proceeds by sector* (1990–2000)

Financials 15%

Telecoms 36%

Other 17%

Transport 6%

Oil and Gas 10%

Power 16%

Privatisation proceeds by region* (1990–2000)

Middle East and Africa 2%

Eastern Europe and FSU[†] 5%

Australasia 8%

Asia 15%

North America 2%

Latin America 15%

Western Europe 53%

International privatisation

* Based on data from *Privatisation International*

[†] Former Soviet Union

Activity

Assess the likely impact of international privatisation on:

(a) the competitive environment for firms; and

(b) industrial policy.

Competition law

The growth of large firms operating in oligopolistic or near-monopolistic markets has led governments to introduce competition laws. The case for state interference to promote competition comes directly from economic theory. As we saw in Chapter 5, a high degree of competition leads to the following benefits:

- Lower prices.
- A normal profit level.
- Lower costs of production.
- More consumer choice.

By contrast, monopolies and restrictive practices, where firms band together to agree production quotas and prices or allocate markets, imply high profit-making or inefficiency at the expense of the consumer.

The first laws of importance aimed at regulating monopolies and restrictive practices were introduced in the United States in 1890 and 1914. However, in Europe sympathy for the idea of large-scale production so as to benefit from economies of scale meant that similar legislation was delayed until after the Second World War. The United Kingdom passed legislation for the first time in 1948 when it established a Monopolies Commission (this was renamed the Monopolies and Mergers Commission in 1965, when its brief was extended to mergers and takeovers, and the Competition Commission in 2000); but restrictive practices were not tackled until 1956 and only in 1976 was the Office of Fair Trading (OFT) established at government level to oversee the operation of competition policy. In 1998 a new Competition Act introduced a prohibition-based regime in the UK with much stronger powers for the OFT to investigate monopolies and restrictive practices and to levy fines. The Act brought UK competition more closely into line with EU policy (see below).

Today in most of the major economies firms with a dominant share of their market can be subjected to investigation and fines imposed where abuse is discovered. Similarly, restrictive practices are either prohibited or severely regulated by national governments. In addition, however, firms in Europe are increasingly confronted by the requirements of European competition law. This law applies not only to companies based in the EU but potentially to any company operating in the EU, e.g. a Japanese company distributing goods to one or more EU markets. The European Treaty includes the following two main Articles regulating competition:

- **Article 81.** This prohibits restrictive agreements and practices in so far as they 'affect trade between member states' *and* restrict or distort competition. All agreements have to be notified to the European Commission and those relating to price fixing, market sharing, production quotas, discrimination between consumers, collective boycotts and tie-in clauses are specifically prohibited. An agreement may be exempted from the rigours of Article 81 only where it contributes 'to improving the production or distribution of goods or to promoting technical or economic progress' *and* it allows consumers 'a fair share of the resulting benefit'. Exemptions may be granted on an individual or a block basis. Block exemptions can be given for agreements relating to specialisation, exclusive distribution, exclusive purchasing, patent licensing, and R&D.

- **Article 82.** This prohibits 'any abuse by one or more undertakings of a dominant position within the common market or a substantial part of it' in so far as it affects trade between member states. A 'substantial part' has been interpreted as including any one of the major EU national markets, e.g. Germany or France. 'Dominance' has been defined as occurring where a firm has the power to behave to an appreciable extent independently of its competitors and customers.

European competition law is administered by Directorate General IV of the European Commission which has considerable investigatory powers. Whenever an infringement of the law is suspected, DG IV may examine books and records, enter premises and question management. It may also levy penalties for infringing the law of up to 10% of a company's worldwide turnover. For example, in 1989 BPB Industries was fined more than 3 million ECUs for offering fidelity payments to large customers in return for a promise not to buy from French and Spanish competitors. In 1991, Tetrapak (a producer of cartons for liquid food) was found guilty of using monopoly profits from the sale of aseptic cartons to cross-subsidise entry into the fresh-liquid segments of the market. In a further case, European steelmakers reacted angrily in February 1994 to fines of more than 100 million ECUs imposed by DG IV for allegedly operating a cartel in the sale of steel beams to the construction industry. In administering European competition law, though subject to scrutiny by the full European Commission, DG IV is effectively investigator, prosecutor, judge and jury. An appeal against a DG IV ruling is to the European Court of Justice in Strasbourg.

In addition to monitoring the extent to which companies in Europe conform to the requirements of Articles 81 and 82, DG IV also intervenes where governments are felt to be unfairly subsidising their own firms. Thus the EU has required repayment of French government support to the state-owned car maker Renault and has placed restrictions on state aid to national airlines such as IBERIA. For obvious reasons, however, DG IV has been more effective at prosecuting companies for breaches of the competition rules than it has been in pursuing offending member governments!

Neither Article 81 nor Article 82 directly addresses the subject of mergers. When the Treaty of Rome was drafted in the mid-1950s mergers were far rarer than they are today, especially mergers between companies operating in different EU countries. In response to the trend towards EU-wide mergers, however, the EU member states agreed in September 1990 to extend European competition law to the control of mergers. For many years DG IV had intervened where a European merger created a monopoly which infringed Article 82, but the new powers meant that it could now scrutinise and prevent mergers *before* dominance occurs. The regulation gave DG IV sole jurisdiction on mergers which have an important European dimension, though national governments can request the EU to transfer jurisdiction to them where a merger affects a distinct national market or where it threatens the public interest, e.g. mergers involving national media. Smaller mergers and takeovers, and those where all the companies involved have more than two-thirds of their sales in one member country, continue to be scrutinised under member countries' competition law.

Today, firms operating in the EU need to take care that they do not infringe EU competition law. In the past governments have often turned a blind eye to the creation of national monopolies able to achieve economies of scale and so compete successfully in the international market. This is now no longer so easy in Europe because most mergers of any size have to satisfy the requirements of EU law over which national governments do not have discretion. Therefore, in Europe managerial decisions on restructuring are constrained by the need to satisfy Articles 81 and 82 and the European merger regulations, as well as national competition laws. They can also be affected by European regional policy.

Application 16.2

Vodafone takes over Mannesmann

A threat or opportunity?

In 1999 the British mobile telephone company Vodafone made a successful £77bn hostile takeover bid for the German company Mannesmann. Mannesmann is an important manufacturing firm in Germany responsible for the employment of around 130,000 workers. Whereas the nature of the capital market in the UK is such that hostile takeover bids are commonplace, in Germany hostile bids are extremely rare. Indeed, the Vodafone–Mannesmann deal was the first successful and major hostile foreign takeover in Germany since the Second World War. In Germany the bid resulted in public opposition and pressure on government to intervene and block the deal.

Some German firms have large family shareholdings that limit the possibility of hostile takeovers. Others have a close financial relationship with their banks that also protects them from corporate predators. The German Chancellor, Gerhard Schröder, angrily opposed the Vodafone bid believing that the result would be damaging to German industry and employment. By contrast, most UK politicians and commentators either adopted a neutral stance or welcomed the takeover on the grounds that a free market in corporate control leads to greater economic efficiency. Hostile takeovers are commonplace and accepted in UK industrial policy but not, traditionally, in industrial policy in Germany and the other continental European economies.

The Vodafone–Mannesmann deal was more than simply a controversy over a foreign takeover. It represented the clash of two different approaches to industrial policy. On the one hand, the UK–USA or Anglo-Saxon model leaves industrial restructuring largely to market forces, including the operations of the competitive capital market. On the other, German economic policy since the 1940s has been based around a 'social market' model with a more interventionist approach to industrial structuring and an emphasis on achieving stakeholder consensus in German industry. An interventionist approach to industrial policy was largely abandoned in the UK in the 1980s in favour of market liberalisation.

Activity

On the basis of the above discussion consider the relative merits of the Anglo-Saxon and German 'social market' approaches to industrial policy. Under what circumstances does a competitive capital market lead to an efficient industrial structure?

Regional policy

Ideally, to overcome imbalances in the development of different regions of an economy, labour would move from areas of over-supply to areas of labour shortage, attracted by higher wages. Similarly, capital would move in search of higher returns offered in regions in need of major capital investment. In other words, workers would move in search of capital and businesses would move in search of labour. In practice, however, labour often lacks mobility because it does not have the required skills, or because of language and cultural barriers, family ties, housing costs and so on. Also, investment funds tend to go to those regions which are expanding quickly, where demand is therefore buoyant, and hence the expected rate of return is highest.

The result is often an economic and social divide between the expanding regions of a country with high per capita income growth and low unemployment, and the more depressed regions with lower purchasing power and high unemployment. Not only is this considered to be politically and socially undesirable, it also involves economic waste. For example, capital equipment, including social capital such as hospitals, schools and roads, may be under-utilised in areas of declining population, while expanding areas suffer from increased congestion. Eventually, regional demand and supply pressures can spill over into higher national inflation as wages and prices are bid up in the areas of shortages.

Regional differences in economic performance throughout Europe first came to prominence in the 1920s and 1930s as the old staple industries of the industrial revolution – coal, textiles, iron and steel, and shipbuilding – went into decline. This prompted governments to introduce measures aimed at alleviating the worst social and economic excesses of regional depression. After the Second World War in Europe regional policies were developed at the national level, but more recently there have been moves to develop a co-ordinated regional policy for the EU in response to marked variations in incomes throughout the European Union.

Regional policy takes two broad forms aimed at:

- **Reversing regional decline.** Governments have attempted to attract new industries into the relatively depressed regions by the use of government grants, relocation expenses, a preferential tax regime, providing business premises at subsidised rents, government factory building programmes, land reclamation and more lax planning regulations.
- **Limiting regional expansion.** Governments have limited the building of new factories and offices in areas of high growth in the hope that businesses would locate instead to the more depressed regions. Also, government departments have relocated activities to areas considered to be in need of development.

In the 1980s in the United Kingdom, consistent with its distrust of state intervention, the then Conservative Government reduced the scope of regional aid in an attempt to reduce its overall costs and to target it more productively. By 1979 the 'assisted areas' included over 40% of the UK working population, leading to criticism that regional aid was spread too thinly and perhaps too indiscriminately. Controls on setting up businesses in the prosperous south-east were abolished and in 1988 the Regional Selective Assistance Scheme was introduced, which removed the automatic award of state aid in assisted areas. At the same time, smaller and more focused areas such as derelict land, especially in the inner cities, were identified for aid and Urban Development Corporations were established. Between 1981 and 1991 regional assistance to depressed areas fell from around £1.8 billion to just under £1.4 billion in 1990/1 prices. In other countries there has been a similar reassessment of the benefits of traditional regional policies.

Economists Moore, Rhodes and Tyler who studied the operation of UK regional policy concluded (in 1986) that it had been beneficial and had helped to create around 784,000 new jobs between 1960 and 1981. By contrast, critics of state aid to the regions, which include free-market economists, argue that the policy is expensive and unnecessary – market forces can solve the problem. They point to evidence of labour and capital responding to price signals (for example, around 11,000 jobs relocated from high-cost London in 1990 alone). These same critics of regional policy also cite the high level of taxpayer subsidy that has traditionally been associated with regional policy. Critics of regional policy who object to the principle of state involvement would prefer to see regional deprivation solved by removing what they see as impediments to the mobility of labour and capital, namely, national wage bargaining, planning restrictions which limit the building of new factories and housing estates, and long-term unemployment and other welfare benefits.

As in the case of competition policy, the EU is taking a greater role in regional development throughout Europe. Regional differences within the EU seem to have increased since the 1970s, while the creation of a single market and monetary union, which rules out member countries devaluing their exchange rates to gain competitive advantage, will probably further exacerbate regional differences in economic performance in Europe in the future. Currently, the most prosperous parts of the EU are largely within the area encompassed by the 'golden triangle' of Milan, London and Frankfurt. By contrast, all of Portugal, most of Greece, parts of northern Europe, Calabria in Italy and parts of Spain have incomes per head that are well below the EU average.

To even out European incomes EU aid is directed especially at the following:

● Declining rural areas.

● Long-term and youth unemployment (through training and retraining programmes).

● Areas of industrial decline (e.g. coal and steel areas).

● Regions designated as 'less developed', which includes most of Southern Europe.

● Investing in infrastructure schemes, e.g. roads and telecommunications, and promoting energy conservation in more backward regions.

EU money must be additional to funds that the national government has already agreed to spend. Member governments submit five-year development programmes detailing how the allocated money is to be spent and regional and local authorities must be involved in the planning process. Regional funding is then allocated via the national governments.

EU regional policy is administered by the Regional Directorate of the European Commission (DG XVI). DG XVI oversees expenditure out of the European Regional Development Fund (ERDF) first established in 1975. Within the ERDF, 'structural funds' have been allocated covering three broad areas: the regions, social needs and declining farming areas.

Concluding remarks

The previous chapters in this book are primarily concerned with the firm's 'internal environment'. In other words, they are concerned with matters which managers can influence or control directly, notably demand, costs of production, employment levels, levels of investment and the 'marketing mix'. By comparison, the role of government may seem remote and uncontrollable. Yet governments today in *all* modern economies (and in many less advanced ones) intervene on a continuous basis in markets. Hence, they are just as significant to the firm's 'competitive environment' as competitors and suppliers. In Chapter 1 we introduced Michael Porter's notion of the five forces – the power of buyers, the power of suppliers, the threat from potential entrants, the threat from substitute products and actual rivalry in the market. It might be more useful, however, to think of the competitive environment in terms of a 'six-forces' model with government intervention being the influential sixth force. Recognition of the importance of government should trigger a search by firms to minimise the costs and to maximise the possible benefits of state intervention.

Government intervention in the economy requires good forecasting of economic trends so as to ensure appropriate intervention. Similarly, firms need to be able to forecast market trends so that management can take appropriate and timely pricing, output and employment decisions. In the next chapter we turn to the subject of business forecasting.

Key learning points

- A **PEST analysis** is concerned with identifying and evaluating the political, economic, social and technological factors likely to impact on the business in the time period under study.
- There are four main areas of **state intervention** in the market: macroeconomic policy, industrial policy, competition law and regional policy.
- **State intervention** may be justified from a number of perspectives: to encourage or discourage consumption where there are appreciable external benefits or external costs respectively; to regulate the level of economic activity; to protect consumers and employees; and to alter the free-market distribution of income and wealth.
- **Market failure** occurs where the market price fails to reflect the true social costs and social benefits of a transaction.

- **Externalities** are a cause of state intervention and arise when some of the benefits or costs of consuming a good or service spill over to others.

- A **public good** is one where there is significant market failure resulting from the conditions of non-excludability and non-rivalry. A **private good** is excludable and rival.

- A good or service is **non-excludable** when non-payers cannot be excluded from benefiting from the consumption of the good or service or cannot be excluded except at too high a cost.

- A good or service is **non-rival** when its consumption by one person does not reduce another's ability to consume.

- **State failure** occurs when state intervention in the market economy leads to a lower level of economic welfare.

- The level of **macroeconomic activity** is affected by the relative size of injections into and leakages out of the economy at any given time, where injections are investment spending, government spending and export revenue, and leakages are savings, taxation and import spending.

- **Accelerative industrial policies** are designed to speed up the adjustment process within economies in terms of industrial restructuring, while **decelerative policies** are intended to slow down the pace of economic change.

- The various types of **industrial policy** in relation to accelerative or decelerative objectives may be categorised into four broad areas aimed at a 'national champion' strategy, the development of 'sunrise industries', a 'lame duck' strategy and 'problem industries'.

- **Industrial policy**, in general, is faced with the choice between picking winners and supporting losers.

- **Privatisation** and **market liberalisation** policies are pursued so as to increase economic efficiency by replacing state ownership with private ownership and by opening up monopoly markets to competition.

- **Competition policy** is concerned with promoting competition in the economy. A high degree of **competition** leads to a number of benefits, namely: lower prices, a normal profit level, lower costs of production and more consumer choice.

- **Article 81 of the European Treaty** prohibits restrictive agreements and practices in so far as they 'affect trade between member states' *and* restrict or distort competition.

- **Article 82 of the European Treaty** prohibits 'any abuse by one or more undertakings of a dominant position within the common market or a substantial part of it' in so far as it affects trade between member states.

- **Regional policy** takes two broad forms aimed at (a) reversing regional decline, or (b) limiting regional expansion.

Topics for discussion

1 In what ways do governments impact on business decision-making today?

2 Under what circumstances might governments improve economic welfare by interfering in market transactions? What forms might government intervention take?

3 Using an appropriate diagram critically discuss the use of government subsidies to higher education.

4 Consider the different forms industrial policy might take and the implications for corporate strategies.

5 What are the key features of competition policy in your country?

6 Comment on the likely impact of regional policy on business strategy.

7 What do you understand by 'state failure'? When is state failure most likely to arise?

8 Undertake a PEST analysis for a business with which you are familiar, emphasising, in particular, the ways in which government policies might impact, favourably and adversely, on the business.

17 Business and economic forecasting

Aims and learning outcomes

In order to develop strategic plans and to respond effectively to changes in the economic environment, every business organisation needs to have some idea as to the magnitude of its likely future sales. In Chapter 2 we introduced the concept of the demand function, which is concerned with the relationship between consumer demand for a good or service and a range of factors including own price, the price of complementary and/or substitute goods, consumers' expectations, population changes, etc. Firms that devote sufficient resources to derive the nature of the relationship between these factors and their future sales will be in a strong position to gain a significant competitive advantage in the market place over rivals who pay less attention to demand estimation. Of course there are many successful and profitable firms that employ few if any formal estimation procedures. In the complex world of business and commerce today, however, there is clear evidence that the necessity for and popularity of formal estimation techniques is growing.

Understanding the nature of the market place and the reactions of consumers to changes in demand conditions is the first step towards effective forecasting of future sales and the development of a sound business plan. Business forecasting is, therefore, a critical management function – without 'good' forecasting the firm and its management are likely to miss important business opportunities. For example, forecasts of demand will be central to the decision on whether or not to build new production capacity; while decisions about whether to increase or decrease retail prices may depend crucially on forecasts about raw material prices. Forecasting business and economic trends is, of course, not an exact science – if it were, then no company would ever be taken by surprise and face the threat of unplanned closure! Nevertheless, there are well-established procedures available to management to eliminate as much guesswork as possible from business planning. These procedures, if followed methodically and correctly, should ensure that the final forecasts of sales and general economic indicators are more reliable than those based purely on intuition or hunch.

It is not possible to provide a comprehensive treatment of demand estimation and forecasting techniques in a single chapter; in particular, a detailed treatment of the appropriate mathematical techniques is well beyond the scope of this book. Instead, the purpose of this chapter is to provide a broad overview of the subject, touching on most of the major aspects. It should lay the foundations for further study by the interested reader.

The chapter covers the following aspects of business and economic forecasting:

- Interpolation and extrapolation from data.
- Collecting information on consumer behaviour.
- Statistical estimation of demand relationships.
- Forecasting demand.

Learning outcomes

This chapter will help you to:

- Appreciate the importance of *forecasting* in the context of strategic planning and development.

- Distinguish between the *estimation of relationships* between key business variables and the use of data to forecast future business and market trends.

- Understand how the demand for a product or service can be estimated and the technical steps involved, using cross-sectional or time series data.

- Select an appropriate method for collecting information about consumer behaviour in relation to a firm's products which form the basis of demand estimation and forecasting.

- Categorise various methods of *market experiments* including sales-wave research, simulated store techniques and test marketing.

- Avoid the common pitfalls in business and economic forecasting, particularly concerning the dangers of spurious correlations, data mining and the misinterpretation of statistical results.

- Grasp the principles of various forecasting techniques, involving *trend projection*, the use of *leading indicators* and *econometric modelling*.

Interpolation and extrapolation from data

At the heart of business and economic forecasting lies two central themes:

- The estimation of demand relationships.
- Forecasting demand.

Information used for these purposes may be categorised as either *cross-sectional* or *time series* in nature. The former is concerned with data recorded at a point in time (such as sales in each of a company's stores in a particular period), while the latter refers to data collected over successive time periods (such as the company's total sales revenue over a number of years). The estimation of demand relationships can involve both types of data while, in general, forecasting demand uses time series information to assess trends and changes from one time period to the next.

Statistical analysis can involve decisions concerning *interpolation* and *extrapolation* from the data employed. The distinction between these concepts is explained as follows:

341

- **Interpolation and estimating demand relationships.** Estimation is concerned with deriving the best specification of the demand function, that is, with *explaining* the relationship between the quantity of the product demanded by consumers and the factors that influence this demand. Interpolation is the prediction of a value of demand from a value of an explanatory variable which lies within the range of observed values. For example, suppose that we wish to estimate how sales change as advertising expenditure changes in June 2001 and we have quarterly data on sales and advertising spend for March, September and December between 1997 and 2001. The value can be estimated by *interpolation*. This involves computing the missing sales value within the range of the recorded observations of the advertising expenditure.

- **Extrapolation and forecasting demand.** Forecasting can form the basis of both short-term and long-term decisions. For example, a study of the pattern of sales for the past few weeks will help the firm to plan short-term production, inventory or advertising expenditure over the next few weeks. At the same time, demand estimation of a longer time span (perhaps many months or many years) will enable the firm to determine the requirements for new production capacity, say, over the next decade, and to plan the development and introduction of new product lines and markets. Forecasting is thus concerned with the *extrapolation* or projection of future behaviour on the basis of past behaviour. Extrapolation can also involve backward projection.

The meaning of interpolation and extrapolation are illustrated in Figure 17.1 below. It will be appreciated therefore that demand estimation and forecasting, both in the short term and in the long term, can provide a useful basis for strategic planning and development of any business.

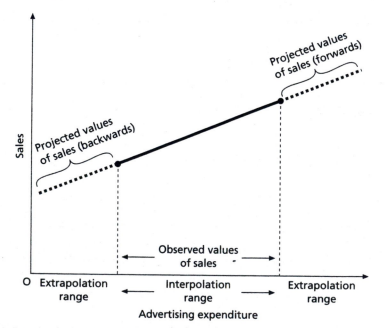

Figure 17.1 Extrapolation and interpolation

Collecting information on consumer behaviour

In general, demand estimation is concerned with the identification and measurement of the factors that jointly determine the demand for a firm's product(s). As we saw in Chapter 2, the most important determinants are likely to be:

- The own price of the good in question.

- The price of the good relative to the price of substitute and complementary goods.

- The level of advertising expenditure for the good as well as on complementary and substitute products.

- Income levels of potential buyers – who may be individuals, households or even other firms or the government (both at home and abroad).

- Changes in consumers' wealth (both actual and expected).

- The cost and availability of finance (in terms of the rate of interest and credit terms available to potential customers).

- Changes in consumers' tastes and preferences and in their perception of the quality of the good relative to other goods.

- Consumers' expectations about future prices and the availability of the good.

- Changes in population in terms of age structure, growth, regional distribution, etc.

We also saw in Chapter 2 that we can estimate the responsiveness of demand for a product with respect to changes in its own price, i.e. the *price elasticity of demand*. This concept is not confined to own price changes but is applicable equally to any of the other determinants of demand listed above, such as income or advertising expenditure, as well as to changes in the prices of substitute or complementary goods. Such information about the relationship of the level of sales to each of these determining factors provides management with key data upon which to base production levels and to formulate strategy in terms of marketing, pricing, etc.

There are several methods available to help management collect information about consumer behaviour in relation to the firm's products and which form the basis of demand estimation and forecasting. These may be broadly categorised under the headings of:

- *Consumer surveys*; and

- *Market experiments*.

The most common source of information, however, is the historical record of sales collected by the firm itself about existing products. This will include details about sales levels, prices, advertising expenditure, production and design changes, etc., and anything else that may be thought to have an impact on consumer demand for the firm's products. This internal information may be augmented by information on external factors such as consumer income, the general level of retail prices, population changes, competitors' performance, credit conditions, etc., and any other external factors that may be thought to be relevant – including the weather for example! Before seeing how the information relating to these internal and external variables can be used statistically to estimate demand relationships it is useful to summarise the key features and limitations of consumer surveys and market experiments.

Consumer surveys

In essence, consumer surveys seek to discover the future buying intentions of consumers by eliciting their probable reactions to a range of conditions concerning price, advertising spend, product quality and design, and so on. The firm may carry out its own consumer interviews or it may commission a market research organisation to conduct interviews on its behalf. For example, a random sample of consumers could be asked how much of the product they would buy if its price was reduced by 5%. This would help the firm to derive an estimate of the price elasticity of demand. The product's consumers could be asked to state the current price of the product – if awareness of the price is low this might suggest that demand for the product is relatively price insensitive!

The major limitation of consumer surveys and of all such interview techniques is that the questions being asked are hypothetical – they are 'what if' scenarios. Answers to such questions may prove to be inaccurate in the sense that consumers may not *actually* behave in the manner indicated. A great deal of skill is required on the part of the institution conducting the survey to ensure that the questions are not misleading and that they are framed in such a way that the respondent is not enticed into giving the answer the firm wanted in the first place. In general, consumer surveys are likely to be better at providing qualitative information about general market reactions rather than the concrete quantitative data which are needed for statistical demand estimation.

Market experiments

Rather than pose hypothetical questions to potential customers, the firm may opt instead to carry out a direct market experiment in order to test buyers' reactions to actual changes introduced, while attempting so far as is possible to keep other market conditions stable or under control. For example, the product in question may be offered at different prices or in a range of designs or packaging, while using the results from a control group of buyers for which no corresponding change is made for comparative purposes. Other controlled laboratory-type experiments could involve giving money to buyers and telling them to shop in a particular supermarket. By varying prices, design, shelf location, etc., the experimenter can analyse consumer behaviour in a controlled environment. In these ways, the firm can estimate price and income elasticities of demand for various buyer groups and product ranges.

The main drawback of such market experiments is that consumers participating in them know that their actions are being monitored. This may distort their normal buying patterns and hence invalidate the experiment! In addition, market experiments can be very expensive to set up and administer. The sample size must be sufficiently large to provide reliable results, increasing the costs still further. Against these drawbacks must be set the possibility that a market experiment may be the only reliable source of demand information available to a firm intending to launch a new product. The experiment in this case is a trial run and should be in a segment of the market which is regarded as representative of the whole market.

In general, the different methods of market experimentation employed by firms fall under one of the following three headings:

- Sales-wave research.

- Simulated store techniques.

- Test marketing.

We comment briefly on each method in turn.

Sales-wave research

This involves the selection of a group of consumers, supplying them initially with the product at no cost. Sometime later the same product is then re-offered to them for sale along with competitors' products at prices which can then be varied a number of times. This method is sometimes employed in the soap powder industry, for example, where initially a bottle of fabric softener may be given away, free of charge, with every packet of soap powder sold and subsequent purchase results analysed. This type of experiment enables the firm to assess the rate of repeat purchases and to estimate the impact of different competing brands. Attitudes to different packaging designs can also be monitored in a similar way.

Simulated store techniques

These techniques involve the establishment of a sample group of shoppers who are shown a number of advertising commercials for a range of products, including those for a new product to be launched by the firm, and then giving them some money to spend (or to keep!). Purchases of the new product and of competitors' products by the sample group can then be monitored. Discussions may be held with the customers to discuss their buying preferences with later follow-up interviews to find out if these preferences have changed.

Test marketing

This involves actually selling the product in a limited number of locations with different packaging or advertising campaigns in order to test market reaction. The scale of the test marketing may be fairly small, based in only a few shops, or it could be a full-scale experiment spread across many regions of the country.

Consumer surveys and direct market experiments are important sources of qualitative information concerning consumer reactions and can provide useful broad indications of the likely scale of demand. However, more 'scientific' techniques are available for demand estimation, the most important of which is based on *regression analysis*. The principles of this technique are set out below.

Statistical estimation of demand relationships

Using internal data relating to sales levels, prices, advertising expenditure, etc., and external data relating to the wider economic environment such as consumers' income, credit conditions, population changes, etc., it may be possible to estimate statistically the demand function for a product using the technique of *regression analysis*. The basic principles involved in using this technique are well-established and straightforward, although there are a number of important statistical problems involved in arriving at reliable estimates. A detailed treatment of these problems is not appropriate for this book but we shall deal later with one particular difficulty referred to as the *identification problem*. It will be sufficient for our purposes here to outline the steps of regression analysis. These are illustrated in Figure 17.2.

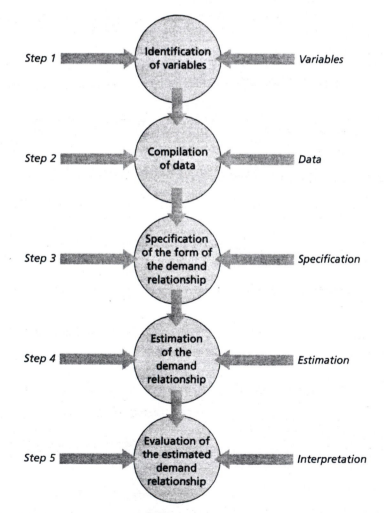

Figure 17.2 Steps of regression analysis

Step 1: Identification of variables

Ultimately, identification of the appropriate variables to be used as the basis for determining demand will depend on a combination of judgement, observation and understanding of fundamental economic principles and relationships – all of which are encapsulated within the demand function (Chapter 2). It involves identifying those factors which are likely to be the most important determinants of demand for the good in question. As the analysis proceeds, this list may be increased or reduced as we learn more about the impact of certain variables on consumer demand.

Step 2: Compilation of data

A data set will need to be compiled for each of the variables which are expected to influence demand. Much of this data will be internal, while other data will be external but may be readily available from public records including government statistical sources. Other data may have to be especially generated, for example, via customer surveys and market experimentation.

Step 3: Specification of the form of the demand relationship

The nature of the relationship between the quantity of a good demanded and the variables which influence or determine this demand may not always be a simple one. The analyst will need to test various specifications of the relationship to discover the one which provides the best explanation or 'best fit'. It should be noted in this context that care should be taken to avoid data mining which may lead to identifying spurious relationships or *correlations* between variables (see p. 359) – there should be some sound theoretical basis for the estimated relationship.

The simplest and most common case is that of a linear relationship, such as:

$$Q = a + bP + cA + dY + e$$

where
    Q is the quantity of sales (referred to as the *dependent variable*),
    P is the price of the good in question,
    A is advertising expenditure, and
    Y is real disposable income per head.

The factors which affect Q are referred to as the *explanatory* or *independent* variables since they are intended to explain the observed variations in sales (note that we could, of course, add many more potentially relevant explanatory variables).

In this demand relationship, a, b, c and d are known as the *regression coefficients* and show by how much sales (Q) will change for a unit change in the associated independent variable, assuming all other independent variables are unchanged. For example, if b is estimated, using regression analysis, to equal −2.0, then for every $1 increase in the price of the good, sales will fall by 2.0 units.

The last term, *e*, in the demand relationship is referred to as the *error term* and reflects the fact that the expression above is unlikely to explain fully all of the variation in sales. In other words, the *e* term captures the effect on sales of all the determinants that are not specifically included in the relationship. These might include irregular events such as strikes, severe winters, earthquakes, etc. as well as any errors in the input data sets. Demand estimation is not a perfect science – the world of business is never a certain one and hence the error term, *e*, reflects the proportion of the variation in sales that we have not been able to explain. Of course, as our knowledge of the market place increases and as the input data and demand estimation improve, the significance of the error term should decline.

The expression above assumes that sales are linearly related to the specified determinants. It may arise, however, that a more accurate expression for the relationship is in terms of a *multiplicative* or *exponential* form such that:

$$Q = aP^bA^cY^de$$

This form is commonly found in the estimation of relationships. By taking logarithms of both sides of the expression we can convert this equation to one which is log-linear in form:

$$\log Q = \log a + b\log P + c\log A + d\log Y + \log e$$

The attractiveness of this form stems from the fact that we are now able to read off elasticity values directly: the estimated value for *b* now represents the price elasticity of demand, *c* represents the advertising elasticity of demand, while *d* represents the income elasticity of demand. In the earlier linear case, these coefficients only measured the absolute (rather than proportional) change in sales for a unit change in *P*, *A* or *Y*.

Step 4: Estimation of the demand relationship

The most commonly used procedure for estimating the demand relationship is known as the *method of least squares regression*. In essence, this enables us to find the values for the regression coefficients *a*, *b*, *c* and *d* defined above which give the best fit of sales (*Q*) to its determining variables (for example, *P*, *A* and *Y*). The method works by finding the values for the coefficients which minimise the sum of the squared positive and negative deviations of the actual (observed) sales values from those predicted by the fitted relationship. Figure 17.3 shows the principle of least squares regression for a simple case involving only one explanatory variable, say advertising expenditure, *A*. The relationship may be expressed as:

$$Q_t = a + cA_t + e_t$$

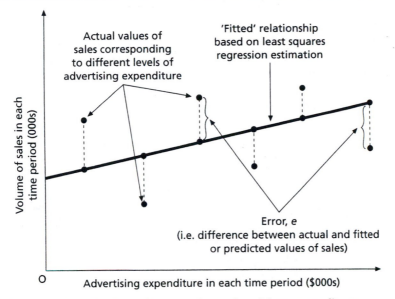

Figure 17.3 Regression of sales volume against advertising expenditure

The subscript *t* in the above expression refers to time and the relationship indicates that, for any particular time period *t*, sales (*Q*) are estimated to be positively related to the level of advertising expenditure (*A*) as shown in the figure. The estimated value for *a*, the intercept term, shows the level of sales suggested by this equation that would be achieved in the absence of any advertising (i.e. *A* = 0). The value of *a* is an indicator of the position of the graphed relationship, while the value of *c* provides an estimate for the slope showing the effect of a change in the absolute value of advertising on the absolute volume of sales.

In this simple example, it is fairly easy to draw by eye the line passing through the actual plot of sales and advertising expenditure values which gives the 'best fit'. In most situations, however, there will be more than one explanatory variable – indeed there could be very many specified in the relationship – and hence we must use the technique of 'multiple' regression, rather than 'simple' regression. Conceptually, the least squares technique is the same in both cases though we cannot adequately show the relationship graphically. Fortunately, a wide range of computer program packages are readily available, such as Excel and Minitab, which remove much of the mental effort from estimating the demand relationship.

Step 5: Evaluation of the estimated demand relationship

Once the demand relationship has been specified and the estimates derived for the coefficients we then need to stand back and assess the plausibility of the results. Some of the questions to be asked are: Does the estimated relationship seem plausible? Does it contradict what has happened in the past? Is it in agreement with the relationships suggested by economic theory? Also, how reliable are the resulting statistical estimates?

Fortunately, most computer regression analysis programs automatically produce a range of statistics which help us to evaluate the *reliability* of the estimated coefficients. Two particular statistics are especially important in this respect, namely, the 'multiple correlation coefficient' and the 'standard error of the estimate'. The former measures the proportion of the total variation in the observed sales figures that is 'explained' by the estimated equation. It is thus an overall measure of the strength of the relationship between sales and the explanatory variables specified in the result. The standard error of the estimate allows us to attach a 'degree of confidence' to the estimated value of sales based on the regression equation. We can then state with, say 95% confidence, that the actual sales level will fall within a certain range of variation around the estimated value of sales. It should be clear that the higher the value of the multiple correlation coefficient and the lower the value of the standard error of the estimate, then the more confidence we can have in our estimated demand function as an accurate representation of the true relationship between sales and the explanatory variables. In a similar way, from the standard errors for each of the independent explanatory variables we are able to reach a view about the reliability of the predicted relationship between demand and each of the variables. For example, we can reach a view about whether the predicted relationship between advertising and sales is statistically significant.

The above discussion is intentionally only a very brief summary of regression analysis. Also the technique is not without problems and challenges for the analyst. We have already noted the requirement for adequate data on the relevant dependent and explanatory variables. This is the first major hurdle in demand estimation. Another problem which may arise involves the possibility that the explanatory variables themselves may be statistically correlated. The extent to which this problem exists – referred to as the *degree of multicollinearity* – will result in unreliable estimates of the coefficients for the individual explanatory variables. There are statistical techniques available for minimising this problem but they are outside the scope of this book.

In general, it is important to stress that the statistical estimation of demand relationships based on regression analysis does not provide an *exact* measure of the link between demand and its determinants. It simply shows the 'best-fitting' relationship, i.e. that which fits the existing data best! In some cases this best fit may in fact be very poor and hence of little value to management in estimating and forecasting the level of demand for the product.

A further problem, and one which we briefly referred to earlier, is known as the *identification problem*.

The identification problem

The simplest illustration of the identification problem arises when we attempt to relate the price of a good to its sales over time. For example, a manager given the task of estimating the demand curve for a particular product might, understandably, plot the quantity demanded in 2001 against the 2001 price, the quantity demanded in 2000 against the 2000 price and so on. If the resulting plots of points for 1999–2001 were as shown in Figure 17.4, it would be tempting for the manager to conclude that the demand curve for the product is DD.

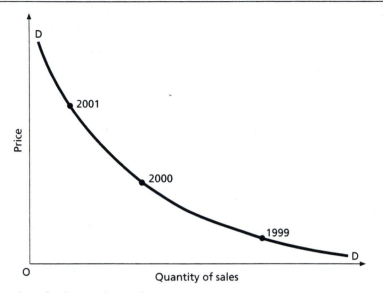

Figure 17.4 Plot of sales against price

This approach, however, is seriously flawed because the market price at any point in time is determined by both the demand and supply curves, if the market is competitive. Specifically, the equilibrium value of price will be at a level where the demand and supply curves intersect, showing the quantity that consumers are willing to buy and suppliers are prepared to supply at that price. It is very likely that the demand and supply curves for the product will be different *each year*. For example, as shown in Figure 17.5, the supply curve may have shifted (from S_{1999} in the year 1999 to S_{2000} in

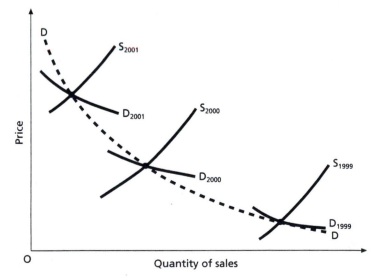

Figure 17.5 The identification problem

2000 and to S_{2001} in 2001), representing a change over time in the underlying conditions of supply. In addition, the demand curve may also have shifted (from D_{1999} to D_{2000} to D_{2001}) reflecting a change in the conditions of demand, e.g. a change in incomes. If we superimpose the curve DD from Figure 17.4 shown by the dotted line in Figure 17.5, it will be seen that this is not a good estimate of the demand curve for the product in *any* of the years, 1999 to 2001 (compare the slope of DD with the slopes of D_{1999}, D_{2000} and D_{2001}). Thus there exists an identification problem in estimating the precise demand relationship.

The problem arises because of the need to hold constant the other non-price variables or 'conditions of demand' such as incomes, the prices of other goods, consumer tastes, advertising expenditure, etc. which affect demand, when constructing the demand curve. In practice, we cannot be sure the demand relationship was constant during the period 1999–2001. If the relationship had been fixed then, as the supply curve changed each year, we could be confident that DD does accurately represent the price/quantity demand relationship. As Figure 17.5 shows, shifts in the supply curve each year would map out various points on the demand curve.

This raises the problem of how to estimate a demand relationship if it has not remained fixed in the past. There are many solutions to this problem, some of which are simple and others which are very complex. Certain statistical techniques recognise that demand and supply quantities are determined simultaneously by price and that both of these curves shift in response to non-price variables. In essence, these techniques solve the identification problem by estimating a model of demand made up of a number of simultaneous equations, rather than a single equation.

Forecasting demand

So far we have discussed how firms can estimate the way in which consumer demand for their products responds to changes in price and other determinants. We have summarised how the causal link between the level of demand and its determinants may be quantified using regression analysis. However, in order, for example, to plan for production, inventory or advertising expenditure, in the short term and longer term, the firm must attempt to estimate future demand for its products – planning, therefore, necessitates *forecasting*. We now turn to describe those forecasting methods which are most commonly employed in business. At the outset it ought to be appreciated that all forecasting techniques should be treated with a degree of caution because none can be described as infallible. But, the fact remains that businesses (as well as governments) have little choice but to make forecasts, albeit crude ones, in order to formulate decisions and future plans. Sometimes the forecasts arrived at will be implicit (based perhaps on 'know-how' and 'hunch' or even 'trial-and-error') while at other times they will be explicit (based on some formal statistical techniques). The key challenge is to arrive at the best method for producing the best forecasts – 'best' ultimately can only be decided, of course, on the basis of comparing forecasts and actual outcomes.

The various forecasting methods can be grouped conveniently under three headings, namely:

- Trend projection (or trend extrapolation).
- Leading indicators.
- Econometric modelling.

A fourth method, *survey analysis*, could be added to this list, but we have already covered this in our earlier discussion of demand estimation.

The choice of the most suitable method to be employed will depend on the answers to a number of questions relating to the forecasting problem at hand. The questions are as follows:

- **How far forward do we need to forecast?** A technique suitable for short-term projection may not be at all relevant for longer-term forecasting and planning.
- **What degree of accuracy is required in the forecasts?** Forecasting can be an expensive exercise and hence management must weigh up the cost of achieving greater accuracy against the additional benefit which they can expect to derive.
- **How quickly is the forecast needed?** Short-term forecasts, by definition, need to be derived quickly, but they are likely to have only a short life span in the sense that they will quickly become outdated.
- **How accurate and complete are the underlying data which form the basis of the forecasts?** No forecasting technique can make up for inadequacies in the primary information available.

We now discuss each of the three forecasting methods listed above, keeping these questions to the fore.

Trend projection

The simplest type of forecasting method is a straightforward projection (or extrapolation) from the trend of past sales data. This is particularly useful when management is interested in arriving at short-term forecasts because it can reasonably be assumed that the behaviour of sales in the recent past will be a useful indicator of their behaviour in the near future (for example, the demand for bread in shops on each normal week day is unlikely to change significantly from one week to the next). In general, sales figures for many consumer goods tend to display stable behaviour over time.

Trend projection is not concerned with an explanation of *why* sales vary over time; we are not interested in estimating a demand relationship. Instead, the aim is more limited in that it is restricted simply to predicting the future volume of sales, without quantifying responsiveness to the various factors which determine demand. Since time and observations of past sales are the only variables to be used, the technique of trend projection is also frequently referred to as 'time series analysis'.

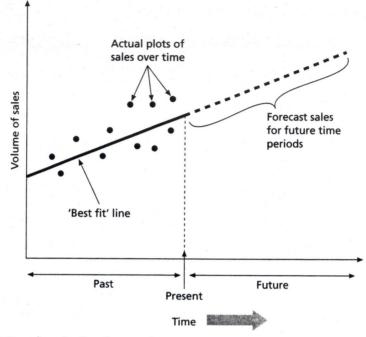

Figure 17.6 Trend projection forecasting

The simplest form of trend projection is illustrated in Figure 17.6, where the level of sales in recent time periods is represented by dots. The solid line provides the 'best fit' to these sales volumes, fitted by simple linear regression (as described earlier in this chapter) or simply by visual inspection. The broken line represents an extension of the sales trend into the future and is based solely on the assumption that the past trend will persist in the forthcoming time periods. In strict trend projection exercises there is no attempt to adjust the forecast to allow for a possible change in any of the causal factors which determine sales.

A more sophisticated approach to trend projection breaks down the time series of past sales data into four components (this is often referred to as the *decomposition method*). These components are as follows:

- **Trend (T).** This shows long-run changes in the data which result from fundamental developments in population, economic prosperity, technology, etc.

- **Seasonal variation (S).** During the year, demand for many products is likely to change with the season (for example, the demand for ice-cream in the summer and the demand for toys at Christmas). This problem is addressed by the use of *seasonally-adjusted* data.

- **Cyclical variation (C).** Sales and company performance may be subject to more or less regular fluctuations every few years, perhaps broadly in line with the general ups and downs *either* of the wider economy or in the company's particular industry sector.

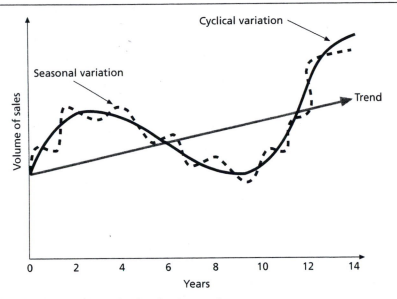

Figure 17.7 Decomposition of sales data over time

- **Random shocks (R).** Sales may sometimes fluctuate as a result of random and unpredictable events such as floods, wars, strikes, etc. This component would also include any other irregular variation in sales which is unexplained in terms of any causal factor (this random variation might simply be due to a sudden change of consumer tastes, for no predictable reason!).

Figure 17.7 shows these components in terms of a hypothetical example based, say, on the sales of domestic electric cooling fans over a period of fourteen years. Decomposition of the data will show that there is (a) a rising trend in sales perhaps associated with rising real income and a greater demand for comfort; (b) a seasonal pattern of demand with peaks in the summer and troughs in the winter (not surprisingly); (c) a cyclical pattern associated perhaps with the underlying performance of the economy in terms of growth and government economic management; and (d) irregular shocks arising from events such as sudden interest rate surges impacting on consumer incomes, power cuts, etc. (the effect of these random shocks, while perhaps not obvious from the graph, is included as part of the otherwise unexplained variations in the short-term regular patterns).

As with regression analysis for demand estimation, many computer packages are available which break down time series data into the above four components. There is little need, therefore, to elaborate further on the underlying technical procedures. It is worth noting, however, that different approaches to decomposition can be adopted, depending on how one judges the four components to be related. Essentially, two choices are available:

- The additive approach.
- The multiplicative approach.

355

The components of the time series may be viewed as an *additive model* such that the sales data (Q) may be decomposed as:

Additive model

$$Q = T + S + C + R$$

where T is the trend value of sales, S represents the seasonal variation component of sales, C the cyclical variation and R the random shocks.

Alternatively, the relationship may be stated in terms of a *multiplicative model* whereby:

Multiplicative model

$$Q = T \times S \times C \times R = T.S.C.R.$$

A number of statistical procedures can be used to check the appropriateness of the model chosen and to improve further the quality of the forecasts made based on the decomposition method. For example, quite simply the accuracy can be checked by 'back-forecasting'. This involves using the model to estimate demand for an earlier period for which actual sales data are available and checking the estimated result against the actual figures.

Leading indicators

Another common approach to planning used by business economists is to try to discover the correlation between sales and other economic variables over time. There are many examples where movements in two or more economic variables are closely associated, with changes in one variable being followed more or less consistently by changes in the other. For example, as real disposable income rises in the economy, the demand for most consumer goods eventually increases, the time lag being longer perhaps for the more expensive items such as durables (e.g., cars and houses) and shorter perhaps for items such as clothing. It is therefore extremely helpful to management if a variable or group of variables can be found whose time series leads the sales figures for the firm's products. Information about such variables, referred to as *leading indicators*, is a great aid to demand forecasting.

Most governments devote a great deal of effort to analysing the behaviour of a wide range of economic variables over a long period of time. The aim is to find out whether each economic indicator turns downwards before, at, or after the peak of a business cycle, and whether it turns up before, at, or after the trough. Variables that go down before the peak and up before the trough are called *leading indicators*; variables that move in tandem with the business cycle are called *coincident indicators*, while variables that go down after the peak and up after the trough are referred to as *lagging indicators*.

Some examples of leading indicators used in many countries in forecasting trends in the economy are the following:

- New housing starts.
- Stock Exchange indices.
- Price-to-unit labour cost ratios.
- New orders for durable goods.
- Orders for new capital goods and equipment
- Changes in manufacturing stocks.
- Changes in consumer credit.

These variables tend to turn upwards before an economic trough is reached in anticipation of a future recovery, while they also tend to slow down in advance of a peak in expectation of a subsequent economic downturn. Similarly, coincident indicators often include changes in corporate profits, gross domestic product, and employment; while lagging indicators may include changes in long-term unemployment levels, retail sales, personal incomes and retail prices (since inflationary pressures can be slow to respond to a general economic downturn).

The use of leading indicators as a sales forecasting technique is applicable mainly to short- and medium-term forecasts. This is because there may only be a relatively short time lag (say, a few months) between a change in the leading indicator and a corresponding movement in sales. Moreover, management may be reluctant to rely too heavily on this method for longer-term forecasting because it does not provide an explanation for sales, but merely helps to identify turning points in the direction of movement of sales. The method is also unable to indicate the magnitude and exact timing of any subsequent change in demand. However, the method is usually an inexpensive one – very often, the leading indicator information will be published by the government statistical office!

Econometric modelling

We have already described how econometric modelling can be used to estimate demand relationships. Once this relationship has been specified it can be used as a tool for estimating future demand by including forecast values for the determining variables. For example, it will be recalled that sales (Q) were estimated as a function of price (P), advertising expenditure (A) and disposable income per head (Y), such that:

$$Q = a + bP + cA + dY$$

The error term, e, is not included explicitly here because any error will be reflected in the accuracy of the forecast itself when compared with the actual outcome. Forecasts for Y will be available from the government statistical office, while forecasts for P and A will be available from the firm itself since the firm controls these variables (note that earlier we stated that the equilibrium price is determined by demand and supply; of course, there is nothing to stop the firm setting whatever price it likes but it will have to accept whatever demand arises at that price – it cannot control price and demand independently). The forecasts for *P*, *A* and *Y* will therefore provide a basis for forecasting sales (*Q*) from the demand relationship.

The above example is a fairly trivial one, involving only a single demand equation. In reality, multi-equation models are likely to be necessary involving a great number of determining variables and complex mathematical manipulations. The principles,

---

Application 17.1

Forecasting demand for health care

An industry in crisis?

In the UK, the National Health Service (NHS) is in a state of crisis. After fifty years of universal health care provision, the Service is in need of urgent treatment as more than a million people await operations and as more and more people who can afford to do so are turning to the private sector. It is a crisis in which patients reaching the front of a year-long queue to go into hospital may face cancellation on the very day of their operation, due to an inadequate supply of nursing and other key medical resources. It is a crisis of a system totally unable to cope with a routine winter influenza epidemic. It is a crisis in which you may have to wait several days for an appointment with your general practitioner, and in which the likelihood of that GP giving you a prescription for the necessary but expensive medicine is said to depend on a 'postcode lottery'.

It is a crisis in which the World Health Organisation (WHO) reported (in June 2000) that, in an international league table ranking the overall performance of health systems throughout the world, the UK languishes in eighteenth place (and in a rather alarming twenty-sixth position as regards its per capita expenditure on health care).

Increased resources on the supply side

The answer to the crisis would appear to be the provision of an increase in NHS resources, or, to put it another way, to facilitate a rightward shift in the position of the supply curve. The Government has announced major increases in investment in the NHS, well above the rate of inflation, for the years ahead: the measures are expected to raise health spending to 7.6% of GDP by the year 2004. Emergency plans are also in place to cut waiting list times.

A growing demand for health care

But will these measures be sufficient to restore some sort of equilibrium to the Service? Many observers are pessimistic as a result of the expected future growth in the demand for health care. The government recognises the challenges posed by a moving demand target – as one government minister put it, 'the NHS is rather like a supertanker out at sea. It is difficult to turn it around and steer a new course'.

Activity

You have been appointed as a consultant by the government with responsibility for forecasting the demand for health care in the UK over the next decade. How would you approach the task? What factors are likely to be the key drivers behind a growing demand for health services?

however, are the same and, fortunately for management, the job of econometric modelling can be left to economists and statisticians.

Many multi-equation models are used by a number of government and private sector organisations throughout the world. These models contain large systems of equations variously intended to explain the level of expenditure by households, business investment expenditure, national output and employment, wages, retail and wholesale prices, interest rates, construction activity, etc. Like all forecasts, however, the reports issued by these institutions are far from perfect. As a result, they often attract considerable criticism, especially from business, because of inaccuracies in some of their forecasts (with the benefit of hindsight of course!). Nevertheless, in the absence of a superior alternative, forecasts from econometric models such as these continue to be widely used by business and government as the basis for discussing future policy and business strategy decisions.

Econometric modelling has an important advantage over the other two forecasting methods of trend projection and leading indictors outlined above. An attempt is made to account for future sales in terms of causal relationships using anticipated future values of those factors that are believed to affect demand. A more detailed understanding of 'cause and effect' helps management to accommodate changes in assumptions about future events in a more systematic way. This in turn facilitates the development of a range of scenarios and the formulation of appropriate business responses. In addition, the forecaster has the opportunity to improve the accuracy of the forecasts as time passes by adding new, up-to-date information into the forecasting model – there is, therefore, an adaptive learning process. At the same time, however, it is important to recognise the danger of using econometric models simply as 'number crunching' or 'data mining' devices, i.e. churning out forecasts under a vast spectrum of scenarios (some realistic, some fanciful, some bizarre!), especially since it is not very difficult to produce endless forecasts using today's computerised technology. It is vital that forecasting models are carefully and methodically constructed, representing a sound blend of economic theory and reliable statistical methods, if they are to be of use.

Concluding remarks

In this chapter we have described the fundamentals of demand estimation and forecasting. From even this treatment of the basic principles of the subject presented here, it will be clear that forecasting is one of the most challenging aspects of business analysis. It is also an area of business which, in recent years, has increased dramatically in importance as competition has grown both domestically and globally. The reader should not, however, be daunted by the technical aspects of forecasting, some of which we have mentioned in this chapter. The advent of user-friendly personal computers has circumvented the mysteries of the 'statisticians' black-box'. Nowadays, there is little need for managers to be fully conversant with the underlying technical aspects of forecasts. More important is the ability to interpret computer-generated results correctly, with this interpretation complemented by good judgement and sound managerial experience. However, a degree of scepticism about all forecasts is useful. It helps to avoid the danger of placing undue emphasis on hard, cold numbers. The numbers should represent only one component of sound management decision-making.

The next chapter provides a summary of many of the key concepts in business economics discussed in this book in the form of a checklist for managers.

Key learning points

- Understanding the reactions of consumers to changes in demand conditions involves estimating the nature of demand relationships within the range of observed explanatory variables and forecasting future demand patterns from values of variables which lie beyond the range of observed values. The former is concerned with **interpolation** and the latter **extrapolation**.

- The methods available to help management collect information about consumer behaviour as the basis of demand estimation and forecasting may be broadly categorised under the headings of **consumer surveys** and **market experiments**.

- **Consumer surveys** seek to discover the future buying intentions of consumers by eliciting their *probable* reactions to a range of conditions concerning price, advertising spend, product quality and design, and so on.

- **Market experiments** seek to test buyers' reactions to *actual* changes introduced, while attempting so far as is possible to keep other market conditions fairly stable or under control.

- In general, the different methods of **market experimentation** fall under one of three headings: *sales-wave research*, *simulated store techniques*, and *test marketing*.

- **Regression analysis** involves five key steps: the identification of variables, compilation of data, specification of the form of the relationship, estimation of the relationship, and evaluation of the estimated relationship.

- The most commonly used procedure for estimating the relationship between variables is known as the **method of least squares regression**. In essence, this enables us to find the values of the coefficients of the explanatory variables which minimise the sum of the squared positive and negative deviations of the actual (observed) values of the dependent variable from those predicted by the fitted relationship. This enables us to derive a mathematical relationship providing the 'best fit' between the dependent and explanatory variables, which can be shown graphically.

- Evaluation of the **reliability of estimated coefficients** is commonly based on the multiple correlation coefficient and the standard error of the estimate.

- The **multiple correlation coefficient** measures the proportion of the total variation in the observed dependent variable that is 'explained' by the estimated relationship – it is thus an overall measure of the strength of the estimated relationship.

- The **standard error of the estimate** allows us to attach a degree of confidence to the estimated value of the dependent variable based on the regression equation.

- The various **forecasting methods** may be grouped under three headings, namely: *trend projection* (or trend extrapolation), *leading indicators*, and *econometric modelling*.

- The **choice of forecasting method** depends on how far forward we need to forecast, the degree of accuracy required in the forecasts, how quickly the forecasts are needed, and how accurate and complete the underlying data are which form the basis of the forecasts.

- The simplest type of forecasting method is a straightforward **trend projection** (or extrapolation) of past data. This can be particularly useful in arriving at short-term forecasts.

- **Time series data** may be broken down into four components: trend (T), seasonal variation (S), cyclical variation (C), and random shocks (R).

Topics for discussion

1 What factors are likely to affect the market for houses and the determination of house prices:
   (a) nationally over time; and
   (b) locally at a point in time?

2 You have been asked to write a report on the future of the market for men's clothing by a major clothing manufacturer.
   (a) Outline briefly the structure that the report will take, highlighting the main steps of the final analysis
   (b) What factors do you consider will be the most important in determining future sales of the company's products?

3 You have been appointed by the board of an upmarket cosmetics producer to prepare a report concerning a new product launch. Briefly describe how you would assess:
   (a) The launch price of the product.
   (b) Future sales, short term and long term.
   (c) The likely reaction of competitors.
   (d) Profitability of the new product.

   You have also been instructed to identify different ways in which the new product may be test-marketed, justifying clearly your preferred method.

4 Samuel Goldwyn once stated: 'Never make forecasts, especially about the future.' Discuss the pitfalls involved in making business forecasts. How are these pitfalls best avoided?

18 Business economics – a checklist for managers

This book has been concerned with investigating various aspects of business economics and has highlighted the importance of an understanding of business economics in the preparation and development of an effective business strategy.

To stay ahead of the competition and to anticipate and react effectively to changes in markets requires an understanding of the forces of demand and supply and their impact on prices and outputs in different market environments. In particular, firms operating in markets where competition is imperfect (hence having less elastic demand curves) typically have far more discretion over prices and outputs than firms operating in highly competitive markets. This suggests a strategy of product differentiation as an obvious option. The alternative, supplying undifferentiated products (products with high cross-price elasticities with substitutes), implies a need to be the low-cost producer since competition will centre on price, as emphasised by the perfect competition model. In addition, as we have seen, the precise response to market signals in terms of the price–output strategy adopted is dictated by the objectives of management – what goal or goals are being pursued? A firm that is intent upon maximising short-term profit will pursue a different price and output configuration than, for example, a firm more concerned with maximising sales revenue. This led on to a discussion of pricing strategies where it was observed that, as price is only one of a number of factors likely to determine consumer demand, attention should be paid to the complete 'marketing mix'. In turn, management should not lose sight of the importance of sound employment policies and investment appraisal when adjusting output to meet changes in demand, issues explored in Chapters 13 and 14.

We concluded our review of business economics with a discussion of natural resources, the role of government in the economy and the subject of business and economic forecasting. The market for natural resources, including land, cannot be ignored because of the importance of natural resources as inputs to a number of industries and the growing public interest in 'green issues'; while governments today play a central role in determining the economic environment in which businesses operate. Government policy can make or break the best planned and executed business strategy. Lastly, our approach to the subject of business forecasting was premised on the belief that when walking through a tunnel it is better to have at least partial light rather than complete darkness. In other words, in business some knowledge of likely future trends, for example in sales, and hence some knowledge of the relationship between demand and the factors impacting on demand, is superior to complete ignorance (or indifference) to the future.

We conclude this overview of business economics with a checklist drawn from the principles explored in the book. The list provides a brief summary of the key topics discussed in the earlier chapters. But the main purpose of the list is to allow busy managers speedily to review their knowledge of their firm's economic environment, both internal and external, with a view to identifying the degree of competitive advantage (or disadvantage!) which exists and thus to identify those areas where more knowledge or information is needed. The list is presented as a series of key economic questions and is summarised in Figure 18.1 as a 'wheel of fortune'!

Learning outcomes

This chapter will help you to:

- Integrate the many dimensions of business economics and decision-making explained in this book.
- Better understand the complexity of questions facing management in their pursuit of successful corporate and *business strategies*.
- Understand that business economics provides insights into important factors involved in the achievement of *sustained competitive advantage*, while recognising that the subject rarely provides precise answers.

Checklist for business success

Understanding the business objectives

- What are my objectives for each of the products, e.g. short-term profit maximisation, sales maximisation (increasing market share), etc.?
- Who are my stakeholders?
- Does my stakeholder analysis suggest pursuit of objectives other than the maximisation of shareholder value or profit maximisation?
- Are current product prices set at a level to achieve the desired objectives?
- Is my competitive strategy primarily focused on being the lowest-cost producer or does it rely more on product differentiation?
- If my products are neither the lowest-cost nor sufficiently differentiated ('stuck in the middle'), what action might be taken to change the product focus and how might rivals react?

Understanding the competitive market

- In what types of markets do I operate (highly competitive, monopolistic, etc.)?
- What are the implications for setting prices and achieving profits in the short and long run?

- How do my main competitors set their prices and determine their expenditure on other aspects of the 'marketing mix'?
- Is there a threat from new competition?
- What barriers to entry into my markets exist and can be legally reinforced?
- Do I understand the limitations imposed by domestic and international competition law on my business and the possible strategies that I may pursue?
- What does new competition imply for my competitive position over the longer term?
- How might I best respond to changes in the market by altering the 'marketing mix' for my products?
- Would either a 'penetration' or 'skimming' pricing strategy be advantageous in achieving my desired business objectives?
- Under what circumstances would a predatory pricing policy make good commercial sense?
- When might non-price competition be superior to competing purely on price?
- Under what conditions would cost-cutting not make good business sense?

Understanding consumer behaviour

- Do I know how different market factors affect the demand for my products and hence do I know (even in general terms) the demand function for each of my products?
- Is it likely that my prices will have to be changed in the immediate future and if so what are the own price elasticities of the products?
- Are the prices of substitute and complementary products likely to change and if so what are the relevant cross-price elasticities of my products?
- What is the income elasticity of demand for my products and what is the forecast for income changes in the next few years?
- Is it possible and would it be useful to have a statistician/economist estimate the demand coefficients for my products?
- Is price set mainly with a view to consumer demand or mainly with a view to covering supply costs (e.g. a 'cost-plus' pricing policy)?
- Is my pricing strategy consistent with my overall business objectives?

Understanding the costs of production

- How elastic is the supply of each of the products I produce and hence how fast could I respond to changes in demand?
- How might supply elasticity be increased?

- What is the current marginal cost for each of my products and is it rising or falling and why?
- What does the nature of my marginal cost structure mean for my future competitiveness?
- Is there evidence of diminishing returns given current plant size?
- What does the evidence on diminishing returns imply for my investment programme in my business?
- Am I getting the maximum economies of scale in production, and if not why not?
- How do economies of scale affect my competitive position?
- Is there scope for reducing X-inefficiency in my business and how might such savings be best achieved?

Understanding business finance and the investment decision

- What are the various sources of finance available to me to fund my business decisions?
- What are the implications for the weighted average cost of capital?
- To what extent would raising capital through the equity markets be preferable to debt financing investment projects?
- How are investment decisions made within my business?
- Are discounted cash flow estimates consistently used in investment appraisal?
- What regional and other government financial incentives might be accessed?
- What is the opportunity cost of capital investment – alternative business investment opportunities or a relatively risk-free return in a bank account?
- What costs and benefits (internal and external) are taken into consideration in investment appraisal in my business?

Understanding the employment decision

- Do decisions on employment take into account the marginal revenue product (i.e. the added value) of labour?
- What criteria are used to establish wage rates in my business?
- What factors determine the supply of labour to the business?
- What are the implications for labour supply of current demographic trends?
- What action is being taken to anticipate unfavourable movements in labour costs?
- Are current wage differentials economically justified?

Understanding the external environment

- Is there a regular briefing in my company concerned with developments in the macroeconomic environment and related government policy and their likely impact on the business?

- Do I know what would be the demand for my products if interest rates rose or fell, or if the exchange rate depreciated or appreciated, or if there was a change in the rate of growth of consumer spending or investment?

- In developing business plans do I make use of any macroeconomic forecasts prepared by the various forecasting bodies in my country?

- Are there any likely changes in the political, economic, social and technological (PEST) environment which will impact on my business in the future?

- How should I respond to these events?

- How does competition policy impact on my business?

- What are the implications for the business of changes in the market for natural resources including land?

- What is the effect of environmental legislation?

- How might our approach to 'green issues' be better managed?

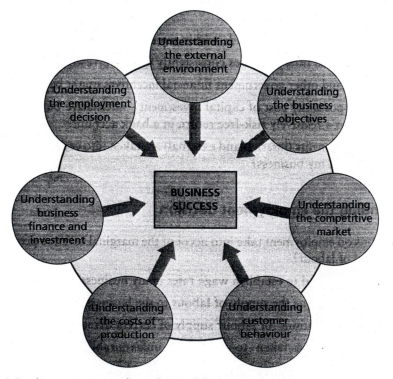

Figure 18.1 Business success – the 'wheel of fortune'

The above lists are not intended to be exhaustive – indeed, they could not be exhaustive since what is important to one business may not be important to another. They are simply intended to provide a *basis* for identifying those economic factors which impact on any business with a view to provoking a search for the relevant answers. For example, in some businesses land and other natural resources play an especially important role. In other businesses labour and capital inputs are much more significant.

Business economics is best viewed as a tool kit for analysing competition and market behaviour. Economists can provide insights into real-world business problems though rarely precise answers. It is ultimately the manager who has to take the difficult decisions of business on a day-to-day basis and after weighing up the alternatives. Hopefully, however, this book will assist managers and students of business (future managers) to understand the challenges they have to face in the competitive economic environment in which they function. Hence, hopefully the book will contribute to sounder business decision-making in what is an increasingly complex business and economic environment.

Topics for revision

1 Set out an economic strategy for a small-scale food retailer threatened by the possible entry into its market of a competitor which is part of a large national chain of supermarkets.

2 Is it sensible for a firm to react to new competition by reducing price? Justify your views.

3 When is cost-cutting not a sustainable, long-term competitive strategy?

4 What non-price strategies should be considered as a reaction to new competition?

5 Taking an industry with which you are familiar (the one you work in or one you have studied), set out the key economic variables that you feel determine business success.

6 Do the same for a *particular* firm in this industry, and indicate the main future competitive threats and actions the management should take.

7 In the case of this firm, indicate the main future threats that are likely to come from the *macroeconomic* environment.

accelerative industrial policies are designed to speed up the adjustment process within economies in terms of industrial restructuring.

activity-based costing attempts to apportion joint or common costs across goods and services according to their contribution to production so as to minimise distortion of resource allocation.

allocative efficiency denotes the optimal allocation of scarce resources so as to produce the combination of outputs which best accords with consumers' demands such that no other allocation of resources would produce a higher level of economic welfare.

arc elasticity measures the responsiveness of demand between two points on the demand curve, calculated as

$$\frac{(Q_2 - Q_1)}{(P_2 - P_1)} \times \frac{(P_2 + P_1)}{(Q_2 + Q_1)}$$

Article 81 of the European Treaty prohibits restrictive agreements and practices in so far as they 'affect trade between member states' and restrict or distort competition.

Article 82 of the European Treaty prohibits 'any abuse by one or more undertakings of a dominant position within the common market or a substantial part of it' in so far as it affects trade between member states.

average physical product is the total output or physical product divided by the number of units of labour employed.

average revenue is the total revenue divided by total output or the revenue earned on average for each unit sold.

average total cost (ATC) is made up of average fixed cost plus average variable cost.

bargaining power of buyers is concerned with understanding how much leverage a firm's buyers (customers) have in determining the price of the product or service offered for sale.

bargaining power of suppliers is concerned with the degree of competition amongst input suppliers which determines the availability and price of inputs to the firm.

bargaining theory of wages suggests that wage determination is a matter of 'negotiation' between 'determined' unions on the one hand and 'intransigent' employers on the other.

barometric price leadership arises when a firm assesses changes in demand and cost conditions and alters its price.

behavioural theories reject the notion of maximisation in favour of a less strong goal of 'satisficing' and are concerned with the firms' actual behaviour with attention focused on the internal decision-making structure of the firm.

boundary of the firm can be explained by *transaction cost* theory and the *resource-based* theory of the firm.

bounded rationality exists where consumers act rationally, given imperfect information.

breakeven pricing requires that the price of the product is set so that total revenue earned equals the total costs of production.

budget line is a line showing the alternative combinations of goods and services that can be purchased by a consumer with a given income facing given prices.

business ethics is concerned with the social responsibility of management towards the firm's major stakeholders, the environment and society in general.

capital is a factor of production which includes all physical (manufactured) factors that are used in the production of other goods and services – for example, plant, machinery, buildings and business fixtures and fittings.

ceteris paribus (or simply, *cet. par.*) is a Latin term meaning 'other things being equal'.

change management is concerned with bringing about organisational change and managing the forces for and against change within any organisation (perhaps analysed using a *force-field mapping*).

cheating behaviour includes secretly selling a lower price than agreed so as to gain market share at the expense of other cartel members.

cobweb theory explains the path followed in moving towards an equilibrium situation where there are time lags in the adjustment of either supply or demand to changes in prices.

coefficient of elasticity is measured as the percentage change in quantity demanded divided by the percentage change in the relevant variable.

collective bargaining refers to arrangements between employers and trade unions regarding the setting of wages and conditions of work.

collusive price leadership exists where firms in an oligopolistic market, either explicitly or tacitly, collude on price.

competence theory is concerned mainly with explaining why some firms add more value that other firms.

competitive advantage is concerned with assessing and adapting to dynamic forces in the global economy.

competitive spectrum illustrates the extent to which competition in the market place can range from, at one extreme, *pure monopoly* (sole supplier) to the other extreme of *perfect competition* (very large number of small suppliers selling identical products or services).

competitive strategy is concerned with how management formulate and implement strategies to maximise and sustain the firm's competitive advantage in the competitive environment.

competitive tendering is the opening up of certain state-supplied services, such as refuse collection and hospital cleaning, to private firms and introducing more competition in other areas of public procurement, notably defence contracts.

conglomerate integration occurs when a firm enters different markets or industrial sectors perhaps in order to spread the risk involved in doing business.

constant returns to scale arise when the volume of output increases in the same proportion to the volume of inputs.

consumer equilibrium describes how consumers maximise their total utility by distributing expenditure so that the ratio of marginal utilities for all the goods and services they consume, at any given time, is equal to their relative prices.

consumer surplus is the excess of the price which a person would be willing to pay rather than go without the good, over that which he or she actually does pay – this is also sometimes referred to as *consumer's rent*.

consumer surveys seek to discover the future buying intentions of consumers by eliciting their *probable* reactions to a range of conditions concerning price, advertising spend, product quality and design, and so on.

consumer's demand curve relates the amount the consumer is willing to buy to each conceivable price for the product – also simply referred to as the *demand curve*.

consumer's rent – see *consumer surplus*.

contingent-claim contracts may specify certain circumstances under which the contract or part of it takes effect or can be adjusted or renegotiated.

core competence is something that gives a firm a distinctive competitive advantage in the market place.

corporate growth maximisation model suggests that management seek to maximise the growth of the firm subject to an optimal dividend-to-profit retention ratio, in order to safeguard the firm from a hostile takeover bid.

corporate-level strategy is concerned with the development of strategy for the entire organisation, including all of its operational subsidiaries and divisions.

cost–benefit analysis is a method for assessing capital projects where it is important to take into account all of the impacts of the investment decision, including the effects on people, other firms, regions and so on, i.e. taking into account the total social or external costs and benefits of a capital investment project.

cost function shows the relationship between the cost of the output and the cost of inputs used.

cost leadership strategy involves the firm in minimising its costs of production so as to become the lowest cost producer in the industry.

cost-plus contracts are contracts which allow for additional or unexpected cost overruns.

cross-price elasticity of demand indicates the responsiveness of the demand for one product to changes in the prices of other goods and services and is calculated as:

$$\frac{\text{percentage change in the demand for A}}{\text{percentage change in the price of B}}$$

cross-sectional data are concerned with data recorded at a point in time.

decelerative industrial policies are intended to slow down the pace of change, usually through financial aid, and are usually directed at industries in serious decline.

decreasing returns to scale arise where the volume of output rises less quickly than the volume of inputs.

degree of competition (rivalry) in the market is concerned with understanding the nature and impact of rivalry amongst *existing* firms in the market place.

demand is the amount consumers are willing to buy at a given price and over a given period of time.

demand curve relates the amount that consumers are willing to buy to each conceivable price for the product.

demand for labour is a derived demand, i.e. people are employed for the output they produce.

demand function expresses the quantity demanded of a product or service over a given time period, in relation to the most important factors which determine demand.

differentiation strategy involves the development of customer loyalty by a firm through product development, branding, advertising, etc., without necessarily producing at lowest cost.

diminishing marginal returns refers to the situation whereby, as we apply more of one input to a fixed amount of another input, then after some point the resulting increase in output becomes smaller and smaller.

discounting is concerned with the fact that costs and benefits arising in future years are worth less to us than costs and benefits arising today.

dominant firm oligopoly exists when one firm has a competitive advantage over other firms in the industry – notably a cost advantage – and produces a large part of the industry's output.

dominant strategy occurs where the same policy is suggested by different strategies.

duopoly describes a market situation in which there are only two suppliers.

dynamic cost reductions arise from efficiency gains and are associated with new developments in products and production processes over time.

dynamic efficiency gains represent lower costs of production or higher productivity associated with new developments in products and production processes over time.

economic efficiency is concerned with the use of scarce resources to achieve stipulated economic ends.

economic rent represents the earnings to a factor of production over and above its opportunity cost or the minimum payment needed to keep it in its present use, known as the *transfer earnings*.

economies of scope arise when the cost of producing two or more different outputs by one firm are lower than would be the case if each output was produced in separate firms.

elasticity of demand for labour measures the responsiveness of employment to a change in wages, calculated as:

$$\frac{\text{percentage change in number of employed}}{\text{percentage change in the wage rate}}$$

elasticity of supply is defined as the percentage change in quantity supplied divided by the percentage change in the price of a good or service.

elasticity of supply of labour is a measure of the responsiveness of the supply of labour to a change in the wage paid, calculated as:

$$\frac{\text{percentage change in supply of labour}}{\text{percentage change in the wage rate}}$$

enterprise initiatives represent the redirection of state funding and other support towards retraining programmes and assisting the start-up of small enterprises with venture capital.

envelope curve shows how the long-run average total costs of production change as output continues to rise over the long run; this represents the *envelope* of all the possible short-run average total cost curves relating to different scales of production.

environmental scanning involves identifying and evaluating external drivers of change affecting the business at both macro and micro levels.

equilibrium price is the price at which the quantity demanded by consumers and the quantity that firms would be willing to supply are the same.

estimation is concerned with deriving the best specification of the functional relationship between dependent and explanatory variables.

experience curve shows how unit costs will fall over time as experience of producing and selling a good or service increases; in other words, how costs of production decline as the *cumulative volume* of output rises – also known as the *learning curve*.

explicit collusion includes the creation of a formal restrictive practice or cartel between producers, where prices may be jointly set and markets shared out.

external diseconomies of scale arise when costs rise as the whole industry expands in a particular area.

external economies of scale arise at the industry level and are generally associated with growth in output over time in *the industry* leading to a lower cost of production.

externalities represent negative outcomes of the market mechanism and arise when some of the benefits or costs of consuming a good or service spill over to others.

extrapolation is concerned with the forecasting or projection of future behaviour on the basis of past behaviour.

factors of production may be broadly categorised as natural resources (including land), labour and capital.

first-degree price discrimination arises in the case of a producer selling each unit of output separately, charging a different price for each unit according to the demand function.

fiscal policy refers to the use of government expenditure and taxation.

fixed costs are costs of production which do not vary as output changes.

flow of capital is the increase in the stock of capital over a given time period resulting from new capital investment.

focus strategy involves the firm in using either cost leadership or differentiation in a narrow segment of the market to gain advantage over more broadly based competitors.

force-field mapping is concerned with the identification of the blockages to change and how a desired change may be best achieved.

forecasting methods can be grouped conveniently under four headings, namely: trend projection (or trend extrapolation); leading indicators, econometric modelling and survey analysis.

full-range pricing means that the firm may be content to earn little or no profit on certain products, preferring to use them as 'loss leaders' to attract consumers who then (hopefully) buy the higher-profit items.

functional-level strategy deals with decision-making at the operational level of the organisation involving the various departments of marketing, finance, personnel, operations, R&D, etc.

game theory explores more complex oligopoly situations based on interacting decision-takers (players) and different outcomes (pay-offs) associated with different competitive strategies.

gearing ratio is the proportion of debt to equity finance raised by a firm – also known as the *leverage ratio*.

generic strategies refer to the choice between pursuing a market strategy based on *cost leadership, differentiation* or *focus*.

Giffen products arise when as price *rises*, more of the good in question is bought – resulting in what appears to be an *upward* sloping demand curve, contrary to the normal law of demand.

globalisation is concerned with the development of competition on a worldwide basis, involving large flows of products and services and international capital across national boundaries.

horizontal integration occurs when two or more firms, at the same stage of production, integrate – usually leading to less competition in the product market (and hence more market concentration).

human capital is concerned with the skills, talents and abilities of the labour force and which leads to a higher marginal physical product of labour.

incidence of taxation relates to the allocation of the burden of taxation, i.e. who bears the tax.

income effect relates to the fact that as the price of a good or service falls, consumers are in effect better off and hence able to buy more of the good, while the opposite applies in the case of a price rise (the change in price is equivalent, in effect, to a change in income though *actual* income is unchanged).

income elasticity of demand measures the responsiveness of quantity demanded with respect to (real) income variations, calculated as:

$$\frac{\text{percentage change in quantity demanded}}{\text{percentage change in real income}}$$

increasing returns to scale arise where the volume of output *rises more quickly* than the volume of inputs.

incremental pricing deals with the relationship between larger than strictly marginal changes in revenues and costs associated with managerial decisions.

indifference curve shows all combinations of two goods or services that yield the same level of utility or satisfaction so that the consumer is indifferent between each combination.

industrial policy in relation to accelerative or decelerative objectives may be categorised into four broad areas aimed at a 'national champion' strategy, the development of 'sunrise industries', a 'lame duck' strategy and 'problem industries'.

inferior goods are goods of which consumers buy less when real incomes rise.

injections into the economy are investment, government spending and revenue from exports.

internal diseconomies of scale result in rising long-run average costs.

internal economies of scale arise where there is a large output of goods or services which lowers long-run average costs. Economies stem from the more effective use of available internal resources resulting in higher productivity and lower costs.

internal rate of return is defined as the rate of interest that equates the present value of a project's net cash flow to the initial capital investment outlay.

interpolation is the prediction of a value of a dependent variable from a value of an explanatory variable which lies within the range or observed values.

inverse pricing rule suggests that social welfare is maximised by applying a higher price mark-up to consumers with the more price-inelastic demand and is associated with two-part tariffs.

isocost line shows the combination of two inputs which can be purchased for the same total money outlay.

isoquant curve shows in graphical form different combinations of factor inputs that can be used to produce a given quantity of a product.

isoquant map is a collection of ranked isoquant curves that shows in graphical form a firm's increasing output when moving outward from the origin using larger quantities of factor inputs.

kinked demand curve theory is concerned with the reactions of firms to an increase or reduction in the price charged by one firm in the market; this model is associated with *price rigidity* ('sticky' prices).

labour productivity is defined as output per unit of labour employed in the production process.

law of demand states that there is an inverse relationship between the price of a good and the quantity demanded, assuming all other factors that might influence demand are held constant (i.e. *ceteris paribus*).

law of diminishing (marginal) returns arises in the short run such that when one or more factors of production are held fixed, there will come a point beyond which the additional output from using extra units of the variable input(s) will diminish.

law of diminishing marginal utility is concerned with the tendency for marginal utility to fall as more units of a good or service are consumed at any given time.

leakages from the economy are savings, taxation and expenditure on imports.

learning curve – see *experience curve*.

leverage ratio – see *gearing ratio*.

logistics is the study of the organisation of supply and distribution chains so as to minimise costs.

long run represents the *planning horizon* of the business in which all factors of production may be varied in order to alter the scale of production.

macroeconomic activity is affected by the relative size of injections into and leakages out of the economy at any given time, where injections are investment spending, government spending and export revenue, and leakages are savings, taxation and spending on imports.

macroeconomic environment comprises the general economic conditions of the larger economy of which each firm forms a part.

macroeconomic policy is concerned with regulation of the level of economic activity.

macro-environmental analysis is concerned with identifying external trends relating to political, economic, social and technological developments which are likely to impact on the firm.

managerial utility maximisation model argues that managers seek to maximise their own self-interest based on the achievement of goals such as high salaries, authority over staffing, discretionary investment expenditure decisions, fringe benefits, etc.

marginal analysis reminds us that most choices involve relatively small (incremental) increases or decreases in production or consumption.

marginal cost pricing involves setting prices, and therefore determining the amount produced, according to the marginal costs of production, and is normally associated with a profit-maximising objective.

marginal costs are the additional costs incurred in producing a very small increment or one more unit of output and will only depend on changes in variable costs in the short run because fixed costs are unaltered as output changes. In the long run, however, marginal costs reflect changes in the total costs of production since all inputs are variable.

marginal physical product is the addition to total physical product as an extra unit of input is employed.

marginal rate of technical substitution is the ratio of the marginal physical product of two inputs in the production process; i.e. the amount by which it is possible to reduce one factor input and maintain a given level of output by substituting an extra unit of the other factor input.

marginal revenue is defined as the incremental change in total revenue and is usually measured as a firm sells one more or one less unit of its output.

marginal revenue product of labour under conditions of imperfect competition is affected by the marginal physical product of labour (MPP) and changes in marginal revenue MR, so that $MRP = MPP \times MR$.

marginal social benefits reflect the degree of external benefits from consumption.

marginal social costs reflect the degree of external costs from consumption.

marginal utility is the amount by which consumer well-being or total utility changes when the consumption of a good or service changes by one unit.

marginal value product of labour under conditions of perfect competition is the value added to production by employing one more person, calculated as follows: $MPP \times P$, where MPP is the marginal physical product (i.e. the volume of output added by employing one more person) and P is the constant price at which the output sells.

market demand curve for a good or service is derived by summing the individual demand curves of consumers horizontally.

market experimentation falls under one of three headings: *sales-wave research, simulated store techniques*, and *test marketing*.

market experiments are concerned with testing buyers' reactions to actual changes introduced, while attempting so far as is possible to keep other market conditions stable or under control.

market failure occurs where the market price fails to reflect the true *social benefit* of consuming a good or service and the marginal cost fails to reflect the true *social cost* of providing the good or service.

marketing mix takes into account other factors than price that influence consumer demand.

mark-up pricing is similar to breakeven pricing, except that a desired rate of profit is built into the price (therefore this pricing is also sometimes referred to as cost-plus, full-cost or target-profit pricing).

maximax strategy involves choosing the strategy that has the best possible outcome.

maximin (regret) strategy involves choosing the strategy which supports the best possible outcome from among the set of worst possible outcomes.

method of least squares regression enables us to find the values for the regression coefficients which give the best fit.

microeconomic environment deals with the operation of the firm in its immediate market, involving the determination of its prices, revenues, costs, employment levels and so on.

micro-environmental analysis focuses on the nature of the competitive environment of the firm at the industry or market level.

minimax strategy involves choosing the strategy which minimises the maximum opportunity loss associated with what might turn out to be a wrong decision.

minimum efficient scale represents the technical optimum scale of production for the firm, corresponding to minimum unit costs over the long run.

minimum wage legislation prevents employers from exploiting workers by offering wages at levels which society may consider to be unacceptable – the result may, however, be higher unemployment.

mission encapsulates the firm's overall values and general aspirations usually captured within a formal *mission statement*.

mission statements set out the overall values and aspirations of a firm.

monetary policy refers to the use of short-term interest rates and monetary control techniques.

monopolistically competitive markets exist when there are many sellers but there is also some degree of product differentiation – this form of market structure is also sometimes referred to as *imperfectly competitive*.

monopoly exists where the market is supplied by one firm producing a product for which there is no close substitute – a monopolist, therefore, tends to be a *price-maker*, in that the firm is able to set a price in the face of little or no competition. In practice, the term monopoly is often applied also to markets that are *dominated* by one firm.

monopsony refers to the situation where there is a single buyer of particular goods and services or particular factor inputs.

multicollinearity involves the possibility that explanatory variables may be statistically correlated.

multi-form structure exists when parts of the company operate with considerable managerial independence, especially in terms of day-to-day decision-making.

multiple correlation coefficient measures the proportion of the total variation in an observed dependent variable that is 'explained' by the estimated relationship – it is thus an overall measure of the strength of the estimated relationship.

multi-product firm has to take into consideration not only the impact of a price change on the demand for the product, but also the impact on the demand for the other products in the firm's product range. Pricing policy, therefore, involves obtaining the desired rate of return from the full product range rather than from individual products.

Nash equilibrium arises in *game theory* and represents the outcome where each player chooses his best strategy given the expected actions of the other players.

natural resources, including the supply of land, are an important input into the production process, alongside labour and capital.

negative discrimination can occur in labour markets, for example on grounds of race, sex, creed, physical disabilities, etc., leading to a lower demand for labour from these groups.

net present value (NPV) is the discounted value of the cash flow over the life of a project – see *discounting*.

normal products arise when quantity demanded rises as incomes rise and falls as incomes fall.

normal profit is the minimum profit which must be earned to ensure that a firm will continue to supply existing good or service. In incorporated firms it is equivalent to the 'cost of capital', namely the interest charges on loan capital plus the return to equity investors that must be paid if creditors and investors are to put their capital into the firm. In non-incorporated enterprises (sole traders and partnerships) this is the profit that ensures that a sufficient number of people are prepared to invest, organise production and undertake risks in an industry (including the return to risky 'entrepreneurship').

objectives set out precisely the quantitative or qualitative goals through which the firm's mission is to be achieved.

oligopolistic competition is a form of imperfectly competitive markets and arises where there exists a small number of relatively large firms which are constantly wary of each other's actions and reactions regarding price and non-price competition. There is therefore a high degree of *interdependence* in oligopolistic markets between the competing firms and while, in principle, the products on offer may be undifferentiated, in practice some differentiation usually exists.

operating period – see *short run*.

opportunity cost of any activity is what we give up when we make a choice, i.e. it is the loss of the opportunity to pursue the most attractive alternative given the same time and resources.

paradox of value concept helps to understand why the value (i.e. price) of a good or service is determined by its relative scarcity rather than by its usefulness.

Pareto optimum exists when resources cannot be reallocated so as to make one person better off without making someone else worse off.

payback method judges investments in terms of how quickly they generate sufficient net returns (income less operating costs) to cover the initial investment outlay on the capital project.

pay-off matrix summarises the possible outcomes associated with various strategies.

peak-load pricing involves charging higher prices for certain products or services at times of peak demand to reflect the higher marginal costs of supplying products at peak times.

penetration pricing – see *promotional pricing*.

perfectly competitive markets are markets which are made up of numerous small firms each offering *identical* or *homogeneous* products with complete freedom of entry for new firms and exit from the market and in which each firm has no control over the price of the product – each is a *price-taker* rather than a *price-maker* – and must accept the price determined by the interaction of the overall market supply and demand.

perfectly elastic demand arises where the demand curve is horizontal such that any quantity of the product can be sold at a certain price.

perfectly inelastic demand arises when the demand for a product is entirely unresponsive to any change in price – the demand curve will be a vertical line.

PEST analysis is concerned with detailing the main political, economic, social and technological factors impacting or likely to impact on the firm.

planning horizon – see *long run*.

point elasticity measures the responsiveness of demand to a change in price with reference to a single point on the demand curve, calculated as:

$$\frac{(Q_2 - Q_1)}{(P_2 - P_1)} \times \frac{(P_1)}{(Q_1)}$$

Porter's Five Forces Model describes the competitive environment and profitability as being determined by the following forces: the bargaining power of buyers; the bargaining power of (input) suppliers; the threat from potential new entrants into the market; the threat from substitute products or services and the degree of competition (rivalry) in the market.

positive discrimination can occur leading to increased demand for labour from particular groups in society.

price discrimination represents the practice of charging different prices for various units of a single product when the price differences are not justified by differences in production or supply costs. Successful price discrimination requires an absence of arbitrage opportunities and differing elasticities of demand in the various markets.

price efficiency occurs when inputs into production are optimally employed, given their prices, so as to minimise production costs.

price elastic refers to products with a price elasticity of demand greater than 1.

price elasticity of demand measures the responsiveness of quantity demanded of a product to changes in its 'own price', calculated as:

$$\frac{\text{percentage change in quantity demanded}}{\text{percentage change in the price of the product}}$$

price inelastic refers to products with a price elasticity of demand of less than 1.

price mechanism describes the way in which the prices charged for goods and services determine how scarce resources are automatically allocated in a free market economy.

price-cap regulation sets the firm's maximum price according to the economy's rate of inflation less an amount to reflect anticipated efficiency gains by the firm.

principal–agent theory recognises the growth in managerial capitalism and the complexity of modern organisational structures based on a *growing separation* between the owners of the firm (the principals) and the firm's senior management or directors (the agents).

prisoner's dilemma highlights how two or more players, acting in their best personal interest, may choose an inferior outcome than if they had colluded. This analysis neatly illustrates why firms have incentives to form cartels and why cartels often break down.

privatisation and market liberalisation policies are pursued so as to increase economic efficiency by replacing state ownership with private ownership and by opening up monopoly markets to competition.

process innovation is concerned with improving the existing methods by which outputs are produced so as to lower the costs of production.

processualist view of strategy recognises that some elements of a planned strategy are abandoned or disregarded as the external environment of the firm changes or because of changes within the internal management of the firm.

producer surplus is the additional revenue that accrues to a firm when units of output are sold at a price which is in excess of the marginal cost of production.

production function is a mathematical expression which relates the quantity of all inputs to the quantity of outputs.

production innovation involves the introduction of new goods and services.

production possibility curve shows the maximum output of two goods or services that can be produced given the current level of resources available and assuming maximum efficiency in production.

productive efficiency occurs when a firm minimises the costs of producing any level of output, given existing technology.

productivity of the firm is the efficiency with which resources are used to produce output.

profit maximisation rule states that profits are maximised where marginal cost equals marginal revenue.

promotional pricing occurs when the price is set low in order to help a firm to enter the market against existing competitors, attract consumers to the new product and gain market share – also known as *penetration pricing.*

property rights define the ownership of property, the uses to which property can be put, the rights of others over the property and how property can be transferred.

public good is one where there is significant market failure resulting from the conditions of non-excludability and non-rivalry in the market.

quasi-economic rents occur when a factor of production earns economic rents that are competed away in the long run as the supply of the factor of production is increased.

Ramsey pricing rule – see *inverse pricing rule.*

rate-of-return regulation involves the state setting a maximum price that the firm can charge consumers according to the firm's costs of production and after allowing for a normal rate of return on investment.

regional policy takes two broad forms aimed at reversing regional decline and limiting regional expansion.

regression analysis involves five key steps: the identification of variables, compilation of data, specification of the form of the relationship, estimation of the relationship, and evaluation of the estimated relationship.

reliability of estimated coefficients is commonly based on the multiple correlation coefficient and the standard error of the estimate.

resource allocation is concerned with decisions regarding *what, how,* and *for whom* to produce and in a market economy the *price mechanism* is the major determinant of these decisions.

resource-based theory is concerned with the assets, skills and knowledge (i.e. core competencies and distinctive capabilities) which are (a) specific to the firm, (b) difficult to imitate and (c) give the firm a distinct competitive advantage in the market place.

returns to scale are concerned with improvements in productivity arising from a change in the scale of production.

sales revenue maximisation model concludes that management which attempt to *maximise sales revenue* will tend to produce at a higher output level, set lower prices and invest more heavily in measures that boost demand than management which attempt to maximise profits.

satisficing arises when, faced with incomplete information and uncertainty, individuals are more likely to be content to achieve a *satisfactory* level of something rather than to strive to *maximise* goals.

satisficing behaviour is an explanation of managerial behaviour which is associated with behaviouralist theory and argues that there is no single objective of the firm; instead, there are multiple goals which emerge from the potential for conflict amongst interest groups within the firm, such that the aim will be to achieve a satisfactory performance for each of the goals without necessarily any single, maximisation objective.

second-degree price discrimination involves charging a uniform price per unit for a specific quantity or block of output sold to each consumer.

short run is the time period during which the amount of at least one input is fixed in supply (e.g. the amount of capital equipment installed or in some organisations the number of personnel employed) but the other inputs can be altered; in essence, the short run is the *operating period* of the firm, where the management has already made a technical decision about the production process.

shut-down point in the short run exists when price has fallen below average variable costs. In the long run the firm will wish to cover its total costs.

skimming policy arises when price is set high initially to cover large unit costs in the early stage of the product life.

social welfare relates to the well-being of society and reflects both private (internal) and public (external) costs and benefits stemming from production of goods and services.

specific tax is a tax which is levied at a fixed rate per physical unit of the good or service.

spillover effects reflect the consequences, both positive and negative, that a particular activity may have on other parts of a business.

spot contracts are contracts which are negotiated and completed at one point in time.

stable cobweb describes a situation where price moves towards the equilibrium.

standard error of the estimate allows us to attach a degree of confidence to the estimated value of the dependent variable based on the regression equation.

state failure is the term used to refer to the economic distortions caused by wasteful public spending, taxation disincentives and economically damaging regulation, leading to a lower level of economic welfare.

static cost reductions tend to occur in the short run and are associated with improving *existing* products and production methods.

stock of capital is the quantity or value of the total capital invested within the firm.

strategic business units are the separate parts of an overall organisation which will have their own specific strategic decisions and objectives.

strategic positioning involves the firm identifying what competitive stance it should take in the market.

structure–conduct–performance paradigm is based on the idea that the structure of the market (namely, the number of suppliers and their market shares) determines the conduct or behaviour of management, and that this in turn affects the performance of the industry in terms of prices, profits, etc.

substitution effect relates to the fact that as the price of a good or service falls, it becomes relatively cheaper than alternatives. Hence, there is a tendency for consumers to switch towards the product in question, substituting more of it for other goods. The opposite outcome occurs, of course, when there is a rise in the price of the product.

sunk costs refer to unrecoverable costs associated with entering a market.

supernormal profit is any profit earned above normal profit and is a form of *economic rent*.

supply chain focuses on the supply of physical inputs to and outputs from productive activity by a firm relating to inbound logistics, operations, outbound logistics, marketing and sales and after sales service.

supply curve shows the amount that a firm is willing to supply at all possible market prices.

supply of labour is determined by demographic factors, the wage rate and other employment inducements, barriers to entry into different occupations and labour mobility.

SWOT analysis involves consideration of a firm's internal strengths and weaknesses in the context of the opportunities and threats which it faces.

tacit collusion occurs where firms do not formally collude but nevertheless undertake actions that are likely to minimise a competitive response, e.g. avoiding price cutting or not attacking each other's market.

technical efficiency occurs when inputs of the factors of production are combined in the firm in the best possible way to produce the *maximum physical output*.

technically optimum output is the output at which average costs are at their lowest.

test marketing involves selling a product in a limited number of locations with different packaging or advertising campaigns in order to test market reaction.

third-degree price discrimination involves charging different prices for the same product in different segments of the market. The market may be segmented by geography, by type of demand, by time, or by the nature of the product itself.

time series data are concerned with data collected over successive time periods.

total costs of production are made up of *total fixed costs* and *total variable costs*.

total fixed costs are fixed at all levels of output.

total physical product is the total output in physical (rather than value) terms when factors of production are employed.

total revenue is equal to the unit price multiplied by quantity sold.

traditional theory of the firm is based on the assumptions of perfect knowledge and profit-maximising behaviour.

transaction costs are the costs of negotiating, monitoring and enforcing market contracts for the inputs of goods and services.

transaction cost theory is concerned with the costs rather than the benefits of different ways of organising production.

transfer pricing relates to the internal prices at which factor inputs and products are transacted between various subsidiaries of an integrated organisation.

trend projection is concerned with predicting the future value of a variable, without quantifying responsiveness to the various factors which might determine this value.

two-part tariff is concerned with levying a charge per unit according to units consumed *plus* a fixed charge to reflect overhead costs.

unit or unitary elasticity of demand arises when the shape of the demand curve is a rectangular hyperbola such that at any point on it the value of elasticity is equal to *unity* (the area under the curve remains constant as price changes).

unitary form structure arises where tight control is imposed on the various parts of a company from the centre on day-to-day operations.

utility describes the pleasure, satisfaction or benefit derived by a person from the consumption of goods or services.

valuation ratio for any company is its current share price multiplied by the number of its issued shares divided by the net book value (assets less liabilities) of the company.

value chain analysis is concerned with the different stages of the production of a good or service from initial inputs to after-sales service. It identifies where value is created (or lost) at each stage of the supply (production and distribution) process.

value chain management is about managing each stage of the supply chain so as to maximise competitive advantage – see *supply chain*.

variable costs are those costs of production that vary as output changes.

Veblen products display perverse price–demand relationships whereby the quantity demanded varies directly with a change in price.

vertical integration is the bringing together under one ownership and control of different stages in the production of a given good or service.

weighted average cost of capital is a weighted average of the costs of using retained earnings, loans and equity finance.

weightless economy relates to the fact that information and knowledge, although embodied in capital and labour (e.g. a highly educated workf5ace) need to be recognised as critical inputs to the economy.

X-inefficiency indicates the extent to which the costs of production are above the minimum average cost due to waste and organisational slack given the existing scale of production.

Index